RUSSIAN

AMERICA

Pavlovsk

Kodiak I

Queen Charlotte Is

Arkhangelsk
(Sitka)

ENGLISH

Baranov I

AMERICA

Vancouver I

Fort Ross

SPANISH

E A N

San Francisco

AMERICA

SANDWICH IS

MEXICO

Quest for
Empire

oximate

DEDICATION

To my family doctors:

My husband George
My son Ronald
My daughter-in-law Jean

Quest for Empire

The Saga of
Russian America

By
Kyra Petrovskaya Wayne

ISBN 0-88839-193-5 (Hard Cover)
ISBN 0-88839-191-9 (Soft Cover)
Copyright © 1986 Kyra Petrovskaya Wayne

Cataloging in Publication Data

Wayne, Kyra Petrovskaya
Quest For Empire
(The Saga of Russian America)
I. Title
PS3573.A95R8 1986   813'.54   C86-091517-4

Printed in the United States of America

Published simultaneously in Canada and the United States by

HANCOCK HOUSE PUBLISHERS LTD.
19313 Zero Ave., Surrey, B.C. V3S 5J9

HANCOCK HOUSE PUBLISHERS INC.
1431 Harrison Avenue, Blaine, WA 98230

TABLE OF CONTENTS

ACKNOWLEDGEMENTS

The author wishes to express her gratitude to Dr. Richard A. Pierce, Professor Emeritus of History, Queens University, Kingston, Ontario, and to the late Esther Billman, curator of the Sheldon Jackson Museum, Sitka, Alaska, for their help and encouragement in creating this book.

Cover picture by A. Greeley Wells, Jr.

INTRODUCTION

This book is a work of fiction set in a period of American history when the Russian tsars reached out to take a share of the New World. Several of the principal characters and many of the peripheral figures lived and left accounts of their activities. These people and their attitudes toward the events of their lives have been woven into the story with concern for the authentic flavor of the period and accuracy in respect to time and place.

A list of characters will help the reader to identify the players in the drama, while an epilogue provides information about the later days of the historical figures.

LIST OF PRINCIPAL CHARACTERS

THE RUSSIANS
Alexander Andreyevich Baranov, Glavny Pravitel, the first
  Governor of Russian America
Grigory Ivanovich Shelikhov, a rich merchant and explorer,
  founder of the Shelikhov-Golikov Fur Prospecting Company
Ivan Kuskov, Baranov's deputy
Timofei Tarakanov, a promyshlenik, a hunter
Father Nektarii, Russian Orthodox priest
Antipatr, Baranov's son from his native wife
Nikolai Petrovich Rezanov, the Envoy to the World, a per-
  sonal friend of Tsar Alexander
Annushka, (neé) Shelikhova Rezanov's wife
Tsar Paul, assassinated in 1801
Tsar Alexander, his son
Count Peter von Pahlen, Governor-General of St. Petersburg,
  one of the conspirators against Tsar Paul
Count Nikolai Rumyantzev, Imperial Minister of Commerce
Ivan, Rezanov's serf
Dr. Langsdorff, Rezanov's physician
Captain-Lieutenent Urey Lysainsky, captain of the *Neva*
Captain-Lieutenant Iohann Kruzenstern, captain of the *Nadezhda*
Lieutenant Nikolai Khvostov, captain of the *Younona*
Midshipman Gavriil Davidov, later captain of the *Avoss*
Nikolai Isayevich Bulygin, captain of the *Nikolai*
Anna Petrovna, his wife

THE INDIANS
Ska-out-lelt, Chief of the Tlingits
Kot-le-an, his heir
Water Blossom, later baptized Anna, Baranov's Kenaitze wife
Marinka, Timofei's Tlingit wife
Takat-kija, Marinka's mother
Ka-too-woo, a Quillayute woman
Utra-Makah, Chief of the Makahs

THE SPANIARDS
Don José Arillaga, the Governor of Alta California
Don José Darió Argüello, Commander of the presidio de San Francisco
Doña Ignacia, his wife
Lieutenent Don Luis Argüello, his son
Señorita Concepción Argüello (Concha), his daughter
Father Uriá
Father de la Cueva, Franciscan priest
Father Landaeta, Franciscan priest

THE AMERICANS AND THE BRITISH
Henry Barber, captain of the *Unicorn* (British)
Joseph O'Cain, captain of the *O'Cain* (American)
John D'Wolf, captain of the *Juno* (American), later the second mate on the *Younona*
James Brown, captain of the *Lydia* (American)

Chapter 1

The old wooden warehouse burned like a torch, flames roaring up between the tall hemlocks and tinting the snow orange and red. Baranov watched helplessly. He pressed his hand against the throbbing wound in his thigh, trying to stop the blood that spilled into the snow beneath him.

The bodies of three Russian hunters lay nearby, victims of the same Chukchi band that had wounded him and carried off a year's catch of precious sables. Worse even than the pain in his leg was the knowledge that he was ruined. Only the stubborn refusal to let the Chukchi have the final victory—his death in the snow—made him rise despite the agony in his thigh. Leaning on his musket, clutching at his blood-soaked pants leg, he hobbled away.

"I am sorry, my dear Baranov, that a misfortune brought you to accept my offer to sail for America. But I must confess I am selfishly delighted that you have finally agreed to become one of us!" Grigory Shelikhov smiled cordially. "Life as a Russian *promyshlenik* on the American shores is not much different from life in Siberia. After all, a fur hunter is a fur hunter, eh? Of course, you must still rely on natives to work for you. But instead of the Siberian Chukchi or Buryati, you'll deal with Aleuts, simple, gentle people."

At the mention of the Siberian tribesmen, Alexander Baranov's face had flushed beneath his unkempt beard. "Chukchi!" he spat the word like a curse.

"May those bastards simmer in hell!"

Shelikhov looked at his guest with sympathy plainly showing in his face. A merchant himself, Shelikhov well understood Baranov's anger. Shelikhov too had faced ruination and had known the helpless anger of one who had been betrayed. But he had always survived, and Baranov would survive too, he thought. Baranov would recover from the loss of money and furs and men just as he had healed from the wounds the Chukchi had given him.

There was steel in this small, stocky gamecock, and loyalty too. "Fate has given me just the kind of leader I need to settle the American shores," Shelikhov thought.

The two men were seated in deep leather chairs facing one another in Shelikhov's handsome English-style study. A huge globe stood on a pedestal in the center of the room. Hundreds of books lined the walls, their gold embossed bindings shining dimly behind the glass-fronted cases that reflected the flickering fire in the open grate. There were etchings of ships in full sail, pictures of the hunt with horsemen dressed in red coats.

A manservant in gray waistcoat, breeches and knee-high boots brought in a silver tray with a crystal decanter and two small glasses rimmed with gold.

"Claret?" Shelikhov smiled at his guest. "Or would you prefer a *charka* of vodka?"

"Vodka," Baranov blurted, eyeing the delicate glasses and the dark red wine with suspicion.

"In that case I'll join you. Akim, bring us some *zakuski*."

The servant left quickly and reappeared with a larger tray laden with bits of smoked fish, sausages, some marinated mushrooms, pickles and slices of bread and butter. Next to the food were several decanters of different kinds of vodka.

"Tell me, Alexander Andreyevich," Shelikhov said, "did the Chukchi leave you nothing?"

"The bastards left me less than nothing." Baranov washed down a bit of sausage with a gulp of vodka of a size that both surprised and amused Shelikhov. "I am in debt to everyone. My hunters. My suppliers. My credit is gone. I am totally ruined. I am surprised that you still have enough confidence in me to offer me a position."

He held the empty glass out for the servant to refill. He had tried to make his last remark in a lighter tone, but it was clear he was touched by Shelikhov's trust. "If there's anything I learned from this disaster, it is that one can never sell the natives firearms. They almost killed me with the same guns I taught them to use. Once those wild people think they have the upper hand, they take what they want."

"Very wise," Shelikhov said. "*Za vashe zdorovie.*" They touched glasses and drank one another's health.

For a moment they studied one another. Shelikhov saw no sign the vodka dimmed the alert sparkle in Baranov's heavy-lidded blue eyes. The smaller man with the receding, light-colored hair and the unruly beard had an open manner that inspired trust. At forty-five or so he was the right age to seem fatherly to his young hunters, but not too old to seem infirm. His patched boots, coarse jacket and trousers would also serve to make him seem closer to them in rank, one of their own.

For his own part, Baranov was surprised by the clean-shaven Shelikhov. The man was tall and rather plump although large-boned and sturdy looking. His head was covered by a powdered wig and his coat and breeches appeared to be silk like his white stockings. On his feet he wore elegant black leather shoes with silver buckles. "If I didn't know he was a tough trader and a daring explorer, I'd mark him down as a fop," Baranov thought. Although Baranov knew they were both of the same social class, Shelikhov seemed like a noble and he like a rude peasant. Baranov promised himself to buy new clothes before he left for America. He would uphold the honor of his post as *Glavny Pravitel* for all of Shelikhov's American holdings.

Shelikhov picked up a piece of smoked sturgeon. "The company will advance you the necessary sums to pay your suppliers and hunters. Although, frankly, I don't see why you need to pay the hunters anything. They knew the work was dangerous. Flood, fire, thieves, poor sable crop—it's all part of the job. No furs, no pay, that's the rule. They would not hold you responsible."

"They are *my* men," Baranov interrupted. "They trusted me. I'll pay them for their losses. And I'll pay the widows too, even if it takes me a lifetime."

Shelikhov smiled. "Not a lifetime, Alexander Andreyevich. We'll see you have enough to pay all your debts and take care of your family for the next five years. You'll also have ten non-voting shares in the company. Should you find new lands and establish new settlements, there will be bonuses. We don't want you worrying about old debts while you manage our interests." He smiled at Baranov and nodded to the servant to pour them another vodka. "We need a manager who can deal not only with the natives, but also with the officials in the Ministry of Commerce in St. Petersburg. One who can write reports and read dispatches. Not many can. We need a man who would share our vision of the Russian empire spreading to the shores of the American continent. We think that you are that man, Alexander Andreyevich."

"I am your man," Baranov said, rising. They shook hands.

For the next several weeks Baranov was occupied with the preparations for his journey to America. He chose the fifty *promyshleniki* who would accompany him to Kodiak Island. He selected his men with great care, picking those with skills in addition to their abilities as fur hunters. He needed carpenters, blacksmiths, shipwrights and sailmakers. Men who could become the nucleus of the future Pacific empire. He conferred with Shelikhov almost every day, and his admiration for the old trader grew. Perhaps Shelikhov dressed like a fop, but he had a mind as tough and nimble as anyone Baranov had ever met.

As the time of his departure grew near, Baranov realized that he had to face another problem; one that he kept pushing out of his mind, the problem of his wife. "I should have taken time to visit her," he thought, telling himself at the same time that it would have been really impossible. Marfa lived hundreds of miles away, in the western part of Russia, while his journey would take him in the opposite direction. He had to sail across the ocean before the winter weather made the sea too dangerous. "Nothing good would come of it anyway," he thought sadly. "Marfa and I have been strangers for years, and I have never even seen my daughter. No, it's better that I don't see them and open the old wounds."

He arranged with the Irkutsk office to send Marfa her substantial annual stipend. Then he put her out of his mind.

On the last day before his departure, Baranov appeared in Shelikhov's house for a final visit. He bought himself a new suit of clothes, complete with a silk cravat, and a pair of buckled shoes, not as fancy as Shelikhov's, but frivolous enough to make him feel foolish. He felt awkward in his knee britches and wrinkled hose, in his tight waistcoat, but he endured his discomforts stoically. The worst discomfort was the absence of his face whiskers. Baranov had them shaved, exposing his face for the first time since he was a lad of eighteen.

When he stared at his pale, naked face in the barber's mirror, his first thought was, "It can't be me. I have never looked so silly." He shrugged. He was an official now. He must look the part.

The servant escorted Baranov into the formal parlor and asked him to sit down.

Baranov looked around. The elegant surroundings made him uneasy. Baranov was more at home in thatch-roofed peasant huts or hastily built *zemlyanki*, shelters, half-buried in the ground.

The Shelikhov parlor was furnished with fragile-looking gilded furniture in French style, with a large carpet of flowers, birds and cupids spread in its center. Several ornate bronze clocks placed on thin-legged tables, ticked nervously, as if each clock tried to be louder and faster than the others.

A huge portrait of the master of the house dominated the room. Shelikhov was painted attired in court dress, with a sword at his side, like an hereditary nobleman, a spyglass in his right hand and a ship in full sail in the background. His handsome, clean-shaven face was framed by the white lace of a jabot and his head was covered with a curled, powdered wig. A huge round medal suspended from a moiré ribbon was clearly visible among the folds of his lacy jabot. It was an impressive image of a gentleman explorer and nothing in it suggested Shelikhov's humble beginnings.

Baranov glanced at his own reflection in the huge gilded mirror above the fireplace. He saw a small balding man with a naked face in ill-fitting clothes perched cautiously on the edge of a delicate chair. He looked uncomfortable and even foolish, Baranov thought, a far cry from the image in the portrait.

Shelikhov entered. With outstretched arms he crossed the room to greet his visitor.

"Alexander Andreyevich, what a pleasure!" he exclaimed. He pretended not to notice Baranov's drastic change of appearance. He concealed his disappointment. After all, he thought, he is only trying to imitate me.

Baranov at once felt better. "I am glad that you don't make fun of me," he said wryly. "I decided to start my new life with a new appearance. Since I am an official now, I might as well try to look like one."

"Make fun of you? To the contrary, you look very well, indeed, in the European attire."

Baranov shifted in his chair uneasily. "I don't quite agree, but I suppose I'll get used to it. Meanwhile, I feel naked, with my face and my legs uncovered!" They both laughed.

Baranov departed from Irkutsk the next day. His party traveled along the Lena river on several galleys, first to Yakutsk, then, on horseback, accompanied by a Cossack convoy, across the formidable Dzhugzhur range toward Okhotsk where a ship was waiting to take them to America.

The journey took them more than three months. It was August when they finally arrived in Okhotsk.

Captain Dimitri Bocharov, of the cargo vessel the *Three Saints*, was anxious to leave. "Only six weeks of relatively calm weather remain. I am unwilling to challenge the ocean beyond September!" he exclaimed dramatically, instead of greeting the new arrivals.

"I am ready to leave this minute if you wish, Captain, providing that the ship is fully loaded, which I doubt is possible," Baranov replied calmly.

Captain Bocharov turned crimson, realizing that he sounded childishly petulant. He smiled with embarrassment and said, "I didn't mean to be so boorish...Welcome aboard!" he offered his hand.

"I like him," Baranov thought. "He's a decent lad. He doesn't insist on having the last word."

"We'll start loading the ship immediately. I, too, would rather not tangle with the ocean during the stormy season. As it is, I don't know how I am going to survive the voyage. I have never been at sea before," Baranov smiled at the young captain.

"You'll do just fine, Your Honor! After a day or two of seasickness, you'll get your sea legs and you'll be one of us!"

"Your Honor!" Baranov was startled to hear this new form of address. "That's right, from now on, I will be addressed as 'Your Honor!' I like it. I truly like it!" he thought.

The *Three Saints* departed from Okhotsk on August 19, 1790. It was a clear bright day with a brisk wind which snapped gaily at the sails. The ship was heavily laden with supplies for the colony on Kodiak Island and it squatted in the water deeper than captain Bocharov thought was prudent. But he realized that his ship would be the last of the season to reach the colonies; there would be no more ships until April or May of the next year. The settlers needed the cargo of provisions, weapons and ammunition. He allowed the ship to be loaded to its full capacity, including several head of cattle and sheep stabled in the holds.

From the start of the voyage, Baranov fell victim to seasickness. The constant pitch and roll of the ship made his stomach heave and churn. His fifty recruits did not fare any better. They were landlubbers. Their previous experience with sailing was limited to small river boats and rafts. Once in the open sea, they draped themselves on the bulwarks, vomiting overboard. They were useless as deckhands. The captain, his first mate and a cabin boy had to work the sails by themselves.

Baranov willed himself to stay on his feet. The sight of him, so frail, so small and yet so determined to remain among his men, instead of seeking comfort inside his cabin, inspired the men to fight their own discomforts. As captain Bocharov had predicted, eventually his passengers became used to the constant movement of the ship. Soon, they were able to hold their food and some even began to learn their new duties as sailors.

By September 4, the *Three Saints* sailed out of the Kurile Straits into the open ocean. Baranov, no longer suffering from seasickness, sat on the bridge watching his men scurry on the deck, the captain teaching them the rudiments of sailing.

"Such a tiny chip of wood and canvas, the ship is... And just look at this intrepid little thing braving the waves, all alone in this immense ocean!" Baranov thought fondly.

A few days later, the first mate discovered that the fresh water barrels were leaking. Captain Bocharov at once established strict rationing. Each man was allotted four cups of fresh water every twenty-four hours. The lack of potable water soon began to show its effects. Several men became dehydrated, burning with fever.

"They'll die if we don't get fresh water," Bocharov reported to Baranov.

"What do you suggest we do?"

"Put in at the first island where we can get to a stream of sweet water, Your Honor."

"Do it!" Baranov commanded.

They sailed for several more days. The captain reduced their water rations for the benefit of the sick, but every day there were more of them, suffering from dehydration.

The *Three Saints* passed by small volcanic islands, but the parties sent ashore in search of fresh water returned empty-handed.

Finally, on September 28, the voyagers reached a large island in the Aleutian chain. It was Unalashka. Captain Bocharov knew that there was a sweet water river emptying into the bay.

They dropped anchor. The longboats were lowered and two groups departed for shore, carrying repaired water barrels.

The *Three Saints* was ready to sail for Kodiak on September 30, but that night a sudden squall hit the ship. The vicious wind pushed her forward, toward the rocky shore. The vessel dragged her anchor until she ran aground.

All through the stormy night, huge waves rolled over her deck. The hatches were ripped away and the ship began to fill with water. The cattle in the hold were the first victims of the storm. The cows, the bull and the sheep, which were to become breeding stock for the colony in Kodiak, all drowned.

Captain Bocharov commanded the men to abandon ship. At low tide next morning the crew unloaded whatever cargo they still could save, hurrying to reach the shore before the next high tide.

The storm raged for a week. When it finally subsided by October 6, the ship was no more. The *Three Saints* had capsized and broken up with the pounding waves.

Baranov gathered the men around him. "Well, *bratzi*, we'll have to winter on this God-forsaken island. But at least, we are all here. No one drowned. So, let us give thanks to the Almighty for sparing our lives." He made the wide sign of the cross over his chest. The men followed his example.

"Now, first of all, we must dig out several *zemlyanki* to shelter us against this damned weather!" he continued. "Then we'll send scouts to investigate if there are any tribes living on this island. And, of course, we'll have hunting and fishing parties to keep us supplied with food. Cheer up, *bratzi*! Pretend that we are back in Siberia. Instead of the ocean, we are in the taiga. We all know how to survive in the wilderness.

We have done it before, so this shouldn't be much different!"
he said, noting their gloomy faces.

The men eyed the black ocean and its angry white caps
with hostility. They were accustomed to dangers and depri-
vations in the forests, but the ocean threatened them with a
new, mystical power which they could not comprehend.

"I'll send a party to Kodiak to alert them about our misfortune," Baranov promised. "Meanwhile, cheer up *bratzi*,
next spring we'll be in Kodiak!"

They dug out deep square *zemlyanki*, then reinforced
them with salvaged lumber from the ship and piled sod on
the lumber to insulate the roofs.

Inside the shelters they made firepits for cooking and
warmth. Smoke escaped through a hole in the roof.

Baranov divided his men into several working parties giving each group special tasks—hunting for sea lions, fishing,
making salt from sea water and curing sea lion skins for making the native boats called *baidarki*. He made the men rotate
in their duties so that no one would become bored with his
job. Life was boring enough as it was, he thought.

"When spring comes, *bratzi*, we'll pile up in our boats and
paddle away from this miserable island!" he kept reminding
his men lest they become disheartened by their first misfortune in America. He knew that many were already cursing
the day when they signed up to join him.

He dispatched captain Bocharov to chart the Unalashka
shores. "While the weather holds, we might as well make
use of your skill, Captain," he said. "Take the longboat and
make your scientific observations. We'll need the maps and
the charts for our future navigation of these waters."

By November, when the long, dark winter set in, Baranov
and Bocharov pored over the charts by the light of a seal oil
wick. They learned to eat roots and brew tea with grasses;
they ate sea lion meat and crabs. Baranov noted in his journal
that he ceased craving bread and sugar.

One day several Aleuts came to the Russian camp. The
natives brought along bunches of dried fish. The Russians
celebrated the occasion with wild dances, soon joined by the
Aleuts.

Baranov promptly rewarded the Aleuts with handfuls of

colorful beads. After that, the Aleuts became frequent visitors at the Russian camp.

Baranov proclaimed them subjects of the Russian empire. The Aleuts joined Baranov's men eagerly, hunting sea lions for them, bobbing over the winter ocean in two or three man *baidarki* made of animal skins.

To make the act of acquiring Unalashka official, Baranov commanded that a specially minted copper marker be buried in the ground proclaiming the territory as belonging to Russia in perpetuity.

He was surprised how busy he seemed to be. He kept a journal describing their daily life. He made plans for the future, never once doubting that come spring, he and his men would be in Kodiak. He wrote to Shelikhov, knowing that his letters would not reach Siberia for at least a year, or possibly longer, but informing him of his plans to build ships in Kodiak, proposing to sail them south to the edge of the European settlements.

He commissioned the Aleuts to build several large *baidarki* of animal skins, suitable for carrying all his men to Kodiak.

Spring was coming. Baranov wanted to be ready to depart from Unalashka with the first mild weather.

By April, three large *baidarki* were built. Baranov made his men draw lots to see who would remain on the island to guard the cargo and tackle, who would go with captain Bocharov for further exploration and who would try to reach Kodiak.

All three *baidarki* set out. Two of them, under Bocharov, began charting the islands, while Baranov and sixteen of his men set a course for Kodiak.

When they reached Kodiak Island in June, ten months had passed since they left Okhotsk.

Chapter 2

The Russian settlement at Three Saints Bay on Kodiak Island consisted of several exposed wooden shacks and a dilapidated warehouse, gray from the constant rains. It was a far cry from what Baranov had imagined it to be. Somehow, Shelikhov had given him the impression that the settlement was a thriving community, ready to become the Russian capital of the Aleutian Islands.

He saw disappointment on the faces of his men as well. They too, expected the settlement at Three Saints Bay to be more substantial.

"Never mind, *bratzi*," Baranov said quietly. "We are here to set things straight. We'll build our town ourselves!"

He began his inspection at once. He discovered that the local Aleuts worked willingly for the Russians but the natives of the neighboring islands were still hostile and had to be constantly bribed to assure their loyalty.

To his dismay, he found that there were several competing Russian companies. The merchants from Tula, Vologda and Yakutsk tried to outdo one another, killing otter and sealion without a thought of preserving the herds. They abused the natives as well, contributing nothing for their welfare, often cheating them out of their shares.

It became clear to Baranov why Shelikhov was so insistent upon having a monopoly from the government to establish a single trading company. He could foresee the total devastation of the fur-bearing animals within a short time if the present conditions of fierce rivalry among the traders continued.

Baranov began his reforms by moving his headquarters to a new location, away from the unscrupulous competitors.

He chose St. Paul's Harbor at latitude 57 degrees 36 minutes and longitude 152 degrees 8 minutes. The harbor was protected from the ocean by two small islands which acted as breakwaters. The tiny settlement, which was already there, could be easily enlarged since there was an abundance of building timber in the surrounding forests.

Baranov began construction of his town without delay. By the end of summer he had two dozen sturdy wooden huts, a steam bath house, and a large warehouse, built of hewn logs. On the top of the hill he planned to build a church. High palisades, surrounded by stockades and watchtowers, rose around the town; on the outskirts, special dwellings were built for the Aleuts.

Flushed with the success of his undertaking, Baranov called the first meeting of the settlers. He looked proudly at the bearded faces before him, then smiled broadly. "Well, *bratzi*, you've done it! We have our town now, our Pavlovsk!" he began. "I want you to treat it as if it were the town of your birth. I want you to respect it, as if your own mothers and fathers lived here. This is not foreign land anymore. This is *Russia*! So, I want you to behave here as you would in Russia." He paused, then continued with new emphasis, "Now, I know that many of you sleep with the native women. I don't mind. But I do want you to treat them as your true wives. I want you to raise your children by these native women as good Russians. Soon we'll have our church finished and we'll have a priest. He'll baptize your children and your wives. Meanwhile, *bratzi*, use your spare time during the winter and learn the native tongues from your women. I can't tell you how important it is for your survival in this land to know the native tongues. So, use your time of leisure well, *bratzi*!"

Before the winter set in, Baranov made several trips by *baidarki* to the Yakutat Bay where another Russian fort was established on the mainland. He chose Ivan Kuskov, a book keeper from Irkutsk to be his deputy. Kuskov struck him as being a capable, quiet man, literate, but not overly ambitious, good qualities for a second in command. He appointed Kuskov to head the Yakutat settlement.

On his return trip from visiting Kuskov, Baranov and his party camped on the sandy shore of a small island. It looked deserted. Baranov placed guards around the camp and stretched out under his *baidarka*, using it as a shelter. Tired after many hours of paddling his boat, Baranov instantly fell asleep.

He was startled from his sleep by shouts of the guards.

"The savages!" they yelled firing into the darkness. The Russians grabbed their muskets, opening fire at the invaders. The attackers were certainly not Aleuts.

"They must be the Tlingit Indians. We must be on their territory," Baranov thought as he reloaded his pistol.

The Indians were wearing their full war regalia of wooden armor tightly joined by whale-gut thongs. Their faces were hidden by masks carved to resemble fearsome bears, wolves and ravens. Their heads were protected by wooden helmets attached to neck coverings which looked like yokes worn by oxen. Their armament consisted of spears and arrows and they wielded sharp daggers made of bone.

The Russian bullets splintered the wood coverings or ricocheted off the Tlingit armor, causing almost no damage.

Baranov felt sharp pain as an arrow pierced his left shoulder. He gritted his teeth and pulled the arrow out. He fired point blank at a towering Indian. The man fell, hit in the abdomen.

"Aim at their bellies!" Baranov shouted. The Russians lowered their aim, felling several attackers.

The battle was quickly over. The Tlingits retreated under concentrated fire, leaving their dead and wounded.

The Russians watched the suddenly quiet shore nervously. The Indians had vanished.

Baranov doubled the guards around the camp. Cautiously, the *promyshleniki* crept toward the wounded enemy. The Indians were still capable of treachery, they thought.

"Don't harm the prisoners. We need them as hostages," Baranov commanded.

He took his coat off. His arrow wound was deep. It pulsated with blood which spilled down his arm in spurts.

"Someone, take a look at my shoulder." One of the men knelt on the ground next to him.

"You'd better lie down, Alexander Andreyevich," he said. He tore a strip of his shirt off and began to bandage Baranov's shoulder.

"I cannot lie down. I am too excited. We beat the bastards off!" Baranov beamed. "What are our losses?" He demanded more soberly. "Anyone killed?"

"Two Russians and ten Aleuts killed and almost everyone

wounded," reported Tumanin, one of Baranov's old friends. Tumanin's left arm was hanging lifelessly, an Indian arrow having splintered it at the elbow.

"Dear Lord... Two Russians and ten Aleuts dead! I swear, I'll make the bastards pay dearly for that!" Baranov cried out.

"They have already paid dearly. We killed fifteen and have taken seven prisoners," Tumanin said.

At dawn, the Russians buried their fallen comrades and threw the bodies of their enemies into the ocean to show their contempt. They tied the prisoners with seal gut thongs and loaded them into the *baidarki*, paddling away from the unfortunate camp.

Baranov learned from his prisoners that the Tlingits had attacked his party by mistake. The Tlingits were at war with the Chugach tribe and mistook the Russian encampment for the one of their enemies. "Mistake or not, the savages must be taught a lesson!" Baranov fumed. "We'll avenge our dead. One of these days we'll even the score!"

Despite his threats, Baranov was kind to his prisoners. He intended to set them free, but not before they taught him their tongue. He already knew quite a lot of Aleut language and he was eager to learn Tlingit. His plans for the future depended upon his proficiency in native tongues.

His wound was healing badly. He was often feverish, suspecting that perhaps the arrow was poisoned. Since there were no doctors, he ministered to his ills himself, using the old peasant remedies, such as chewing moldy bread and cobwebs and applying the sticky mass directly to the wound.

Late in October, an English ship, the *Phoenix*, belonging to the East India Company, arrived in Pavlovsk, one of its masts broken, and in need of replacement.

Baranov received the Englishmen cordially. He surprised them by the peculiar Russian custom of hospitality by inviting them to bathe in his new steam bathhouse.

It was difficult to converse with his visitors: neither party spoke the language of the other.

In desperation, Baranov tried a few words of German, which he still remembered from his youth, when he worked in Moscow as an apprentice in the household of a German merchant. The English captain, Jeremy Moore, responded.

He too, knew a little German! The connection was established.

Captain Moore invited Baranov to visit his ship. Eagerly, Baranov climbed aboard.

It was the first time that he had seen a real ocean-going trading vessel. Despite the broken mast, the ship looked fit, every coiled rope in its place, all sails neatly furled. "Quite a difference from the chaos on our ships," Baranov thought, promising himself to demand order on any Russian vessels under his command.

He noticed with interest the precautions taken by the English against the natives. Decks were shielded against the arrows by huge bullock-hide screens. "Perhaps we can do the same, when we sail into the Tlingit waters," he thought.

Baranov assigned his best men to assist the Englishmen in replacing the mast.

While the work was being done, he visited the ship almost daily, becoming especially friendly with the first mate, Joseph O'Cain, a sailor from Boston.

A week passed too soon. The mast was replaced and the *Phoenix* was ready to depart. In gratitude for his help, Captain Moore offered Baranov an unusual gift—a young Bengalese slave named Richard.

"He's a bright lad. He speaks several languages. He'll teach you English," the captain said, nodding toward a slightly built, brown-skinned youth with dark velvety eyes.

For a moment Baranov was confused. In Russia only the nobility had the right to own slaves. "I can't accept," he said.

"Nonsense. Take him, he's yours!"

"Perhaps he won't want to stay with me?"

"Of course he will."

"Ask him, just the same."

Captain Moore turned to Richard. "Are you willing to stay as a servant with Mr. Baranov?" Richard nodded. "Well, then it's settled. He's yours!"

Baranov grinned at the dusky youth. "Please tell him, sir, that I am not a slave owner. If Richard wants to work for me, he'll work as a free man, free to leave my employ at his pleasure."

Captain Moore shrugged, but translated his words.

A slow smile spread over Richard's face. He fell on his knees and kissed Baranov's hand.

"No...no...get up, young man," Baranov stuttered in embarrassment.

"He'll be not only your servant, he'll be your friend," captain Moore chuckled.

During the following several years Baranov searched for a suitable harbor further south. He traveled by *baidarki*, accompanied by Richard and several Aleuts. He adopted the native form of dress of animal skin garments, lacing them to his boat in Aleut fashion. More than ever he realized that he needed ships for his explorations. Paddling in native boats was exhausting and progress was very slow.

"I need ships!" he wrote to Shelikhov. "How can we push the borders of the Russian empire further east if we have to do it in animal skin boats? The English are breathing down our necks. Their famous captain George Vancouver has been charting in these waters for several years now. Soon, the English will be arriving here, bringing shiploads of settlers, while we are still paddling our *baidarki*! I will build my own ships! God knows, there's plenty of quality timber to do so!"

Shelikhov fully agreed with his *Glavny Pravitel*. To aid Baranov in his new undertaking, he engaged a young Englishman, one James Shields, who had served as a lieutenant in a Siberian regiment and, who happened to know shipbuilding. No one seemed to know how an Englishman had found himself serving in the Russian military forces. Shelikhov couldn't care less. He was only interested in whether Shields could build and sail his ships.

He dispatched the Englishman to his office in Okhotsk with instructions to build an oceangoing vessel for the colonies in America.

Shields proved to be an excellent find. Within a year he built a sturdy two-master, which Shelikhov christened the *Orel* after the eagle symbol of the Tsars. At once he outfitted the *Orel* with shipbuilding materials and sent her off to Baranov, with James Shields as her master.

Not knowing that a new ship and a qualified shipwright were coming his way, Baranov was following his own plan of shipbuilding.

He formed a new fort in Chugatsk Bay at Kenai Peninsula, naming it *Voskresensk* (Resurrection). There was a plentiful supply of tall straight timber, so necessary for making masts and yardarms. However, there was nothing to use as tar or pitch.

"*Bratzi*, you must invent something to take care of this!" Baranov appealed to his men. The *promyshleniki* pondered the problem. Someone came up with the idea of boiling the sap of several varieties of fir trees found around Voskresensk. It produced a sticky, waterproof gum, which proved quite suitable for their purpose.

In 1794, the first Russian ship, built in America, was launched. Baranov named her the *Phoenix.*

Meanwhile, James Shields had arrived. He examined the *Phoenix*, amazed at the Russian ingenuity. Everything on the *Phoenix* was built by men who knew nothing about shipbuilding. She was no beauty to look at, yet she was as seaworthy as any vessel he had seen. He pronounced her an excellent ship.

"I feel like getting drunk!" Baranov exclaimed happily, which he proceeded to do in the company of Shields, whom he appointed to be the master of the *Phoenix.*

Baranov ordered two more ships of smaller capacity to be built closer to Pavlovsk, on Spruce Island. The following year they were completed. He named them the *Olga* and the *Delfin* (Dolphin). His fleet was growing.

All through the following years the intrepid company ships kept crossing the ocean, taking the fur pelts back to Russia, bringing to Baranov more hunters and adventurers. Some of the ships never reached their destinations. The fragile vessels and the inexperienced seafarers were no match for the fierce Pacific storms, but others came through unscathed. Among them was the *St. Simeon*, which brought a young Siberian lad, Timofei Tarakanov, to America.

Chapter 3

Timofei Tarakanov arrived in Russian America in 1797 when he was barely seventeen. Over six feet tall, and still growing, he moved with an awkward grace of a young colt unaware of his burgeoning strength, his muscles rippling and straining under the confines of his outgrown shirt. His curly hair and the soft fuzz sprouting on his chin and over his broad chest, were the color of shelled corn, giving him a shimmering golden appearance. He greeted the world around him with the eagerness of an inquisitive child, his eyes deep blue, like his native Lake Baikal, where the tall lavender mountains cast their image on the fathomless green waters.

Timofei's lively intelligence had attracted the attention of the old Prince Ozhogin, on whose estate Timofei's father served as a bailiff. "Teach him to read and write. If he's good, I'll take him into my house as a page," the Prince told Timofei's father.

The lad was dispatched to the village priest. For four years he struggled with the lives of the saints, the only book the pious priest would use, learning to read Church-Slavonic, an archaic dialect used only in the liturgy.

Proud of Timofei's progress, the priest recommended that the lad continue his education by entering a monastery as a novice.

"A monastery! I don't want to be a monk!" Timofei protested to his father. The scholarly seclusion of the monastic life held no appeal for Timofei. "I don't want to be a page either and empty Prince Ozhogin's chamberpots!"

Timofei had a different ambition. "I want to be a Cossack," he thought.

All his short life he had dreamt of the time when he

would be old enough to join the Cossacks, the descendants of the brave men who had taken Siberia from the Tatars. Peerless horsemen, the Cossacks led free lives in their fortified settlements, obeying only their own elected commander, God and the Tsar, in that order. "God is high up, the Tsar is far away, while our commander is right here!" was the Cossacks' credo.

As soon as he turned sixteen, Timofei stealthily crept out of his village and plunged into the *taiga*. He carried a musket, a flint, a bag of shot and a ram's horn of powder, all taken from his father's house. Stuck in his belt was an axe, which he honed to razor sharpness. Slung on his left shoulder in the manner of the village beggars was a canvas bag that held a loaf of his mother's bread, five onions and a handful of salt, wrapped in a clean cloth. He was barefoot, having never worn shoes except in winter. His curly head was covered by a shaggy fur *shapka*, in which he had snagged his fish hooks for safekeeping.

Timofei had no fear of the silent *taiga*. His father had taught him how to track an animal, how to shoot a musket, how to lure trout. He knew how to build a brush *shalash* and how to set traps, and how to find his directions from the sun and dipper stars. Like all peasant children he had learned to recognize the edible mushrooms and berries. "I can survive in the forest indefinitely! The *taiga* will provide me with all my needs," he thought, full of optimism.

He had never seen a Cossack settlement. He had only a vague idea where to look for it. It had been described to him many times by itinerant storytellers who trudged the forest villages and the steppes of Russia regaling their listeners with tales of yore in exchange for a heap of straw for a bed and a meal of bread and boiled cabbage.

Timofei had been their most constant listener since his early boyhood. Their blood-curdling tales of ancient battles against the Tatars were real to him. He imagined himself astride a magnificent stallion with a flowing mane, galloping fearlessly under the Cossack banner to save Russia from her enemies. Sitting on an earthen floor at the feet of a storyteller, Timofei would listen with wonder, dreaming that someday, he too, would become a Cossack.

That day had finally arrived. "I am on my way!"

It was dark in the *taiga*. The tall trees crowded closely

together, their branches entwined and twisted. The slippery narrow path, obscured by the thick growth of ferns, felt damp under Timofei's bare feet. He followed the path that he knew would lead him to a stream, which eventually would end up at the river Shilka. He stepped into the stream, wading knee-high to throw pursuers off his trail, his senses honed to the sounds of crushing underbrush and baying dogs, but all was quiet. Only the crowns of the tall trees whispered and nodded as if in approval of his decision to become a Cossack.

As night approached, there was still no sign of pursuit. Timofei build himself a *shalash*, from fir branches. He did not dare to start a fire. "Smoke or light will give me away," he thought as he curled up on a bed of pine fronds, falling asleep, with a chunk of bread still in his fist.

In the morning, as a precaution, Timofei took his *shalash* apart and threw the branches into the stream. They floated away instantly.

He made the sign of the cross. Then he scanned the trees for green-gray moss growing on the southern sides of their trunks. It pointed unfailingly toward his destination.

Once more Timofei was on his way. Day after day, he trudged in a southerly direction, surrounded by the monotonous dense forest of towering dark trees and thick underbrush. He could barely see the path made by the animals on their way to the river. His bread and onions were long gone, but there were pine nuts and berries in abundance. He trapped squirrels and roasted their tiny carcasses over the fire at night. He was no longer afraid to light the campfire.

But Timofei was growing weak. His mind often played tricks on him, making him suddenly hear his mother's voice or smell the aroma of her cooking. Circles of red and yellow began to swim before his eyes. He pushed on, his naive faith that he would find the Cossacks, still unshakable.

"Guide me, dear Lord," he prayed as he staggered forward. He lost count of the days since his departure from the village. Was it a week? A month? He did not care. It seemed to him that he was forever walking through the *taiga*, that there was no end to the forest.

Timofei's perseverance was finally rewarded; he came upon the Cossack settlement exactly as described by the garrulous itinerants and forever imprinted on his brain.

The Cossacks expressed no surprise at the shaggy youth's sudden emergency from the *taiga*. They were accustomed to sheltering runaway serfs and escaped convicts. They accepted Timofei without questioning and put him to work caring for a flock of chickens. "Chickens!" Timofei felt disappointed.

Very soon he began to feel discontented. Life among the Cossacks was the same as in his own village. The Cossack huts were no different from those he knew, small and squat, roofed by rotting sod, with crooked windows covered with mica.

Timofei loathed his assignment to the chicken yard. "Had I stayed home, I would have been a page by now in Prince Ozhogin's mansion!" he thought, forgetting how he had once hated the idea. "Who is to teach me how to tame wild horses or swing a sabre?" Timofei was deeply disappointed. In fact, no one swung the sabre anymore. The weapon hung as a decoration in the Cossacks' houses next to the icons of the saints.

The Cossacks did not live in the fortified camp of Timofei's imagination, in a brotherhood of men, but instead led sedate married lives with their families. Their legendary horsemanship and their dare-devil raids had long since become the folktales of the past. The Cossacks were now farmers. They eked out a living from the barren Siberian soil like everyone else.

Timofei thought of returning home. The fear of punishment kept him among the Cossacks. "I will be flogged, for sure, and perhaps be conscripted for twenty-five years into a punitive army battalion," he thought wretchedly, having heard about the usual punishment for peasants.

Then, good luck struck. A recruiter had appeared among the Cossacks, seeking men to sail across the ocean to hunt otter in America. Timofei signed up for five years without hesitation. "I will become a *promyshlenik*, a fur hunter in America!" he decided. "America? Where is it?" He did not know. The priest who had taught him how to write was weak in geography. But it did not matter. He would go to America, he decided, wherever it was.

The *St. Simeon* was a small but sturdy looking brig. She squatted in the water like an old hen, grown broad of beam, her two sails patched up like a peasant quilt.

Timofei had never seen an ocean-going vessel. It was hard for him to imagine how such a small ship, laden with thirty people and dozens of crates and barrels of cargo, could float without sinking. Even harder was to imagine how she could sail across the ocean. She sat too low in the water, her bulwarks almost touching the lapping waves.

There was no turning back. Resolutely, trying not to show that he was afraid, Timofei stepped aboard.

The *St. Simeon* departed from Okhotsk sailing through the turbulent Kurile Straights hugging the coastline. Her skipper, an old *promyshlenik*, guided her by visual contact with the land, relying on luck, ignorant of the art of navigation. No one aboard the *St. Simeon* knew any better.

Good luck and good weather favored the *St. Simeon*. She arrived unscathed, some six weeks later, in the harbor of St. Paul in Kodiak Island.

Timofei's heart sank as he stepped ashore, his legs shaky after weeks on the pitching ship.

The tiny community of Pavlovsk was buried in spring mud. A small church and several long, low company warehouses were the best buildings in the village.

Baranov's foothold in America did not impress Timofei Tarakanov.

Timofei moved into a communal hut reserved for bachelor hunters. It had rows of crude wooden bunks lining its walls. Its slimy floor had never been washed. Timofei felt it was not much cleaner than a Cossack chicken yard.

Chill rain pounded Pavlovsk for weeks at a time only to be replaced by milky fog brewed up by the warm Japanese current. Although the harbor never froze, few ships ever braved the foggy, stormy shores. Yet ships were the lifeblood of the colonies, for its inhabitants could not raise crops to feed themselves.

Trapped on the cold, rainy island that was in darkness for half the year, the morale of even the hardiest hunter sagged. Most turned to drink for comfort. Eagerly they saw to the "education" of young Timofei.

They called him *bogatyr* after the golden-haired hero of folk legends.

But when Timofei passed one of the tests of a true *bogatyr* and straightened out a horseshoe, they saw new possibilities in him. They egged him into wrestling matches with local champions, winning bets on his crude strength. They also saw that Timofei had his first woman. They plied him with vodka and pushed him atop a dark-haired, slit-eyed woman. Through a haze of vodka, Timofei was both frightened and

bewildered by his fishy-smelling, groaning bunkmate. But
the native woman was anxious to please. Timofei's youthful
lust got him through the experience.

The hunters greeted his initiation into manhood with
more vodka and wild dances. Timofei laughed in embarrassment when the woman left. He wanted desperately to please
his new friends. He craved their approval. He felt very lonely.

Becoming a *promyshlenik* proved to be even harder than
trying to please his friends. Timofei had to learn to hunt from
a weightless *baidarka*, as it pitched over the waves.

"Dear God, I'll never learn how to paddle this cursed
boat!" he agonized as he retched over the side of the *baidarka*
until his guts felt as if they were going to spill out along
with the bitter bile. He cursed his fate which brought him
to America. He faced the heaving sea with hatred. "For the
next five years I will be in this prison like a *katorzhnik*, at
hard labor!" he thought, steeling himself for the battle with
the relentless ocean.

An elderly Aleut patiently taught Timofei the ways of
handling the boat, of throwing a harpoon and shooting an
arrow. "The precious otter pelt must be protected from musket fire. It ruins the fur. Only harpoon and arrows are used
to kill otter," the Aleut taught him. He knew that the lad
would overcome his dread of the sea; he was strong and smart;
he would learn.

After a while, Timofei did learn to trust his little *baidarka*,
so flimsy, yet bobbing easily on the high crests of the waves.
He became proud of his new skills with a harpoon and an
arrow. He discovered the beauty of the endless panorama
of the ocean. His bouts of seasickness had disappeared. He
began to enjoy his freedom. He stopped thinking of himself
as a runaway youth, lonesome for his homeland. He began to
think of himself as a free man.

The future no longer seemed dismal to Timofei. He was
a man now. He had grown to his full height of six feet four
inches, his chest broad, as if sculpted. The peach fuzz of
youth was gone from his cheeks. Instead, Timofei's face had
hardened, framed in golden whiskers that mingled with his
curly hair.

No one dared try to force him to drink anymore. The
men sought his friendship, in awe of his strength. The Aleut
women argued with one another who was to share his bed.
Several offered to become his "wife", but Timofei was not

interested in any permanent arrangement. "What will I do with a wife? I am too young," he laughed off their proposals.

But a vague feeling of disappointment with his life began to trouble him again. Paddling a *baidarka* and hunting otter was very dull. Timofei craved adventure of a different sort, his head still full of dreams of glorious deeds that he wished to achieve. What deeds exactly, he could not tell. He only knew that he was capable of more than his life seemed to offer. "I am a literate man, after all... "

Timofei's chance to prove himself came in the spring of 1798. Because he could read and write, Baranov chose him to become his aide. Baranov was planning to annex an island held by the Tlingit Indians.

"Now, at last the real adventure!" Timofei thought. "Perhaps there will be a fight!" Still remembering his boyhood dreams of glory in battle, Timofei prayed for a fight.

"I am convinced that it is my destiny to add a new jewel to the crown of Russia—the American mainland. The time is ripe," Baranov wrote in his journal. He pored over the crude map of the North American continent. Only the shorelines were drawn; the middle of the continent remained basically blank, ready for exploration. "The British and the French and even the Boston Yankee traders are on the move in the Pacific. I have been watching them competing for the undiscovered lands, already outflanking the Spanish, although Spain has a chain of military forts along the coast north of Mexico!"

Baranov planned to outwit them all. "Russians must have the Pacific!" he wrote, underlining the word "must". "We'll start modestly, by building a fort close to the mainland. I am convinced we can succeed."

He had found a suitable site for such a fort. It was a large island, hundreds of miles south of Kodiak, but only a short distance from the mainland. It was perfect. It had plenty of sweet water and a large natural harbor. There was an abundance of timber for construction and shipbuilding. The island bore no traces of being previously claimed by any of Russia's rivals, although it was heavily populated by the Tlingit Indians. But this fact did not bother Baranov. "The Tlingits are savages. They have no concept of ownership of the land. Besides," he wrote, "we can deal with them in the same manner we have dealt with the Aleuts. We'll bribe

them, make them Russian subjects and put them to work for
the Crown. It worked with the Aleuts. No reason that it
should not work with the Indians."

His cynicism notwithstanding, Baranov had pursued a
liberal policy toward the natives. He scrupulously paid them
for their work and he built a school for their children, donat-
ing the money out of his own funds. He allowed the Aleuts
to live by their own rules, not interfering with their customs
of worship nor with the rearing of their children.

His tolerance of the native customs had paid off. He
won their trust. The Aleuts welcomed Russian settlements
on their islands and they worked for Baranov willingly, hunting otter and seal. "I like the Aleuts. Their happy disposi-
tion is such a contrast to our dour Russians!" Baranov often
thought.

The peace between the Russians and the Aleuts was disturbed when the Synod in St. Petersburg had decided that
the natives must be converted to Christianity. An Archdeacon and six priests and monks were dispatched to the Aleutian
Islands to begin a mass conversion of the natives.

The Aleuts eagerly flocked to the church to be baptized.
None of them understood the meaning of Christianity. They
worshiped the sun, the wind, the bear and various carved
images, following their ancient pagan customs, although they
crowded the church on Sundays.

The priests were powerless to stop the heathen practices
of their converts.

"Let them be," Baranov admonished the priests. "Let
them worship their idols, they do us no harm!" The priests
were incensed. During Baranov's absence from Pavlovsk,
they raided an Aleut village and burned the wooden idols.
The priests demanded that the Aleuts worship the invisible
God, a concept the natives could not grasp. Outraged by
the destruction of their effigies, the Aleuts assaulted one of
the priests. Archdeacon Nektarii, in retaliation, burned their
village and boats and took away their children.

In one act of zealous brutality, Nektarii had destroyed
the carefully built trust that Baranov had cultivated between
the Russians and the Aleuts.

Upon his return, Baranov summoned Father Nektarii to
his office. The priest, a young and gaunt man with a fanatical
fire in his close-set eyes under bushy brows, refused to sit
down. He stood at the door of Baranov's small office filling

it with his hostile presence. His black beard and long black tresses blended with his black cassock and tall black hat. A gold cross dangling over his chest on a long heavy chain was the only relief from his dark countenance.

He faced Baranov defiantly. There was no remorse on his hard face, no pity in his harsh eyes.

Baranov pleaded that the Russians must be tolerant of the ancient ways of the Aleuts. "Give them time, Father. In another generation they will learn to love our Lord and will embrace our faith. What good is faith if it is not freely given? Let them keep their idols. They do no harm."

Nektarii was adamant. "How dare you talk to me about waiting for another generation!" he thundered. "How dare you defend the heathen effigies! You are no better than a heathen yourself. Unless you recant, I forbid you to enter the church!" He shook his long finger under Baranov's nose.

In turn, Baranov became livid with anger. Jumping to his feet, he pounded his fist on his desk, glaring into the bearded face of his towering adversary.

"As the Lord is my witness, I won't allow you to mistreat my people! I'll punish the guilty, but I won't allow you to destroy the rest of the people. It took me years to win their trust, and I will not let you wipe it out overnight. I forbid you and your priests to leave Pavlovsk. Should any of you be seen in the Aleut villages, I'll confine you to the stockade. I swear!"

Nektarii glowered at him. Then, turning abruptly, he stalked out of Baranov's office, the skirts of his cassock flapping like the wings of a menacing bird.

He made good his threat. Baranov was forbidden to attend the Church services shortly after.

Baranov suffered his humiliation in silence. "The truth will prevail," he thought. "I will not allow anyone to harm my Aleuts. They are my children, they depend on my protection." Deeply religious, Baranov prayed before the icons in his house.

The antagonism between Baranov and the clergy grew. The priests wrote vicious letters to the Synod in St. Petersburg, denouncing Baranov as the Antichrist, a heretic, demanding his recall.

Baranov fought back. He wrote letters of his own, to Shelikhov, to the Ministry of Commerce, even to the Synod, protesting the priests' meddling into his administration of the colonies. He wrote that Russia needed the good will of the natives if she were to expand her influence in the Pacific.

He was locked in battle with the priests, neither side giving in. As he finally departed for his negotiations with the Tlingit Indians, the problem was still far from being solved.

Baranov had a dreadful premonition that the conflict, like a boiling volcano, was going to erupt, spreading its poisonous lava of destruction on everyone.

Chapter 4

"It's a formidable flotilla, Timosha," Baranov chuckled to Timofei as they stood by the helm of a small brig, the *Olga*, observing hundreds of *baidarki*, ready to begin their voyage into the Tlingit lands. "*S Bogom!*" He glanced at his sister ship, the *Ekaterina*. She was ready also. "Raise the flag!" he commanded.

Timofei pulled on the ropes and the Imperial double-headed eagle slowly began to rise, unfolding and fluttering in the wind.

Baranov saluted, his hand at the visor of his battered *kartuz*, a merchant's hat. His expression was solemn, his small body all but lost in oversized Aleut clothing made of sealskins. His sandy hair, beginning to turn white, struggled from under the *kartuz* in unkempt thin strands. His aging face was sagging and so was his body, but to young Timofei, Baranov was a figure of might. Baranov was a hero, a giant, on the threshold of claiming new territory for the motherland!

Timofei was bursting with pride of being chosen to accompany Baranov. "I'll show him of what I am capable!" he thought eagerly.

"Make sail!" Baranov commanded firmly.

Two weeks later, Baranov's flotilla reached the narrow bay studded with dozens of small green islands. From a distance the brushy little islands looked like floating Cossack hats.

The ships dropped anchors near the largest island. The Aleut *baidarki* arriving in small clusters during the next three days soon choked the bay. There were five hundred and fifty of them, each with two or three men. The boats bobbed gently on the calm rippling sea, protecting the two ships within their floating circle. The impassive Aleuts dozed in their boats as if in cradles once the paddling was over.

Baranov swept the area with his telescope.

The islands were silent. It seemed that nothing had ever disturbed their serenity, that no human being had ever stepped on their shores.

Baranov knew that this serenity was deceptive. From his previous exploration of the region he had learned that the large island was teeming with Tlingits. They were probably watching his flotilla at this very moment, he thought.

He sighed. "Well, we might as well disembark," he said to himself. "Let's go!" he ordered.

Baranov chose Timofei to row him ashore. Timofei's huge hulk would be most impressive, he thought. Baranov wanted to win the Indians' trust by coming to them unarmed, showing no fear, accompanied only by one man. However, as a precaution, he told his gunner aboard the *Olga* to load the cannons and shoot point blank should the Indians show any signs of hostility.

As Timofei rowed closer to the silent shore, a large group of Indians suddenly sprung from the underbrush that grew thick and verdant at the water's edge.

"The bastards look fierce," Timofei thought in alarm. He had become accustomed to the Aleuts, to their flat, gentle faces and narrow eyes that would light up in a friendly smile at any provocation.

The Tlingits were a different people. They were as tall as the Russians. Their well-proportioned naked bodies glistened from frequent applications of halibut oil. Their faces were painted in black and white stripes with touches of red and yellow. They wore rings in their high-arched noses. Pieces of bone pierced their lower lips. Their heads were elongated since infancy by exaggerated special binding and by applications of goosedown, which they patted into their hair.

The Indians, armed with slender spears and bows and arrows, aimed their weapons at the Russians.

"I don't like it," Baranov muttered. "They have their hair in a *whaler's knot*. They tie their hair this way only when they are on the warpath. Or hunting whales." He stood up in the boat and spread his arms wide to indicate that he was not armed. "Spread your arms," he said sharply to Timofei.

The Tlingits lowered their bows and spears.

"A close call," Baranov smiled nervously as Timofei beached the boat.

The Russians stepped ashore. "We come in peace," Baranov said at once to the Chief, distinguished from the others by a tall funnel-shaped hat woven of grass and consisting of several tiers to denote his importance. "We brought gifts." He motioned to Timofei to open the bag that he carried over his shoulder. "Look at these beads!" Baranov reached into the bag for a colorful strand. He spoke in Tlingit, having learned it from his own Indian wife.

Timofei, who already spoke fluent Aleut and was fast learning the Tlingit tongue, could follow most of Baranov's talk with the Chief.

"I am the Big White Chief," the Governor proclaimed solemnly, thumping himself on his chest. "I come in peace with gifts for your people. My name is Ba-ra-nov."

"My people call me Ska-out-lelt. I belong to Raven kwan," the Chief replied.

"My kwan is Double-headed Eagle. Do you see those floating houses?" Baranov pointed to the ships rocking gently at anchor. "Look at their tops. Do you see the double-headed eagles?"

"I see them." The Chief and his warriors squinted against the sun at the Russian Imperial eagles waving from the top of the masts.

"My kwan wants to be brothers of your kwan. This is for you." Baranov handed the Chief several strands of beads. "And for you and for you." He distributed handfuls of beads among the warriors. They took them greedily, delighted like children by their brightness.

"Come with me," the Chief said gruffly, turning towards the woods.

Baranov followed without hesitation. "Come on, Timosha, it's safe now. They won't cause any trouble. They are too curious to see what we've got for them!"

Only in Siberia had Timofei seen such tall and thick trees. On the Aleutian Islands the trees were stunted and gnarled by persistent gales. Here, they were verdant and full, exuding a wonderful scent, reminding him of Siberia.

A huge crowd of Tlingits waited for them at the clearing. They milled around several large windowless wooden houses decorated with striking designs of monstrous snarling beasts and predatory birds. Each single narrow entrance had been fitted into the gaping mouth of a monster, creating the impression that once one had stepped over the high threshold, one was swallowed by the beast. Timofei made the sign of the cross, to ward off evil.

The Chief led his guests into the largest house set apart from the others. His warriors crowded behind.

In the center of the house a fire was burning in a pit surrounded by sooty stones, the smoke escaping through a hole in the roof. Several women wearing seashell necklaces, but otherwise totally naked, tended the fire.

Timofei had never seen so many naked women. His eyes involuntarily followed every movement of their bouncing breasts, every shift of their round buttocks, drawn particularly to the junction of their legs. He hoped that Baranov had not noticed his interest in the women. Timofei's encounters with the Aleut women had never quite rid him of the teachings of the Siberian priest. Nakedness and the feelings it stirred still made him feel ashamed.

The Chief invited his guests to the fire. Haughtily he indicated where they were to sit on a grass mat as he settled himself on a broad carved seat resembling a throne, towering over his visitors.

"Why did you come?" he demanded, staring at Baranov.

"I want a strip of land on your island to build houses for my men." Baranov was cautious. He did not want to alarm the Chief by asking for the whole island.

"It's a big island. Enough space for everyone. You must want something else," the Chief said suspiciously.

"No. Only enough space to anchor my ships and build my houses."

The Chief had no objections to sharing the island, but he did not trust that the Russians would deliver the gifts as promised. He demanded that the gifts be brought from the ship immediately. Until then, the White Chief of the Double-headed Eagle would be the prisoner of the Ravens.

Baranov agreed. "My man will fetch the rest of the gifts. But send your own son to my ship. He'll be our hostage until I return."

The condition was accepted. The Indians appreciated the value of hostages. It assured protection against treachery.

The Chief's son, a boy of about fifteen, stepped out of the ranks to accompany Timofei back to the ship.

Timofei hesitated. He did not want to leave Baranov alone in the hands of the Indians.

"Go!" Baranov commanded sternly. "I'll be all right."

Baranov resumed his bargaining. In return for a large part of the island, he promised the Chief to protect him against his enemies.

The Chief laughed. "I am of the kwan of the Raven... I fear no one!" He struck his smooth, glistening chest with his fist.

When Timofei returned an hour later, followed by several men bent like itinerant tinkers under the weight of the bags of glass beads, and clanking pots and pans, Baranov's negotiations had been successfully completed. He was seated now next to the Chief on his carved seat, sharing a meal of smoked fish.

He grinned at his men. "The bastards swallowed it hook, line and sinker!" he exclaimed happily. The Ravens also smiled, nodding their elongated heads, not realizing that they had just lost their island.

Baranov named the new fort "St. Michael."

Timofei enjoyed working on the construction of the fort. It was exciting to see the stockades and block-houses rise where once there was an impenetrable virgin forest. Felling giant trees, uprooting ancient stumps which spread their tentacles deep into the ground, he felt his strength swell and expand. He liked to feel the axe in his hands as he hewed out logs for building the barracks and then, the small individual houses for married *promyshleniki.*

Soon the men would be settled down there with their Aleut wives and children brought from the Aleutian islands.

Timofei watched them, suddenly envious. The men looked so content in their snug little huts, he thought. He suddenly wanted to find a woman for himself, as well. "I am ready to settle down. Fort St. Michael will be my home. I have built it with my own hands. There's nothing waiting for me in Russia," he thought. "Nothing."

He liked the Tlingit women. They were taller and shapelier than the Aleuts, and their noses were not as flat, which appealed to him. "Some of them are real beauties," he thought. He asked Baranov's advice.

"By all means, take a wife! A fellow needs a woman," Baranov agreed. "Indian squaws make good wives," he added, thinking of his own Indian woman waiting for him in Pavlovsk. "I'll ask the Chief to find you one," he smiled fondly at the young man.

Several days later, the Chief brought to the fort a young copper-skinned woman with firm conical breasts tipped with broad dark nipples. She had long shiny black hair decorated with a single raven's feather. Her strong angular face was dominated by large, dark, luminous eyes, which reminded Timofei of a she-deer. Her thin, slightly arched nose bore a faint tattoo as delicate as a spider's web. Its tracery spread from her nostrils to her high cheekbones and her stubborn chin. Her lips were soft and full, the color of crushed raspberry.

She wore only a short apron of cedarbark. Her hips and breasts were bare. Timofei could not take his eyes off them. He bought her outright, not bothering to bargain for her price. He named her Marinka, thinking a Russian name and a Russian husband would make her a Russian wife.

Baranov blessed Timofei and Marinka with an icon of St. Michael and pronounced them married. It had no legal meaning, but Baranov always insisted on performing the ceremony. It kept the men in line, he thought, preventing them from changing their women. It also obligated them to take care of their offspring.

Freed by the "wedding" Timofei found he could not stay away from Marinka's ripe young body. Whenever he could he tasted, nibbled and squeezed. When she worked, he rubbed against her and fumbled under her cedarbark skirt. He spent every spare moment with Marinka, avoiding his fellow *promyshleniki*.

He chuckled at himself in the role of a husband. "I never thought that I would be so happy!" His days were filled with anticipation of the night when he would sink into the warm, moist body of his Marinka.

As for Marinka, she gave him her body but nothing else. It annoyed her to be constantly touched, squeezed and probed. Timofei's passion interfered with her work and disturbed her sleep. She showed no interest in learning to be a Russian wife either. She refused to wear the voluminous *sarafani* of Russian peasant women. She preferred her cedarbark aprons. She continued to decorate her hair with feathers and flowers instead of hiding it under a kerchief as was the custom for married women in Russia. She cooked Indian fashion, using hot stones to boil water. Nor would she try learning Russian words. "I am the daughter of the Raven," she said in Tlingit. "I speak the Raven tongue."

Timofei did not mind. Of course, he would have preferred that Marinka cover her body from the lewd stares of the *promyshleniki*, but it was impossible to argue with her; she could not grasp the idea that running around half-naked was a sin. He laughed at his friends' teasing that he had become a putty in Marinka's hands. The older men pointed their fingers to their heads and rolled their eyes; the young Timofei Tarakanov was obviously crazy!

"Sure I'm crazy," Timofei laughed good-naturedly, "I'm love crazy!" He was oblivious of Marinka's annoyance with his ardor. Barely nineteen, the juices of his manhood flowed powerfully through his body, demanding gratification. He was in love with his Indian wife, unaware that she was unresponsive.

Marinka pined for someone else.

Chapter 5

It took almost two years for the news of Catherine the Great's death to reach Fort St. Michael.

Baranov conducted the funeral service himself. There were no priests yet in Fort St. Michael. The bareheaded *promyshleniki* gathered around him on a clearing, the site of their future church. Fine rain glistened on their hair and beards. Soon the moisture began to run down their cheeks to their necks. They shifted uncomfortably, but no one left the services. They mourned their Tsaritza.

Baranov read from the Bible, his heart heavy. He could foresee many changes in Russia with the demise of Catherine. Although she had not actively supported her Pacific colonies and refused to grant Grigory Shelikhov the monopoly to develop the fur gathering enterprises, she was keenly interested in further explorations of the region. Would her successor follow her policies? What kind of a man was this new Tsar Paul? It was well known, even in the far-off colonies in the Pacific, that the old Empress meant her grandson Alexander to be her successor, yet the dispatch from Irkutsk stated that Paul, Alexander's father, was on the throne.

How did it happen? How was Catherine's desire disobeyed? Was there a plot to eliminate Alexander?

Baranov's mind churned as he read the words of the funeral services without hearing them. He wished that he could have had more information. The future of the Pacific colonies might be drastically changed, he thought. Perhaps, even threatened...

Catherine had died of a stroke, suddenly. She was only a

few days short of her intended date to officially proclaim her eldest grandson, Alexander, as her successor.

Catherine had raised Alexander from infancy. She supervised his education, having him taken away from his parents, preparing him to succeed her. Alexander pleased her. He was kind and gentle and she was sure that he would follow the course that she had charted for him. She knew his thoughts. He was also tall and good-looking, qualities the lusty Empress especially admired in young men. Catherine wrote in her will about preference for Alexander over her own son, Paul. She planned to announce this preference on her name's day, St. Catherine's Day on November the 24th.

She died on November the 6th.

Paul immediately ordered all the papers of his mother and those of Platon Zubov, her last lover, sealed. He secluded himself in Catherine's study with the Foreign Minister, Prince Bezborodko. Together they forced Catherine's desk open in search of one particular document—her will. Paul scattered his mother's papers carelessly off the edge of the desk. Correspondence with the American President George Washington slid to the floor. Paul had no interest in it. His pulse raced. While his hands scrambled the private letters of the Empress of all the Russias, one phrase sang in his mind like a gleeful chant. "Dead at last...dead at last...dead at last!"

He pulled at every drawer of Catherine's elegant desk, emptying them on the carpet in one large pile, not bothering to examine the contents. He wanted only one document: the will.

Prince Bezborodko found it. It was sealed in an envelope, tied with a black velvet ribbon and it bore an inscription in Catherine's own hand—"My will—to be opened after my death in the presence of the Council."

Paul grabbed the envelope. Without opening it, he threw it into the flames of the burning fireplace.

"I have won!" he shouted, not caring who might hear him. The light of the flames danced in his eyes. They glowed insanely as he turned to Bezborodko. The foreign minister felt a shiver of apprehension as he saw the look on Paul's face. "This man will soon control the lives of millions...Including my own," he thought, suppressing a shudder.

"I have won! The throne is mine!" Paul faced the foreign minister triumphantly. "Do you realize what it means?"

"Yes, Your Majesty," Prince Bezborodko bowed low before the new Emperor.

Paul began his reign by immediately demanding allegiance from the Court in the chapel of the Winter Palace.

The first to kneel before him was his wife the Grand Duchess Maria Feodorovna. She kissed the cross and the Bible proffered to her by the Metropolitan Gavriil, uttered a few prescribed words of the oath and then kissed her husband on the eyes and on the lips as was the custom. Then she took her place next to him. She was the Tsaritza now.

Paul's sons, the Grand Dukes Alexander and Constantine, were next. Alexander's handsome face was unperturbed. The old Metropolitan watched him covertly. "What thoughts run through his mind? Does he suffer from crushing aspirations or is he glad that the awesome responsibility is no longer to be his?" he thought as he proffered Alexander the Bible and the cross.

One after another the nobles filed before the new Tsar. His simian face was stony. He glared as Platon Zubov, his mother's last lover, knelt at his feet in subjugation.

He fought with the temptation to kick the hated favorite in the face with his polished Prussian boot. "I can do it, too! I am the Emperor!" he thought as he pushed his hand roughly for Zubov to kiss.

Alexander saw the look of hatred on his father's face. A feeling close to pity for Zubov stirred in his heart. "How low has Zubov fallen in just a few hours!" he thought.

The news of the Empress's death was announced to the people of St. Petersburg by the solemn toll of church bells. By the hundreds, people gathered on the snowy quays of the Neva and on the broad Palace Square, staring at the curtained windows of the Winter Palace, hoping to catch a glimpse of the new Tsar, not knowing whether it would be Paul or Alexander, most of them hoping it wouldn't be Paul.

A day passed without the new Tsar showing himself to the people. Paul waited for his loyal troops from his residence in Gatchina to arrive. He was terrified that Catherine's Guards regiments might stage a coup, arrest him and sweep Alexander to the throne. Locked in his mother's study, suspicious of anyone from her court, he promptly replaced Catherine's advisers with his own men. In less than twenty-four hours Catherine's court ceased to exist.

Paul rubbed his hands with glee as he listened to the familiar sounds of German all around him now. No more would the Tsar's Court prattle in French, the language of that murdering bitch, he thought. He was equally pleased to see the new style of dress. The gentlemen of his court would wear Prussian uniforms, he declared. No more embroidered waistcoats and silk stockings for courtiers. No more gold brocade jackets and lace trimmed shirts. The gentlemen of his court were ordered to don stiff woolen coats and coarse linen shirts and the ladies were reminded of feminine modesty and requested to cover their bosoms.

Paul was delighted that his orders were immediately obeyed.

"What a difference! I am the Emperor of All the Russias!" he thought, in awe of his sudden power. "I am the Emperor!" he repeated aloud, savoring the words.

Changing the Court's appearance was only a small step in Paul's plans in erasing Catherine's memory. He was waiting for the opportunity to display publicly his disdain for his mother, planning to do so during her funeral.

As he worked personally on every detail of the funeral, he did not forget his revenge against Platon Zubov. He had suffered greatly from the ridicule by his mother's young lover. The arrogant Zubov used to treat Paul with open contempt, inspired by Catherine's own attitude toward Paul.

Now it was his turn! He dealt harshly with all Catherine's favorites, but Platon Zubov was the first to suffer his wrath in a subtle way. Zubov was stripped of the title of Prince as well as all estates and serfs and other gifts from Catherine. Then, he was exiled from Russia for five years. "Let the salons of Europe see the Great Whore's gigolo!" Paul laughed cynically.

Having Zubov disposed of, Paul turned his full attention to the funeral. He commanded that his father, the murdered Tsar Peter III be exhumed.

The remains of Peter were taken from within the walls of Alexander Nevsky monastery. The pitiful bones were placed in a new coffin decorated with the imperial emblem of the two-headed eagle. The sealed coffin was placed on a pedestal next to Catherine's, but above hers, reminding the world that Peter was the rightful monarch of Russia, and Catherine merely his consort. A banner placed at the foot of both catafalques proclaimed in Church-Slavonic script—"Divided in life, united in death."

Paul yearned for still more humiliation for his mother's memory. Even in her death she threatened him. He ordered personally the route of the funeral procession.

Early in the morning the cortege formed in the courtyard behind the gates of the Winter Palace. On the Tsar's strict instructions it would follow Millionnaya Street, pass the Hermitage and then turn left on the Kamenostrovsky Bridge over the Neva. Burial would be at the chapel of Peter and Paul Fortress, the resting place of Russian monarchs since Peter the Great. And there were additional instructions.

Before the eyes of tens of thousands who lined the streets, Metropolitan Gavriil and his clergy dressed in black robes embroidered with dark tarnished silver led the way. Hundreds of church banners, icons and crosses held high by the priests swayed over their heads. Behind them, and ahead of the body of Catherine, rolled the black and gold carriage that bore the remains of Peter III. The six black horses pulling the hearse wore headgear of tall black ostrich plumes and their flanks were covered with embroidered blankets.

Peter's special touch was seen in the old man who wore the brilliant colors of Catherine's court and limped along ahead of the cortege. He carried the Imperial Crown on a velvet cushion, looking like a jester in his bright clothes compared to the rest of the somber procession. He was Alexei Orlov, the alleged assassin of Peter III and brother of one of Catherine's former lovers. Beside the carriage walked two of his accomplices, Prince Bariatinsky and Count Passek, ordered into service as pall bearers.

Paul was satisfied. He had denied Catherine the crown she stole, and had paraded the assassins who helped her to get it. He followed the remains of his father, walking alone, unaware of the bitter November cold, the wet snow plastering his bared head. Rivulets formed on the sides of his face as the snow melted, but Paul was oblivious to anything but the sweet taste of revenge.

The second catafalque bearing Catherine, also drawn by six black horses, was surrounded by Paul's Gatchina drummers, as if there were no mourners for her. This was Paul's intent, but the people of St. Petersburg thwarted his plans. They thronged behind her coffin by the hundreds, then thousands. They ignored the first catafalque. Peter had been

Tsar for only six months, and so long ago. Murdered or not, he was a mere abstraction to them. Most of the people had never seen him, but they knew Catherine, who often appeared before them during her thirty-four year reign. They mourned their *matushka* Tsaritza. At the sight of her coffin many fell on their knees in the snow, lamenting her death loudly, tears streaming down their faces.

Paul walked through this display of grief like an automaton, his eyes fixed straight ahead, his face stony.

"Cattle!" he thought. "Filthy Russian cattle!"

Chapter 6

Among thousands of troops along the funeral procession, only the Imperial Guards were allowed to follow the members of the Royal family.

Nikolai Petrovich Rezanov, a young cavalry officer and a close friend of Grand Duke Alexander was one of the Guardsmen. He rode with the funeral procession astride his favorite Arabian mare, Khanum Two, leading a battalion of Izmailovsky Guards.

The horse stepped smartly, lifting her front legs high, her neck curved like a swan's, showing her hours of dressage training. Nikolai, usually so proud of her performance, rode mechanically.

He felt depressed. The ascendance of Paul to the Russian throne threatened his career. "What will become of our country, now that Catherine is no more? What will become of *me*, now that Paul is on the throne?" Nikolai was deeply disturbed by the turn of events. He had high hopes for a brilliant career if Alexander had become the Tsar. Now—his future was uncertain, possibly even bleak. It was no secret in the Guards' circles that he had openly declared his preference for Alexander. He and the Grand Duke had been friends for years... Knowing the new Tsar's vindictiveness, Nikolai suspected that it would not be long before Paul terminated his career in the Guards.

As he rode slowly ahead of his battalion, the resentment against the new Tsar welled up in his heart. "If only the Empress had named Alexander!" he thought ruefully, his lean handsome face grim under the chin strap of his tall cockaded helmet. He touched the emerald ring on his left hand, a gift from the Empress for winning a dressage competition.

"Never mind, *golubushka*, little dove," he murmured softly to his mare. "Even if I have to leave the Guards, I'll never part with you, my treasure!"

Nikolai Petrovich Rezanov was descended from a proud noble family fallen on hard times. His profligate forebears had gambled away the ancestral lands and serfs and forced succeeding generations to rely only on their intelligence to survive. Rezanov's father Peter, deprived of the wealth of his ancestors, had become a distinguished jurist, president of the High Court of Equity in Irkutsk, Siberia. In his later years, he had moved to the capital so that his only son, Nikolai would receive a proper education. Several tutors were hired; by the time the young man entered the Izmailovsky Guards Regiment, his inherent right as a nobleman, Nikolai was as fluent in French, English and German as he was in Russian. On his own, he had learned Spanish, wishing to read *Don Quixote* in the original.

Brilliant in mathematics and philosophy, the young Rezanov read voraciously and secretly wrote poetry. He thought of himself as a disciple of Voltaire and Diderot which was fashionable in the Court of Catherine the Great, who herself had corresponded with the French philosophers.

For a while Nikolai fancied himself a musician, having learned to play the violin well. But of course, the career of a musician was beneath his station as an hereditary nobleman. Most musicians were serfs.

Were he seriously interested in a military career, he could have risen in his elite Regiment to become perhaps a colonel, or even a general, but Nikolai was aloof and sarcastic, seldom taking part in the regimental drinking and gambling orgies. The officers instinctively felt that Nikolai Rezanov was of a superior intellect and was bored by their company.

Nikolai was indeed bored. He yearned for more opportunity to exercise his abilities than a military career would afford. He would have liked to become a diplomat. But to be appointed an ambassador, one had to be very rich to uphold the Russian prestige abroad.

There remained only one way for a penniless officer to become wealthy: a prosperous marriage. Reluctantly, he began to think of it.

Nikolai was extremely handsome. Tall and slender, he had the look of a Nordic warrior, a Viking, with his cold blue eyes and full head of wavy blond hair. He had the pale complexion of a denizen of St. Petersburg, accentuated by his fine, thin-nostrilled nose, stubbornly set mouth and strong chin. He carried himself with the elegant arrogance of the Guards officers, but beneath that mask, there was a sensitive, easily hurt man, painstakingly suffering the humiliations brought upon him by his lack of funds.

A "prosperous marriage" was one of the humiliations. The prospect of a cold-blooded arrangement repulsed him. At thirty-two Nikolai was still a romantic, wishing for a marriage for love; he was not yet ready for a calculated union.

Paul plunged into his new role as the Emperor of all the Russias by ordering the construction of a new fortress surrounded by moats and drawbridges.

Beyond its walls, guarded by his own Gatchina troops, he would be safe. The fear of assassination filled his thoughts, diminished his satisfaction in becoming the Tsar, deprived him of sleep. He trusted no one, not even his wife. He was torn between affection for and mistrust of his son Alexander, who was loved by so many at court and venerated by the Guards. "The Guards! Always the Guards!" Paul thought furiously. It was the Guards who had murdered his father and proclaimed Catherine the Empress. He had a morbid premonition that the Guards might try to dethrone him as well.

To forestall a possible palace revolution, he began to curtail the power of the Guards, by denying them the privileges to which they had become accustomed. He would humiliate them too, he thought. He would appoint as their generals people of lower ranks. The arrogant aristocrats would have to bend, forget their pride and obey former corporals and sergeants. Of course, mass resignations of officers would follow, but it would open the way for appointment of German officers to high positions.

To gain recognition as an absolute monarch and to destroy his mother's international reputation, Paul repudiated her treaties and recalled her ambassadors, replacing them with his favorites, most of them of German ancestry.

The old proud Russian aristocrats were rudely denied access to the new Emperor, their complaints unheard, their advice unheeded. The new favorites clawed their way to the top rungs of success, fighting for the high rewards of titles and lands. Like his predecessors, Paul created scores of new barons and counts, assuring their loyalty to himself.

Shortly after his coronation in April, 1797, which was traditionally held in Moscow, Paul began the reshaping of his empire in earnest.

Nikolai Rezanov watched with horror as Paul turned the glittering capital of St. Petersburg into a military camp like Gatchina, his former residence. Every day Paul personally drilled the troops on the Field of Mars, the broad square near the Winter Palace, striking soldiers and junior officers with his cane for falling out of step, barking out the commands in a high squeaky voice.

Harsh reforms followed. The citizens were forbidden to wear round hats, laced shoes and long trousers. Instead, they were instructed to don three-cornered hats, powder their hair, wear knee-britches, white gaiters or stockings and buckled shoes. To enforce this whim, Paul dispatched two hundred dragoons to patrol the streets of St. Petersburg and punish those who disobeyed the new regulations. Soldiers attacked passersby, snatched their hats off their heads, tore their jackets into shreds and confiscated their laced shoes. Humiliated, the citizens had no choice but to obey the silly order. They began to look and to speak German.

Next, Paul directed his attention to the people's cultural needs and amusements. He forbade dancing of the waltz, considering the dance a French invention.

He deleted from the Russian vocabulary by a special *ukase* such words as 'citizen', 'club', 'society' and 'revolution', considering them subversive and directly responsible for the French revolution. Terrified that a revolution might be staged in Russia as well, Paul proclaimed censorship of all printed material, forbade importation of foreign books and music and finally, established a universal curfew. All streets of St. Petersburg were to be closed at night by striped barriers after nine o'clock. Only doctors and midwives, and a few privileged favorites were issued special passes.

For Nikolai Rezanov the end came when a whole regiment, which had displeased Paul during a drill, was ordered to leave the city immediately, exiled to Siberia.

The terrorized soldiers marched out of the capital in full formation, with their banners unfurled, the officers marching in front.

The citizens of St. Petersburg watched the doomed regiment in silence. No one dared to protest. The Tsar's power over his subjects was absolute.

The harsh punishment of the regiment made Nikolai offer his resignation from the guards.

He rode his Khanum Two to the barracks of the Semeonovsky Guards where Grand Duke Alexander had his quarters.

Alexander sprang to his feet to greet him. He stood more than six feet tall, his shoulders broad, his legs straight, unlike his bow-legged father.

"He looks like a Tsar should look," Nikolai thought fleetingly. "Even in this drab Prussian uniform he looks dashing!"

There was a certain softness about Alexander. Nikolai knew that women found him irresistible. He had curly blond hair, prematurely receding, which did not detract from his appearance. His eyes, strikingly blue, were the color of cornflowers. He was a little near-sighted and he often squinted, which gave him a look of utter attentiveness. His straight nose with narrow nostrils looked as if chiseled and Nikolai often thought that Alexander's profile would have looked marvelous wreathed in a laurel and stamped on a gold coin.

"Ah, Nikolai! At last! I haven't seen you since the funeral, and then we couldn't talk!" Alexander exclaimed cordially.

"Your Highness!" Nikolai bowed.

"Come, come... Enough of this formality. Sit down. I want to talk to you. I need your advice."

"I thought it was I who needed your advice," Nikolai smiled thinly.

"It can wait," Alexander interrupted impatiently. "I want to know what you think of this... this scandal, this embarrassment of sending the whole regiment to Siberia! Really! How did Papá allow himself to be persuaded to do such a cruel thing! It's all his German advisers! They always complain that we Russians don't know the meaning of discipline. But this is not 'discipline'. This is pure inhumanity!" Alexander's blue eyes were welling up with tears. "What can be done?"

"You are the only one, Your Highness, who can do anything about it," Nikolai said gently. "Try to persuade His Majesty that the unfortunate incident will be exploited by our enemies abroad. They'll consider us barbarians, and worse...

As you know, Russia is trying to negotiate certain treaties with England and France, right now... I think it would be beneficial not to attract too much attention to our domestic problems," he concluded, choosing his words carefully.

"Yes! Yes, I'll talk to my father. I'll request an audience with him right away!" Alexander exclaimed enthusiastically. "You're a born diplomat, Nikolai!"

"And perhaps, I would have been one, if you were the Tsar," Rezanov thought as he smiled.

"What was it that you wanted to talk to me about?" Alexander reminded.

"I have decided to tender my resignation from the Guards."

Alexander looked at him pensively, saying nothing. He was aware of the unrest among the Guards.

"What will you do in civilian life?"

"I don't know yet."

"If I were the Tsar, I would appoint you as my ambassador to some great country!" Alexander laughed. "England, perhaps!"

"But you are not the Tsar," Nikolai thought. Aloud he said, "Try to convince His Majesty to rescind his order."

Alexander was able to persuade his father to recall the regiment. The condemned soldiers, already on the march for a week, returned to the capital, still in formation, dully submissive to their fate.

But the officers, most of them the scions of the best Russian families, burned with hatred for the Tsar. They swore vengeance.

"What should I do, Father? It's obvious that I must find some form of employment, now that I've resigned from the Guards."

Nikolai sat in his father's study in the modest house on the Fontanka Quay.

The elder Rezanov frowned. Like his son he was tall and lean, his lined face still handsome, his silvery mane glistening, reflecting the light of the candles in the tall candelabra.

"I think we should visit Count von Pahlen. He has managed to stay in power after the Empress' death. Perhaps he might have a position for you in one of the ministries... Yes, let's pay a visit to Peter Alexeyevich!"

A carriage was ordered and the two Rezanovs departed for Count von Pahlen's mansion.

A servant announced their arrival. The Count greeted them at the door of his study furnished in luxurious French style, in complete disregard of the Tsar's wishes to abolish French influence.

"*Bonjour, mes amis! Quel bon chance de vous voir!*" he exclaimed warmly, ignoring the *ukase* to speak German.

Count Peter von Pahlen, although of German ancestry, thought of himself as a thoroughly Russian patriot. Of medium height, well proportioned with broad shoulders made to look even broader by the heavily fringed gold epaulets of a general, Count Peter von Pahlen was a skillful diplomat. He had survived several palace purges following the death of Catherine, rising to the high post of Governor-General of St. Petersburg.

He won the new Tsar's trust by refusing to intercede on behalf of his own son who was arrested on Paul's orders. Instead of pleading lenience for the young officer, von Pahlen declared, "Sire, it will be beneficial for the rascal to be incarcerated. You've performed an act of justice!"

Paul was impressed. Von Pahlen became his confidant. The Tsar entrusted him with several important posts in the government, such as the presidency of the College of Foreign Affairs and management of the postal service. The police were already under von Pahlen's command as the Governor of St. Petersburg.

"What can I do for you, my friends?" he inquired, inviting the Rezanovs to sit down. A servant in a powdered wig and a brocaded livery coat brought them glasses of claret. "I heard that Nikolai has tendered his resignation from the Izmailovsky regiment. Is it true?" he continued.

Nikolai nodded. "Yes, Peter Alexeyevich. I find it impossible to remain in the Guards. For many reasons," he added with a special meaning.

"I understand. So, now, you'll need a civilian position that pays well and allows room for advancement, *n'est pas?*" he winked broadly at Nikolai.

"Yes."

"Well, I just happen to know that there's an opening in the department of petitions at the Senate. The position is that of a deputy, but the gentleman who is heading it now is due for retirement... Are you interested?"

"Thank you, Peter Alexeyevich, I am indeed very interested. Thank you very much!"

"Don't mention it. It's my pleasure to help an old friend." He smiled at the elder Rezanov. "Too many important papers get lost in our governmental offices run by little people in Prussian uniforms. We need *our own* men to run the Russian government!" He lowered his voice conspiratorially, knowing that both Rezanovs understood his meaning. They could be trusted in their loyalty to the legacy of Catherine. They could be counted on in their support of Alexander.

Nikolai moved out of his quarters in the barracks of the Izmailovsky regiment and into his father's house without regret. He dismissed two of his servants, keeping only his serf, Ivan, as his valet.

His horses he sold, except for his precious mare Khanoum Two; he would never part from her, he thought. Khanoum Two would stay in his father's stable until he could afford quarters of his own and a place to keep her. If his work went well he might be able to move soon.

The job in the department of petitions required that he read hundreds of letters addressed to the Tsar, asking for favors, demanding justice, crying for help. Some he prepared to pass along to von Pahlen for further screening, others he rejected with formal notes. But one letter from Grigory Shelikhov, a Siberian fur merchant, was of special interest to Nikolai. He knew that Grigory Shelikhov was an old friend of his father. He read the letter twice and took it home to show it to his father.

The elder Rezanov read the letter with great concentration. Finally, pushing his spectacles above his forehead, he said pensively, "I believe, Nikolasha, you must make sure that Shelikhov's plea reaches the Tsar's ear. Look, he's not asking much. My wily friend is clever. He doesn't request any money from the Crown, only that a government official be sent to visit his offices and perhaps the newly claimed territories in the Pacific. He just wants to demonstrate how much his company had already accomplished in securing the land and its wealth for Russia. Just listen to what he says... " Peter Rezanov unfolded the letter and pushed his spectacles back on his nose.

"The waters around the islands off the American continent are teeming with fur-bearing animals," the elder Rezanov read aloud. "If Russia fails to advance her claims on the region, the British, the French, the Bostonmen, will soon dominate the ocean trade. All we need is Your Majesty's blessings. With God's help, we'll advance the borders of Your Majesty's empire to the American continent."

"You see," Peter Rezanov peered at his son over the letter, "if my old friend dares to ask for inspection, his affairs must be indeed in pretty good order. He must be quite confident that the government will be impressed with his achievements in the Pacific. What's more, Nikolasha, I think that it ought to be *you*, who will be this 'government official'," Peter Rezanov pointed his finger at Nikolai.

"I?"

"Yes, my dear, *you*. It could be of enormous importance for your career. When you succeed in persuading the Tsar to become interested in the expansion of the Pacific empire, your rewards will be enormous. So, take my advice, talk to Count Rumyantzev and ask him to deputize you to go to Irkutsk to examine Shelikhov's warehouses and see his accounts. When you return, you will present your findings and your own recommendations to the Tsar."

Nikolai looked at his father for several moments without speaking. Then he nodded. "I like the idea. I have been looking for a long time for an opportunity to explore the world beyond the salons of St. Petersburg," he smiled. "Going to Irkutsk, and possibly even to the Aleutian Islands sounds exactly what I would like to do! I'll talk to the Minister tomorrow." He rose to leave. He carefully placed Shelikhov's letter into a red morocco leather folder. He kissed his father on the cheek and left the room.

Peter Rezanov watched through the window as his son mounted Khanum Two and cantered out of the courtyard. "I do hope that Nikolai will be able to advance Shelikhov's cause," he thought. "It could be very good for all concerned, " he smiled to himself. "Grigory's two daughters should be old enough to marry by now... A man could do worse than become a son-in-law to that fortune," he thought.

Chapter 7

Grigory Shelikhov had been waiting impatiently for a reply from the Tsar, but month after month had passed without a word from the capital.

He paced the floor of his spacious study, then stopped at the window covered with delicate spiked designs of hoarfrost. He breathed on the glass and made a little round spot. He pressed his eye to the melted spot, peering at the snow-covered yard where servants were exercising his sturdy Siberian horses.

He watched them, thinking of the elegant, high-stepping St. Petersburg horses and how they would not have lasted a day in the brutal Siberian winters of sixty and eighty degrees below zero. Shelikhov sighed. "If only I knew someone at Court!" he thought bitterly. As a member of the lower class, he could not hope for a private audience with the Tsar without the intervention of someone highly placed.

A bell rang in the front hall, interrupting his thoughts. Shelikhov heard a servant opening the door. The deep voice of a stranger inquired whether the master was at home. Shelikhov went to greet the unexpected guest.

"I am Nikolai Rezanov. I believe you know my father." Nikolai removed his sable hat and bowed to the older man.

"But of course! Come in, come in, be my guest, Nikolai Petrovich!" Shelikhov exclaimed with delight. "Your father and I knew each other quite well when he lived in Irkutsk!"

Nikolai took off his great traveling coat, a *shuba* lined with red fox, asking permission to remove his snow-powdered *valenki*. A servant pulled the felt boots off, replacing them with fur slippers.

Shelikhov led Nikolai into the parlor.

"A glass of vodka?"

"With pleasure. I am frozen to the bone." Shelikhov
clapped his hands and a servant brought in a tray of *zakuski*,
tidbits of meats, smoked fish, and caviar and a sparkling crystal decanter of vodka with two silver tumblers.

Shelikhov poured vodka for both of them. "Your health!"
Each drank it in one gulp. Nikolai felt the *ryabinovka* burn
his throat, then flow downward, spreading fire all the way to
his stomach.

"What brought you to Irkutsk, Nikolai Petrovich?" Shelikhov asked as the servant poured them another cup.

"Your petition to the Tsar. Perhaps I can help you reach
His Majesty."

"You are heaven-sent, Nikolai Petrovich!" Shelikhov
cried happily. "My prayers have been answered!"

That evening Shelikhov introduced Nikolai to his family. His wife, Natalia, was a tall, handsome woman dressed
in the European fashion, looking more like a gentlewoman,
rather than a merchant's wife. Nikolai was accustomed to
traders and their wives who looked and spoke like peasants;
but here was a refined couple who had the appearance and
speech of cultured people. Nikolai knew that Shelikhov was
indeed a man of considerable achievements. His *Journal of
the Voyages to the Coast of America in 1783-1786* had been
published in London in 1795, stirring much interest in that
seagoing nation. Nikolai had read the Russian and the English editions in preparation for his meeting with Shelikhov.
Like its author, Nikolai had been fascinated by the promise of
Empire the new land possessed. Talking with Shelikhov that
day had convinced him that at last he had found his own
goal in life. He would do anything in his power to advance
Russian claims on the Pacific, he thought. He decided to tie
his future to Shelikhov's plans.

These thoughts churned in his mind as he chatted with
Shelikhov's wife.

He heard a rustle of silk.

"Ah, there she is, my *golubushka* Annushka!" Shelikhov
exclaimed, jumping to his feet lightly as if he were a young
lad and not a portly middle-aged man. "May I introduce my
youngest daughter Anna, to Your Excellency?" He took her
by the hand and led her ceremoniously to Rezanov.

"I am delighted, Mademoiselle," Nikolai bowed. Annushka blushed and made a deep curtsy.

"She's adorable!" Nikolai thought watching the fourteen-year-old Annushka covertly. She was very tall for her age and slender. Her budding breasts pushed against the tight bodice of her European-style gown and her smooth white neck rose gracefully over its low cut. She wore her pale blond hair in one long thick braid which was the only "Russian" concession to her otherwise European appearance. She had a pert nose and full pink lips which rose up at the corners, reminding Nikolai of Botticelli's cherubs. She chatted with Nikolai in French, charmingly mispronouncing some words, but at ease in the presence of a stranger, in strong contrast to the behavior of other provincial maidens he had met.

Nikolai was enchanted. "I don't need to look any further," he suddenly thought. "Here she is, my future bride!"

In the days that followed, Nikolai engrossed himself in the examination of Shelikhov's company records. He pored over the reports of Shelikhov's man, Alexander Baranov, who as *Glavny Pravitel*, was hired to govern the enterprises. He examined the crude maps of the Pacific and the Aleutian Islands made by the illiterate *promyshleniki*, who often served as navigators on the company ships, for lack of real navigators. He visited Shelikhov's warehouses, impressed by the quality of furs brought from the American shores. He let Shelikhov talk, eager to learn everything about his enterprises.

Shelikhov was delighted to have a sympathetic listener. He indulged himself in long speeches which he never would have had a chance to make to the Tsar, but which he could deliver now to his new "friend at Court."

"My partner Ivan Golikov and I had founded our company in the early 1780s. From the beginning, we struggled with the indifference of the government toward our enterprise, although the government was always prompt to collect taxes," Shelikhov smiled bitterly at the recollection.

"My father told me that you went to St. Petersburg personally to plead for an audience with Catherine. Did the Empress receive you?" Nikolai asked.

"Alas, no. I spent several months in St. Petersburg being shuttled from one ministry to another, never allowed in Her Majesty's presence," Shelikhov's genial face clouded, his pride still smarting at the humiliating experience.

Nikolai recalled his father's comments. "All that Grigory Shelikhov had accomplished by his visit to St. Petersburg was to receive a medal for his explorations and a jeweled sword, which the Empress sent him. But no monopoly, for which he asked, nor money to build ships for exploration. Catherine decreed that the merchants must use their own money for building ships and a monopoly—of any kind— was against her principles."

Nikolai stared at Shelikhov's portrait where he was depicted wearing his medal and his sword. "He must've had it painted while he was in St. Petersburg," he thought, a wave of sympathy for his host swelling in his chest. How easy it had always been for him, as a nobleman, to see the Empress, or any member of the Royal Family, he thought. And here was this great man, this visionary, who had to bow and scrape before some minor functionaries, trying to make them comprehend his great designs!

"So, my partner and I went ahead and built the ships and the settlements on the Aleutian Islands without the help of the Crown," Shelikhov continued. "Our largest settlement was on Kodiak Island. I named it Pavlovsk, in honor of Grand Duke Paul. I wrote to her Majesty about it, hoping that it would please her."

"The Empress would have liked it better if you had named it after her grandson, Alexander," Nikolai smiled wryly.

"If I only knew!" Shelikhov said. "Anyway, the warm Japanese current kept the harbor open the year around. From that harbor we could launch our incursions into the Pacific. I hired a *Glavny Pravitel*, one Alexander Baranov, a tough, experienced fur hunter, who was perfect for the job."

"I wish I could meet him," Nikolai said. "From his reports it seems that he's devoted to his job and is eager to pursue your plans."

"Oh, yes, he is. He's a very tenacious man. He has already established several new settlements on the islands and has his eye on a new territory on the mainland. He's just the kind of a leader we need."

As the days passed, Shelikhov's zeal to talk about his ambitions never slacked. Once in a while he would stop, suddenly embarrassed that he had been turning their conversations into a monologue, but soon would continue, encouraged by Nikolai's sincere interest.

By the end of the month Nikolai thought that he had learned enough to present an impressive report to the Tsar. It was time to leave, but he delayed his departure from day to day.

The reason was Annushka.

Every evening, after spending his day poring over the company's records and listening to Shelikhov talk, Nikolai relaxed in the company of the Shelikhov women.

He was impressed by his hostess Natalia's knowledge of her husband's business. He did not realize that she had accompanied Shelikhov to the Aleutian Islands.

"It must have been very hard for a lady," he said looking at her with new respect.

Natalia smiled. "It was. We spent a whole winter living in an underground like moles. It was awful!" she shuddered.

"What an unusual family," Nikolai thought, his gaze drifting to Annushka. He liked everything about her. Her soft long hair, her deep-throated laugh, so unusual in a girl her age. She wrinkled her nose when she laughed, and Nikolai thought it was charming. Her eyes, brown, with golden specks, were in strong contrast to her pale blond hair. She had proudly arched eyebrows and long curving lashes which gave her eyes a look of mystery. Her mouth was soft and full and Nikolai knew that it would taste sweet.

"I couldn't do any better if I searched for a bride for a hundred years!" Nikolai thought. "Annushka's perfect!"

On the practical side, Nikolai knew there would be no bar to the marriage. He was poor, but he had something no commoner's wealth could buy. He was a noble by birth and therefore a link to the power that controlled everything. The Shelikhov family would welcome him. Through him Annushka would be elevated to the nobility. Shelikhov's grandchildren would be nobles.

But what about Annushka? Was she interested in him or was she just impressed by a glamorous visitor from St. Petersburg?

That evening Annushka came down to supper with her hair dressed in the French manner, curls cascading along her pink round cheeks.

"I like it better when you wear your hair in the old Russian way, like the Snow Maiden," Rezanov said teasing her. Annushka quickly left the room. When she returned, moments later, her hair was wet but plaited into a braid.

"I wanted to please you, so I stuck my head into a bucket of water!" she announced naively.

Rezanov knew then that he would not be rejected by her. Annushka was in love with him.

Later that night, alone with Shelikhov in his handsome wood-paneled study, sipping cognac, Nikolai asked for Annushka's hand. As he had expected, Shelikhov was greatly honored. He called his wife and Annushka into his study.

"His Excellency Nikolai Petrovich has asked to marry Annushka," he said smiling broadly. "What will you say, daughter?" They all knew the answer.

Shelikhov took the icon of the Virgin Mary off the wall and with his wife at his side, gave his blessing to the young couple kneeling before him. He kissed Nikolai on both cheeks and embraced his daughter, tears glistening in his eyes. "My cup runneth over," he thought.

It was decided to dispense with the traditional long engagement. They must hurry with the wedding so that Nikolai could return to St. Petersburg and present Shelikhov's petition to the Tsar. Still, the family needed at least two weeks to prepare for the ceremony.

Seamstresses, floor polishers, cooks and bakers filled the Shelikhov's spacious house. Horse-drawn sleighs pulled in and out of the yard bringing in bushels of provisions, bolts of Chinese silk, French laces and even fresh flowers grown in the only greenhouse in Irkutsk at the residence of the Governor. The snow was cleared from the street in front of the house twice a day by the prisoners of the local *ostrog*, but new storms and wind would pile it two or three feet high again during the night. In the courtyard quadrangle the footpaths created a giant X. Crossing diagonally from one end of the yard to another, the servants scurried over the paths, hidden up to their shoulders in the snowy tunnels.

Annushka locked herself in her room with her mother and five seamstresses who stitched and embroidered her trousseau and wedding gown. She would appear for a few moments, flushed and pretty, smile at her fiancé, accept a secret kiss, then disappear again behind the closed doors of her maiden domain. Nikolai would hear her clear pure voice singing along with the women working on her trousseau.

"I am a lucky man," he thought.

They were married in the old log church where Annushka was baptized fourteen years before. Her older brother gave her away following the old Orthodox custom. Her parents remained in their house during the ceremony, according to the ancient tradition, keeping the front doors open to indicate that their daughter was always welcome in their home.

It seemed that the whole city of Irkutsk had gathered to celebrate the wedding. The governor, the city officials, the rich merchants, all with their families, crowded into the church, standing with lighted candles, singing lustily, "Many Years of Life." Many more crowded in the church yard.

The priest, in golden robes, led the newlyweds three times around the altar, while the choir sang. The four best men, Annushka's cousins, alternating every few minutes, held heavy golden crowns over the young couple's heads, while her bridesmaids carried the long train of her white satin gown.

The newlyweds were greeted by a crowd of beggars and cripples as they left the church. The cripples swarmed around them, their hands outstretched, their mutilated arms and feet exposed to evoke pity.

Nikolai and Annushka dropped coins in every outstretched hand as the tradition demanded. Now their life together would be blessed by the poor.

A lavish reception awaited them at Shelikhov's house. Wine, vodka, French champagne and huge quantities of foods and sweets were spread on several long tables. The guests attacked the foods and drink.

Soon they grew boisterous, shouting "*gorko, gorko!*" demanding that the newlyweds kiss to "sweeten" their drinks, an old Russian custom at weddings. The young couple obliged and kissed.

"*Gorko, gorko!*" the guests shouted.

Nikolai began to feel annoyed. He always hated drunken crowds. But he suppressed his annoyance, seeing that Annushka enjoyed herself.

"It's her last evening with her family," he thought. "Tomorrow we'll leave for St. Petersburg."

A long caravan of sleighs and pack horses was assembled in the yard of Shelikhov's house. Annushka bade a tearful farewell to her parents. But Nikolai was relieved that she was less emotional about leaving them than he had expected.

Annushka was aware of the importance to her family that Nikolai reach the Tsar as soon as possible.

"*S Bogom!*" Shelikhov lifted the heavy icon of St. Nikolai to bless the travelers. "God speed!"

A convoy of ten armed Cossacks surrounded the covered sleighs where Nikolai and Annushka and her elderly nurse Nikiforovna and two maids were to ride. The caravan was off.

Nikolai dreaded the journey with the extra burden of women, baggage and cumbersome sleighs. As the days passed, monotonous in the sameness of the forest landscape, he became short-tempered and harsh-tongued with everyone except Annushka. She gave him the only joy he had found in the journey. Her eyes had found newness and beauty everywhere. She marveled at the horsemanship of the Cossacks, the patterns of frost in the mornings, the sudden crack of a fir tree split asunder in the frost. Bundled up in a great sable coat, only her face visible, Annushka radiated happiness and wonder.

"I am so happy!" She snuggled close to Nikolai. "Isn't it the most wonderful journey you have ever taken?" Nikolai smiled, ashamed for his outbursts of irritability. Annushka's innocent enthusiasm was contagious. Nikolai relaxed. St. Petersburg was still several weeks away

Chapter 8

The Rezanovs' caravan reached St. Petersburg in early spring. In the city it was still cold, although the ice on the Neva had broken and was floating in huge clumps toward the Baltic. The poplars lining the boulevards at the Admiralty were coming into bud, misted in tender green hues. The air felt fresh and salty as the wind blew from the sea.

Nikolai always like the early spring in St. Petersburg. It was the beginning of a brief period of bright skies and sunshine, culminating in the blooming of the lilacs and the white nights of June. By September the city would gradually return to its perennial fogs and rains which would draw a veil of melancholy over it. There would be three or four golden days of autumn, but by the end of October, snow and a bitter raw winter would settle for a long stay. Nikolai requested an audience with the Tsar, but Paul was in no hurry to receive him. Nikolai had to be patient. He threw himself into supervising the repair and refurbishing of a house, which he had bought, using some of the money from Annushka's dowry, an old stucco mansion on Vasilievsky Island. It was neglected and peeling, but its architecture was of the elegant Italian style. Two broad wings embraced the small round court with a minuscule formal garden. The central part of the building was fronted by a terrace decorated with urns and classical statuary. From their windows they could see the granite embankments of the Neva, and beyond, the Winter Palace.

Months passed. Then one morning a messenger arrived with a summons to appear before the Tsar immediately at his new, still unfinished fortress, the Mikhailovsky Palace.

Nikolai was ready. His thick portfolio of maps and drawings had been packed since the second week of his arrival.

He would show Paul the newly published volumes of writings of the English explorer, George Vancouver, as well as both editions of Shelikhov's journal. He hoped that Vancouver's books would demonstrate better than anything that the English had been extending their empire, encroaching on the north Pacific.

His serf, Ivan, drove him to the palace in Annushka's new carriage. The matching grays stepped out smartly, the carriage barely swaying on its leather suspensions.

At the draw bridge across the moat Nikolai's way was barred by a black and white barrier. Two black and white diagonally striped guardhouses stood at the opposite sides of the bridge, and the guards, shouldering muskets with fixed bayonets, stiffly goose-stepped back and forth between the guardhouses.

Nikolai left the carriage and walked across the bridge on foot. His name was carefully checked on a list by the duty officer. He was allowed to enter the courtyard. Once more his name was checked; he was permitted to enter the vestibule.

Within the palace, his identity was checked again, by an officer who knew him personally, but who went through the procedure nevertheless. Finally, Nikolai was escorted by an aide-de-camp to a large reception room with massive ebony furniture and asked to wait.

The room was dominated by long tables supported by huge solemn figures of bronze sphinxes. Nikolai recalled the contrast of Catherine's reception rooms. They had been full of light, elegant gilded furniture, gleaming statuary and inlaid mosaic Italian tables. Her tapestries had burst with flowers, birds and cupids, while Paul favored bare walls sparsely hung with military banners and Prussian-style weapons.

"Not a vase of flowers, not a mirror, to break the ugliness!" Nikolai thought as he sat down on an uncomfortable straight-backed chair.

Several other men waited to be received by the Tsar. They shifted nervously, glancing at the massive doors of his study.

Nikolai prepared for a long wait, but he was the first to be called in. An aide-de-camp opened the door ceremoniously. Nikolai stepped into the Tsar's study.

It was a large room with three tall windows facing the parade grounds. The Tsar sat behind a desk of shiny ebony, dwarfed by its dimensions.

Nikolai bowed from his waist, waiting to be invited to come closer.

"Nikolai Rezanov?" the Tsar asked nasally in German, although he had met Nikolai many times before. He lifted his protruding eyes from the papers on his desk. His long chin spilled out of the stiff collar of his Prussian uniform. He wore a lacy jabot and a powdered wig with a black ribbon holding the pigtail.

His scrawny neck seemed to stretch and disappear periodically, like the neck of a turtle. His short upturned nose, too small for his long-chinned narrow face, looked like a button, its nostrils like buttonholes.

"At your service, Your Majesty." Nikolai bowed again.

"You may approach."

Nikolai crossed the parquet to the desk and stopped the required three steps away. There was no extra chair. The visitors were not allowed to sit during the audience.

"We have been informed that you have an interesting proposition to present to us. We have read the petition of the merchant, Shelikhov, and we find it to possess certain merits," the Tsar began.

"Yes, Sire. If Your Majesty would permit, I'll follow merchant Shelikhov's presentation by presenting verbally the most important points."

"You may proceed."

"Your Great-Grandfather, Sire, authorized the first expedition to the Eastern Ocean, as the Pacific was known to us in those times."

"Continue."

Nikolai quickly outlined the early explorations and told what he had learned of the current state of Shelikhov's thriving business.

"It's all very interesting," Paul said as Nikolai paused. "We've heard that the waters of the Pacific are so full of sea animals that hunters don't even bother to shoot them. They pull them out of the water. Is it true?"

Nikolai smiled. "No. Not quite, Your Majesty. But it is true, there are millions of seals and otters. Also, such other animals as fox, beaver, mink and bear. There is a great fortune in furs, Sire. However, the fur trade is not the most important aspect of Shelikhov's proposal."

"What is it then?"

"Sire, the Pacific Ocean is the key to many unclaimed territories. For instance, the Sandwich Islands, or as the natives call them, Hawaii."

"Who owns these islands?" Paul's eyes suddenly sparkled with curiosity.

"No one, really, that is, no European power, although it was an Englishman, Captain James Cook who had discovered the islands." Nikolai was encouraged by the Tsar's interest. "The native ruler, King Kamehameha, probably is not aware of the strategic value of his islands. They are at a crossroads of the shipping lanes. The country that possesses the Sandwich Islands will have open sea lanes all the way to India." He paused significantly. He had learned from Count von Pahlen of Paul's particular interest in India.

"Continue."

"To start, Sire, we can lease some land from this Hawaiian king ostensibly for a trading post. We can build a small fort, then bring in settlers and, eventually, troops, to protect the settlers. We can take over the Sandwich Islands one by one, as we have done already in the Aleutian chain." He pointed to the map again. "What we need, Your Majesty, for our advance on the Pacific, is some dedicated Russians and ships. The time is ripe, Sire."

Paul stared at the map. Nikolai continued, "You'll see from my report, Sire, and from these volumes of Captain Vancouver's writings that the English have already claimed a large portion of the Pacific. So have the Spanish. If you allow, Sire, I'll show it to you on the other map."

"By all means." Nikolai unrolled another map.

"This map was prepared by Captain George Vancouver, Sire." They bent over the map, their heads almost touching. The Tsar had a foul odor from his mouth. Nikolai tried not to show his discomfort. He traced the holdings of Spain on the map. "The Spanish have military posts and religious missions all along the coast." He made a sweeping gesture over the map. "They call this region California. The British are here, further north," he pointed to Nootka Sound and the Vancouver Island. "The British had a military dispute with Spain over this territory. They claimed it under right of previous discovery by Sir Francis Drake. The Spanish finally conceded. As you can see, Sire, there's nothing to prevent the British from expanding their claim on the Northern Pacific. They have the ships needed for it. As you know, they have already reached India." He paused significantly.

The Tsar snorted contemptuously. "I hate the British! Such a tiny island nation, how did they manage to grab India?"

"Oh, they are very clever, the British! They always start by offering to trade. Then, when the trade begins to flourish, they offer their assistance to the local rulers in exchange for a token territory. Of course they pledge non-interference in the local and political affairs, but that means nothing."

The Tsar laughed cynically, making a high hiccuping sound, as if gasping for air. "*Divide et Impera,*" he gasped through his laughter. "Divide and rule. Those British bastards are very enterprising, eh?"

"Indeed they are, Sire. They have *the* ships to carry on their ambitions," Nikolai repeated with a special emphasis, which he hoped the Tsar would not miss. "I've heard recently, the British could mobilize more than two hundred ships of the line!"

"To our less than fifty," Paul mumbled, staring at the Vancouver map. "Tell me more about India," he said suddenly.

"Well, Sire, I believe that India will shortly become a colony of the British empire. The British had established their foothold there as early as during the Elizabethan times, through their East Indies Trading Company."

"Trading, again!"

"Yes, Sire. *Trading* company. Just what I suggest we create in the American islands. A *trading* company of our own."

"Go on, about India."

"At present, Lord Mornington, a very shrewd administrator, is the Governor-General. He has a small number of troops at his disposal, but they are faultlessly trained. His officers are in charge of training the local troops for the benefit of the British crown, and his administrators are virtually in every province, overseeing all aspects of civilian life, from trade to justice.

Ceylon has just become a British Crown colony...India is not far behind, I am afraid, unless someone, like Napoleon Bonaparte interferes."

Paul gave him a peculiar look but said nothing. He had his own ideas about Napoleon Bonaparte.

"So, you advise us to become active in the Pacific?"

"Yes, Sire, without delay. It would be relatively inexpensive. If Shelikhov and Golikov are granted the monopoly to trade, they will build the new establishments at their own expense. The government need do nothing until the traders build the forts. Then we will dispatch troops to man the forts and to protect the settlers, the usual procedure in colonization. It would take only a few years, but we would block the British on the Pacific. Or, for that matter, anybody else. The Pacific would become a Russian lake!"

Paul's round forehead furrowed in concentration. "Why then nothing has been done before? According to your report, this information has been available for at least several decades."

"Sire, your Great-Grandfather had died before the first expedition of Vitus Bering was completed. The following monarchs had no interest in continuing Peter the Great's work," Nikolai began diplomatically. He knew of Paul's identification with his Great-Grandfather. The latest proof of Paul's admiration for him was a huge bronze equestrian statue of Peter, which he had commissioned to be placed in front of his new Mikhailovsky Palace. In imitation of the famous monument to Peter erected by Catherine, which was inscribed simply "To Peter the First—Catherine the Second", Paul had ordered *his* monument to read— "To Great-Grandfather from Great-Grandson."

"Your mother, Sire, felt that her interests lay elsewhere, mainly in Europe and in the Bosphorus," Nikolai continued, hinting about Catherine's designs on Constantinople. Shrewdly, he said nothing more, counting on Paul's aversion to his mother's policies.

"The Pacific, a Russian lake, you say? All right, Herr Rezanov, leave your report and maps with us. We shall study them thoroughly and notify you of our decision in due course."

Nikolai bowed. The Tsar rang and an aide-de-camp instantly appeared to escort Nikolai out of the study.

Weeks of waiting began, when Nikolai would rack his brain about some detail he might have left out of his presentation.

"You must be patient," Annushka consoled him gently. "You know how we Russians are, always slow in making up our minds. The Tsar is no different. He too, is *Russian*."

Annushka was pregnant and she secretly hoped that the

Tsar's decision would come after the birth of their child. She was afraid that Paul might send her husband to America.

While no direct word came from the Tsar, Nikolai was encouraged by a promotion to the Privy Council with the rank of High Procurator of the Senate. The post carried a substantial increase in salary.

Then a son was born to the Rezanovs. Almost simultaneously, as if to celebrate the occasion, came the long-awaited *ukase* from the Tsar.

Paul's edict granted full powers to the Shelikhov-Golikov enterprise, which thenceforth was to be known as the Russian-American Company. The monopoly was granted for twenty years with an option to renew. The Company was authorized to conduct trade and to explore the Pacific Ocean and to claim any undiscovered territory for the Russian empire. The company would also be responsible for building settlements and forts, but the government would supply ships and the necessary materials. The government would provide the new territories with settlers, drawn mainly from among exiled convicts and their families.

Nikolai and his friends at court were jubilant. A mansion was bought on the Moika Quay to house the new Company's headquarters. The regional offices and warehouses remained in Irkutsk and on Kodiak Island in Russian America as the territory was to be known.

Alexander Baranov, whom Shelikhov had originally hired as *Glavny Pravitel*, a general manager, would continue in his post as the governor. It would be his duty to settle the new territories.

Nikolai was appointed as the new Company's chief representative in the capital, with a seat on its board of directors.

Nikolai's dreams had been realized.

But it was too late for Shelikhov. Annushka's father died before the good news reached Siberia.

Chapter 9

Nikolai Rezanov's star was rising, but the Tsar's was descending. Hidden behind the thick walls of his new still unfinished fortress, Paul sneered contemptuously at his subjects, but he was afraid to face them. He avoided the contact with anyone but a few trusted friends. The fear of assassination was constantly on his mind. At night he often abandoned his bedchamber for some other room, to confuse his would-be assassins.

Paul confided his fears to Count von Pahlen. "Your suspicions, Sire, are unfounded," von Pahlen declared. "Nothing goes on in St. Petersburg that I don't control. If there were a conspiracy against you, Sire, I would be the first to know through my informers!" The Count's round face shone with earnestness, nothing betraying him as one of the leaders of the conspiracy.

In July, 1799, Paul signed the Charter granting the Russian-American Company a complete monopoly on the Pacific. He issued additional orders: the new Company would be run as a business corporation and control its operations through an elected board of directors. As Nikolai Rezanov had proposed, the Company's territory would extend from the Arctic to the 55th parallel, and from Siberia, across the Pacific Ocean to the American coast, and beyond, as far as was feasible.

At the Russian-American Company's headquarters on the Moika Quay Nikolai was busy settling his father-in-law's estate. Annushka inherited a large amount of the stock in the Company. The Rezanovs were rich. It was time to relax, but Nikolai could not relax. Like most of the nobles, Nikolai watched with alarm the Tsar's new obsession—the conquest of India.

In 1800 Paul made a secret pact with Napoleon Bonaparte who continued to cast his ever-lengthening shadow over Europe. Flushed with victory over the British at Malta, Napoleon capriciously offered the island as a gift to Paul who had recently been elected the Grand Master of the Knights of Malta.

Overnight Paul changed his opinion about the Corsican. He declared that Napoleon was the savior of Europe, instead of its scourge, the restorer of law and order, instead of the ambitious conqueror. He sent Napoleon a message, saying that he did not wish to dwell upon their differences, but rather hoped that together they would bring the world much-needed stability. He thanked Napoleon profusely for Malta, but before he could take possession of the island, the British fleet recaptured it.

Paul went berserk; he declared war on England, his ally of the previous year, seized British ships in Russian waters and imprisoned the crews.

But his most bizarre act was yet to come; Paul ordered an invasion of India.

Twenty-two thousand five hundred troops under the command of General Platov were ordered to march overland toward India, where they were to join forces with Napoleon's armies and together, roust the British out of the sub-continent.

The poorly equipped troops left for Orenburg in January 1801, on the first leg of their campaign. From Orenburg they were to proceed to Bukhara and Khiva and capture the plains of the Indus within three months thereafter. The hapless army had only fourteen cannon and no maps beyond Khiva, but this did not concern the Tsar. It was just a minor detail, he declared. He planned to unite his Cossacks with the French troops not knowing that his new ally, Napoleon, had been bogged down in Egypt. The huge distances between the armies failed to discourage the Tsar; his hatred for England blinded him to reality.

Napoleon, unaware of Russia's lack of preparedness, gambled that it was entirely possible to conquer India with the help of Paul. He had several intelligence reports that India was protected by no more than two thousand British troops.

If Russians, coming down from the mountains and the French, reaching India from the sea, united—the British would find it impossible to hold India.

The Cossack army reached Orenburg, but General Platov refused to move his men any further until spring. "It's madness to march an army across the endless steppes, to expect it to climb the mountains during the winter!" he declared, risking his career by insubordination. General Platov hoped that the absurd idea of the conquest of India would be dropped by spring.

The conspirators in St. Petersburg realized the danger of the new folly of their Tsar. There was no more time to waste.

Count von Pahlen called a meeting at his home, ostensibly to celebrate the opening of the Russian-American Company's headquarters.

Only men were present. Nikolai was surprised to find many senior officers from the Guards regiments seated around the banquet table.

"What's their connection with the Company?" he thought. Soon, however, he sensed that there was another reason for the gathering. As the evening progressed, Nikolai realized that he was attending a meeting of conspirators.

Von Pahlen glanced at Rezanov. "Are you with us, Nikolai? You know as well as we do, that Alexander ought to be on the throne. He was the Empress' choice as her successor. Only her sudden death prevented her from signing the proclamation. We want to follow Catherine's wish. We want to put Alexander on the throne."

"How do you propose to accomplish it?" Nikolai asked. Although he disapproved of many of Paul's actions, he felt grateful to him for following his recommendations and creating the Russian-American Company. He could not participate in a conspiracy against him.

"We'll enlist Alexander's help in persuading the Tsar to abdicate in his favor," von Pahlen answered.

"The Tsar will never agree to that!"

"There are many methods of persuasion," a general of the Semeonovsky regiment said haughtily.

Count von Pahlen smiled placatingly. "Gentlemen, gentlemen! We're talking only of the *voluntary* abdication."

Nikolai raised his hand to silence them. "Wait. I want to know nothing more of your plans. Rest assured that your secrets are buried within my soul."

He rose to leave.

"Nikolai, stay!" von Pahlen begged. Nikolai shook his head. "No, I can't."

"At least, let's drink to Alexander's health. To Alexander!" von Pahlen raised his crystal goblet.

"To Alexander!" the conspirators shouted emptying their glasses and hurtling them against the walls. The crystal splintered into sparkling shards, covering the carpet with hundreds of tiny sharp daggers.

"To Alexander!" Nikolai joined, emptying his own glass and smashing it against the wall. He bowed to the company and left the room.

Next morning Count von Pahlen departed for Grand Duke Alexander's quarters at the Semeonovsky Guards regiment.

Alexander was well aware of the general displeasure with the rule of his father. Paul's latest folly, the conquest of India, was the talk of the salons and the taverns alike. Although he was not eager to become the Tsar, Alexander often thought that he would have conducted the affairs of the country quite differently. He confided his thoughts to a few friends, who instantly informed Count von Pahlen. Alexander was ripe to joint the conspiracy.

The Count entered the Grand Duke's reception room and bowed formally. "Your Royal Highness, I was chosen by the representatives of all the Guards regiments to offer you the Russian throne. Your father is incapable of governing the country. You must save Russia."

Alexander blanched. "You can't be serious Count..." he mumbled.

"I can't be more serious, Your Highness." Von Pahlen began by describing the great threat against Russia created by Paul's thoughtless military adventures. He painted a vivid picture of Paul's dangerous domestic policies, which threatened to bring a general uprising against the Crown. He described brilliantly the mobs which could sweep through the streets of St. Petersburg, destroying everything in their wake.

He reminded Alexander of the lessons to be learned from the French Revolution. He fell on his knees dramatically and begged Alexander to answer the call of his country and save Russia from chaos.

At last Alexander spoke.

"All right, I'll take the throne if my father abdicates voluntarily," he said with a deep sigh as if the weight of the empire was already on his shoulders. "But you must swear that my father will not be harmed in any way!"

"I swear it, Your Royal Highness!" Count von Pahlen vowed solemnly.

The date of the coup was set for March 15th, 1801. The Ides of March, as Count von Pahlen, a lover of classics, had wryly suggested. But it was Alexander, who had advised that the date be moved to March twelfth, when his own Semeonovsky regiment would be on duty at the Mikhailovsky Palace.

Five men were chosen to face Paul: von Pahlen himself, General Levin von Bennigsen, and the three Zubov brothers.

Platon, Catherine's last lover, recently returned from exile, thirsted for Paul's blood. His two brothers, Valerian and Nikolai, demoted by Paul and transferred to provincial regiments, had their own scores to settle.

At dawn, two columns of the Semeonovsky regiment marched from their barracks to the Palace in the normal changing of the guard. Among the soldiers entering the palace guards were the five conspirators.

Semeonovsky officers took positions at every exit, while the five made their way to Paul's study. Two hussars on watch at the door of the study attempted to stop the invaders, but they were quickly overpowered, tied and gagged.

Paul heard the scuffle. Instinctively, he knew that his moment of mortal danger was at hand. It was there, behind his doors. Terrified, frantically dashing about the room, he padded barefooted to the door of his wife's room. It was locked. Ever since Paul had taken a mistress, the Empress kept her door locked.

He ran to the window, but it was sealed for the winter. He could not pry it open. He felt his heart beat wildly as he tried to squeeze himself under the bed. The bed was too low. Desperately, he slipped behind the sparse cover of a Gobelin tapestry hanging in his dressing alcove. The conspirators burst into the bedroom, von Pahlen lingering in the anteroom. The Zubov brothers rushed toward Paul's bed. It was still warm, but empty.

"He's behind the tapestry!" Platon Zubov yelled noticing

Paul's bare feet sticking from under the hanging. The Zubov brothers dragged the Tsar out.

General von Bennigsen kept his head. "Your Majesty, we are here to request your abdication in favor of your son, Alexander," he bowed to the cowering Tsar and extended the prepared document of abdication.

Paul drew himself upright. Bennigsen's tone gave him hope.

"Abdicate? Never!" he replied haughtily, unaware of his comical appearance. The sleeve of his nightshirt was torn and his thinning hair was plastered to his skull with sweat. His knobby bare feet, particularly, gave him a ludicrous air.

"We implore you, Sire," General Bennigsen said.

"Leave us!" Paul pointed to the door. "Guards! Arrest these men at once!" he tried to shout but his voice squeaked, like a small boy's. The Zubov brothers would wait no longer. The youngest picked up a heavy paperweight and threw it into Paul's face. It hit him on the cheek. The Tsar staggered. The three brothers fell upon him.

It was over in seconds. The disfigured body of the Tsar was spread on a bright Bokhara carpet. His protruding eyes seemed to have popped out of their lids like two pale-blue glass marbles. His mouth gaped in a silenced scream, a tumescent purple tongue jutted out.

"My God,!" whispered Bennigsen, nervously making the sign of the cross. "You did not need to go that far!"

Count von Pahlen and General Bennigsen rode together to Alexander's private quarters at the Semeonovsky regiment where he was waiting for the signal that his father had abdicated.

General Bennigsen was visibly shaken, but von Pahlen was calm.

"Your Majesty," Count von Pahlen and the general bowed low before the new Tsar.

"He has abdicated!" Alexander exclaimed, delighted.

"Your father is dead, Sire," von Pahlen said somberly.

Alexander broke out in sobs. "No...No...you promised..."

"Your Majesty, the time has come to reign. Stop being a child!" Count von Pahlen admonished sternly.

Chapter 10

It was announced that Tsar Paul had died of a sudden stroke. There was only a token inquest into his death.

People danced on the streets as it became known that Alexander was now the Tsar and the Emperor of all the Russias.

The country returned to being a nation forged by Catherine the Great. Alexander reinstated Catherine's treaties of friendship with England, and once more united Russia with Austria against Napoleon Bonaparte. The Cossack army, waiting in Orenburg to resume the campaign against India, was recalled.

On the domestic front, Alexander proclaimed several new reforms. He lifted the ban against foreign travel. More than fifteen thousand nobles were invited to return from exile. Censorship was abandoned, the barricades within the capital were removed, special passes required by all walking near Paul's fortress, cancelled. The terror and gloom created by Paul disappeared; people were eager to forget the aberrant Tsar.

After a short affectation of mourning for the murdered Tsar, life at Court returned to its former glitter. For the benefit of the plain people, however, Alexander assumed a modest posture. He rode his white horse Lucinda about St. Petersburg accompanied only by a handful of aides, wearing the simple green tunic of a colonel of his Semeonovsky regiment. He seemed like one of the people. He was approachable.

The people loved it. Alexander often stopped to greet an old man or to smile at a child. Once he had appeared unannounced at the wedding of a shopkeeper and presented the newlyweds with a purse of gold coins.

The people began to idolize him, calling him their guardian angel. With little effort, the twenty-four-year old Tsar became the Father of his people, the one anointed by God to rule over them. The popular opinion made him into a "perfect Tsar."

Annushka was pregnant with their third child when the Rezanovs received an engraved invitation with the Imperial crest.

"A ball! At the Winter Palace!" Annushka cried excitedly. "But I am scared!"

Nikolai smiled at her fondly. "You'll be the most beautiful lady there," he said. He had been preparing his wife for life at Court ever since Alexander had ascended the throne. A special tutor was hired to improve Annushka's French, a music teacher to sharpen her skills on the clavichord and a dancing master to teach her the latest dances.

Annushka practiced diligently, stepping gracefully to the thin scrapings of the violin of her dancing master, an old Frenchman from the court of the Bourbons. Watching her practice, Nikolai felt warm waves of affection sweep over him: Annushka was so eager to please him! She conjugated French verbs, played scales on the clavichord, danced with the old dancing master like a good little girl, anxious to learn, eager for his approval.

"I am a lucky man," Nikolai thought proudly.

Annushka could see the brilliant chandeliers through the tall windows of the Winter Palace even from afar as the Rezanovs were driven to the ball in her elegant little carriage.

They dismounted at the grand entrance and their carriage was instantly waved away by the porters, as another carriage pulled up.

Nikolai led Annushka inside the vestibule. A page removed her velvet cloak and took her husband's cape. Slowly they ascended the marble Iordansky staircase covered with red carpet and lined along the balustrades with larger than life-size classical statuary.

Annushka was dressed in a full-skirted gown of pale green silk, which disguised her pregnancy. Her shoulders and the upper part of her round bosom were bared. Around her slender white neck she wore a magnificent collier of large Siberian emeralds and rose-cut diamonds, a wedding gift from her father. Her arms were encased in long white kid gloves and she carried a fan made of opulent ostrich feathers, tinted to match her gown. Her hair was curled on both sides of her cheeks and topped by a small tiara of emeralds and diamonds.

She trembled with excitement as she ascended the grand staircase holding tightly to the arm of her husband, who looked so handsome, she thought, in his new Court dress with its short jeweled sword. The Tsar had recently appointed Nikolai to be Chamberlain of the Court, gentleman-companion of the Tsar, their old friendship becoming even stronger after Tsar Paul's death. Alexander openly sought Nikolai's opinion on matters of diplomacy and foreign policy, often consulting him before any of his ministers.

Nikolai persuaded the Tsar to become a stockholder in the Russian-American Company. As the Imperial family joined the stockholders, it became fashionable to participate in commercial enterprises; it was no longer beneath the dignity of nobility. Nikolai bought stock in his own name, becoming one of the main stockholders of the Company.

In the opinion of the Court, Nikolai Rezanov was becoming a power to reckon with.

Nikolai led Annushka to one of the gilded chairs lined along the walls of the ballroom. She sat down. She heard the sounds of the orchestra from the gallery above and felt her excitement mount, as the murmur of polite voices, chatting in French, mingled with the sounds of the tuning instruments.

Soon all the chairs along the walls were occupied by the ladies in colorful summer gowns of light silk and lace. The jewels glittered, the men's sashes, stars and cordons competing with the ladies' necklaces and tiaras.

The orchestra struck the national anthem and the ladies rose to their feet. They sank into curtsies and the men bowed low as the Imperial couple entered the ballroom, slowly proceeding to the ornate chairs under a canopy of red velvet tied with gold tassels set on an elevated platform covered with a silk Oriental rug. Alexander and his Empress sat down, ready to receive their guests. The line slowly moved forward as a Majordomo loudly announced the names and titles of each guest.

As the Rezanovs approached the Imperial couple, Annushka made a deep curtsy and Nikolai bowed.

"Why were you hiding your beautiful wife all this time,

mon cher?" Alexander smiled, raising Annushka to her feet and kissing her hand gallantly. Annushka blushed with pleasure.

"Don't hide her from us anymore," Alexander continued. Turning to Annushka he said with a smile, "Madame, your husband and I have been friends for many years. I'm sure you'll enhance our friendship."

Annushka blushed even more as she made another curtsy and Nikolai clicked his heels.

"Yes, indeed," the Empress joined in. "It's a pleasure to see a new pretty face at Court." But there was no warmth in her voice.

Nikolai took Annushka back to her chair. The reception line moved slowly, but Annushka was oblivious to the crowd. She was ecstatic; her hand had been kissed by the *Tsar!*

Nikolai was amused and proud, thinking how Annushka outshone the Court coquettes, the wives of generals and diplomats, many of whom had been his mistresses in the past.

The reception over, the ball began. Flushed dancers soon sought the champagne served by the liveried servants. Annushka sipped it thirstily, her face pink with the excitement and exertion of the dance. She fanned herself with her ostrich plumes.

"Will you do me the honor, Madame?" Alexander stood before her, offering her his arm. Annushka panicked, but Nikolai with a bow to the Tsar took her hand and placed it in Alexander's.

The Tsar led Annushka to the center of the ballroom. She felt all eyes on her as she placed her left arm on Alexander's fringed epaulet.

The orchestra began to play a waltz, a dance introduced to the Court during the last years of Catherine's reign. Alexander swirled Annushka around the ballroom, her feet barely touching the polished parquet.

The Tsar was an excellent dancer and Annushka began to relax. The others joined them, dancing on the periphery of the ballroom, leaving the center for the Emperor and Annushka.

He danced with her twice more. Nikolai was delighted. It was obvious that Annushka, his low-born Siberian beauty, was accepted by the Tsar as an equal to the aristocratic ladies of the Court. Annushka was a success.

She danced with her husband and with the Guards officers, with the Grand Dukes and even with the eighty-year-old gout-ridden Prince Orlov, who could barely shuffle across the floor. She hardly was allowed to sit down. She glowed with happiness.

But on the way home, she confessed to Nikolai that she was glad that she would not have to go to another ball because of her forthcoming confinement.

"But you were such a success!" Nikolai objected.

"To tell the truth, I was scared to death that I might step on the Tsar's toes."

"Well, did you?" Nikolai smiled.

"I don't think so. But he did step on mine, several times." They both laughed.

Chapter 11

Peace and tranquility had returned to St. Petersburg, but trouble was brewing at Baranov's new fort in the Tlingit land. Unsuspected by the Russians, the Indians were plotting to get back their island.

Meanwhile, Fort St. Michael was growing. Several new warehouses were finished and a shipyard was constructed where a keel of the first ship was laid out. Baranov's dream of a self-sufficient colony was becoming a reality. He felt pleased with his choice of the island; he already thought of St. Michael as the capital of Russian America. He began to prepare a house for his own wife and small son. It was time for them to join him.

A new contingent of *promyshleniki* arrived from Russia. They brought along several head of cattle and sheep to begin a program of animal husbandry, another dream of Baranov. He wanted to create a true "Russia" on the green shores of Sitka Bay, a bountiful "Russia" with her herds of cattle and fields of golden wheat. It would take several years, of course, but he had laid the foundation for it.

More houses were built to accommodate the new arrivals. The fort spread out deeper inland.

Foreign ships began to put in at Fort St. Michael, at first for fresh water, then for repairs when they discovered that the Russians were good craftsmen. The colony was beginning to prosper.

But the Chief Ska-out-lelt felt cheated. It was clear to him now, the Russians never intended to stay on the narrow strip of the shore. They wanted the whole island.

As the settlement pushed deeper into the forest, Ska-out-lelt asked Baranov for guns as a payment for the additional land.

"My braves will hunt better," he said.

Baranov refused with an obvious lie, saying, "The white man's gun can be fired only by white men."

Ska-out-lelt became angry. He said nothing more to Baranov. He knew that he must gather his forces and strike before more white men came.

He was waiting for the right moment.

It came shortly after, when Baranov had to depart from the fort to deal with personal problems in Pavlovsk. A messenger from Kodiak Island had brought the disturbing news that Baranov's wife had disappeared and was feared dead.

The Governor sailed for Kodiak Island immediately, leaving Fort St. Michael in charge of a deputy.

The Tlingits and their allies converged on the island during the night. Lying in ambush in the forest surrounding the fort, they waited for a signal, to strike the unwary Russians.

The signal was provided by Marinka.

She saw an opportunity to win for herself the only man she had ever wanted, the powerful young warrior Kot-le-an. She had been promised to him since her childhood, but the Chief, wishing to cement his good relations with the people of the Double-headed Eagle, sold her to the big Russian instead.

The young Kot-le-an did not object. She was only a woman. There were plenty of young women in his tribe.

He gladly accepted several bead necklaces and a hunting knife as his share for selling his intended bride. Not until the maiden was gone from the village did he miss her. He regretted that he had not insisted on getting some other woman for the Russian. He found excuses to go to the fort for a glimpse of her.

Kot-le-an began to scheme to get her back.

Timofei liked the early mornings best. It was quiet, the air felt fresh and chilly, and the birds, just awakening, stirred in their nests. He imagined them stretching their wings, like people stretched their arms, feeling the flow of blood; shaking their wings, like people flexing their muscles.

On such a morning in late June, Marinka begged Timofei to allow her to visit her tribe. "I have not seen my mother in many moons. She's old. I must see her before she is no more."

Timofei hesitated. The Governor's rule forbade such visits. "Let their kin visit them at the fort. It's safer that way. We can keep an eye on them," he had said.

Timofei did not agree. He trusted his Marinka. She was loyal to him. "Go, *golubushka*, my little dove, go and visit your old mother. I'll find something to do while you're away. It's Sunday, I don't have to work today, so I'll go fishing with my Aleut, that's what I'll do!" he said smiling, as he slipped his hand under her apron.

She slid away from his touch. "No time," she said.

Timofei walked with her to the gates of the fort. "She has my permission to leave," he said to the guard on duty. "Go ahead, *golubushka*. Don't forget to come back!" he joked.

Marinka slipped through the stout gates. She noted that the guard did not bolt them after she passed. She ran across the clearing separating the fort from the forest and disappeared under the dark canopy of dense hemlocks.

Once under the protection of the woods, Marinka stopped, panting, waiting. She knew that Kot-le-an was stalking around the fort for a glance at her. The Aleut women living with the Russians had told her of Kot-le-an's passion, teasing her about it.

Marinka's heart pounded in anticipation. She hoped that she would be met. Presently a tall warrior appeared from behind the tree.

"What took you so long to leave, woman?" he asked brusquely, not looking at her.

"The white man wouldn't let me go..."

"What news do you bring of the fort, woman?"

"The big gates are open. There's only one man on watch..." she said eagerly.

"What else?" Kot-le-an demanded.

"The men are drunk most of the time since the White Chief left. The men don't stand watch...Kot-le-an?" she looked at him. He pretended not to notice. "What else?" he repeated gruffly.

"They fight with one another. Then they beat their women."

Kot-le-an grabbed her by the shoulders. "And your white man? Does your white man beat you too?" He looked fierce. "He wants me," Marinka thought proudly.

"Does he beat you?" Kot-le-an repeated.

Marinka hesitated. "No," she said. "He never beats me.

He's good to me." She met his piercing stare. "He's good to me, but I don't want him. I want to be your woman. I want to bear your sons. Take me, I always wanted to be your woman," she said, not lowering her eyes.

Kot-le-an relaxed his grip on her shoulders. "I'll take you. I also always wanted you to be my woman and bear my sons. Go to the shaman. Tell him to purify you from the seed of the white man."

She bowed her head for the first time. She felt contented.

"Go!" Kot-le-an gave her a small push toward the village. Obediently, Marinka walked away.

Kot-le-an raised his arm and made the cawing sound of a raven. He would attack the fort immediately, without waiting for the assistance of the other chiefs. He decided they could join him later in looting the fort, he thought, but the glory of the attack would be his alone. He had plenty of warriors waiting.

He repeated the call of the Raven. At once the silent forest came alive with shrill war cries as the Tlingits swooped on the unprotected fort.

Kot-le-an led the attack. With one blow of his club he smashed the skull of the *promyshlenik* on guard at the gates. Without a sound the man slid to the ground, his knees buckling under him. He remained kneeling at the gate, as if in prayer.

Howling Ravens poured into the fort, scaling the stockades and the fences of the inner fortress with the agility of wild cats.

The *promyshleniki* ran from their houses, loading their muskets as they ran. Some were still only half dressed, having slept late on that peaceful warm Sunday. Taken by surprise, with no one to rally them, the Russians dashed in all directions, confused and terrified.

One of them climbed to the bell tower to sound the alarm, summoning the men who had left the fort to go fishing. An Indian arrow pierced his throat and he fell to the ground, like a sack of flour, the bell tolling for him.

Another hunter managed to load the cannon and fire a single shot that hit nothing. Before he could reload the gun his head was split in two by a mighty blow.

Women screamed as the Ravens dragged them out of their houses. The old ones were dispatched quickly by a slash across their throats; the young ones were corralled into a whimpering cowering crowd. The Indians snatched the infants from their mothers' arms, tore away the older children clinging to their skirts, smashing the children against the walls. They had no use for enemy children.

The Aleuts rose to the defense of their women, meeting the attackers with a shower of arrows, but there were too many Ravens. Tlingit clubs felled Aleuts like saplings.

The Russians, less than two dozen of them, fought their way to a blockhouse. They bolted the stout doors and stared in horror as the Ravens annihilated the Aleuts. The Russians fired their muskets at new hordes pouring through the open gates to join Kot-le-an's men. The Ravens darted along the fort with smoking torches, and where they ran, flames sprung up.

The *promyshleniki* kept firing at the invaders as fast as they could reload,but for each fallen warrior, there were dozens more.

The Ravens rushed to the warehouse as it, too, burst into flame. They flung the doors open, scurrying back and forth like an army of laborious ants, hurrying to empty the warehouse of its valuable furs before it was too late.

A lighted torch, then another one, landed inside the blockhouse. The Russians scrambled for the blazing brands and hurled them back, but they could not get them all. The wooden floor flared up. Frantically, the Russians beat the flames down. The Indians surrounded the blockhouse. A mass of shining copper bodies sealed every escape.

"God bless you, *bratzi*...May He rest your souls!" gasped one of the *promyshleniki* as he writhed on the floor, a poisoned arrow in his belly.

Acrid smoke crept through the walls of the stronghold, choking its defenders. The lower section was already burning. They could hear the fire crackle in the dry timbers.

Eyes streaming, the men reloaded their muskets. "Let's get out of here and die like men!" one cried. They embraced one another briefly. "Farewell, *bratzi*..." Making the sign of the cross, they charged out of the burning blockhouse, shouting and firing their guns. Several Tlingits fell. A narrow path opened, but it closed too quickly. The Ravens surged forward. The Russians went down, skulls smashed by clubs or throats cut by clamshell knives.

There were no survivors except for a few young Aleut women taken as slaves.

The whole fort was ablaze. Dark smoke curled up into the cloudless sky, turning the bright day into twilight.

Kot-le-an, sweat streaming down his massive chest, gathered his men around him. "Cut their heads off," he commanded, pointing at the dead Russians with his club. He was splattered with blood. His heavy whale-bone club was encrusted with the drying brain matter of his enemies.

The sticky heads rolled in the dust and dry spruce needles.

"Impale them!" Kot-le-an turned his back on the pile of his dead adversaries. He had no more interest in them. He had won the battle.

The air around the fort grew oppressive with the smell of smoke and the sickly sweet odor of blood. The insects buzzed over the dead bodies and, on the fringes of the fort, black ravens, the scavenger birds, gathered for a feast.

Warriors collected the heads, impaling each one on a tall stake wrested out of the fence. The heads faced the sea, their bulging eyes reflecting the horror of their deaths. The bodies were thrown into the sea. The enemy spirits must be drowned, the Ravens believed.

A crowd of Tlingit women and children came out of the forest. The women brought food in cedarbark boxes and water in tightly woven baskets. There would be a feast to celebrate the victory.

Marinka was among the women. She carried a basket of fresh spring water. She poured it over Kot-le-an's arms and watched him wash the blood off. She wondered whether he had killed her white man, but did not dare to ask.

"Come!" Kot-le-an ordered brusquely, leading her to the fence studded with the severed Russian heads. "Is he among them?" he pointed to the heads.

Marinka walked slowly past them, recognizing many faces, thinking how curious the heads looked without their bodies. She stared without emotion.

"Is he there?" Kot-le-an demanded.

Marinka walked back, closely examining each head once more. "No. He's not here." She felt a sudden relief that Timofei's head was not among them. She did not dare to face Kot-le-an. She turned away, a little smile curving the corners of her mouth. Her white man had escaped!

Timofei Tarakanov cursed himself. "What a fool I was!

It must have been Marinka who told the Indians that the Governor had left the fort!" It was clear to him now.

Timofei stirred and sighed wretchedly. At once he felt the pressure of a sharp spear between his shoulder blades. He was lying face down on the bottom of a canoe, a naked Tlingit warrior standing astride him. Timofei's bound hands felt numb, the sealgut straps cut deeply into his flesh. His head throbbed with pain and his face felt stiff, caked with dried blood. His left eye was swollen shut.

His nostrils quivered. He smelled smoke, the acrid odor of destruction. "The smoke from cooking fires has a different, friendly smell," he thought. "This must be the smell of death. The fort is burning. It must be all over."

The stench of burning buildings grew heavier. Timofei felt his lungs fill with it. He coughed. "They are taking me back to the fort," he thought in confusion. He heard the rush of water under the hull and the rhythmic sound of paddles as the Indians propelled the canoe forward.

Shortly the boat hit the sandy beach and the Indians jumped out. They did not bother about Timofei. He was tied, hands to feet. He could not escape.

He waited until their footsteps had died away, then struggled in vain to turn over. Unable to move, he breathed shallowly, his body racked with pain. He could see nothing through his only eye but the rough bottom of the dugout canoe.

Timofei concentrated on the sounds. He could hear no Russian voices, only those of the Indians, guttural, excited shouts.

"Everyone's dead," he thought. "Good Lord in Heaven, spare me!" he prayed, paralyzed with terror. Surely, the Indians would kill him upon their return.

The shouts grew closer. Timofei froze. He wished he could become invisible. He shut his good eye, expecting the final blow which would end his life. "Make it quick, O Lord!"

The Indians ignored their prisoner as they returned to the canoe. They laughed and danced, triumphant in their easy victory, their seashell necklaces and ear pendants swaying from side to side as they danced.

They piled bales of pelts stolen from the fort on Timofei's prostrate body, threatening to suffocate him under the soft dead weight.

Timofei felt the canoe slide into the water again. The

Tlingits paddled away from the destroyed fort. The smell of burning buildings and smoldering fur grew fainter.

"Dear Mother of God, spare me," Timofei pleaded. A new hope, timid as a sputtering candle, began to flicker in his mind. Perhaps the Indians would allow him to live.

He thought of the peaceful morning, just a few hours before. The warm day had smelled of fresh grass and sparkled with sunshine. The exhausting months of winter were over; the sky was clear and blue at last, the calm sea reflecting the greenery of the islands as if it were a village pond. The whole archipelago of minuscule green islands, scattered like loose emeralds, lay before Timofei's mind's eye.

He thought how keenly he had been aware of the stillness as he padded his *baidarka*, the Aleut behind him singing, repeating the same three notes of his fishing song. The monotonous melody was soothing like a lullaby. Timofei dozed, he remembered, his fishing lines trailing behind the *baidarka*, water lapping gently against the boat.

His nap had been shattered by the sound of a bell ringing rapidly in alarm, a battery of musket shots, and a single boom of a cannon.

Timofei had stiffened as he heard another outburst of scattered gun fire. Timofei remembered that he had glanced over his shoulder at the Aleut. The man's broad slit-eyed face had a frightened expression. Without a word they had turned the *baidarka* around and paddled back to the fort.

Rounding a small island which obscured their view of the fort, they saw three Russians frantically paddling away from the shore. "The savages! They captured the fort! Flee for your lives!" yelled one of them, Erlevsky, his face twisted with terror.

Timofei's hands had turned to ice as several long war canoes with twenty warriors each shot out of the bay. The canoes surged across the glassy water with terrifying speed.

Within moments the Tlingits were upon them. They cracked the skull of the Aleut with one blow of a heavy paddle. Timofei remembered grabbing for his musket as his *baidarka* had been surrounded and overturned. He felt a deafening blow to his head as he slipped into unconsciousness.

When he regained his senses, he found himself bound hand to foot, lying face down on the bottom of the Tlingit canoe.

Chapter 12

It was well past midnight when the Tlingits brought Timofei, mashed beneath the load of furs, to their village. He felt as if it were his own face and body that plowed a furrow in the wet sand as they beached the canoe.

Curious women and children crowded the shore.

The warriors jumped out, left the fur bales to the women and yanked Timofei roughly to his feet. His bound legs could not support him. He fell to the ground in a heap. The women giggled, while the children circled around, staring at his bearded face and his hairy chest. A warrior cut the straps binding Timofei's feet and pulled him up. The children stepped back. They had been warned by their elders that the white men were dangerous.

Timofei peered around with his good eye, moving his head from side to side like a nervous bird. His injured eye was swollen closed and throbbed with pain. He searched for Marinka among the Tlingit women, but their faces, painted in garish stripes, looked all alike.

The warriors led Timofei toward the great communal house. The mysterious symbols of the Raven's heraldry stared at him from the broad facade. He had to stoop to enter the house through the opening fitted into the gaping mouth of a bear.

It was dark in the house. The stout carved totems of ravens, eagles and bears supporting the roof, cast huge shadows exaggerating their grotesque features. A low fire burned in the pit, the smoke curling up toward a hole in the planked roof.

The warriors pushed Timofei down to the ground in a

corner. As he fell, he heard a stifled sob. "Mother of God, have mercy on my soul," someone cried pitifully in Russian.

"Who is there?" Timofei whispered hoarsely.

"Erlevsky and Vasily Kochesov. Who are you?"

"Timofei Tarakanov. *Bratzi*, what happened? I thought you had escaped."

"The savages intercepted us right after they captured you. We're both wounded."

"And Somov? Wasn't he with you?"

"They chopped his head off as he tried to resist."

"Dear God Almighty" Timofei felt a trickle of sweat crawl down his spine.

Timofei spent an uneasy night drifting in and out of sleep. In the morning an old slave woman brought the prisoners water, but she would not say anything. The warriors were gone and only women bustled around. Their chatter told him nothing of the Ravens' plans for their prisoners.

He looked at his compatriots. Erlevsky was unconscious; the wretched Kochesov, his wounds oozing blood, looked more dead than alive.

"They surely will be killed," Timofei thought. "The Indians don't keep sick slaves." His own hope for survival was in staying strong. Under no circumstances should he look useless to his captors. He recalled the early days at the fort when an Indian had been caught stealing a chicken. To make an example of him for other would be thieves, the Russians kept him in hand and leg irons for a week. When the prisoner was finally released his hands and feet were gangrenous. The Indians had no use for a mutilated warrior. They beheaded him, a shaman performing the ceremony, chanting and dancing around the corpse.

Timofei's ghoulish memories were interrupted by the entrance of Ska-out-lelt. His face was still hidden under a carved helmet of a raven, but Timofei recognized him.

Two young attendants deferentially accompanied the Chief. They removed his helmet and the triangular ceremonial blanket intricately woven with his tribal emblems. A woman then presented the Chief with a large bowl shaped like an animal lying on its back. Timofei knew that it was filled with stale urine, which the Indians used for ceremonial ablutions.

The Chief performed the ritual with slow deliberation.

An attendant held a mirror and Ska-out-lelt carefully re-painted his face in festive colors, different from his war paints.

Timofei recognized the mirror. It was a frivolous boudoir mirror that Governor Baranov had originally ordered from Irkutsk for his own Indian wife.

The Chief combed his stiff hair with a fish bone comb. The attendants sprinkled ashes on his head and then patted handfuls of goosedown, mixing it with his hair. The Chief's head became twice as big. The Tlingits' heads traditionally had been elongated in infancy by special binding as a sign of beauty. Now the Chief's head resembled a sugarloaf.

The attendants helped the Chief to put on a Russian calico shirt printed with red and yellow flowers, a souvenir of the land deal. Ska-out-lelt grinned at his reflection in the mirror, pleased with his appearance. He wore nothing else.

A loud commotion at the entrance distracted the Chief. A young warrior attired in full war regalia and crowned by a shiny black helmet in the form of a raven's head, burst into the house. He was Kot-le-an, the nephew of the Chief and the heir to the Raven kwan.

Kot-le-an motioned to his men. Two of them rushed at the prisoners brandishing sharpened clamshell knives.

Timofei caught his breath. "They are going to slash my throat," he panicked, but the Indians only cut the thongs tying the prisoners' hands. Timofei exhaled with relief. He flexed his arms and shoulders cautiously. The muscles were numb and his fingers had no feeling. Slowly he lifted his arms above his head. He shook his arms and then his hands, hoping to increase the blood circulation. Kot-le-an observed him closely, a glint of triumph in his dark eyes.

Erlevsky and Kochesov could not move. They moaned and Erlevsky mumbled a prayer to the Virgin. Weakened by the loss of blood, they were barely alive. Kot-le-an waved a hand and the slaves dragged the wounded Russians over the high threshold to the clearing outside the house. Their lifeless legs left wavy patterns over the dusty ground.

Timofei was allowed to walk on his own. His legs felt as if they would collapse under him, but he made an effort to hide his weakness.

Hundreds of Indians had gathered at the clearing nearby for the celebration. The chiefs draped in their blankets, their heads crowned with ceremonial masks, paraded around the bonfire. Ahead of each chief, slaves carried large shields of soft native copper. The more shields a chief possessed, the higher was his social rank.

"Several tribes attacked the fort," Timofei realized. Sudden anger scalded him. He had never hated the Indians before. Now he felt the tears of impotent rage gather in his eyes. If he could, he would have rushed at them, strangling them all with his bare hands, he thought.

The warriors tied the captives to trees. Timofei's short-lived hope for survival was extinguished once again. "They are going to torture us before the killing," he thought. Suffocating panic struck in his throat like a ball of cottonwool.

The crowd opened a path for the shaman, an old gnarled man. He was dressed in a torn cedarbark shirt encrusted with dirt. His long gray hair and matted beard stuck out in all directions, like the quills of a porcupine. The shamans never cut their hair; they believed that their mystic power was concentrated in their long tresses.

The Indians feared and respected their witch doctors. No great undertaking was ever attempted without consulting a shaman. The shamans communicated with the dead and could exorcise the evil spirits of those possessed, the Indians believed. The shamans could predict the future and cure the sick. It was the shamans who were to torture the enemy.

Timofei, terror stricken, his heart thumping wildly, watched the shaman approach the prisoners. A young apprentice, wearing only a raven's feather in his hair, followed the shaman, beating a drum.

While the rest of the crowd sat silently, the shaman whirled about the clearing, his shirt ballooning from his wiry body. His skinny legs were stained blue by tattoos up to his buttocks.

The shaman slowly circled Erlevsky. Howling like a wolf, he suddenly grabbed Erlevsky's left hand and, with a sharp pair of clamshells, tore out each of the anguished man's fingernails, starting with the thumbs. Erlevsky screamed.

"Mother of God, help him," Timofei cried wordlessly. Sweat, mingled with tears, ran freely down his face into his beard, making it curl into shiny wet ringlets. "Dear Lord, let him die quickly!" he prayed, turning his face away. But another wild, inhuman scream forced Timofei to look again.

The shaman had started on Erlevsky's right hand. The veins swelled on the wretched man's neck and temples as he fought to suppress his cry of pain. But as each fingernail was torn out, the man cried out in agony again and again, unable to endure the torture.

"Mother of God, have mercy on me! Let me die!" Erlevsky screamed. "Let him die," Timofei echoed in a hoarse whisper.

The shaman lifted his head to the cloudless sky and howled again like a lone wolf as he pulled out the last fingernail. Erlevsky lost consciousness. The shaman circled his victim, crouching almost to the ground, ready to spring on him again. The apprentice shook the rattles in an increased tempo, chanting as he danced around his master. The crowd joined him in the chant.

Timofei stared at his unconscious friend in horror. He saw Erlevsky's head droop over his chest, his hands dripping blood. Fearing the same fate, Timofei begged God to strike him dead now, before the shaman approached him.

"Spare me the torture, dear Lord, take my soul now!"

Against his will, Timofei watched the wild gyrations of the shaman. With a quick movement of his clamshell knife, the shaman made two deep incisions in the skin just below Erlevsky's knees. "Saints in Heaven!" Timofei screamed silently in his head. "The bastard's going to skin him alive!" Timofei looked away just as the shaman pulled Erlevsky's skin down to his ankles. It hung there like a pair of loose stockings, the raw flesh of both legs immediately attacked by swarms of insects.

The spectators cheered.

The shaman then moved to his next victim, Kochesov. Mercifully unconscious, Kochesov was unaware of his horrible fate. The shaman nevertheless performed the same ghastly ritual on him, starting on the thumb of his left hand.

Tongue dry, bathed in a stinking sweat of terror, Timofei knew he would be next. He scanned the crowd wildly, searching for Marinka, desperately hoping she might somehow come to his rescue. He was willing to be judged a coward. He would do anything, anything at all, to save himself from the horrible slow torture. A quick death he could face, but not the torture such as his friends had to endure.

The shaman pulled down the skin on Kochesov's legs but the poor man felt nothing. He was dead.

Timofei was next.

The shaman howled again and commenced with his

macabre dance. "God strike me dead now!" Timofei cried out loud. The shaman was drawing nearer. Timofei stopped breathing. His mouth opened wide in a silent scream. The shaman was now directly in front of him, his clamshells ready to tear out his victim's fingernails.

Suddenly a young warrior stepped out in the crowd. "This man shall live," he commanded sharply. The shaman retreated from Timofei. Kot-le-an, without another glance at the prisoner, returned to his place among the chiefs.

Timofei's life was miraculously spared.

The long summer evening had changed into the twilight of the night. The Tlingits, having eaten and danced around the fire in celebration of their destruction of the fort, now spread their blankets on the ground, settling for a night's rest. The clearing grew quiet.

Timofei, too, sagged to sleep in his tethers, without knowing it.

The sun and the pain of his cramped body awakened Timofei some hours later. The Indians were gone. The mutilated bodies of Erlevsky and Kochesov remained tied to the trees.

In time two sleepy-looking warriors appeared and cut down the bodies, hurling them into the sea. Turning to Timofei, they cut the bindings that held him to the tree. Slowly he sank on the ground, tearing his shirt and skinning his back against the bark. They left him under the tree. He slept again.

Awakening several hours later, Timofei was startled to see Marinka squatting on the ground a few feet away from him. Her hair was plaited in two thick braids decorated with seashells and flowers, her lower lip stretched out by a *labret*, a wooden plug that he had forbidden her to wear. Marinka watched him expressionlessly.

"Marinka!" He gasped. "*Golubushka*, my little dove! You came back to me!" The scene seemed unreal. Timofei blinked.

"You'll go to the Ravens," Marinka said without moving or changing expression.

"Yes! Oh, yes!" he cried in relief. "I'll go with you anywhere!"

"You're a slave," she said flatly. "I'm no wife to you. I am Kot-le-an's woman. I led the Ravens to the fort!" She said proudly. She stood and left without looking back.

Chapter 13

A small boy led Timofei back to the village. Now that he knew his life had been spared, Timofei became aware of his hunger.

"*Utxuh,*" food, he tapped the boy on the shoulder, pointing to his mouth. The boy nodded. He yelled to a woman passing by with a basketful of berries. She stopped and silently allowed Timofei to help himself.

"*Utxuh,*" Timofei repeated, unwilling to settle for a mouthful of sour berries. The child glared at him. "Wait here," he said gruffly, already imitating his elders.

Timofei was determined to get food. Carefully he moved closer to a group of women. They merely glanced at him, concentrating on packing their belongings, preparing for a journey.

"*Utxuh,*" he said again. They paid no attention.

Discouraged, Timofei threw himself under a tree. Every inch of his body hurt. His wrists and ankles were grotesquely swollen, disfigured by ugly bruises from the sealgut thongs. His left eye was totally closed now by swelling, throbbing with pain. "But I am alive!" he thought.

"I'll wait," he said to himself. "The good Lord heard my prayers and saved me. He will provide," he made the sign of the cross. He stretched under the tree and dozed off again, his empty stomach growling.

He was awakened by an old woman gnarled by age like a decaying tree stump. She shook him by his shoulder as her shriveled breasts swayed from side to side. Covering her bony shoulders was a colorful Russian shawl printed with red and yellow cabbage-size roses.

Timofei recognized the shawl. It was one of the items he

had paid to purchase Marinka. It was meant for her mother. And there she was, nearly toothless old crone, smiling at him, proffering him a whole side of dried salmon! Timofei grabbed the fish and tore it apart with his strong teeth.

The women abandoned their tasks and squatted around him in a wide semi-circle to watch him eat. Marinka's mother sat on her haunches, her long flat breasts almost touching the ground, her cedarbark skirt barely covering her bony thighs.

"*Doo Wak,*" she said, pointing to Timofei's eye.

"*Oonah eetee.*" Timofei nodded. Marinka used to say the same word, *oonah eetee,* a wound, before she attended to his cuts and bruises.

The old woman looked back at the circle of women. "*Heen!*" she commanded. One of the younger women, an infant strapped to her back in a cradle board, obediently brought her water. Timofei cupped his hands as she poured. He splashed it over his face, wincing at the sharp sting of pain whenever it touched his eye. But the coolness had a refreshing effect on his disfigured face. He washed the caked blood off and Marinka's mother examined his eye. Mumbling to herself, she rummaged around inside one of her baskets looking for a chunk of dried root. She broke a piece of it off and proceeded to chew it.

She gestured that she wanted Timofei to cup his hands again, and as he did, she spat the dark mass into them. It reminded him of his mother who had treated the wounds of his boyhood in a similar manner, by chewing black bread and cobwebs.

He held the spittle against his throbbing eye. Almost at once the pain subsided. "*Yakei,* good," Timofei smiled at the old woman. "You're better than a shaman!"

She grinned exposing her few remaining teeth. She pointed to the woods. Her kwan was leaving the Raven's village. The celebration was over.

Timofei saw warriors laden with bundles of pelts, disappear under the fringed branches of the hemlocks. The women and children followed, moving single file. Marinka's mother fell into her place, gesturing for him to pick up several bales of otter skins. Timofei picked up the bundles, adjusting the weight by placing the heaviest part on his back, in the hunters' way. Timofei too, fell into line. "Praise the Lord, I am alive!" he thought.

The Indians moved swiftly. The tall, thick trees crowded the path, their giant roots reaching across the trail, coiled against one another as if they were monster snakes locked in deadly combat. The sun never completely penetrated the thick forest, touching only the crowns of the trees with its life-giving rays. The crowns were green and lush, while the floor of the forest remained cold and damp, dense with rotting fallen trees covered with moss, smelling of decay and mushrooms.

The Tlingits moved at a steady pace, disturbing nothing in their wake.

Timofei, too, could move almost invisibly through the forest, he had that in common with his captors. It was part of his upbringing as a boy when his father used to teach him the secrets of the Siberian *taiga*. "Never disturb the forest, my boy," his father used to say. "The *taiga* has a soul, like a person. Everything in nature has a soul, like you and me."

Years later, Timofei had learned that Marinka held the same belief; everything had an immortal soul. Her convictions made it more difficult for Timofei to pursue his duties as a fur hunter.

That Marinka! How he loved her, he thought now as he trudged along the path behind her mother. But Baranov was right. The Indians were savages, and so was she, still a savage, incapable of love. He made an effort not to think of Marinka. It hurt too much. But her copper face and her ripe young body were before his mind's eye. He shook his head trying to change his thoughts. The fort...what had happened there? There was no one he could ask about the massacre; he must have been the sole survivor.

In a few hours the party reached a river which snaked out of the narrow canyon. Timofei breathed deeply as the forest opened for the river; the air became fresh, the cool breeze rustling in the reeds in the shallows.

The Indians halted to build a fire. "Now we'll eat!" Timofei thought, but the fire was used only to light torches that the young boys made from branches wrapped with moss dipped in halibut oil. The torches gave off acrid smoke to protect the travelers against mosquitoes.

Timofei also made a torch. He welcomed the short respite. His feet hurt and were bleeding. He envied Marinka's mother her tough, broad feet. Not a scratch showed on her leathery brown soles.

The sun began to sink, leaving a vivid smear of red beyond the mountains. Instantly the travelers were engulfed by swarms of mosquitoes. The insects formed huge clouds vibrating with a high-pitched buzz. They flew into Timofei's mouth, crawled into his ears and nose, drowned in the moisture of his only good eye. He waved his torch, trying to envelop himself in smoke, but it helped very little.

Timofei cursed as he slapped at the mosquitoes, squashing them against his skin. Even in the Siberian swamps he had never seen such huge and vicious mosquitoes! Every exposed inch of his body was covered now by ugly red welts. He knew that a maddening itch was to follow.

He watched the Indians. They walked steadily, stoically suffering the assault.

Finally, the narrow corridor created by the river, widened. The river split into a delta, sandy and shallow, spilling into the sea. The mosquitoes vanished, as suddenly as they had appeared, driven inland by sea breezes.

Several large canoes rested on the beach, hulls up, like so many dead whales. The Indians pushed the canoes into the water, loaded them and paddled into the open sea.

Everyone paddled. Timofei too, grabbed a paddle, easily falling into the rhythm.

Pale stars appeared on the lavender sky. It was still bright, although it was night time. It felt good to move his arms again after being trussed like a Christmas goose, Timofei thought as he wiped the sweat off his face with his sleeve. He did not care where he was being taken. Somehow, someday, he would find his way back to his own people.

The Indians traveled through the night. Toward morning Timofei saw a large dark forest looming ahead.

The leading canoe slid to a stop. The others followed. The Indians were home.

Timofei saw a village consisting of several tribal houses perched on a high cliff. A steep path winding among the boulders led up to the houses.

Marinka's mother pointed to a cave in the cliff that would be Timofei's home. He unloaded his burden of furs at the entrance to her house and limped back, down the path, toward the cave. He stared longingly at the canoes, empty now, with paddles neatly hidden under their upturned hulls. He dismissed the thought of escape in one of them. They were huge war canoes, requiring dozens of men to paddle them. A small one-man kayak would be necessary for his purpose.

There was no one-man kayak on the beach. But someday there would be, Timofei assured himself.

Timofei found he was not the only occupant of the cave. Two dozen men, women and children, all slaves, were already living there.

They looked emaciated, their ribs and joints protruding under their skins. Their bodies bore tattoo designs but no ceremonial paints. The children, bow-legged, their swollen abdomens grotesque, sprawled listlessly near the fire. A couple of infants suckled at their mothers' sagging breasts.

There were no mats on the dirty ground, no blankets, no utensils of any kind, no food nor water. The slaves lived like animals, held in contempt by the tribe.

"Tomorrow I'll find something better," Timofei thought as he made the sign of the cross, murmured a prayer and, curling up like a dog, fell asleep instantly.

He was awakened by a sharp poke in his ribs. Marinka's mother stood over him, a stick in her wrinkled hands. The cave was empty except for the children who whimpered like blind puppies in their sleep.

The stench of the cave hit Timofei like a blow in the face. It had not been so offensive in the coolness of the night, but now he hurried to crawl out and fill his lungs with fresh salty air.

The old woman pointed to the beach below. "Go," she said. "Food!"

Timofei flexed his stiff muscles and trotted down the well-worn path toward the narrow strip of sand, trying to imprint in his mind every detail of the topography.

The edge of the cliff hung precariously over the water obscuring it from view. For centuries the waves had pounded at the rocky shore, carving intricate passages for the sea to enter during high tide, creating a group of sheer narrow rocks pointing like index fingers into the sky. Colonies of sea birds nested on the rocks filling the air with their cries. The tides regularly filled the space between the rocks, carrying seaweed and kelp, providing a hiding place for myriad of sea creatures. During the low tides, the slaves foraged there for food.

They were there now, searching the kelp for muscles and

shrimp. Timofei joined them, probing among the seaweed with a long stick. Now and then some small creature would wriggle at the end of his stick; Timofei consumed it greedily on the spot. He had learned to eat raw fish from the Aleut hunters. At first he had been repulsed, but his trade as a *promyshlenik* required that he spend many hours at sea, laced into his *baidarka*. It became essential to learn to live like the Aleuts, eating fish raw, as it was caught. He was glad now that he was no longer squeamish.

The debris on the beach was almost bare; the hungry slaves preceding him had thoroughly combed it. However, his search for food was not all in vain; further along the shore, he found several fishing canoes. These small boats could easily be handled by a single man. With a little luck, Timofei thought, he could paddle near the shore, protected by the hanging cliff, until he was out in the open sea. He would fish along the way, as he had done many times before, he thought.

Timofei planned for escape by cautiously exploring his new surroundings.

The village was located near the mouth of the river, surrounded by a lofty forest. A large clearing crowded with seven tribal houses faced the sea.

The site of the village was well chosen. There was plenty of timber in the forest for building houses and canoes. The rapid river nearby jumped with salmon and the rocks jutting out of the sea a short distance away were alive with seals.

"I wish this place were ours," Timofei thought enviously as he split the logs for his mistress' fire. "What a fort we could have built on this spot!"

Chapter 14

As the sun rose Baranov watched Pavlovsk slowly emerge from the mists of the morning. It grew larger by the moment, the outlines of its drab buildings becoming clear as the *Olga* sailed forward at a fast clip. Through his telescope he could see groups of people hurrying out of their houses to greet the ship. He knew how the report of a sail on the horizon would excite the isolated village.

"Drop anchor!" he said over his shoulder to Richard.

They climbed into a *baidarka* which served as a lifeboat on the *Olga*, leaving the remaining two crew members to lower the sails and prepare the brig for anchor. They paddled toward the landing.

"I have your son!" *promyshlenik* Koshkin shouted as he hurried to help Baranov out of the *baidarka.*

"Where is he?" Baranov demanded gruffly. He sensed Koshkin's apprehension.

"He's in my house," Koshkin, all nervous servility, led Baranov to his house. "The little fellow is fine... He wasn't hurt at all...My wife took good care of him," he chattered, wiping his nose on his sleeve.

"Stop snivelling and get my boy."

"Yes sir, yes sir, Alexander Andreyevich, sir," Koshkin all but doubled up in a bow. He flung the door to his house open. Baranov stepped over the high threshold.

The air was oppressively hot and stale. The Russians kept their clay stoves lighted day and night, cooking on one portion and sleeping on broad *lezhanki* built over the stove tops for warmth. Baranov could see several dark-haired children peering at him from the top of the stove like tiny chicks from a nest.

"Poppa!" a child cried. He climbed down from the *lezhanka* and rushed into Baranov's outstretched arms.

He lifted Antipatr, pressing him roughly against his stubbled face.

"I thought you had disappeared like Momma," the child sobbed, his arms wound tightly around Baranov's neck. "I thought you would never come back. I was so scared..."

"Sh-sh-sh...I'm here. I'll never leave you...Don't be scared. Your Poppa's here..." Baranov comforted his son, shaken by the boy's outburst. "I'll talk to you later," he turned to Koshkin. "Thank you for taking care of my son." He carried Antipatr to his own house in the middle of the village.

The house looked deserted. The air had a faint odor of decay; left unheated, the houses quickly developed mildew in the damp climate of Kodiak Island.

"I want this house cleaned, aired and warmed up," Baranov directed Richard, who followed him into the house.

He put the child down, but Antipatr clutched at his leg with both hands. "He's terrified," Baranov thought. "What has happened to frighten him so?"

Two Aleut women, one of them Koshkin's wife, timidly entered the house. They lighted the large clay stove, the warmth soon dispelling the musty odors. The women washed the planked floors and mica-covered windows and dusted the furniture.

Baranov watched them with impatience. He wanted to be alone with his son to comfort and to question him. He knew that he would probably get nowhere questioning the villagers. "They will insist on total ignorance." Baranov knew his men well. "All liars," he thought.

The women finally left. Richard, who lived in Baranov's house, had also discreetly disappeared to his own room, to leave the Governor alone with his son.

Baranov sank into his arm chair, the child on his lap. "Tell me what happened," he said gently. "Tell me everything. You're a smart boy, so tell me all the truth. What happened while I was away? Where did momma go?" He peered into the boy's dark slanted eyes, shiny as plums. "His mother's eyes," he thought as he caressed his thick dark hair. The only "Russian" feature about Antipatr was his pale skin. "My poor little baby...What you must've gone through...Tell me, my baby, tell me what happened to Momma?"

But the child was unable or unwilling to talk. He clung tightly to Baranov, his bright eyes welling up with tears at the mention of his mother.

Baranov gave up questioning him. "Let him get used to the idea that I am back with him," he thought. "I'll talk to Koshkin. He will know what might have made Antipatr so frightened."

He smiled at his son. "I must talk to Koshkin. I'll be right back."

"No!" Antipatr screamed. "You'll leave me like Momma did!" he broke down sobbing.

Baranov gathered him in his arms. "Never! I'll never leave you my *medvezhonok*, my little bear cub"...he cradled Antipatr in his arms, comforting him with kisses, repeating sweet words of reassurance until the child quieted down. "I must wait until he goes to sleep," Baranov thought. "I cannot leave him now."

Toward the evening, Antipatr, exhausted by the emotional reunion with his father, fell asleep. Gently, Baranov carried him to the *lezhanka* and covered him with a quilt.

"Stay with him," he whispered to Richard. "I'll be at Koshkin's house."

Nikita Koshkin had been expecting Baranov. He waited for him, nervously pacing before the table set with a bottle of vodka and a plate of smoked halibut. His Aleut wife and children were shooed out of the room. Koshkin felt guilty that he did nothing to prevent the tragedy of Baranov's wife and child. He waited for the Governor, thinking how he could make himself appear blameless.

Baranov sensed Koshkin's fear but he controlled his rising temper. He sat at Koshkin's table and allowed him to pour some vodka for him.

"Tell me, Nikita, what happened to my wife. Tell me why she suddenly disappeared and why my son is so frightened. I want the truth."

Koshkin shifted in his seat and began, his eyes focussed on the table, afraid to meet Baranov's piercing stare. "She must've lost her mind, Alexander Andreyevich. Only a crazy woman would want to hurt her child."

"Wait, wait! What do you mean—hurt her child? What did she do? How did she hurt Antipatr?" Baranov interrupted.

"Well, sir, she hurled the boy off the cliff during the

night...Only a miracle saved him. He had landed on the juniper bushes instead of on the rocks...I found him in the morning. I heard a child cry, so I went searching and found him, all scratched and bruised, scared to death, but alive."

"Where was my wife?"

"We couldn't find her anywhere...She was gone. Later, we found that one of the small canoes was missing. She must've taken it. We wanted to send a search party for her but we couldn't. The weather turned real nasty. Storms, one after another, made it impossible to send anyone out to sea. She must have drowned."

"But why would she try to kill her child and then disappear, to be drowned?" Baranov peered at Koshkin fiercely. "The bastard knows more," he thought.

"She became crazy," Koshkin mumbled, averting his eyes.

"No," Baranov felt his temper rise. "She was driven to it by something or someone. *You tell me now!*" He pounded the table with his fist, his eyes blazing.

Koshkin paled. "It must have been because of the priest," he finally stammered. "Father Nektarii."

"Father Nektarii!"

"Yes, sir...He was giving Water Blossom...your wife, I mean, the instructions for becoming a Christian..." Koshkin paused.

Baranov waited. He knew that Water Blossom had been obsessed with the idea of becoming a Christian. "She must've gone to Father Nektarii for help, not knowing of my conflict with him about the forcible conversion of the Aleuts. Nektarii must've refused her request..." Baranov thought. "But still, this could not be the reason why she wanted to kill the child and herself."

"Tell me more," he said quietly.

"Well, sir, my wife worked for Father Nektarii. She was there when he cursed Water Blossom and your boy and threw them out of his house. She can tell you, she saw it all with her own eyes!" Koshkin was eager to divert Baranov's inquiry from himself.

"Call her in!"

An Aleut woman entered, grinning and bowing to Baranov.

"Your husband says that you heard Father Nektarii curse my wife and son. Tell me about it."

"I know nothing," Pashka hedged.

"Tell me the truth or I'll have you flogged!" Baranov threatened. He had never flogged anyone, but the threat worked.

"I was doing laundry in the kitchen when Water Blossom came in with your boy. She begged Father Nektarii not to bar her from religious instruction, but the Father wouldn't listen. They argued, Father Nektarii calling her names."

"What kind of names?" Baranov demanded.

"Well, names...You know, bad names."

"What names?" He raised his voice threateningly.

"He called her an 'Indian whore' and your son a *poblyudok*, the son of a whore. Then he said that she was sent to him by the devil himself to tempt him with her flesh. Then he grabbed her and began tearing her clothes off. When she screamed and fought with him, your boy rushed at the priest, pounding at him with his little fists. Father Nektarii then cursed them both and threw them out of his house. I was too scared to do anything, so I hid behind the wash bin. I waited until Father Nektarii left the house, then I ran home."

Pashka paused, then met Baranov's eyes boldly. "It's God's truth," she said.

Baranov believed her. Pashka was among the first Aleuts to be baptized into Christianity more than a decade before. She was known among the settlers for her piety. She told the truth, Baranov thought.

"Thank you," he said rising. "I believe you."

Baranov knocked on Father Nektarii's door. The house was dark and it looked empty although there was a slender column of smoke rising over the chimney. Father Nektarii was in, but he refused to open his door to the Governor.

Baranov returned to his own house. "I'll deal with the bastard tomorrow," he thought. "I know now what happened in my absence...Nektarii's curse terrorized my Water Blossom..." Baranov knew that the Indians feared being cursed more than they feared any threats to their lives. Being cursed meant that their souls and their bodies, would be forever possessed by evil spirits. Their families and their tribes would forsake them lest they become contaminated themselves. "Water Blossom was still an Indian," he thought. "She still believed in her Indian evil spirits even though she was ready to exchange them for our Russian saints..."

He checked the sleeping Antipatr. The boy looked rosy in his sleep, his thumb stuck in his mouth.

"All right, Richard," he turned to his servant. "Go to bed," Baranov said wearily. "I'll turn in myself."

Baranov climbed on the warm *lezhanka* and stretched out next to the sleeping Antipatr. He gathered his child closer to his body looking down at him tenderly. "Poor little *medvezhonok*! How much he has already suffered in his short four-year life!"

He thought back to the time when he first saw Water Blossom. She was given to him by her father, Chief of the Kenaitze tribe that permitted the Russians to build a settlement on their land in exchange for gifts of beads and other small items of trade.

Baranov recalled that he did not want the Chief's daughter but he could not refuse her without offending the tribe. "I'll use her as a servant," he had thought.

But it was before he saw her.

Her name was Water Blossom. She was no more than fifteen. She wore only a short cedarbark skirt and the skin of her long legs and body was a smooth warm copper. Her small breasts were tipped with wide dark nipples. An unusual feature of her high cheekboned face were her long curving lashes, such as he had never seen on an Indian.

Water Blossom had not yet begun to wear a lip-stretching *labret* or the nostril-distorting shells popular with the Indian tribes. She had only a faint tattoo on her cheeks and on her chin, delicate as lace, which gave her face an enigmatic look, as if it were veiled.

He took her to his bed.

Within a year she presented him with a son, whom he named Antipatr. He was happy with Blossom and would have married her had the church allowed him to divorce his Russian wife whom he had not seen for twenty years.

But the church denied his request for divorce. Baranov remembered with bitterness how jubilant his old enemy, Father Nektarii, had become when Baranov's petition for divorce was refused. Nektarii thundered from his pulpit against Baranov, accusing him of deserting his Christian family in order to wallow in sin with a heathen woman. He demanded that his parishioners shun Baranov and his Indian concubine.

"I tried to ignore it," Baranov thought. "I truly tried to

ignore his accusations. And I know my men never thought that I lived in sin. After all, most of them live with the native women without the benefit of a church marriage.

"Blossom, bless her innocent heart, knew nothing of sin or our Russian marriage customs. She knew only that I was unhappy," Baranov thought. "I remember how she took it into her head that all would be well if she became a Christian... She must've thought to surprise me with her conversion..." he thought wryly. "She must've gone to Father Nektarii for guidance, not suspecting what a bastard he was... My poor innocent Blossom... Dead..."

He knew now why Blossom wanted to kill Antipatr. He was cursed. Only his death would free his soul from the evil spirits, she believed. She was ready to kill his body to set his soul free. "My poor innocent Blossom," he agonized. "My beautiful Blossom...Dead...". He lay awake through the night. Finally, as dawn began to break, his eyes grew heavy and he fell into a deep dreamless sleep.

Father Nektarii paced his hut like a caged lion, his mind racing. He had a vision—or was it a dream?—that an angel chided him for not doing the good Lord's work of spreading the gospel among the natives. "I know, you're forbidden to leave the village, but who has the right to forbid you doing the Lord's work?" the angel said before he disappeared.

Who, indeed, Nektarii thought, but that Antichrist, that Baranov, whom he had forbade to enter his church. He, Nektarii, as a good servant of God, did not need to obey Baranov's orders. His orders were from the Lord Himself, through His angel.

He would leave Pavlovsk and go to the Aleut villages to spread the gospel, Nektarii decided. It would please the Lord much more than the nightly flagellations of his flesh to which he subjected himself to dispel from his mind the image of the Indian woman.

Nektarii ordered a novice to prepare a box with sacraments. "Get a two-man *baidarka*. Stock it with food and fresh water. You're coming with me tomorrow," he said gruffly.

The novice bowed, not daring to ask where they were going.

No one saw Nektarii and the novice as they left at dawn. Nektarii paid no attention to the rising wind whipping the ocean. In his mind's eye he saw only God's angel, leading him on his mission.

The seas churned the waves rising like a solid wall before the little *baidarka*. The wind tore the paddle out of Nektarii's hands; soon the novice too, lost his paddle. The *baidarka*, with its helpless passengers, was fast filling with water; Nektarii failed to secure it by lacing their clothing, Aleut fashion, to the boat. In fact, they both were attired in their clerical robes instead of native *kamliki*.

A blast of wind tipped the *baidarka* on its side. They struggled to level it, but a wave tossed it up, spilling them out like peas from a pod.

Neither of them could swim, but even if they could, they were lost, miles away from shore. They thrashed, gulping for air, their lungs fast filling with water.

In a few moments their struggle was over. The water closed over their heads.

The two bodies, horribly swollen and almost unrecognizable, were washed ashore a week later. Father Nektarii's eyes were eaten by fish but his gold cross was still around his neck. It became entangled in his long beard along with sea weeds.

Baranov sent a messenger to the Kenaitzes, hoping against all odds that perhaps Blossom had returned to her tribe. But the messenger brought back the reply that the Kenaitzes had not seen her.

It was obvious that Water Blossom was dead. Baranov prayed for her soul. He mourned her deeply, the only woman he had ever loved.

He put the thoughts of punishment of the villagers out of his mind. They could have done nothing, really, to save Blossom from the venom of Nektarii, he thought. They too, were afraid of him.

He began his preparations to move the offices of the Company to its new headquarters in Fort St. Michael, knowing nothing about the massacre, unaware that Fort St. Michael had ceased to exist.

Late one night, Baranov heard the door of his front room being opened and a blast of cold night air rush in. The flame of his candle wavered, almost extinguished by the blast.

He lifted his eyes from the journal he was writing. Standing in the open door frame was Blossom.

Emaciated and trembling, she clutched at the door, her cedarbark skirt in tatters, her bare breasts and arms, her thighs and legs scratched and covered with welts of insect bites.

"I killed my child," she whispered hoarsely, her red-rimmed eyes feverish.

He rushed to her. "No, no, you did no such thing!" he cried, trying to lead her into the room, but Blossom fought him, clutching to the door for protection. She stared at him wildly, only half-recognizing him, not understanding what he was saying, her inflamed brain throbbing, pounding at one thought—she had murdered her child.

"Look! Look over there, at the *lezhanka*! There's your son, he's safe!" Baranov begged her, realizing that Blossom was delirious, afraid that she might disappear again as suddenly as she had reappeared.

He felt her body relax a little and he took advantage of it. He loosened her grip on the door and pushed her gently into the room.

"Look, there he is, sleeping..." Baranov repeated softly.

Slowly, Blossom turned her head toward the sleeping child. It seemed to Baranov that she did not recognize the boy. Quickly Baranov closed and bolted the door.

"Do you see? He's safe, our little Antipatr," he whispered taking her by the shoulders and leading her toward the boy.

Blossom made several steps and stopped, staring at her sleeping son. Baranov waited, afraid to move.

Blossom lifted her hand and stroked the child's hair. Then she pressed her haggard face against his little body. Antipatr stirred in his sleep and smiled. "Momma," he said without awakening.

Blossom shut her eyes as one tear after another slid slowly down her thin cheeks.

Chapter 15

Timofei sat hunched over near the fire, his naked body covered with gooseflesh. The fire flickered as blasts of wind swished through the cave. There was no rain but he knew it would come momentarily.

Dark towering clouds chased one another, collided and regrouped like echelons of titanic warriors. Thunder shook the earth and lightning split the turbulent sky, illuminating angry waves crashing at the foot of the cliff.

The slaves huddled together in their cold cave, their angular faces like stone carvings in the lightning flashes.

As the first heavy drops began to fall on the stony path, each drop splintering into a minuscule fountain of its own, Timofei watched them, dully. "There will be no food in the morning," he thought. "The beach will be flooded..."

Timofei tried to remember how long he had been a slave of Marinka's mother. Three days? Or—was it four? Or five? He could not tell. The long hours of daylight in the summer months were deceptive. One could hardly tell when the day began and ended.

Morning came. The storm subsided to a monotonous drizzle.

The slaves did not stir. They knew that the passage under the cliff would be flooded; no one could forage for food there for some time to come. They would suffer hunger until the water subsided.

Timofei was unwilling to go hungry. Decisively he trotted out of the cave, his body glistening with rain as he made his way to his mistress' house.

"*Utxuh*, food." he demanded, pointing to his mouth. He

had half expected that the old woman would call for help and the warriors would throw him out.

Instead, she grinned. She pointed to a space at her fire and said "*woetch-di-k-ri-ta*, you sleep there."

Timofei sat down. The welcome warmth of the fire enveloped him as if it were a blanket. "What's your name?" he asked.

"Takat-kija."

There was no word in the Tlingit language to express gratitude, so he said in Russian, "*spasibo.*"

Takat-kija rummaged inside a large cedarbark box decorated with the tribal symbols of birds and animals. She paid no attention to Timofei, mumbling to herself. Finding what she wanted, a triangular fringed blanket woven of cedar fibers, she handed it to Timofei. She pointed then to the fish, curing under the eaves, inviting him to help himself.

Eagerly, Timofei grabbed the largest chunk of fish he could find. Takat-kija watched him benevolently.

"Dear Lord, you've answered my prayers!" Timofei thought as he chewed vigorously on the tough fish.

In the days that followed, Takat-kija treated Timofei as if he were a member of her tribe, and not a despised slave. She made a poultice for his eye and covered it with a soft patch of cedar fibers. She allowed him to keep the cedar fiber blanket, to which she added a sleeping mat of reeds.

Timofei luxuriated in his new feeling of safety as he lay wrapped in his blanket at night, his back turned toward the fire. The peaceful sounds of people asleep, their rhythmic breathing, gentle snoring and an occasional deep sigh, comforted him.

The fire light played on the planked walls of the house. The carved totems supporting the roof looked even more mysterious at night. Their shadows danced on the walls as the monstrous animals scowled at him exposing their fangs. For the first time, Timofei tried to decipher their intertwined forms.

"These bastards are such good carvers," he thought. "Even my Marinka could carve a fine bear." The thought of Marinka was like a sharp stabbing pain. "How could she hate me so?"

In the morning, still thinking of her, he asked Takat-kija about Marinka. He had never bothered to learn his wife's tribal name. Pointing to himself he used a Tlingit word for wife, *doo shut*.

Takat-kija bent over, cackling. She beckoned to the other women, chattering too fast for him to understand. The women shrieked with laughter, pointing at the new slave, who was demanding a wife.

Timofei watched a group of warriors depart to hunt whales. The village grew quieter.

Timofei scanned the beach for canoes, thinking of escape, but the warriors were not so careless. The beach was empty. To fill his free time, Timofei made a pair of soft slippers of rabbit skins for Takat-kija, a craft he had learned from an Aleut. Delighted as a child she showed the slippers for all to admire. Encouraged by her reaction, Timofei made her a long shirt of sealskin stomachs, another craft of the Aleuts. These garments, *kamliki*, were watertight and windproof. The Aleuts laced such clothing to their kayaks with animal gut thongs to keep water out. As a shirt, the *kamlika* would be comforting for Takat-kija's arthritic body, Timofei thought.

She broke into a joyous dance as she slipped the shirt over her head. Timofei watched, pleased with her delight. "She's really quite sweet," he suddenly thought. "What does your name mean?" he asked, smiling. He knew that Indians gave themselves names of animals and birds; women were often named after flowers and trees, but he had never heard the word "takat-kija."

"It's a bird. Very small. It flies very fast," she flapped her arms in imitation of a hummingbird. "I'll do my name dance now." She began to move in a circle, flapping her arms. Her age and rheumatism robbed her of agility, but she danced with the dignity of a proud young beauty.

Impulsively, Timofei joined her, whirling around her in the Cossack way, "*v prisyadky*," throwing his legs in front of him while moving in a squatting position. Exhilarated by his dance, he stuck two fingers into his mouth and whistled wildly. The old woman demurely moved in a dance of her own, paying no attention to him.

A group of children and then the women began to gather around, attracted by Timofei's hoots and whistles. Soon there was a large crowd watching.

Finally, Takat-kija stopped. "I'm tired," she limped toward a shade tree.

"Me, too," Timofei collapsed on the ground next to her. The crowd dispersed instantly.

As he lay, panting, Timofei thought, "A few days ago they wanted to kill me, and now I *dance* with them!"

Takat-kija tapped him on his shoulder. "You are a good man, White Slave. Make another shirt for the Chief, my brother. He's very sick." She hobbled away.

Timofei knew now why he was allowed so many privileges. As sister to the Chief, Takat-kija held a special place of honor within the tribe. Her son would be the next chief. Tlingits, Timofei had learned from Marinka, passed on leadership through a female line, to a nephew, rather than to a Chief's own sons. If Takat-kija liked him, she could permit him anything she wanted. Her good will could insure his survival; it might even lead to his escape, he thought.

He began making a *kamlika* for the Chief. The curious women watched him stretch and fit together elastic pieces of sealion intestines and stomachs. The Tlingits did not know that the intestines could be stretched into large parchment-like skins and stitched together with the thinnest sinews. The Tlingits made their garments out of cedarbark.

The secret of an Aleut watertight garment was in the sewing. The overlapped pieces had to be stitched one to another without passing the bone needle through. The needle could prick only the underside of each skin, never passing from one side to another. It was a tricky process requiring a lot of care, but as long as the skin remained unbroken, the garment was watertight.

The women were eager to learn the new skill. Soon several of them were seated under a tree next to Timofei stitching up the pliable skins.

Timofei watched his pupils proudly. They had dexterity he could not match. "Like in a Siberian fur factory," he said to Takat-kija in Russian. She nodded several times as was Tlingit custom, as if she understood.

Timofei labored over the *kamlika* for several days. He wanted it to be the best. Should he fail to escape and be forced to spend the winter with the tribe, he wanted to be sure of the Chief's friendship.

He fitted the pieces carefully together. "How big is your brother? As big as me?" he asked Takat-kija.

She giggled, making a funny slurping sound. "No one is as big as you. If you were a Tlingit you would be a totem."

He laughed.

"My brother is no bigger than me," Takat-kija continued. "The evil spirits invaded his body. He'll die soon."

In the afternoon Timofei completed his *kamlika*. Takat-kija took him to her brother's house.

The old Chief reclined in front of the fire. He was emaciated, wrapped in several blankets like an infant. His face, without the garish paint, looked sad.

"I brought you a gift," Takat-kija said, squatting before her brother. "My white slave made it for you."

The Chief lifted his hooded eyes at Timofei. For a moment there was a sparkle of amusement in his stare; he had never seen such a giant of a man before.

"What kind of a gift?" he rasped. Takat-kija nudged Timofei. "Give it to him." Timofei unfolded the shirt before the dying man.

"It will keep you warm," he said.

The old man struggled to sit up. With the help of his sister and two other women, his wives, he pulled the *kamlika* over his head. Exhausted by his effort, he fell back on his blankets.

"I like it," he said faintly, closing his eyes.

"Come," Takat-kija tugged at Timofei's arm, "He will die now. Let him die in peace."

Another week passed but Timofei became indifferent to the passage of time. One day was exactly like another, the sun never leaving the sky long enough for the darkness to descend. Timofei's eye had healed but the sight was gone. He took his loss stoically. He had become accustomed to use only one eye during the healing process.

"Better one eye than none," he repeated a proverb he had heard as a boy.

Nobody watched him closely any more, so he used his new freedom to prepare his escape. He was almost ready to try to get away when he was awakened from sleep by Takat-kija.

"You must leave," she said shaking him by the shoulder. "At once," she pointed to the entrance of the house.

Dimly silhouetted against the entrance, were the forms of several warriors.

"You go with them," Takat-kija said, and pushed him along.

The warriors surrounded Timofei and pinned his arms.

Outside, in the milky light of the summer night, Timofei could see the warriors more clearly. They were naked, wearing only raven's feathers in their hair. Their bodies shone with sweat and halibut oil, their faces were smudged with war paints.

They trotted to the beach where they pushed Timofei into a waiting war canoe and launched into the waves. Timofei glanced at the cliff. A few people lined up along it, watching him leave. They stood draped in their blankets, motionless, like a row of carved chess figures.

As the canoe picked up speed, he noticed one lone figure raise its arm as if in a farewell salute.

"Takat-kija," Timofei thought. "This must be very serious if she could not save me." He huddled his great body deeper into the canoe to avoid the chilly salt spray.

Chapter 16

The Indians paddled through the night. Timofei watched the pale stars fade, then the bright orange colors of the sunrise appear. He shivered. His naked body was covered with gooseflesh. He envied the Indians. Their brown hairless bodies glistened with sweat, the muscles of their arms and backs bulging with the effort of paddling. They felt no cold.

"Where are they taking me? Have I been sold to some other tribe?" It seemed unlikely that a simple transaction such as selling a slave would require such an escort.

The canoe skimmed smoothly over the calm sea. The Indians paddled inexhaustibly. The rings in their noses, the seashells in their earlobes and the raven feathers decorating their hair nodded rhythmically, following every movement of their bodies. Their eyes were cast down as they totally concentrated on paddling.

The sun rose above the horizon and its warm rays caressed Timofei's body.

"*Doojin,*" an Indian sitting in the prow pointed to Timofei's arms. They were swollen and almost black from the tight bindings. A warrior bent over and slashed them through.

"*Yak-ei,* good." Showing his knowledge of proper Indian manners, Timofei nodded several times. He was ignored.

He moved his arms, flexing his muscles from the shoulders down. Feeling the warm blood surge to his fingertips, he raised himself to a sitting position, then to a kneeling one, like the Tlingits. Picking up a spare paddle from the bottom of the canoe he began to paddle. The warriors paid no notice.

Toward evening the travelers reached a small sandy island studded with gnarled trees stunted by the northern winds. The Indians leaped out. They flexed their arms and legs.

Timofei followed them in their exercises, the numbness in his body gradually disappearing.

The warriors built a fire and stretched out on the sand around it, gesturing to Timofei to join them.

"*Utxuh*", food. One of them opened a cedarbark chest containing dry fish. He threw a fish toward Timofei.

"*Yak-ei!*" Timofei caught the fish and smiled. He took it as a good omen that they invited him to share their meal.

After eating, the warriors fell asleep, wrapped in their blankets. Timofei spent the night shivering, tending the fire, acting as unwilling lookout.

Early in the morning the Indians smeared their faces and bodies with fresh war paint and donned their masks. They were transformed into snarling wolves and grinning frogs, curved-beaked eagles and sharp-billed ravens. Did they expect to go into battle? Timofei was too tired to worry anymore. He curled up on the bottom of the canoe and was lulled to sleep by the rhythmic sounds of the paddles.

When he awoke some hours later, he saw the familiar Sitka Bay and small green islands dotting the sea around Fort St. Michael.

"It can't be true," he thought, sitting up abruptly. He made the sign of the cross to dispel the devil's illusion. Yet, there it was, Fort St. Michael, right ahead of him, and in the bay, two ships at anchor, one flying an American flag, the other British.

He saw too that the fortifications were nothing but charred walls and half-burned structures. The fence around the high palisades was almost intact, but to his horror, it was studded with the severed heads of the fort's defenders. The heads, dried and shrivelled in the sun, their eyes pecked out by seagulls and ravens, grinned at Timofei, exposing their teeth in a ghoulish grimace.

The Indians paddled straight to the ships. Timofei could make out their names: The *Unicorn* under British colors and farther at sea, the *Alert* under the American flag.

"Look, there's Timofei Tarakanov!" someone aboard the *Unicorn* yelled in Russian. "Timosha, *golubchik*, little dove, son of a bitch, you're alive, glory be to the Lord!"

The Indians halted at the port side of the sturdy, well-tarred British schooner, the *Unicorn*. At once a rope ladder was thrown down by the deckhands. Six Tlingits climbed up, leaving one warrior in the canoe.

Timofei leaped to his feet. Not caring whether his quick movement might overturn the canoe, he scrambled up the ladder. He had nothing to fear anymore. The sailors had their muskets aimed at the Indians.

He was seized in a powerful bear hug by his friends Plonikov and Baturin.

"*Bratzi*, I can't believe it! I am free!" Timofei sobbed, laughed and slapped his friends' backs. He kissed their bearded faces, tears running down his cheeks. For the first time he realized that he was naked.

"For God's sake, give me a pair of pants," he begged his friends. They roared with laughter. The English sailors laughed too, for his plight was evident to all. One scampered below decks and brought back a pair of trousers and a woolen shirt. Jumping on one foot in his eagerness to find the pant leg opening, Timofei finally got into the trousers. They were too short, barely covering his knees, but they were *trousers*! He laughed with relief.

"How did you know where to find me?" he cried, hugging his friends again.

"We'll tell you later. First, you must meet Captain Barber, the master of the *Unicorn*. He made the arrangements for your deliverance," Plotnikov said.

Timofei saw a short graying man with a ruddy complexion dressed in an old blue naval uniform. His bowed legs were encased in hip-high fisherman's boots which made him appear even shorter than he actually was. One of his epaulets was torn off and the tunic was smudged with grease. A few gold buttons were missing as well, proclaiming that the captain was no more a member of His Majesty's Navy, but rather fended for himself as a merchantman, commanding the splendid three-masted schooner.

"Welcome aboard," Captain Barber greeted Timofei, extending his hand with a broad smile. "Do you speak English? What's your name?"

"My name is Ti-mo-fei Ta-ra-ka-nov," Timofei replied, carefully enunciating every syllable. "Sir," he added respectfully as an afterthought. He and his friend Plotnikov had learned quite a lot of English from the British and American sailors who regularly visited Fort St. Michael and traded with the Russians. He was glad that he had not forgotten it.

"Welcome, Mr. Tarakanov. My men will give you something to eat as soon as we finish our little transaction with these splendid gentlemen," Captain Barber sarcastically indicated the warriors standing on deck in various poses of defiance. "They think they are through with me! Ha! Little do they know me." The captain's laugh was a mirthless explosion. "Tell them to bring the furs on deck," he turned to Plotnikov. "Tell them also that they won't see their chiefs unless I have all the pelts at once!" Plotnikov translated the message.

"Yak-ei!" The commanding Indian nodded imperiously, his arms crossed over his chest. He motioned to a warrior to climb down into the waiting canoe. The man tossed several bales over the bulwarks, carrying the last one on his shoulder. The carved wolf mask partly obscured his face but there was no mistaking his expression. It was full of contempt.

"The prisoners, sir," reported a deckhand, saluting smartly to Captain Barber.

"Ah, yes, here they are. The brave chiefs!" the captain snorted.

Timofei heard the sound of iron chains as they struck the narrow ladder leading to the deck. Presently two Tlingits appeared on the bridge.

They were Ska-out-lelt and Kot-le-an.

Timofei gasped. No wonder the Indians hurried to bring him back to the fort! The two most important Tlingit chiefs had been held hostage for his release.

The chiefs were shackled to one another. Kot-le-an glared at his captors, holding his head high.

A piercing war cry rose from the shore. Armed Indians appeared among the ruins, aiming their spears and arrows at the ship.

"The idiots!" the captain sneered. "As if they have a chance against my cannons!"

Ska-out-lelt raised his chained arm and the wail ashore stopped. The adversaries, the white men and the red, glowered at each other. The chiefs did not want to plead for their freedom; Barber, wishing to prolong the chiefs' humiliation, was loath to grant it to them.

Timofei felt that he must speak up. "I beg your pardon, sir," he said respectfully, in his halting English. "This young Chief is an honorable man. He saved me from torture. I beg you to release him and his uncle."

"There's no such thing as an honorable savage," the captain snapped. However, he ordered the blacksmith to remove the hostages' irons and release the chiefs.

They climbed down the rope ladder into the waiting canoe. It moved swiftly away. The war masks obliterated the human features of its passengers. From a distance it looked as if totem carvings had suddenly come to life, moving toward the ghost of a fort.

A loud shout greeted the chiefs as they reached the shore; then all was quiet again. The Indians vanished into the ruins.

Timofei, his stomach full of real, cooked meat and English gin, rested in a hammock lent by a sailor. Plotnikov and Baturin sat on the deck next to him, smoking fine English tobacco, a gift from the first mate.

"Tell me, *bratzi*, how did you escape?" Timofei said, "The bastards captured me off shore while I was fishing. I know nothing about what had happened at the fort."

"We were lucky," Plotnikov said, puffing slowly on his pipe, his broad pock-marked face sad with his recollection. "We too, were outside the fort at the time. It saved our lives. I was in the pasture, checking my sick cow."

"And I was looking for wild strawberries in the forest with my woman and child," interrupted Baturin, a young *promyshlenik* who had only recently arrived from Russia. "The child was crying, so my woman took him home. That was the last time I saw them, my Masha and Petrusha. God rest their innocent souls." He made the sign of the cross, his angular face with a hooked nose looking more Tlingit than Russian.

"I was checking my cow, as I said," continued Plotnikov, "when I heard the bell ringing in alarm. I ran toward the fort, but before I reached it, the gates were barred."

"So, it saved your life," Timofei said.

"Yes. I saw the savages attacking the fort so I crept into the woods and dug a hollow in the loose ground. I covered myself with branches and ferns. I could see the fort clearly from my hiding place. I thought our cannon would drive them off, but the Indians were just too many, hundreds of them. The attack was too sudden.

"I stayed in my hiding place," he continued. "I saw the fort burn. I watched them ransack the warehouses and set our shipyard afire. The bastards killed anything that moved, people, dogs and even the cows as they returned from pasture." Tears glistened in his eyes. He brushed them away angrily.

"Not *everyone*. They missed the three of us and eighteen Aleut women," Baturin corrected.

"Eighteen women!" Timofei whistled. "Where are they?"

"On the *Alert*. Two days ago they were here, but now it's the Americans' turn. It's only fair that all sailors get their turn with them."

Timofei nodded. "What happened next?" he asked Plotnikov.

"I hoped the savages would leave when they burned the fort. I had nothing to eat for two days. I planned to sneak into the fort and search for food. Then, saw a sail on the horizon. I prayed that the ship was heading for our harbor. I waited several hours until she dropped anchor. Then I made a dash toward the water. The English had already discovered that the fort had been sacked: it was still smoldering. They saw me right away. They lowered a boat to pick me up. Later, the captain sent a party ashore to search for other survivors. There were none."

"And you? How did you escape?" Timofei turned to Baturin.

"After my woman returned to the fort, I continued my walk, going further and further into the woods. The day was so beautiful!" Baturin said. "Then I heard the alarm. I ran back toward the fort, but the bastards saw me and shot at me. They missed, but I fell. I pretended that they got me. I hid in the woods for the rest of that day. I could see nothing, but I could smell the smoke. I wept. I cursed. I prayed. What chance did a handful of our men have against hundreds of savages?"

They fell silent, puffing on their short English pipes.

"As night fell," Baturin resumed his story, "a young Aleut woman with an infant appeared. She told me she was Kochesov's woman."

"Kochesov was tortured to death," Timofei said. "I saw him die."

"God rest his soul," Baturin made the sign of the cross. "I told the woman to stay with me. We hid in the forest for another day, then made our way to the shore. I hoped to find a canoe and perhaps some food. Then we saw this ship at anchor. A most welcome sight! I told the woman that I would swim to the ship and get help." He paused and broke into laughter. "In my eagerness, I had forgotten that I can't swim! I went into the water waist deep. I moved my arms as I have seen other men do, but each time I let my legs go I started to sink. It was at least a half-mile I would have to swim, and there I was, unable to do anything but sink! I returned to our hiding place and confessed to the woman that I did not know how to swim. She shoved her baby into my arms, took off all her clothes and slid into the water. Slick as a seal, hardly making a ripple, she swam right to the ship! Captain Barber dispatched the boat at once. The rest you know."

"And the child?"

"He died a few days later. He was already too weak." They fell silent again. The calamity that befell the fort and their friends was overwhelming.

"Tell me, how did the English arrange for my release? How did they know where to look for me?" Timofei asked.

"A stroke of good luck!" Plotnikov exclaimed, his face lighting up in a smile. "The savages played right into the captain's hands by offering to trade furs stolen from our fort for guns and powder. And you know the Chief, that greedy bastard Ska-out-lelt! He came aboard, strutting on the deck, dressed in a Russian shirt, with no pants, his bare ass showing. Captain Barber instantly seized him. I translated the captain's demand that all Russians and Aleuts be freed and all stolen furs be brought aboard the *Unicorn*, or the Chief would be hanged. As soon as the messengers returned to the fort, we saw another canoe speeding toward the ship. Two chiefs arrived to negotiate the release of Ska-out-lelt. That Kot-le-an was one of them. Captain Barber commanded that they be seized also.

"During the next several days the Indians brought back eighteen Aleut women and a few bales of fur, but the captain insisted that there must have been more survivors and certainly more bales of fur. He gave the Indians a few days of grace to deliver the furs and to find survivors."

"We learned from the women that three white men had been dragged away in a canoe," Baturin added. "It must have been you and Erlevsky and Kochesov."

"The bastards returned with a dozen more bales of otter pelts and two male Aleuts, but no Russians. While we were questioning the Aleuts, one of the chiefs made a dash toward the rail. The sailors grabbed him. That's when the captain had the chiefs put in irons and ordered his men to hang the one who tried to escape. The sailors strung him from the top yard. The captain threatened that the remaining bastards would be hanged also, if no white prisoners were delivered to the *Unicorn*."

Timofei shook his head. "Hanging the chiefs would have sealed my fate. The savages would have never released me if the chiefs were already dead. Do you suppose the English will take us to their country now?"

"If there were only the three of us, they probably would. But what will they do with the Aleuts?"

"They can sell them to the Americans," Baturin said.

"Americans buy only black slaves," Plotnikov reminded him.

Their questions were soon answered by Captain Barber. "As soon as the women are brought back from the American ship, I'll sail for Kodiak Island," he told his Russian charges.

"God bless you, sir!" they shouted.

Captain Barber waved their thanks away with a modest smile.

Chapter 17

Brisk wind filled the sails of the *Unicorn*, pushing her toward Kodiak Island. The August air was crisp and cold in the mornings, forecasting an early autumn. Timofei, Plotnikov and Baturin watched the horizon, each wanting to be the first to sight Pavlovsk. They could almost hear the peal of the church bells announcing their arrival.

Captain Barber too, was anxious to reach Pavlovsk, for reasons he did not share with the Russians. The friendly captain saw a chance for profit, perhaps even a small fortune. He smiled every time he saw the three rough *promyshleniki*. To Barber they represented a quiet cottage in Dover and an end to sailing. The Russian Governor would pay well for the return of these sturdy lads, especially that amiable one-eyed brute. Nor would Barber regret the chance to unload the women before his crew began to fight over them. As it already began to happen, the ship seemed to reverberate with clandestine encounters between his sailors and the women. Yes, indeed, he thought, Pavlovsk would be a happy anchorage.

When the *Unicorn's* lookout yelled from the crow's nest, "Ahoy, I see the mountains!" Barber began to prepare for his meeting with Governor Baranov.

He had his tunic cleaned and all the missing buttons replaced. His torn epaulet was resewn. He replaced his scuffed boots with silk stockings and silver buckled shoes.

The Russian Governor was known among the trading captains as a shrewd dealer. It wouldn't do to appear shabby and eager. He imagined Baranov as a powerfully built giant of a man, imperious in his bearing, a cold and arrogant aristocrat. "These bloody Russians are all giants," Barber grumbled.

By the time the *Unicorn* dropped anchor in a cove at the harbor entrance, Barber had fluffed his hair into a pompadour and completed the picture of what he took to be that of a "prosperous English gentleman."

"Captain, Governor Baranov is approaching," the first mate reported.

"Ah, that was quick," Barber thought. To the mate he said "Are you sure that it is *the Governor?*"

"Yes sir, I recognized him. I've met him before."

Barber was perplexed. He was prepared to pay the Governor a courtesy call and had a longboat waiting to take him ashore; now, the Governor himself was coming to the ship. He took his spyglass out of its leather case and followed the first mate to the bridge.

He could see nothing but a small native boat with two men paddling. He turned to his first mate. "Do you mean the Governor is in that little kayak?"

"Yes sir, the older man is Governor Baranov!"

Barber peered through his telescope, transfixed.

The Governor was about Barber's own age, in his late fifties, maybe older. What was left of his hair looked pure white, and stood in wispy tufts around his shiny scalp, like the fuzz on a nestling.

Baranov's appearance was surprise enough, but to see that so important a man was actually paddling himself in a native craft accompanied by a dark-skinned servant instead of arriving in an official launch with a retinue of honor guards, was a shock.

Barber folded his telescope. "Well! I'll be damned!" Barber snorted. "Prepare the refreshments in my quarters," he commanded over his shoulder.

The *baidarka* was now under the curved portside of the *Unicorn*. Like a cork, it bobbed up and down, close to the ship. Baranov extended his arm to steady it against the sturdy hull of the schooner. The deckhands lowered the ladder. The servant, Richard, climbed up first. Small and agile, he vaulted over the ship's railing.

Baranov's ascent was clumsy and laborious. He was in no hurry, oblivious of his awkwardness. Puffing heavily, he readily grabbed his servant's hand and allowed himself to be pulled over the rail.

Unflustered, Baranov extended his hand to captain Barber with a cordial smile.

"Welcome to Russian America," he said in Russian. "Are you here to trade or has some misfortune brought you to Pavlovsk? No ships ever come here for a social visit," he joked. Richard translated his words into sing-song English.

"Your Excellency, you guessed it, a great misfortune of yours has brought us to your harbor. Perhaps you will accompany me to my quarters where we can talk and share a cup of whiskey," captain Barber smiled pleasantly.

Baranov looked surprised but bowed and followed the captain.

Barber waved Baranov to the single arm chair in the cabin and seated himself on a stool at his small desk. The cabin boy brought in two tankards, a large platter of sausages and cheeses, and a loaf of freshly baked bread. The captain tossed him a key for his sea-chest, which the boy caught in mid-air.

"Get us a bottle of my Scotch whiskey," Barber said. "The one under the Bible." While the boy looked for the whiskey, Barber surreptitiously observed his guest. He noticed that Baranov must have been quite stout at one time, but now his fleshy jowls hung flabbily as if he had lost weight. He was dressed in shabby sealskin native garments and scuffed leather boots. An onion-shaped gold repeater watch attached to a heavy gold chain festooned his chest from one side pocket to another. There was a glimpse of a gold baptismal cross from under Baranov's soiled undershirt.

"How can this shabby *muzhik* be in command of this vast territory?" the captain thought, watching his guest attack the plate of sausages and cheese.

Baranov sliced off big chunks with his hunting knife, chewing vigorously and washing his food down with huge gulps of whiskey. He belched several times. Barber noticed Baranov's calloused hands, the broken, dirty fingernails.

The captain was disgusted. He had expected quite a different representative of the Tsar of Russia.

"He must be a real peasant, like my hostages," Barber thought. He observed with distaste how Baranov shared his food and drink with his servant, both using the same tankard.

"Tell the good captain that we have been nearly starving in Pavlovsk," Baranov instructed Richard. "Tell him that this is the first real white man's food I have eaten in more than two years. Bread and cheese! Sausage! He probably won't believe that we have been subsisting on dry fish, like the natives, that we haven't eaten baked bread for more than two years."

"Does he know why I'm here?" Barber thought with alarm. "Is that the reason for the show of poverty?" But he smiled cordially and spread his arms expansively. "Eat, eat," he urged, "there's plenty."

"Ask the good Captain what misfortune brought him to our shores," Baranov reminded Richard, his mouth stuffed with sausage.

"Quite simply, sir, we have at great risk to ourselves, brought you some poor wretches who survived the massacre at Fort St. Michael," Barber said. "Three Russians and twenty Aleuts, eighteen of them women."

"What are you saying?" Baranov demanded in English. His face had blanched. A piece of sausage fell from his hand.

"You did not know, Your Excellency?" Barber replied. "I am truly sorry to bring such evil news," he said. His expression was sympathetic, but it was only a mask for his delight. In his mind the price for the survivors soared.

"Dear God! The Fort is gone?"

"Quite gone, Governor, burned to the ground and all who were in it, save for the handful we rescued."

"I must see them at once," Baranov said. His mind was still reeling from the shock. He could not see the smug expression on the Englishman's face.

"Of course, Your Excellency," Barber responded smoothly, "but before I allow them into your presence, I must have your assurance that I will be properly reimbursed for all the risks I have taken to deliver them into your safekeeping. I realize, of course, that you might not have adequate compensation with you, so I will be perfectly satisfied with your signature on a simple promissory note." Barber reached into a drawer in his desk.

"How much?" Baranov suddenly sensed the situation and scowled.

"Fifty thousand pounds, Your Excellency," replied Barber, with a pleasant smile. "In gold."

"Fifty thousand pounds!" Baranov's flushed face became distorted with anger. "That's out of the question!"

"Sorry, Your Excellency, but those are my terms. My ship, my crew and I, personally, have endured great danger in order to save your men and women. I must be properly reimbursed."

"Where is your spirit of Christian charity?" Baranov lapsed into Russian, jumping from his chair in agitation. "Where is your code of chivalry at sea?"

Richard faithfully translated the angry torrent of Russian words.

"My dear sir, chivalry at sea has traditionally been the subject of high rewards," the captain sneered. "Without the prospect of high rewards, one would never risk one's neck for the sake of strangers." Barber saw no reason to hide his dislike any longer. He could not comprehend how the Russian monarch could have given so much power to such a barbarian.

"I want to see the Russian survivors." Baranov ignored the change in his host's manner.

"Not yet, Mr. Baranov," the captain parried, changing his form of address from the respectful "Your Excellency" to a mere 'Mister'. "I must be assured that I will be reimbursed."

"Bastard!" Baranov swore in Russian. Richard did not translate the remark. "Tell this blood-sucker I don't have any gold. Tell him that I have had no communication with Russia for almost three years! Tell him that because of storms we lost several ships carrying money and supplies. Tell him that I myself haven't been paid my salary for three years. Tell him that our people in Pavlovsk have been starving. Starving! Oh, the hell with the bastard! Don't tell him anything! Just ask him the names of the survivors," Baranov sighed resignedly.

When Richard translated only the request for the names, the captain smiled thinly. "Good," he thought with satisfaction, "the *muzhik* has realized that he cannot bluff his way among English gentlemen." Aloud he said, "I am holding three Russian men—Tarakanov, Plotnikov and Baturin. Also, eighteen Aleut women and two Aleut men."

"Tarakanov, Plotnikov and Baturin—my best men!" Baranov exclaimed. "I must see them!" he demanded again in English.

"Not until I have your word about payment," the captain insisted dryly, his teeth on edge.

"I can't pay. I have no money. None."

"Then, unfortunately, I must sail away with my prisoners." Captain Barber no longer called them his guests. "I will sell the women in America or Europe. Men might find them as exotic as Africans. As for your Russians, well, they will serve as seamen to pay for their freedom."

Baranov glared. "I will give you my answer tomorrow," he growled as he stomped out of the cabin toward his frail sealskin boat.

"Right, *Excellency*," the captain bowed.

"The bastard!" Baranov muttered as he climbed into his *baidarka* with Richard. "This scurvied son of a bitch! He has me over a barrel!"

Below decks, Timofei, Plotnikov and Baturin wondered why they were locked up and being treated as prisoners just when they should be going home. They did not know of Baranov's visit.

The captain suffered pangs of greed through a restless night. He regretted that he had not asked for more. "I should have demanded seventy-five or even a hundred thousand pounds!" In the morning Barber impatiently scanned the shore of Kodiak Island through his telescope. Once again, he saw the little *baidarka* pitching on the choppy waves, Baranov and Richard paddling expertly. The captain strained his eyes, trying to see whether Baranov was bringing the sacks of gold coins. All he could see were the two leather clad figures seated waist-deep in a flimsy kayak looking as if they were a part of it.

"The money is on the bottom of the boat," Barber told himself, but he had an annoying premonition that the Governor was arriving empty-handed.

"Did you bring it, Mr. Baranov?" he yelled, the moment the boat was within earshot.

Baranov scowled. He made a few strokes with his paddle and brought the *baidarka* into the shadow of the *Unicorn*. He grabbed the rope ladder the moment it was lowered and climbed aboard, Richard following. Neither carried any bags.

The captain took the visitors to his cabin but this time offered neither food nor drink.

"I cannot meet your demand!" Baranov snapped in English the moment the door of the cabin was closed. "I have no money. None. I haven't been paid by my government for more than three years; I haven't paid my hunters for more than two years; several of the ships sent from Russia went down in storms. We lost dozens of men, all our cargo and money. The colony in Pavlovsk is practically starving. Now you say St. Michael is burned and our people are killed. Do you want to pick our bones?"

Captain Barber was unmoved.

"I'll make a deal. I'll pay you in furs," Baranov said resignedly.

The captain frowned. He still did not believe that the Governor of such a vast territory as Russian America had no money.

"I'll pay you five thousand pounds in furs," continued Baranov. "Sea otter skins will bring a high price in Canton. The Chinese will pay you in gold!"

"Five thousand pounds in furs!" Barber exclaimed indignantly. "For the rescue and the upkeep of twenty-three people! You must be joshing, sir!"

"The rescue cost you nothing. I am sure the Indians brought the prisoners aboard the ship. I know their ways. As for the upkeep, the women probably paid for it with their bodies while my men, I am sure, made themselves useful. Five thousand pounds worth of furs is quite generous."

"Sorry. Your offer is unacceptable to me."

"Let me talk to my men!" Baranov responded angrily.

"That is out of the question. Tomorrow I weigh anchor. I have no more time to waste. Good day, sir." Barber coldly showed his visitors out of the cabin. "Five thousand pounds in furs!" he thought indignantly.

As the hours slowly dragged on, the captain began to have second thoughts. Doubts began to gnaw at him. "What if the Russian really don't have any money? What will I do with the prisoners? It will be months before I reach a port where I can sell the women. Meanwhile they will eat like horses...They'll become pregnant..."

He regretted now that he had not accepted Baranov's offer. Five thousand pounds in furs would have indeed brought a huge profit. What should he do if Baranov failed to return?

Baranov did return, the same afternoon, paddling his kayak, but this time he was surrounded by a fleet of forty native boats, each with two or three men.

The show of force made the captain bristle. He saw that Baranov's men, armed with muskets, bows and arrows, outnumbered his crew. Should they try to board the ship, the *Unicorn* cannon could hold them off, but some Englishmen might die too. For the moment Barber toyed with the idea of firing a warning shot, but he held back. He would talk to Baranov first.

Baranov and Richard climbed the rope ladder. The boats

surrounded the *Unicorn* like so many water bugs around a floating leaf. The Aleuts remained seated in their little crafts, bobbing on the choppy waters around the ship, their paddles in horizontal position. They showed no hostility.

"Welcome aboard," the captain greeted Baranov courteously, extending his hand. Baranov ignored it. He planted himself firmly on the deck, his short legs widespread to brace himself against the roll of the ship in the increasing wind. His manner was one of suppressed fury.

The thought flashed through Barber's mind, "He'll never pay me fifty thousand. He *really* doesn't have it!"

"I came here to make my final offer," Baranov said. "I'll pay you ten thousand pounds worth of furs. I cannot pay more. It's all that I have in my stores. If you don't accept it I'll take my people by force."

Barber pretended indignation, but mentally he leaped at Baranov's offer.

"You propose to take my prisoners *by force*? What *force*? These few savages in their little boats made of animal skins and sticks of wood? With one salvo of my cannons I can sink your 'fleet'! Besides, what is to prevent me from taking *you* as my prisoner?" The captain sneered.

"I thought of the possibility," Baranov replied evenly, his worn face showing no surprise. "My men on shore are watching your ship through their telescopes. Should they detect any movement among your sails, any movement at all, they will open fire from our shore batteries. My men in the boats will board your ship."

Barber looked into Baranov's eyes and knew the truth.

"You would die too," he said. His voice was strained.

"If need be," Baranov replied. There was a lengthy silence.

"Very well. Bring the furs," Barber said. "You leave me no choice."

Baranov waved a handkerchief and the boats moved closer to the ship. The crew lowered several more ladders. The Aleuts scurried bearing bales of pelts.

Baranov supervised the unloading. When the last bale was dumped on deck and the men returned to their waiting boats, he turned to captain Barber again.

"Here you are. Ten thousand pounds worth of furs. Now I want my people."

"Mr. Coleridge, please bring our guests," Barber said to

his first mate. Now that the furs were piled on deck, Barber was prepared to be pleasant.

Presently Taranakov, Plotnikov and Baturin were led on deck.

"*Detushki!*" Baranov cried, rushing with outstretched arms toward them, tears streaming down his weathered face. "My children!"

"*Batushka!*" They embraced, laughing and crying.

A crowd of Aleut women emerged from below deck and giggling shyly, climbed over the side to the waiting boats.

"It was a pleasure to do business with you, sir," the captain said to Baranov. A mere glance at the bales told him the furs were of the finest quality. He knew he would easily sell them in Canton. Counting the furs delivered to him by the Tlingits as ransom for their chiefs, it would be the most profitable voyage of his entire career, he thought gleefully. It was a fortune!

Baranov bowed curtly to the captain and climbed down the ladder to his *baidarka*.

Timofei hesitated at the ladder. He did not understand why the English had kept him and his friends locked below decks for two days, but now that they were reunited with their *nachalnik*, he held no grudge. He stepped toward Barber. "Thank you, sir, for saving our lives," he said. "We are grateful to you forever."

The captain shook his hand and slapped him on his back. "Don't mention it laddie. I did only what any good Christian would have done."

Baranov snorted, "You should have cursed the bastard instead," he muttered to Timofei in Russian. "Oh, well, you're still wet behind the ears. You'll learn."

Chapter 18

Timofei shared a *baidarka* with Plotnikov. They did not talk. Their eyes were on the tiny cluster of wooden huts and a diminutive church nestled at the foot of the craggy mountain.

"The bells!" were the only words Plotnikov spoke, his round, pock-marked face breaking out in a wide grin. Timofei smiled and nodded. They rested their paddles and listened to the faint sound of church bells ringing with joy, celebrating their deliverance. They could see a black-cassocked novice jumping up and down on the ground next to the belfry, pulling the yet invisible ropes.

They glanced at the *Unicorn*. The ship was tacking, turning back into the open sea.

The first *baidarka* carrying the women reached the shore. The villagers grew wild with joy, surrounding the survivors in one noisy huddle. They hurled their *shapki*, fur hats, up in the air in their excitement, shouting and swearing, sobbing and laughing.

Baranov watched their rejoicing as he beached his *baidarka*. The enormous sum he had paid for the rescue of his people was well spent, he decided. He was anxious to query his men about the massacre, but he knew he had to wait. A ceremony of thanksgiving and a service for the souls of the departed must come first.

On a high palisade, the priests waited. Gold glittered on the church banners, the evening sun reflecting on the embroidered vestments of the clergy, contrasting with the severe black attire of the novices.

Baranov slowly ascended the steep staircase leading to the palisade, the survivors and the villagers following him. All knelt before the sacred icons as a new priest, Father Afonasii, solemnly approached them swinging his *kadilo*, a censer filled with aromatic incense.

The *promyshleniki* clasped their *shapki* to their chests, their eyes reverently focussed on the gold cross held high by a priest.

Timofei knelt on the dusty ground next to Baranov. His heart was overwhelmed with joy for his deliverance. Like a child, he promised the Lord that from now on, he would be good, he would stop drinking, he would never fight, or gamble, and he would write to his parents. He could not think of any other "sins" that he might have committed. He was torn between the selfish feeling of joy that his life had been spared and a feeling of—almost—remorse, that he had survived while the others had so horribly perished. He was ashamed that he had begged the Lord to spare him above the others.

He kissed the cold silver frame of the icon as the novice passed it by him.

He glanced at Baranov. The Governor lay prostrated on the ground, his forehead touching the dust. Timofei noticed that Baranov had visibly aged during the past months. His sparse hair was white. He moved around with difficulty as if his whole body ached.

Baranov prayed with deep concentration. His mind was bursting with conflicting feelings of gratitude for the deliverance of his men, with desperation over the lost fort, with pity for his demented wife, anger for the deaths of hundreds of good men.

He prayed silently for their souls and for the soul of his old enemy, Father Nektarii. He forgave him the pain which Nektarii had inflicted upon him. There was no hatred in his heart for Nektarii.

Timofei helped Baranov to rise to his feet. The Mass of Thanksgiving was nearing its end. The priests chanted, the kneeling hunters responded. Finally, the priests carried their banners and icons back into the church. Father Afonasii blessed the crowd and retreated behind the church doors. The service was over.

The villagers surrounded Timofei, Plotnikov and Baturin, anxious to hear about the massacre, but Baranov led the three survivors toward his house. "You can talk to them later," he said firmly. "Right know, I want to talk to them myself. Go!" He shut the door.

Alone with their *nachalnik*, the three men fell on their knees. Bowing low to Baranov they touched the floor with their foreheads.

"God bless you *batushka*, for our ransom." They groped for Baranov's hands trying to kiss them. Embarrassed, he hid his hands behind his back.

"Come, come, *bratzi*, you know that's unnecessary," he grumbled, touched nevertheless. "You are worth every damned pelt I paid for you! Sit down now. Tell me what happened at the fort. Tell me everything!"

The men rose clumsily to their feet, wiping their eyes and noses on the sleeves of their shirts. Baranov felt a surge of pride as he looked at them. Such men these were! Moved to tears and laughter in a moment, but tough as walrus hide in hard times. How good it was to have the trust and affection of them all, he thought.

Baranov gestured toward the benches around the table that was laden with maps and bookkeeping ledgers. "Let's have a little something to eat and drink!"

Timofei had been in Baranov's Pavlovsk house many times before. It was made of huge uneven logs, with tufts of dry moss protruding between them, built in the manner of a Siberian "*izba*". Three small windows draped with hand-loomed Russian towels embroidered in red thread with snowflakes and roosters, faced the harbor. In the right-hand corner of the *izba* gleamed the silver frames of three icons. Tiny votive lights flickered under them, giving the room a cozy air. At the far end, behind a curtain of calico, Timofei glimpsed a pile of bearskins spread on the floor.

There, holding the curtain with one hand, stood Water Blossom.

"She's beautiful," Timofei thought. "Even more beautiful than my Marinka." He still felt a twinge of pain at the thought of Marinka, even though she had betrayed them all. His mind's logic could not overcome his feelings.

Next to Blossom stood Antipatr, clutching his mother's skirts, peering shyly at the strangers. His dark, slanted eyes were serious. His raven-black hair was in strong contrast to his pale white skin.

Timofei smiled at the child and won an instant smile in return. "I wish I had such a son!" he thought as Blossom brought in a plate of smoked fish and a bottle of vodka. She cleared the place on the table.

"We don't have much to offer," Baranov apologized. "The ships with provisions never reached us. Storms, as usual." He shook his head sadly. "Tell me now from the beginning what happened at Fort St. Michael. And you, Timosha," he turned to Timofei, "tell me how you lost your eye."

It was past midnight when Baranov clicked open his onion-shaped watch and announced that they must go to sleep. They would talk more in the morning.

"Cover the windows. We need a few hours of rest," he told his wife. Silently she went about hanging Indian blankets over the windows. The red and orange streaks of another dawn already colored the horizon.

They rolled up in blankets spread on three huge bearskins, each of them with a plump, square Russian pillow. Timofei stretched on the soft, deep fur, his head and shoulders resting on the pillow. "A pillow, like back home in Russia!" he chuckled to himself. He fell asleep instantly.

Baranov could not sleep. He lay quietly on the *lezhanka* watching the ever-brightening fingers of light stretch through the cracks where the Indian blankets did not quite cover the windows. Blossom and the child were asleep next to him, the boy sucking his thumb. Baranov's mind raced over the story the men had just told him. It was obvious that the island must be retaken from the Tlingits. The fort must be rebuilt. It was also obvious that this time he would have to use force. The Indians would not surrender the island without a fight. When he finally drifted off to sleep, his old shoulder wound was throbbing.

Chapter 19

Timofei woke up with a start. It took him a few moments to realize where he was. So much had happened to him in the past weeks, he thought. He made the sign of the cross before the icons, then careful not to awaken the others, pulled his boots on and made his way outside.

The air was bitingly cold. Autumn was approaching rapidly. He could smell it in the air, that peculiar scent, the mix of smoke from clay stoves, the warm smells of cowsheds and the bittersweet aroma of haystacks already beginning to decay. The smell reminded him of home. These last days of summer, with their harbingers of the winter to come, were always full of melancholy in Russia.

Timofei strolled along the wooden boardwalk laid out in the middle of the muddy street, toward the palisade. Down below, at water's edge the hunters were already loading their boats. Timofei watched them, thinking that soon he, too, would be among them.

He squinted his eye against the brilliant reflection of the sun rising over the water. He thought that he saw an outline of a ship. He opened his eye wider. There was no doubt, far out on the horizon there was a ship in full sail.

"*Ko-rabl!*" he yelled, waving his arms. The people on the beach turned in the direction he was pointing. They, too, saw the ship.

"*Ko-rabl!*" they shouted, dropping their work, running up the palisade to awaken the villagers. Timofei ran back to Baranov's house.

The church bell began to toll, telling the news in measured tones. People spilled out of their houses, many still half-dressed, scurrying to the palisade.

Baranov met Timofei halfway. He was fully dressed in his usual native attire, but for the special occasion of greeting a ship he wore his three-cornered official hat with plumage. Richard ran behind him, carrying a telescope. Together they pushed their way through the crowd. Baranov leaned on the wooden fence surrounding the palisade, training the telescope on the fast approaching ship.

"She's an American schooner," he announced. "I can see her flag. I think I can make out her name. It says O-C-A-I-N. It must be 'Honest Joe' O'Cain!" Baranov laughed.

"Prepare the guest house for the sailors. See that the bathhouse is hot. The men will appreciate our steam *banya* after being at sea. The captain will stay at my house," Baranov told Richard. "I'm looking forward to seeing the old bastard, O'Cain," he thought fondly.

The *O'Cain* lowered her longboats and the sailors piled in, leaving aboard only a watch crew.

"Joseph, my friend!" shouted Baranov in English from the palisade. "Welcome to Pavlovsk!"

O'Cain waved his cap with its shiny black visor. "Good to see you, Alex," he yelled in reply. He stood in the bow of the leading boat, dressed in a long black coat, his trousers tucked inside the knee-high black boots, a colorful scarf wound carelessly about his neck, the wind playing with its ends. Joseph O'Cain was about forty-five, a tall man of spare build, with curly red hair and a bristling short beard framing his face. He wore no moustache, shaving his upper lip clean, which made him look like a Quaker preacher. His face and the back of his hands were thickly covered with freckles, making his skin look as if it were scalded. His eyes were icy-blue, turning to a pale, watery color when he was drunk, which was quite often. His red eyebrows grew close together, creating an unbroken bushy line above his aquiline nose. He was known as a fine sailor, a shrewd trader and a trustworthy friend.

He jumped out of the boat and clasped Baranov in a bear hug, the Governor all but disappearing in his arms.

"What brings you to Pavlovsk?" Baranov queried as he led O'Cain toward his house.

The captain sucked on his unlit pipe and answered through his clenched teeth, "A proposal...A deal. Do you recall when we saw each other last time, over two years ago, you gave me a list of things that your colony at Fort St. Michael needed? Well, since St. Michael is no more, I brought the cargo here, to Kodiak Island."

"So you have heard," Baranov said mournfully.

"Of course I have heard! I learned about the sack of the fort when I stopped at the Sandwich Islands. Shall we trade your furs for my cargo, old pal?" O'Cain slapped Baranov heartily on the back. Baranov shook his head sadly.

"Sorry, Joe, but my warehouses are empty. I have just paid ransom for my people to that bastard, Barber, on the *Unicorn*. Ten thousand English pounds worth of furs! I am wiped out."

O'Cain whistled in surprise. His sharp brain churned, searching for another possibility.

"I'll tell you what," he said, as they reached Baranov's house. "Lend me your hunters and *baidarki* and I'll hunt otter in California waters. There's plenty of otter there but the Spaniards do nothing about it. We'll go fifty-fifty. You take my cargo in exchange for *baidarki* and the Aleuts. In six months I'll be back with enough otter to make us both rich. Agreed?"

"Let me think," Baranov replied slowly. "I have never subcontracted my hunters before. Besides, it is dangerous to poach in Spanish waters. Their coast is fortified, isn't it?"

"Let me worry about that. I'm willing to take my chances against the Spaniards. I have a fast ship and a few cannons of my own," O'Cain grinned.

The offer was tempting, but Baranov never made impulsive decisions.

"Let me think it over," he repeated, inviting O'Cain to join him at the table and filling their glasses with vodka. "To our reunion!" he lifted his glass.

Baranov accompanied O'Cain back to his ship. "Show me what you have brought," he said.

"All this!" O'Cain exclaimed, making an expansive gesture with his freckled hand. "All this is *for you*, my friend!"

Baranov went from one box to another. Tea, flour, sugar, salt pork, crates of fresh vegetables and fruits which O'Cain picked up in the Sandwich Islands...

In another part of the ship he saw muskets, barrels of gunpowder and shot, boxes of nails, bolts of woolen and cotton cloth, thread, needles and crates of hand tools. Everything that Baranov had ever hoped to receive from Russia during the past three years was there, in the spacious holds of the *O'Cain.*

"All right," Baranov said, making the decision. "It's a deal!" They shook hands firmly.

"However, you'll have to pay the Aleuts. I have no money. I'll lend you sixty Aleuts with their boats. You'll pay them two and a half Spanish piasters for each otter skin. And two hundred and fifty piasters to the family should the man be killed."

"Agreed. What else?"

"They take commands only from one of my men. He will be in full charge of the Aleuts."

"Agreed." They shook hands again, and headed for the captain's quarters to seal the deal with strong Yankee whiskey.

Within hours, the American sailors and the villagers moved the cargo to Pavlovsk's warehouses. The colony on Kodiak Island could face the winter.

The *O'Cain* was ready to depart.

Baranov chose Timofei to be in charge of the sixty Aleut hunters. He knew their language and he spoke some English. He was an experienced hunter himself and the Aleuts liked him. They would obey him.

Timofei felt honored that Baranov entrusted him with such a responsibility.

Warmly dressed in furry Aleut clothing, his spirits soaring, he climbed into the leading *baidarka,* waving his paddle to the villagers as they gathered on the palisade to see them off. Timofei's partner, his friend, Grishka, began an Aleut song about their journey. It was going to be a good hunt, he sang. No one will drown and all will become very rich.

The ship's guns fired a salvo to bid farewell to the colony. The lone cannon of the shore battery replied with a modest salute of its own. The villagers watched the *O'Cain* tack as she slowly turned around, her sails filling with wind. Thirty *baidarki* lined up in her wake, like a flock of ducklings following their mother.

Timofei liked to watch the American sailors as they scurried up and down the rigging, performing the rites of sailing men. "How I wish that I were a sailor!" he often thought.

The *O'Cain* and its flotilla sailed steadily south, staying within sight of the coast. A week after leaving Kodiak Island, the lookout sighted the first group of otter. The playful animals showed no fear of the approaching armada. Driven by curiosity, some of them swam close to the *baidarki*, peering at the invaders with innocent bulging eyes, unaware of the danger. The others slept peacefully on kelp beds, lying on their backs with their front paws crossed over their bellies, like fat contented humans.

Timofei always liked otters. It amused him to see how the otters used "tools". They pounded on the hard mussel shell with a stone until it would burst open. He enjoyed watching the females play with their young, tossing them up in the air, catching them in their paws before they plunged into the water; suckling their pups, lying on their backs in the position of nursing human mothers.

Timofei hated to kill these friendly trusting animals; they reminded him of playful puppies of his childhood. He was full of remorse hearing the anguished cry of a mother otter as her young was hit with an arrow. She would tear at the arrow with her teeth and claws, then realizing that her pup was dead, charge at the hunters in desperation, committing suicide.

Years ago, Timofei had confessed to Marinka that he detested killing animals. Marinka did not laugh, as he had expected. She understood his misgivings. Her Indian gods permitted killing of animals only when one was hungry, or in need of clothing, she told him.

"When you kill animals—the spirits get angry. You must ask the spirits to forgive you."

"How do you ask forgiveness of the spirits?" Timofei remembered asking her.

"You explain to them why you kill the animals. They understand."

Timofei sighed. That Marinka! How he still missed her!

He signaled to form a wide arc encircling the kelp beds. The Aleuts paddled carefully so as not to alert the animals. The arc completed, Timofei raised his paddle, silently praying to the animal spirits for forgiveness.

A shower of arrows descended on the unsuspecting otters. Some were killed outright and the Aleuts pulled them out of the water with long hooks; others dived, trying to escape. Otters could not stay long under the water; every few minutes they surfaced for air, to be met by another barrage of barbed arrows. Swimming inside the blockage of *baidarki*, the terrified animals came up for air each time more exhausted.

The kelp beds turned red, the Aleuts paddling through the sea of blood, collecting every slain otter, clubbing those still alive.

The sailors from the *O'Cain* watched the slaughter with morbid fascination. Most of them were glad they did not have to participate in the carnage.

The hunt over, the Aleuts paddled ashore and made camp on the beach. They skinned the otter, wasting nothing. The meat was eaten, the intestines stored, to be made later into ropes and thongs, the stomachs into buoys. The Aleuts stretched the skins on sticks to allow them to dry in the wind. Later on, they would scrape the skins of every remnant of fat and tissue.

Timofei kept scrupulous account of every pelt taken aboard the ship. Occasionally, he climbed aboard the *O'Cain* for a glass of whiskey with the sailors, but returned to his Aleuts at night to share their meager meal and hastily build shelters. Lying under his *baidarka* wrapped in a wolfskin blanket against the bitter cold of the night, Timofei watched the play of the northern lights over the darkness that was the ocean and the sky, united as one, infinite and mysterious.

Often he could not sleep. He would still see before him the reddened kelp beds and hear the pitiful cries of the frantic animals, trying to escape.

"I wasn't meant to be a *promyshlenik*," he thought with distaste. "I should have been a sailor."

Imagining himself at the helm of some marvelous schooner, such as the *O'Cain*, eventually would relax him. He would fall asleep only to be awakened at dawn by Grishka, shaking him by his shoulder.

"Time to hunt, master. Good day to hunt. Kill many otter!"

The *O'Cain* reached Alta California waters and remained there for almost six months. When she finally returned to Pavlovsk laden with furs, there had been enough profit in the expedition to satisfy all.

"Let's do it again next year," captain *O'Cain* said, toasting Baranov on the eve of his departure.

"We shall see." The Governor smiled. "Next year I may

not have enough men left for your expedition. Next year I will need every man and every *baidarka* from here to Yakutat! I'm going to take my fort back from the Ravens!"

Chapter 20

In the early spring of 1803 Annushka was ready to deliver Rezanovs' third child. Nikolai worried about her. Her previous two pregnancies had been difficult ones. He dreaded the approaching hour of delivery. Annushka lay in her high bed under a brocade canopy of blue silk, propped against several square pillows. She was beginning to feel the first pangs of labor.

The pale sun of the northern spring poured through the tall windows of her bedchamber, making the tiny particles of dust dance in its shafts of light. The cool breeze moved the lace curtains, beyond which she could see the broad expanse of the Neva sheathed in granite.

The serf women of the Rezanovs' household clustered around her bed with clean towels and sheets, ready for the arrival of the midwife.

Rezanov's two young children, a boy and a girl, were sent to his parents' house across the river, lest Annushka's screams of childbirth frighten them.

Nikolai sat at her bedside, holding her hand. He watched her flushed face anxiously, keenly aware of her contractions as she squeezed his hand involuntarily each time she felt the pain.

A group of young serf girls, gathered in the corner under the icons, sang old Russian songs, trying to distract her. Between her spasms, Annushka gamely joined the girls, knowing all the songs by heart.

As the pains grew, beads of perspiration began to gather on her smooth brow. Her old nurse, Nikiforovna, standing at the head of her bed, wiped them away with a damp towel.

"Where's the midwife?" Nikolai muttered nervously, wincing at his wife's suffering.

"You'd better leave, master," Nikiforovna said. "This is no place for a man. Now it's for us, the womenfolk, to take care of my *golubushka*, my little dove."

"Yes, Nikolasha, you'd better go. I'll be fine..." Annushka smiled weakly.

Nikolai bent down to kiss her cracked lips. "I'll be in my study," he said, leaving the room with relief.

Nikiforovna shooed the singers away. It was not proper for unmarried women to be present at the birth of a child. The girls quickly left the room, glad to be relieved from watching their mistress' agony.

The nurse and four older women resumed their vigil at Annushka's bed. The contractions came one after another, barely allowing her to rest between them. Soon her moans became cries, which in turn changed to screams.

Nikolai paced the floor of his study, his hands pressed against his ears. Annushka's screams filled the house. The maids, the grooms in the stables, the cooks in the kitchen, stopped in their work, making the sign of the cross, murmuring prayers for their mistress.

At last a carriage arrived, bringing the midwife. Nikolai watched her through a window as she crossed the cobblestone yard, a stout middle-aged woman in a white bonnet, carrying a large heavy satchel.

"At last!" he thought with relief. It would not be long before Nikiforovna or Ivan would burst into his study announcing the birth of his new child.

The midwife pulled the sheet off Annushka's body. "How long has it been?" she demanded.

"At least four or five hours," Nikiforovna volunteered. She was illiterate and could not tell time.

Annushka shrieked. When the contraction subsided, she whispered hoarsely, "Do something. I can't stand it anymore. Do something...Anything!"

"You must be patient, Your Excellency. God meant women to suffer. Bear with it," the midwife cooed patronizingly, settling herself in a comfortable chair. She knew that it would be a long wait.

An hour passed, then another one, with Annushka's screams permeating the house.

"Do something!" Nikolai shouted to his valet. "Tell them

to do something! I'll go insane knowing that she's suffering!" He rushed downstairs to the salon, hoping that Annushka's screams would be muted by the distance.

The midwife finally decided that the time had come to assist Annushka. She could see that her patient was exhausted. "Bring my satchel," she commanded. A woman quickly scampered to do her bidding. The midwife opened the satchel and pulled out a horse yoke. The women grabbed the yoke from her, holding it two on each side, while Nikiforovna and the midwife helped Annushka out of her bed.

Her head spun and her legs felt shaky. The nurse and the midwife led her slowly to the women waiting for her with the yoke.

"What are you doing?" Annushka cried, recoiling from the oval horse collar.

"Don't worry, *golubushka*, it won't hurt much," Nikiforovna soothed her. "Just slip through the yoke, and the baby will pop out in no time!"

Annushka screamed, terrified, "No!"

"Yes, yes, *golubushka*, you must!" The old nurse pushed her gently. "You must. It's the only way to squeeze the babe out!" she explained kindly. "Yes, Your Excellency," joined the midwife, "It's the *only* way!"

Annushka tried to fight them off, but another contraction doubled her up in pain, making her sag in their arms. The six women quickly slipped the yoke over her head, pushing it down over her bulging body.

"No! No! Nikolai!" Annushka screamed in terror. "You're killing me!" They pushed the yoke lower.

Nikolai heard her calls for help, but he presumed that it was all part of the mysterious process of birthing. He paced the salon, waiting for a messenger to announce that the child had been born. "The birthing room is surely no place for a man," he thought.

The yoke would not budge over the thickest part of Annushka's abdomen. The women, covered with perspiration, breathing heavily, pushed it, inch by inch, over her body. Nikiforovna wiped Annushka's face with a towel, anguished that her beloved mistress was suffering such an agonizing childbirth. She would have preferred not to use the yoke, but who was she to disapprove the methods of the learned midwife, she thought.

The women pushed harder and Annushka passed out. She

lay huge and motionless on the flowered carpet at the foot of her bed, the women on their knees, still struggling with the yoke.

Finally, they forced it over her belly and down to her knees. They lifted Annushka's lifeless body back on her bed.

The women made the sign of the cross piously before the icons.

"It won't be long now," the midwife said. "Pack the yoke into the satchel. The master shouldn't see it. The nobles don't appreciate our ancient peasant ways," she said, feeling superior.

The women packed the yoke back into the satchel. The midwife locked it with a key.

Nikiforovna anxiously watched Annushka's suddenly peaceful face.

"Are you sure that she's just fainted?" she said, fear creeping into her voice.

"Of course. They often do," the midwife replied. She took Annushka's wrist nevertheless, and felt for a pulse. There was none.

"Call the master!" the midwife raised her voice in alarm. "I think she's dead. Not a word about the yoke!" she hissed hysterically.

The women, shaken, stared in terror at the midwife's contorted face. They all could be accused of murdering their mistress, they suddenly realized.

Nikiforovna fell on her knees at the bed. "We only wanted to help!" she lamented. The other women cowered around the bed, unwilling to be the ones to summon Rezanov. Finally, the midwife gathered her wits and rushed out of the room in search of Ivan.

"Tell the master..." she began. "Tell him...that her Excellency has died in childbirth. The baby has killed her!"

Nikolai burst into the bedchamber. Annushka was already covered with a sheet, her damp blond hair neatly combed.

Sobbing, he threw himself on her motionless body. Six lamenting women lay prostrated on the floor under the icons, their faces hidden. Nikiforovna howled like a she-wolf.

One by one the servants filed into the room, standing around the bed in a semi-circle, sobbing, murmuring prayers for their young mistress and her unborn child who they had heard, had murdered her.

Like an automaton Nikolai went through the formalities of the funeral service, receiving condolences from his friends and colleagues and from the Emperor, who attended the services.

Woodenly, Nikolai walked bareheaded behind Annushka's catafalque to the cemetery, counting his steps mechanically, never able to go beyond a hundred, starting his count over and over again. He threw the first handful of earth on the white coffin containing the remains of his beloved wife and the unborn child, still nestled inside her body. Ashen-faced he stood between his parents at the graveside, thinking of the long years ahead without Annushka, without ever seeing her lovely face, without ever hearing her voice or her laughter.

The boys' choir from the Tsar's own chapel sang the funeral hymn as shovelsful of earth began to fall with dull thuds on the nailed lid.

A small mound of earth rose above the grave. Later, it would be supplanted by a marble sculpture of a kneeling angel with Annushka's face and a cherub; the sculptor was already at work on the monument.

Nikolai was led away from the grave by his parents as if he were still a little boy. He followed them into their carriage, settling on a small seat opposite them as he used to when he was a child.

"Are you sure dearest, that you wouldn't want us to stay with you?" his mother said as the carriage stopped in front of his suddenly empty house.

"I'm sure, Mother. Ivan'll be with me." He kissed his mother's cheek and embraced his father.

"We'll take good care of the children," his mother smiled through the tears as the carriage pulled away.

"Thank you, Mother," he muttered, not caring whether she had heard him.

Chapter 21

Nikolai grieved for his wife in the seclusion of his book-lined study. Ivan spread a bed for him on his uncomfortable slippery leather sofa; Nikolai refused to enter the bedchamber where Annushka had died. He locked himself in the study, pacing the floor for hours or lying on the hard sofa, staring at the ceiling, lost in a void, seeing images and hearing snatches of conversations which made no sense. Ivan brought him his food, which he would leave mostly untouched. He stopped shaving and soon his face was covered with thick stubble, which grew into a beard, making him look like a Siberian convict.

Weeks passed. The faithful Ivan suffered watching his master. "He's killing himself with grief," he agonized, sitting in the kitchen with the other servants. "He doesn't talk, he doesn't cry, he doesn't pray. He doesn't even get drunk like any Russian would!" The servants shook their heads in pity.

Finally, Ivan made a decision. He went for help to Rezanov's parents.

They set out immediately for Vasilievsky Island with the children. They hoped that seeing his children would snap Nikolai out of his depression.

At the house Nikolai entered the salon trailing the long skirts of an old silk robe with worn out elbows. Underneath, his fine linen shirt was spotted with food. He was unshaven; his hair looked greasy, reaching down to his shoulders. There was dirt under his fingernails and he smelled of stale sweat.

The children shrunk away from him, but he seemed not to notice. He sat on the edge of his chair, listless, ready to flee.

"Nikolasha, what has happened to you!" Mme. Rezanov

cried, bursting into tears. Seeing their grandmother cry, frightened by the stranger, who they were told was their father, but who did not look at all like their father, the children, too, began to sob.

Nikolai winced in pain. "I'm sorry, Mother, I have an excruciating migraine. Please don't cry. And take the children away."

Mme. Rezanov weakly waved her hand to Nikiforovna who stood at the door, sniffling discreetly. "Take the children to their rooms, nanny, please," she said, wiping her eyes with a perfumed lace handkerchief.

"You misunderstood me, Mother," Nikolai interrupted coldly, raising his voice slightly, "I would like you to take the children back to *your* house."

"Of course, son, we'll be glad to," his father said quickly.

"Thank you," Nikolai stood up. "Goodbye now...I must lie down. I have a headache. Goodbye." He left the room without a glance at his children.

They ran to their grandmother, sobbing. "You poor little orphans," she wailed like a peasant woman, hugging them to her ample bosom.

"Where's your master?" Count Rumiantzev inquired in a cheerful booming voice, winking at Ivan conspiratorially.

"This way, Your Excellency," Ivan led the Count to Rezanov's study.

Rumiantzev flung the doors open. "Here you are, Nikolasha!" he cried loudly, ignoring the stagnant atmosphere of the room, the leftover food on a plate, and a milk ring which stained a priceless volume of Aristotle. "Open the curtains," he ordered cheerfully. "It's so dark here that I can't see my own nose!" he laughed, playing the game of not noticing anything unusual about his friend.

Ivan quickly drew the heavy draperies apart, letting the sunlight pour through the dusty windows.

"Ah, this is better!" Rumiantzev exclaimed. "Now, let us alone, my good man." Ivan closed the double doors carefully. He made the sign of the cross, feeling assured now that the Count would help his master.

Nikolai watched his enthusiastic friend apathetically. Rising from his sofa he tightened the sash of his soiled robe. The Count could see that Nikolai was very thin.

"I came here to convey a proposition from the Emperor,"

the Count began. "Remember, some years ago, when you and I discussed the future of Russia with the Emperor? Before he became *the* Emperor?"

Nikolai barely nodded.

"Well, the time has come," Rumiantzev continued. "Alexander is sending two new frigates, which we have just purchased from England, on a voyage around the world. Just as he had promised to the late Empress that he would. The first circumnavigational voyage of the Russian Imperial navy!" Count Rumiantzev grew more excited as he talked. "What's more, the Emperor is following *your* general plan."

Nikolai smiled thinly through his scraggly beard. "Yes, it sounds exciting," he said politely, without interest.

"That's not all. His Majesty wants *you* to head this historic expedition!"

Nikolai shook his head.

"Impossible. I'm in no condition to take any assignments. Look at me! I'm ill."

"Nonsense. All you need is a good bath, a shave and a haircut! Ivan!" Rumiantzev clapped his hands.

Ivan appeared immediately.

"Bring hot water, soap and towels and give your master a shave and a haircut. Also tell them in the kitchen to heat plenty of water for a bath!"

"Yes, sir!" Ivan grinned from ear to ear, saluting Rumiantzev with military smartness. He had not forgotten from the years he and his master had spent in the Guards.

Within minutes Ivan was back with the necessary equipment, paying no attention to Nikolai's weak protestations. He encircled his master with a crisp white sheet, preventing him from moving his arms, and began to clip away at his long greasy hair.

Meanwhile, Count Rumiantzev continued to talk, pacing the room as was his habit.

"His Majesty has chosen two of our finest young naval officers to command the frigates. Both of them have seen service in the British navy, and have traveled around most of the world while serving in England. You know one of them. He's Captain-Lieutenant Kruzenstern."

"Who's the other?" Nikolai asked through a closed mouth, trying to avoid a mouthful of shaving foam. It was the first spark of genuine interest he had shown since Rumiantzev had arrived. The Count felt encouraged.

"Captain-Lieutenant Urey Lisyansky. A fine officer. The frigates are christened the *Nadezhda* and the *Neva.* His Majesty has kept asking about you all these months, wondering why you were not seen at Court. I told him that I would pay you a visit—and here I am!" he laughed heartily. "He wants you at Court. I am here to convey his *order.*" Rumiantzev knew that he could go that far with impunity. Alexander, indeed, had been asking about Rezanov, expressing concern over his health.

Nikolai began to object, but Rumiantzev interrupted, this time without artificial brashness. "I think, Nikolasha, you have mourned Annushka long enough. You must accept her death and go on living yourself. You have two small children who need you. You have elderly parents who need you. You have friends who need you. Your Sovereign needs you. Your *country* needs you!" he said a bit pompously, but meaning every word of it. "You can't be selfish in your grief."

Ivan finished his ministrations and covered Rezanov's face with a hot towel. When he removed the towel, a new man sat grinning weakly at Rumiantzev. "I thought I would never be interested in anything again," Nikolai said, "but you have made me want to get out of here and *see the new ships*! You're right. Life must go on. Tell His Majesty that I am ready to accept my assignment."

Rumiantzev embraced him. "I knew we could count on you!" he exclaimed.

After the Count left, Nikolai slowly walked to the doors of his bedchamber.

He flung the doors open, gazing at the wide bed where now he would sleep alone. He closed the doors gently behind him. He fell on the bed, burying his face in a pillow, sobbing the long-suppressed tears that would finally bring him relief.

Chapter 22

Dressed in his Court uniform, which now hung loosely on him, Nikolai was driven in Annushka's carriage to the Winter Palace for an audience with the Tsar.

Ivan, in a footman's livery, rode next to the coachman, beaming with happiness. Life was going to pick up again at the house on Vasilievsky Island, he thought.

Nikolai leaned back on the velvet cushion of the carriage, breathing in the fresh salty air blowing from the Baltic. The feeling of being alive overwhelmed him. The sounds of the city, the snorting of the horses, the sight of the people busy with living, filled him with a sudden yearning for life. His heart ached at the thought of Annushka, but at last he felt he was able to face her death.

The carriage arrived under the portico of the inner court of the palace and two footmen sprang up to take the bridles of the horses.

Rezanov placed his plumed hat on and stepped down. He was ushered into the Tsar's private study.

Sun poured through the two tall windows facing the Neva, its rays resting on the thick Oriental carpet, awakening its brilliant colors, making it look as if a handful of rubies, emeralds and sapphires were carelessly tossed over its surface.

Tall Chinese vases on the malachite pedestals decorated the room. A small elegant desk inlaid in mother-of-pearl with many secret compartments and drawers, nestled between the windows. On the top of the desk stood a small marble bust of Voltaire, smiling slyly. In the corner of the room, a tall Holland stove of dark blue ceramic tile was lit, radiating warmth, often needed during the cool damp summers of St. Petersburg.

Alexander sat at his desk, apparently just finishing a letter. Nikolai stopped at the door, his plumed hat under his left arm, waiting to be invited to approach the Tsar. No more could he call him by his first name. No more could he sit down in his presence without being invited to. Alexander was now the Emperor of all the Russias.

"Ah, Nikolai! At last! We've been missing you at Court!" Alexander exclaimed cordially, standing up to greet Rezanov.

"Your Majesty," Nikolai bowed and clicked his heels.

"Come in, *cher ami*, I have truly missed you!" the Tsar embraced Nikolai, leading him to a dark red leather sofa. Nikolai waited respectfully until Alexander sat in a chair opposite the sofa. "Thank you, Sire," he bowed and then lowered himself onto the sofa.

Alexander smiled. His blond hair and sideburns curled around his handsome youthful face, but on the top of his head there was already a pink bald spot, like a monk's tonsure.

"I am so glad to see you looking so well!" The Tsar slapped him on the knee of his velvet britches. He himself was attired in the colonel's uniform of his Semeonovsky Guards regiment with its immaculate white kid leather britches and high polished boots. "Nikolai, I was most sorry and grieved at your loss of Annushka. You must be very thankful for your great memories and your fine children. You *do* feel better?" he asked with genuine concern.

"Yes, Sire, I am fine now. I am awaiting your orders."

"I am delighted. I'll come straight to the point. Count Rumiantzev had suggested that we appoint you as our Envoy Plenipotentiary to Japan. As you know, Japan is a closed kingdom, which no European power except the Dutch has been able to penetrate. For some reason, the Japanese trade only with the Dutch, even though Russia is their closest European neighbor.

"Aside from trade, we would like to deal directly with Japan in case our ships get wrecked within their territory. As you know, with the increased travel between Siberia and Russian America, we have increased shipwrecks. The Japanese intern our sailors and confiscate our cargo and the only way we can get our men back is through the good offices of the Dutch. It takes years to get the diplomatic negotiations going!" Alexander paused, a look of frustration on his unlined face.

Nikolai listened attentively.

"So, my friend," Alexander continued, "We have decided to try a direct approach to Japan. Why should we always depend on a third party to do our bidding? We should deal with Japan directly, to our mutual benefit."

Nikolai waited. Alexander stood up and went to the window. He gazed at the placid Neva, as he continued, "We have always thought of you as a brilliant diplomat, Nikolasha. You have been our most trusted friend. Will you accept the appointment?"

Rezanov stood up and bowed. "Your Majesty, I am deeply honored. I appreciate your trust in me. I accept this appointment with pride and gratitude."

"Good! We have been advised by our ministers to use the occasion of the circumnavigational good will voyage of the *Nadezhda* and the *Neva* for establishing diplomatic relations with Japan." The Tsar smiled. "You won't have much time to arrange your affairs before you leave. The frigates will be ready to sail in a week."

"I am ready now, Sire," Nikolai smiled.

"*D'accord*! A long sea voyage will be good for your health. It will put color in your cheeks," he joked, leading Nikolai to the door. "Count Rumiantzev will see to all the details."

Rezanov bowed deeply to the Tsar. The short audience was over.

Nikolai immersed himself in preparations for the journey. While before he seemed not to care whether he was dead or alive, now he worked with furious energy, going over every detail of his forthcoming mission to Japan. He felt flattered that the mission, and even the itinerary of the voyage, followed closely his own original suggestions of some years ago.

The plan was simple: the two ships would sail from Kronstadt to Copenhagen, then across the English Channel to Falmouth, and from there on to the Atlantic Ocean. Once in the open waters of the Atlantic the frigates would set their course southwest making scientific observations along the way, drawing new maps of the seas and the lands, and perhaps making new discoveries. They would cross the equator and follow around the Brazils and Cape Horn into the Pacific Ocean. In case they became separated, the frigates would rendezvous on the Sandwich Islands. The *Nadezhda* would proceed then to Kamchatka, to be restocked, while the *Neva* would sail for Kodiak. This stop was especially intriguing to Nikolai. Now he would be able to investigate the Russian-American colonies for himself and finally meet with the legendary Alexander Baranov.

Nikolai was full of optimism once again. He would win over the Mikado and open trade with Japan, he thought. The mission was just what he needed.

The *Nadezhda* was loaded with a special cargo of gifts for the Mikado, worth more than three hundred thousand rubles. Not knowing what curiosities might appeal to the mysterious ruler of Japan, the Russians gathered an assortment of gifts varying from two huge bevelled mirrors in elaborate gilded frames to an elephant-shaped clock set with emeralds and diamonds that once belonged to Catherine the Great; from a fine precision-made microscope, to gold-inlaid pistols, sabres and muskets. Silks, velvets and brocades were packed in crates along with European laces and Tatar carpets.

In addition to the gifts to the Mikado, the *Nadezhda* carried a large personal cargo of Rezanov's books, paintings and curios, which he intended to leave in Russian America, as a nucleus for a future library and perhaps even a museum. He had ambitious plans for Pavlovsk as a cultural oasis on the Pacific; now, he felt it was an excellent opportunity to realize these plans.

The second frigate was loaded with a more prosaic cargo for Russian America. Boxes of tools, saws and axes, sail canvas and rope, kitchen utensils and ordinary food staples such as flour and sugar, all items perpetually needed in the colonies, filled the holds of the *Neva*. Both frigates were heavily armed; the *Nadezhda* carried sixteen heavy caliber cannons and the *Neva* fourteen.

From the beginning, Nikolai ran into a conflict with Captain Kruzenstern, the master of the flagship *Nadezhda*, who had objected to having Rezanov's mission dominate and possibly obscure his scientific expedition. Kruzenstern wanted the journey to be solely a voyage of discovery. He wanted to survey exotic shores, to draw maps of unexplored regions and to present the Emperor with a new atlas of the world. The journey, the way he saw it, should provide an opportunity of bestowing his own name on the still unknown islands and straits.

Instead, the ships were to be used as a means of transportation for Rezanov and his embassy.

Kruzenstern tried to block Rezanov's mission. "No Russian ship is ever allowed to anchor in Japanese harbors," he argued. "The country is sealed against the Europeans."

Count Rumiantzev had heard that argument before. He produced a Japanese document written in 1793 and given to a Russian captain, Adam Laxmann, in gratitude for rescuing shipwrecked Japanese fishermen and returning them to their country. The document stated that the Kingdom of Japan would permit *one* Russian ship to enter Japanese waters as a gesture of good will.

This permit had never been utilized; the document had been misplaced at the Ministry of Commerce, then forgotten. By chance, Rumiantzev came upon it. The document was still valid.

Kruzenstern argued no more.

Nikolai saw Alexander once more before his departure. This time the Tsar received him formally, along with the commanders of the frigates.

The captains, wearing their summer parade uniforms of white and gold, with full sets of decorations, fidgeted with the tassels of their swords, feeling ill at ease in the splendor of the Winter Palace.

The Tsar's adjutant, young Prince Vasily Obolensky, kept glancing nervously at the clock on the mantel. Only three minutes before the Tsar would enter the reception room...But where was Rezanov?

He arrived, unperturbed, and took his place between the captains, but a step ahead of them.

Kruzenstern envied Rezanov's cool self-possession, which seemed to make him the master of any situation. The good-hearted Lisyansky frankly admired Rezanov's aristocratic aplomb. "Nothing fazes him," he thought.

The Tsar entered, surrounded by his ministers and aides. He greeted Nikolai and the captains. "We are proud of you," he said embracing Nikolai with his usual familiarity. "At ease, at ease," he smiled at the captains who stood at attention, their hands raised in salute.

"Russia is proud of you," the Tsar continued, his eyes suddenly misty with emotion. "You are our Russian Columbuses, our Magellans, our Vasco de Gamas!" He seated himself and motioned to Count Rumiantzev to read a proclamation by which he granted a pension for Kruzenstern's wife and

Lisyansky's parents. In addition, both captains were awarded the Order of St. Vladimir.

Kruzenstern, not a rich man, fell on his knees, kissing the Tsar's hand. Lisyansky, embarrassed by Kruzenstern's servility, was at a loss as to how to express his own gratitude. Finally, he blushed deeply, clicked his heels and stretching at attention again, exclaimed much too loudly, "Thank you, Your Majesty, you are far too generous!"

Nikolai was amused by the little scene. He watched it with a thinly concealed smile. He despised Kruzenstern's groveling, but he liked Lisyansky's boyish embarrassment and obvious sincerity. "I would rather sail on his ship, than with this Prussian. Lisyansky is a true *Russian!*" Nikolai thought.

"As for you, my dear Nikolai Petrovich, as the leader of our expedition," the Tsar turned to Rezanov, "we wish to bestow upon you the rank of High Chamberlain of the Court and appoint you the Actual Counsellor of the State." Alexander smiled. "We must make sure that no one outranks our Envoy to the world, mustn't we?"

Nikolai suddenly understood how Kruzenstern must have felt; he, too, had an urge to fall on his knees before his generous monarch.

Alexander continued, "We also award you the order of St. Andrew." He motioned to a page, and the boy proffered to him a large flat box of red Moroccan leather. Inside, on the bed of red velvet, lay a long gold chain interspersed with colorful enameled plaques, attached to a pendant of St. Andrew, the highest decoration of the land. A many-pointed brilliant star, pinned to a wide sky-blue moiré sash, lay at the bottom of the box.

Alexander slipped the chain and the pendant over Nikolai's head, while Count Rumiantzev encircled his chest with the moiré sash, attaching the star to the right side of his coat.

"Thank you, Your Gracious Majesty," Nikolai bowed.

"You well deserve it, my friend," Alexander said kissing him on both cheeks. Then, turning to Kruzenstern and Lisyansky, the Tsar slipped their medals, dangling on striped moiré ribbons, over their bowed heads.

"When you return in three years, we'll celebrate the success of your journey with a national holiday!" the Tsar smiled. The captains saluted. Alexander patted Nikolai on his shoulder. "*S Bogom*, God speed," he said as he left the reception room, his attendants crowding behind him. The

captains turned about face smartly and marched out of the
room.

Count Rumiantzev remained. "Don't leave yet," he said
to Nikolai. "Well, Russian Columbus, how do you feel now?"
he laughed heartily, slapping him on his back.

"I feel wonderful! Ready to conquer the world!"

Rumiantzev winked. "I'll tell you a secret. When you
return, you'll be rewarded with the title of Count. But not
a word about it! His Majesty wants it to be a surprise!" he
whispered conspiratorially.

On August 8, 1803, the *Nadezhda* and the *Neva* were
ready to start the first Russian circumnavigational voyage of
the globe.

The populace of St. Petersburg was in a frenzy of pa-
triotic hysteria. Thousands of people lined along the sandy
shores of the Gulf of Finland waiting for the ships to pass on
the first leg of their journey. Hundreds more piled up into
boats of every description, hurrying to Kronstadt, a naval
fortress on the Gulf protecting the approaches to St. Petersburg, hoping to follow the ships for a short distance.

Elegant brigantines of the rich bedecked with garlands
of flags and flowers, full of fashionably dressed ladies and
gentlemen, competed with rowboats of the poor for a better
glimpse of the stately frigates.

Music filled the air. The marine band blared the martial
tunes, while the small boats around the frigates vibrated with
their own music of balalaiki, flutes and human voices raised
in boisterous songs.

The Emperor himself arrived with his suite on his private
galley to inspect the ships.

"Attention on deck!" the bo'swain's pipes whistled
shrilly. Alexander and his Empress ascended the ladder leading to the *Nadezhda*, followed by their suites of admirals, ministers and ladies-in-waiting. They were met by the enthusiastic young crew dressed in crisp white uniforms, shouting
oo-rrah, as the Emperor passed them in review. The officers,
in their dazzling parade uniforms, stood at attention, their
left hands on the hilts of their swords.

The Empress presented each sailor and officer with flowers.

Wearing the official uniform of the diplomatic corps, his
white-plumed hat firmly set on his blond wavy hair, Nikolai

waited for the Imperial couple to approach his own small entourage of six aides, including two Japanese interpreters.

"This is for you, Monsieur Rezanov. For good luck." the Empress handed him a small velvet box. Inside was a miniature portrait of Alexander painted on ivory and surrounded by a delicate frame of tiny pearls and diamonds.

"Your Majesty, I am speechless," Nikolai murmured, kissing her gloved hand. "I'll treasure it forever." She smiled and followed her husband, the wind playing with the ribbons of her pale-blue bonnet.

Nikolai was profoundly touched by her gift. The Empress did not like her husband's Russian friends. Being German, she felt uncomfortable among the Russians whose language she found difficult to learn. Although baptized into the Orthodox faith, the former Maria-Luisa of Baden thought of herself as a German princess rather than a Russian Tsaritza. Given the new name of Elizaveta Alexeevna, she settled quietly in the Winter Palace, suffering bad health most of her life. She was convinced that her husband's subjects did not like her for not producing an heir to the throne.

Nikolai knew that the Empress disapproved of his marriage to Annushka, whom she considered far beneath his social class. She was heard making disparaging remarks about Annushka, calling her 'that Siberian tradeswoman,' which the Court gossips were quick to convey to him.

When Annushka died, he received a letter of condolence from the Empress, but she did not attend the services in Annushka's memory, although Alexander and the members of the Court stood at her open coffin in the church and most of them accompanied it to the cemetery.

Nikolai was astounded by the Empress' unexpected gift. He interpreted it as her shy bid for forgiveness.

The band struck "God Save the Tsar." Alexander and his suite departed for the inspection of the *Neva*.

The ceremony continued. The elderly Metropolitan Yevgeny, formidable in his tall golden mitre and heavily embroidered vestments, blessed the ships. The clergy chanted as he slowly went around the decks swinging his censer, blessing the sailors. Bareheaded, they knelt, their round caps pressed to their hearts. The Archdeacon followed the Metropolitan carrying a gold cross, which he proffered to each sailor to kiss.

On a special barge towed close to the frigates, the boys'

choir from the Tsar's private chapel burst forth with the Lord's Prayer. The noisy citizens in their little boats scurrying like waterbugs around the frigates, quieted down listening to the children's pure voices. The men bared their heads, the women dabbed at their eyes with their handkerchiefs, all moved by the solemnity of the occasion and the sweetness of the boys' singing.

The Metropolitan sprinkled holy water on the cannons and then blessed the officers kneeling on the bridge.

The ceremony was over. The clergy proceeded to their barge, while the children sang.

It was time to leave. The Tsar's galley was rowed out of the way.

"Make sail," commanded Kruzenstern.

"Make sail," echoed Lisyansky on his ship. The sailors scampered up the rigging for the last display of naval dexterity. They looked like flocks of white doves lined up at even intervals on several levels of the yardarms.

The frigates were towed out of Kronstadt harbor. Martial music blared as the ships' sails snapped, filling with wind. The stately three-masted frigates slowly glided past the surrounding flotilla of small boats. The shore batteries fired salvos of salutes. The frigates replied, blasting the air with their guns. The naval ships in the harbor joined in the cacophony by firing their cannons as well, while their signal flags semaphored the messages of good luck and fair weather to the *Nadezhda* and the *Neva*.

As the frigates picked up speed, the private boats began to fall behind. Soon the frigates were sailing alone, past the palaces of Peterhof and Oranienbaum, the granite embankments of both towns black with people who came to watch the ships. Russia was proud of her explorers who were to carry her flag around the world for the first time.

The evening sun reflected like molten gold in the windows of the palatial residences lining the seashore. Nikolai observed through his telescope the famous Peterhof staircase made of fountains and studded with gilded statuary. The fountains were turned on and the water rose high in the air, sparkling and shimmering with the colors of the rainbow. In the center of the water display rose a monolithic statue of Samson tearing a lion apart, shining like pure gold in the rays of the setting sun.

"It's a good omen, that my last glimpse of Russia should

be the statue of a man conquering a beast," Nikolai thought wryly, turning toward his cabin.

"It's good luck, Your Excellency, to see gold on the day of a long journey," said Ivan, his ever-present servant.

"Fool's gold, my friend," Nikolai retorted.

Chapter 23

From the beginning of the voyage Nikolai was haunted by echoes of melancholy. He fought it by trying to write his observations of the voyage, but often he found himself staring at the blank page as a memory of Annushka flooded his mind. He tried to concentrate on the mission ahead, but Annushka seemed to dominate his thoughts. The pain of her loss was still acute. It would crush in on him until he could do nothing but lie helplessly in his bunk, head throbbing, stomach in spasm, thinking of his beloved Annushka. His misery was increased by seasickness, which Dr. Langsdorff, his personal physician, could do little to ease. It was only through his powerful will that Nikolai could force himself out on deck and converse with others.

Yet, Nikolai's intellect was too well trained and too active to be chained to his depression. While the frigates lay becalmed at anchor in Copenhagen, he forced himself to leave his cabin and join Captain Lisyansky for a little sightseeing. They hired a rowboat that took them to the famed castle in Elsinore, the setting of Shakespeare's *Hamlet*.

"You spent your time in England well," Nikolai said to the young captain after Lisyansky finished reciting in English the lines from the play as they stood upon the misty battlements. "Not only have you sharpened your skills as a naval officer, but you educated yourself in poetry as well."

Lisyansky blushed with pleasure. A compliment from the taciturn Chamberlain was uncommon. "I love poetry, Sir," he replied modestly.

Urey Lisyansky had just turned thirty, but he was highly valued by the Admiralty as one of its ablest officers. He had been sent to serve in the British navy as a midshipman. Now, years later, he was placed in command of the *Neva*, the frigate he had personally selected for purchase in England for the voyage around the world.

Nikolai liked the young man. Slender and of medium height, Urey Lisyansky had curly brown hair which cascaded from his head joining his sideburns, framing his still boyish face in its luxuriant growth. His warm expressive brown eyes were shaded by long thick lashes, which gave him the look of a romantic hero.

Lisyansky had many talents, as Nikolai was soon to discover. He was a gifted artist and cartographer. He had already compiled a thick folder of drawings, sketching his impressions of different lands that he had visited during his several voyages around the world with the British navy. He made maps and charts of the seas and islands, which the Admiralty found most useful. Nikolai wished that Lisyansky's ship were his flagship. He would have preferred to have Lisyansky rather than Kruzenstern as his shipboard companion.

The wind was rising. They could see the pennons on the masts flutter where only a few hours earlier they hung limp. They hurried back to the ships.

Their pleasant interlude was marred by harsh words of captain Kruzenstern when Nikolai stepped aboard the *Nadezhda*. "I demand, Your Excellency, not to delay the departure of my expedition," he said irritably, loud enough for the crew to hear.

Nikolai blanched. "You *demand*?" he repeated. "May I remind you, Captain, that *I am* the head of this expedition," he said icily, turning his back on Kruzenstern. The encounter upset him. The tone of his relationship with Kruzenstern was set for the entire voyage, just one more source of anger and frustration that filled Nikolai's black moments.

As the journey progressed, Nikolai gradually became a better sailor. Although he never fully shook the tendency to seasickness, by the time the frigates passed through the Spanish waters at the island of Tenerife he began to call himself jokingly "a seasoned seadog".

They spent their first Christmas away from their homeland among the hospitable people of Santa Catalina, a Portugese island off the coast of Brazil. Nikolai saw that the men were exhausted by their long voyage and needed a rest ashore.

He ordered a two week halt to restock the ships with supplies and fresh water and to repair damages suffered during storms.

By March the voyagers reached the infamous Cape Horn. Instantly, the frigates were picked up and tossed about by huge waves whipped up by constant savage gales. Rain lashed at them and their passage was often threatened by floating icebergs. Trying to ride out the storms, the frigates became separated. Such a possibility had been anticipated throughout the voyage. The captains had an agreement to meet at certain ports along the route should they become separated. Their next point of meeting was to be in the Sandwich Islands, in the harbor which the natives called Pearl.

Nikolai had no way of knowing if the *Neva* had survived the passage around the Horn.

Shaken but intact, the *Nadezhda* entered the Pacific Ocean.

No one was in the condition to celebrate the occasion. Nikolai and his aides huddled in their cabins, too seasick to care. The officers and the crew, exhausted from battling the weather, were only too glad to reach the calmer seas. Those not on watch slept, caring nothing about the Pacific. Soon the floes of ice, which so hindered their passage, began to disappear. The warm winds from the tropics aired the ship's canvas and dried the sailors' musty clothes.

Nikolai's mood improved as the *Nadezhda* sped toward the Sandwich Islands. They rose out of the mist, mountainous and lush with tropical vegetation. The trade winds pushed the frigate forward, until she tacked into her anchorage.

To Nikolai's delight, he found that the *Neva* was already in the harbor. Through his telescope he saw her double-headed eagle pennant flying from the topmost spar. He sighed with relief. The expedition's little fleet was still intact.

Lisyansky met Nikolai on the landing. "Thank God, you're safe!" he exclaimed shaking his hand vigorously. "I worried about you."

"I can say the same," Nikolai smiled. "Any damages or losses?"

"No, sir. We are all well and the ship rode out the storms admirably," Lisanyansky reported cheerfully.

Another ship anchored at Pearl brought less happy tidings. The *Unicorn* was in port and Captain Henry Barber was quick to inform the Russians of the loss of their fort St. Michael and the massacre of its inhabitants. He described with a flourish his own role in rescuing twenty-three people, exaggerating his personal danger in doing so.

Nikolai decided to split his expedition and speed the *Neva* to Russian America to aid Governor Baranov. Other foreign captains had told him of Baranov's determination to assault the Indians and retake the fort during the summer. The *Neva* had no time to waste. It was already August and if the attack was not mounted soon, the Indians would be safe for another year. The foul winter weather would protect them from a Russian assault, and by the next year, the *Neva* would have moved on and her crew and guns could be of no help to Baranov.

"There is much more at stake than one destroyed fort," Nikolai explained to the officers gathered in his elegant cabin panelled in polished teak. "The full prestige of Russia is at stake. We cannot allow savages to push us off land that we bought. Captain Lisyansky will sail to Russian America as soon as his ship is refurbished. He will place himself and his ship at the disposal of Governor Baranov."

The *Neva* sailed northeast a month later. The *Nadezhda* set her course in the opposite direction, northwest, toward Kamchatka, from where she was to proceed to Japan.

It was decided that the frigates would meet in Canton, China.

It was not until August, 1804, that Baranov's attack force was finally gathered for the assault on the Ravens.

Every adult male was mobilized. Members of the clergy were excused, but a priest volunteered to accompany the armada to celebrate Mass when the fort was retaken. And to bury the dead.

Baranov sailed on the *Olga*. Brigs, rebuilt that spring, followed, leading the convoy of three hundred *baidarki*, each with two Aleuts. They fanned out in the wake of the ships like strands of oblong beads used for barter with the natives. Two hundred more Aleuts with their boats would joint Baranov in Yakutat.

The rugged armada arrived at Yakutat harbor two weeks later. Even before reaching the harbor, Baranov could see the tall masts of two home-made ships, the pride of Ivan Kuskov.

"He did well," Baranov thought. "And so did I, by sending him to Yakutat..."

Kuskov worshiped the governor. He had modeled his own

life after Baranov by marrying a native woman and by learning native dialects.

Slight of build, prematurely balding, Ivan Kuskov suffered from severe near-sightedness and had to wear thick spectacles. They perched on his thin long nose, constantly falling
off. To reduce the danger of breaking the precious lenses,
Kuskov attached the glasses to a sealgut string, wearing them
around his neck like a necklace.

By those who worked with him, his puny body and
his near-sightedness were soon forgotten. Ivan Kuskov had
proven himself as a good administrator, able to share equally
the hardships of primitive life and its small triumphs.

"I shed tears for you," Kuskov whispered in Baranov's
ear as they embraced. "When I heard that Fort St. Michael
was burned, I feared that you, too, were killed. How fortunate
that you were not there at the time! But come! Let me show
you our new brigs!" He pointed proudly to his two crudely
built ships, their sails fashioned from old patched up canvas,
but furled expertly like on a British man o' war ready for
inspection. Kuskov swore that they held wind and would
tack as easily as any sails he had ever worked with. "We call
them *Yermak*, for the conqueror of Siberia, and *Rostislav*, a
hero of our folklore," he said with a smile.

"I'm proud of you, Vanya!" Baranov squeezed his friend's
hand, his eyes glistening with emotion. "Now, let me see your
tubs. I want to examine them at close range!"

Timofei and Kuskov rowed him to the *Yermak*, the larger
of the two ships. Baranov climbed aboard with difficulty,
breathing in short, spasmodic gasps.

He examined the ship from its top deck to its holds,
smacking his lips in approval. "Wonderful, just wonderful,"
he kept muttering to himself.

The *Yermak* was fifty-one feet long and had over one hundred tons capacity. Baranov was amazed by the ingenuity of
Kuskov's men. They had utilized rusty bent nails and bolts
wrested out of shipwrecked vessels. They made rigging from
rotted ropes, reinforcing the hemp with twigs and whalebone.

Baranov was equally pleased by the *Rostislav*, a vessel
of eighty-five tons capacity, ten feet shorter than the *Yermak*. Overwhelmed with pride Baranov seemed to have grown
in stature by the time Timofei and Kuskov rowed him back
ashore. Solemnly he faced his men.

"Well, *detushki*," he said to the men from Yakutat, "you

performed a miracle. You built two ships out of scraps, with your bare hands!" he exclaimed, his eyes welling up with tears again. "And you, *detushki*," he turned to the men from Pavlovsk, "you restored the worthless wrecks which no one thought would ever float. You made them seaworthy again. I am proud of you, my friends. Now, all we have to do is flush the savages from our fort!"

The men shouted "*Oo-rrah!*" throwing their *shapki* up in the air.

"I'll tell you later, *bratzi*, how we'll do it. Right now, I must talk to my officers." He turned toward Kuskov's house, the officers following.

"I'll sail on the *Yermak*, which will be my flag-ship." Baranov addressed the officers gathered around the table. "Timofei Tarakanov will take the *Olga*. Can you handle her, Timosha?"

"Sure, Alexander Andreyevich, I can handle her!" Timofei exclaimed eagerly.

"Fine. Kuskov, Podgash and Petrovich will command the other brigs. There are a hundred and twenty of us Russians; select thirty men each for your crews. The Aleuts will follow the ships in the *baidarki* and you, the captains, decide who will be in charge of each Aleut group. Choose their *nachalniki* wisely. You know how much the Aleuts fear the Indians; don't expose them to danger unnecessarily. We'll meet at Fort St. Michael in the old harbor. We'll start the action against the bastards when all ships are in place. "*S Bogom*, God speed!"

A large crowd assembled on the beach around the priest. Dressed in his church vestments he administered absolution. The men were leaving for battle; some would not return. They had to be cleansed of sin. The bare-headed *promyshleniki* knelt on the stony ground before the cross held by the priest's helper. Murmuring Church-Slavonic prayers, going from one man to another, the priest laid his hands on their bowed heads.

The Aleuts were next, eight hundred of them. They did not understand the ceremony, but were eager to have the protection of the Russian God as well as their own deities. The Governor too, knelt and kissed the cross.

"*Na ko-rabli!*" Baranov rose with effort to his feet and waved them toward the sea.

The Aleuts rushed to their *baidarki* while the Russians

clambered aboard the ships. Dozens of *baidarki* pulled the four ships slowly out into the open sea. As the tow lines were gathered, the *baidarki* fanned out in the wake of the ships.

Timofei navigated the harbor on his own. Baranov noted that Timofei brought the *Olga* out as if he were a seasoned sailor.

The Aleut women on the beach raised a mournful chant. They knew that many of their men would not return. The men ignored them. They felt exhilarated. The *promyshleniki* thirsted for Tlingit blood and even the peaceful Aleuts were infected by their urge for revenge.

But the women chanted, mournful and sad.

Once in the open water, Baranov commanded from the bridge of the *Yermak*, "Make sail!" The ship lunged ahead. The other ships, encumbered by slow-moving *baidarki* in long stretched convoys, were soon left behind. Only the swift little *Olga* kept up with the *Yermak*, but then she too, began to lag behind.

Baranov peered through his telescope. The sea was dotted with hundreds of little *baidarki* as they followed the ships. "What a beautiful sight!" he thought. It was a perfect day for sailing, warm and sunny, with just enough wind to make it easy for the *baidarki* to keep up with the ships.

"I'm on my way!" he murmured to himself. But before he would truly be on his way, he wanted to visit Blossom. He had sent her and Antipatr for a long visit to her native village. "I may not return from this expedition," he thought as he set course toward the Kenaitze village.

"Poppa!" Antipatr ran into his arms. Baranov caught the child and lifted him up. "How you've grown, my little bear cub!" he exclaimed, kissing the boy. Antipatr was dressed as an Indian, wearing only a scant cedarbark loincloth.

Baranov sighed imperceptibly... "This is not the kind of life I had envisioned for my son. He looks like a savage!" he thought. He reminded himself that at least for the time being he could do nothing about his son's upbringing. As long as he was preoccupied with the retaking of the fort, he could spare no time for his family.

"Where's Momma?"

"There." The child pointed toward the Chief's house. Blossom stood at the entrance, framed by the gaping mouth of a giant frog, the symbol of her family. She still looked gaunt but she smiled at him. She ran toward him, like in times of long ago, her hair glossy and bountiful, trailing down her back like in the days when he had first met her.

"*Golubushka*, my little dove," he embraced her.

That night he fell asleep, his head on her shoulder, feeling peaceful, the *Yermak* gently rocking, like a child's cradle.

In the morning they parted. Blossom left in a *baidarka* with the promise that soon they all would be together again.

"Make sail," Baranov commanded. He watched Blossom and Antipatr wave to him from the shore, surrounded by a crowd of Indians. He noted that Blossom had donned a dress and Antipatr was wearing a shirt over his loin covering.

The crowd and the shore shrunk away until Baranov could see only a bright red dot, his wife's red dress. She was still there, waving, until the ship disappeared on the horizon.

Baranov decided to sneak up on the Tlingits through an inland passage. He wanted to make sure that the Ravens had not built more fortifications. He had no charts of the inland passage, no records of depth soundings, nothing but his intuition that the passage was navigable. Gambling that the *Yermak* would make it, he entered the dark unexplored channel. At once the ship was caught in the surging swirling high tide, which nearly smashed her against a high cliff. The passage was extremely narrow. The air felt damp and cold, reminding Baranov of the deep cellars in his native village of Kargopol, "or a grave," he thought. He shuddered at the thought. "No. I am not ready for the grave. Not when I am so happy." Blossom's face floated before his mind's eye.

Sheer cliffs rose on both sides of the channel, cutting the wind off, making tacking impossible. The *Yermak's* yards scraped the icy walls.

The ship drifted forward with slackened sails, at the mercy of the current.

Hours later the tide ebbed. The passage emptied of water with astonishing speed. The *Yermak* found herself in shallows, barely above the jagged bottom. Baranov cursed. Any moment he expected to hear the tearing sound of the ship's sheathing as the *Yermak* would scrape the bottom. He prayed, waiting for the tide to fill the narrow strait and float the ship again.

As the new tide came in, it rushed with the speed of churning rapids. The *Yermak* was lifted and carried forward. The men pushed the ship away from the walls by long poles, waiting for the terrifying sound of ripping boards should the ship crash against the cliffs. This nightmare of high and low tides repeated itself several times, playing deadly games with the *Yermak*. Baranov thought of turning back but in the narrow channel the men could not tack to turn the ship around.

Then a new danger threatened the embattled ship. Ice floes, torn off the glacier walls, appeared in the passage. Some were small and they parted before the *Yermak's* bow, while others loomed menacingly almost as tall as the ship, threatening to squeeze the intrepid brig. The men pushed at them with their hooked poles but the floes brushed against the ship, leaving deep gashes. The *Yermak* groaned and sighed, complaining like a live being.

For four days the exhausted crew struggled with murderous tides, until the *Yermak*, shaken and bruised, was spewed out of the narrow channel into the deeper and calmer waters of Chatham Strait. At once the wind filled her sails and she darted forward, like a liberated seabird.

Across the strait, among the thick stands of spruce, rose the slender columns of totems, once bright with paint, now weathered and peeling. A small Indian village consisting of four tribal houses nestled at the feet of the totems. Baranov scanned the village through his spyglass.

Groups of Indians gathered on the sandy shore, watching the ship. As the *Yermak* tacked closer to shore, the Indians scattered back into the woods.

"They're afraid of us, the bastards!" Baranov laughed.

The *Yermak* sailed on, close enough to the shore to note the similar reaction of the Tlingits at several other villages: at the sight of the Russian ship, they ran into the woods.

"They recognize our flag," Baranov thought. "They know that we are going to punish them for the destruction of the fort and the deaths of our men." Yet Baranov was wise enough to think about a truce. He would offer peace should the Ravens voluntarily abandon the island. "The thoughts of revenge are sweet, but the reality demands a cooler head," he told his men.

There was no way to surprise the Tlingits, once his ship was observed, so Baranov decided to send a message to Ska-out-lelt. "Give him something to chew on."

He sent several armed men ashore to capture a hostage to act as his messenger. Shortly they returned with an elderly but fierce-looking Tlingit. They had tied his hands behind his back and placed a rope around his neck, leading him as if he were a trained bear.

The old man's face and torso had been intricately tattooed, the designs becoming part of his skin coloration. He wore long ear pendants of iridescent sea shells and a copper nose ring.

"Quite a dandy!" Baranov chortled. "Tell this savage that I am the Great White Chief come to take back the fort. Tell him I want to parley with the Ravens." Although he spoke the Tlingit dialect well, and all the Ravens knew it, Baranov deliberately ignored the prisoner. He wanted his contempt carried as part of the message. Ska-out-lelt would read it as strength.

A *promyshlenik* translated the Governor's message. The Indian stared stonily ahead, his face immobile as if carved of mahogany. He showed no emotion when the rope around his neck was removed and his hands unbound. Baranov told him that he was free to go. The Indian leaped overboard, strong as a young warrior, as he dived into the icy water.

Baranov sighed enviously. The man was old, at least sixty or more, yet he had the body and the strength of a young athlete. Baranov glanced at his own round abdomen which protruded alarmingly with each passing year.

The Indian was gone. The message would be delivered, as Baranov had planned, fortified by the old man's observations of the ship and its well-armed crew.

"Let's go!" Baranov commanded.

The flotilla lay at anchor in view of the destroyed fort. All ships had arrived intact after a six hundred nautical mile journey and now they waited for the Governor. Eight hundred Aleuts made their camp on the shore, their *baidarki* lined up in precision just above the water line.

As the *Yermak* sailed closer, Baranov could see through his spyglass the *promyshleniki* armed with their heavy Moscow muskets standing guard around the camp. It was protected against a sudden attack by barricades of fallen trees and a chain of campfires which kept it well illuminated. The fort beyond the camp looked deserted, but Baranov did not trust the quiet ruins. The Ravens were there, ready to do battle.

The *Yermak* rounded the last small island in her approach to the line of the anchored ships. Suddenly a wonderful sight appeared before Baranov and his crew.

A beautiful naval frigate, the *Neva*, a magnificent three-masted, three hundred fifty ton man o' war, flying the proud colors of Russia, lay at anchor further at sea.

"Dear Lord, you've heard my prayers!" Baranov exclaimed, making the wide sign of the cross over his chest. "The ship arrived just in time!"

The Tlingits, too, had seen the frigate. They were confused. The ship carried a shield on her prow with the symbol of the double-headed eagle split in the middle. They had destroyed that shield when they burned the fort, yet there it was again shining brightly, reflecting the sun off its surface, perplexing the children of the Raven. Watching the white men and the Aleuts dig in on the beach, the Tlingits listened to the chants of their shaman, but he could perform no magic. He could bring no sudden storm to scatter the ships over the rocks. He could not disperse the men on the beach.

The Ravens prepared for battle.

Exultant at his sudden turn of fortune, Baranov was eager to visit the *Neva*. He took a bath in a barrel of fresh water. Richard shaved him and trimmed his hair. Then he laid out Baranov's only linen shirt. He had no other Russian clothes. He was forced to wear his usual native attire over his clean shirt.

"I hope the captain won't mind my wild appearance," he muttered nervously. He felt intimidated by the nobility, that aloof class of exalted families from which the Naval Academy drew its officers.

"The captain should be honored to meet you, sir."

"Thank you, Richard. You're a true friend." Baranov straightened his three-cornered plumed hat over his brow. That hat! It surely had seen better days, he thought, but it was the only symbol of authority that he possessed.

He had no proper launch either to take him to the *Neva*. A *baidarka* was lowered and he and Richard climbed into it.

"What the hell, let them see us the way we are, poor but

proud!" Baranov said as he nosed the *baidarka* toward the frigate.

The lookout on the *Neva* yelled the prescribed question, "Who goes there?" to which Baranov replied loudly, "The Governor of Russian America, Alexander Baranov!"

He heard the whistle of the bo'swain's pipes and shouts of command, "Attention on deck!" A ladder was lowered, an intricately constructed stairs with a handrail and polished copper hinges, reaching down to the water. Baranov ascended it slowly, trying to overcome his sense of insecurity and maintain his dignity.

A crew of handsome bearded sailors in crisp uniforms was lined up to greet him. At the head of the line stood the clean-shaven officers, resplendent in their white summer tunics with shiny gold buttons and epaulets, their short gold-hilted swords at their sides.

The captain of the frigate, a good-looking young man in his early thirties greeted Baranov with a stiff salute.

"Welcome aboard the *Neva*, Your Excellency. I am Captain-Lieutenant Urey Lisyansky. At your service!"

The captain clicked his heels and bowed to Baranov. "I have orders from His Excellency Chamberlain Nikolai Petrovich Rezanov to be at your complete disposal."

"My good sir, you can't imagine how happy I am to see you!" Baranov exclaimed. "You're truly heaven-sent in answer to my prayers!"

Chapter 24

"I'm so glad that we could be of help, Your Excellency," Lisyansky began, showing Baranov into his cabin. With a nod, Baranov accepted a glass of port offered to him by the orderly.

Baranov and Lisyansky liked one another immediately. It was one of those instances when two people instinctively felt drawn to one another from the first moment of their meeting, even before they had a chance to get acquainted.

"Will you come with me, Captain, and see for yourself my attack force?" Baranov said, unwilling to waste time on socializing.

"I'll be delighted."

"No use wasting time," Baranov said apologetically, suddenly realizing that he might have been rude by cutting short Lisyansky's hospitality.

A launch was lowered. It was manned by a dozen armed sailors with a midshipman at the stern. The sailors raised their oars vertically in a salute as Baranov and the captain stepped into the boat, to the shrill whistle of the bo'swain's pipe. The midshipman barked a short command and the men lowered their oars. They rowed in unison, oars slicing the dark green water at the same angle, raising hardly a splash.

"How did they ever learn to row with such precision?" Baranov watched the sailors with admiration.

"We train them well in the Navy. Just before we changed our course for America, we encountered a British frigate at the Sandwich Islands. The English sailors challenged our boys to a rowing contest and our lads won!" Lisyansky smiled.

Baranov looked at the captain's bronzed young face thinking, "Proud of his crew. I like his style very much."

The boat slid gently into the pebbled beach. Baranov and Lisyansky disembarked. As far as they could see, the narrow strip was covered with crude shelters made of overturned *baidarki* propped on paddles.

Groups of *promyshleniki* rested by the camp fires, cleaning their muskets; the others stood watch on the perimeter of the camp.

Lisyansky was impressed that Baranov knew all the Russians and the Aleuts by name, addressing them in fatherly tones. They replied in kind, calling him informally, *batushka*, or Alexander Andreyevich. Everywhere the Governor was met by expression of good wishes, inquiries about his health, and the health of his family.

They reached the end of the camp. A sturdy barricade of huge tree trunks rose ahead.

"Well constructed!" the captain said to the men on guard at the barricade. "How many troops have you altogether, Excellency?" he asked Baranov as they turned back.

"Eight hundred Aleuts, one hundred and twenty Russians, four hundred *baidarki* and four and a half ships. I count the *Olga* as half a ship."

"In that case, you can count the *Neva* as a ship and a half," Lisyansky retorted pleasantly. "And how many Indians are there, do you suppose?"

"Hard to say." Baranov squinted toward the forest. "There could be a thousand or more. Most likely they have received reinforcements from other tribes."

"Before we return to the *Neva*, may I inspect your ships? I'm curious to see for myself how you were able to build these ships virtually with your bare hands," Lisyansky said.

Baranov smiled proudly, "You're damned right we built them with our bare hands! We built *everything* around here with our bare hands!" Embarrassed by his boasting, Baranov paused, then said simply, "of course, Captain, you are most welcome to see our ships. We'd be honored."

The sailors rowed them slowly around each ship. Captain Lisyansky was curious about the structure of each vessel, how she sat in the water, how she was tarred and how well she was balanced. He pounded on each hull with his fists and listened to the ship "breathe," as if he were a doctor, placing his ear directly against the ship's rough siding.

Lisyansky climbed aboard each ship, easily scaling the rope ladders. He examined the rigging, amazed at their in-

genious composition of hemp, whalebone and twigs. He went
down into the holds, bending under the low-slung beams. His
white tunic became grimy, tar smudged, one of the sleeves
ripped on a nail. But he continued his inspection, oblivious
to anything but his fascination with these rough-hewn ships.

"Remarkable!" he finally exclaimed. "I have been around
ships all my life, sent to the Naval Cadet Corps when I was
eight. I have seen all kinds of ships: German, French, English
and even Turkish. I have been aboard Yankee schooners.
But I must confess, I have never seen ships like these, built
without the help of naval architects, without the proper tools.
I congratulate you, Mr. Governor, your men have performed
a miracle!"

Baranov smiled. "I am glad that you approve of us. But
ships are not the only things that we can make. You should
see what we have done on Kodiak Island! We have a brickyard
there to make ballast, and a foundry and a gunsmithy. We
have a school for the Aleut children. But here I go, boasting
again!" he laughed.

"You have every right to boast, Excellency."

They reached the *Neva* and the bo'swain piped them
aboard.

"What is your plan?" Lisyansky asked when Baranov
settled comfortably in an easy chair in the captain's spacious
cabin, a glass of port in his hands. Baranov was relaxed now.
He sensed that the captain had become his true ally.

"I'll try a parley, first. Should it fail, I'll try to encircle
them and cut them off from the sea."

"A parley! An excellent idea! Perhaps we can avoid
bloodshed. When do you propose to start?"

"Right away. I'll dispatch a messenger and demand
hostages. Without hostages we can't trust the bastards."

"Will you dine with me, Mr. Governor?" Lisyansky
asked pleasantly.

"With pleasure, captain. *After* we finish with the savages.
I am just sorry Chamberlain Rezanov couldn't come with
you."

Lisyansky smiled. "Chamberlain Rezanov has an even
more important task to accomplish. The Emperor has entrusted him with opening diplomatic relations with Japan."

Baranov said no more. For him there was nothing more
important than to recapture his island.

For the rest of the day Baranov paced the deck of the *Yermak*, waiting for some signal that the Tlingits would talk. Then a canoe appeared, with a single man paddling. The canoe approached the *Yermak*, but the Tlingit ignored the rope ladder that was lowered for him. Standing up in the canoe, he tossed on deck a cedarbark basket. He departed at once.

Baranov motioned to Timofei to open the basket. Inside was a severed head of the Russian messenger.

Baranov grew livid with rage. He paddled out in his *baidarka* to the frigate and clambered aboard.

"We'll attack at once! We must avenge our murdered brother!" he shouted angrily. "No use trying to talk with these bastards!"

"Shouldn't we wait until the morning?" Lisyansky suggested.

"I can't wait that long! They murdered my man!"

"We must wait, Your Excellency. We need time to move the ships closer to shore. It will take time."

Baranov frowned. He realized that Lisyansky was right. He sighed resignedly. "Oh, what the hell! You're right. Do what must be done. I'll go back to the *Yermak* and work on my tactics for tomorrow. Go and rest, my friend. We'll have much on our hands tomorrow." His fury, quickly aroused, quickly subsided under the pressure of common sense.

"Yes, I'd better rest," Lisyansky thought, as he took his tunic off and stretched out on his bunk. It had been a long, exciting day. He thought that he ought to jot down his impressions of the Governor, to describe the affairs of the day, but he fell asleep before his resolve took any form. An orderly removed his boots and unbuttoned his shirt, not daring to wake him up to remove the rest of his clothing.

The captain was awakened within an hour by the excited voice of Baranov who burst into his cabin unannounced. "Captain, come with me quickly!" he called urgently. Lisyansky pulled his boots on and followed Baranov to the deck.

Resting on the calm waters between the *Neva* and the *Yermak* was a slender war canoe with a high prow carved to resemble a raven. Twenty warriors knelt on its bottom, their paddles across their knees. At the bow stood a splendid young warrior attired in a fringed cedarbark blanket and a scanty loin cover, his head crowned with a helmet representing the

Raven. It was Kot-le-an. The young chief's face and body, as those of his warriors, were painted in broad stripes of red, black and white. Pointing to the *Neva*, Kot-le-an delivered a long speech in the guttural Tlingit tongue. Baranov answered, but the warrior interrupted him angrily with another tirade.

"What is he saying?" Lisyansky asked.

"He ordered the *Neva* to leave. He will allow you to leave if you surrender the double-headed eagle from your prow."

"Very generous of him," Lisyansky smiled.

"I offered him a truce," Baranov said. "I am willing to forget our dispute if the Ravens leave the island. I demanded hostages of course, the children of the chiefs."

"Did he accept your offer?"

"No."

The Indian canoe sped back toward the island, Kot-le-an standing in the bow impassively, like a carved figure.

"What will happen now?"

"They'll confer among themselves and perhaps decide to accept my offer. Nothing much will happen tonight, I'm sure. They'll be arguing all night. So go back to bed, captain. Good night!" Baranov motioned to the sailors to lower the ladder.

"He behaves as if the *Neva* were his own ship," Lisyansky thought. Baranov's lack of etiquette amused him.

Lisyansky returned to his cabin.

Early in the morning Baranov burst into his cabin again.

"Sorry to intrude on you like this, Captain, but it won't wait. I have some wonderful news. My scouts have just reported that the Tlingits have abandoned the village. They moved to their fort, the *kekoor*. They are clever bastards. I am going ashore to celebrate. Will you join me?"

"But of course!" Hastily pulling his clothes and boots on, Lisyansky hurried after Baranov.

The excited crowds of *promyshleniki* and Aleuts waited for them ashore.

"The savages ran away!" the men shouted in greeting, jumping up and down like children.

Surrounded by his men, Baranov entered the abandoned village. He planted the Russian flag, proclaiming the new fort would rise on that spot. He named it *Novo-Arkhangelsk*, New Archangel, in honor of the first Russian seaport on the shores of the White Sea.

The *promyshleniki* shouted themselves hoarse in delirious celebration of their bloodless victory but Baranov knew that the task of expelling the Tlingits from the island was far from accomplished. It was made even more difficult by the Ravens' fleeing to the *kekoor*.

Baranov divided his Aleut troops into two columns, planning to lead one himself, entrusting another to Kuskov.

"We must storm the *kekoor*," Baranov announced to Lisyansky. "Please lend us three or four of your small caliber cannons."

He knew the topography of the *kekoor*. It was hidden behind a wall of huge boulders and set in a clearing, deep inside a thick stand of spruce and hemlock. It was well fortified by huge tree trunks laid in depth on several levels. Baranov hoped that the concentrated fire at close range would split the fortifications and expose the fort.

Lisyansky dispatched several of his gunners to accompany Baranov's troops while he anxiously watched the progress from the bridge. He wished that the operation had been better organized, preceded by an artillery barrage, but perhaps Baranov knew better how to proceed. After all, he had dealt with these Ravens before, Lisyansky thought. Besides, the rocky coast and the shallow waters made it impossible to move the ships in the proper position for a successful artillery assault. The location of the *kekoor* was way out of the range of the ships' guns.

Baranov began his attack. He placed Timofei in charge of the Aleuts who were to pull four small cannons taken off the *Neva*. "We'll shoot at the walls point blank," he told the gunners. He was full of optimism. Puffing heavily, Baranov climbed over the boulders along with his men, a loaded pistol in his hand.

The assault columns advanced cautiously, encountering no resistance. "Perhaps the Ravens had abandoned the *kekoor*," Baranov thought.

Suddenly the rocks above the advancing Russians exploded in rapid musket fire. The Tlingits, well hidden, fired with deadly accuracy. The Aleuts panicked. They ran back to the beach in disorder. The cannons were abandoned. Timofei rushed to one of the cannons, pushing it down the hill. Other *promyshleniki* followed, pulling the precious cannons back to the pebbled beach.

The Russians took cover behind the boulders trying to stop and regroup the fleeing Aleuts.

The Tlingits spilled out of their fort. With blood-curdling yells they rushed at the *promyshleniki*, shooting their arrows, throwing their spears as they ran.

Lisyansky watched in horror through his telescope as the first wave of Indians fell upon the Russians. Wielding their Yankee-bought muskets like clubs they knocked the Russians off their feet, while the second wave of Tlingits finished them off by slashing their throats.

The Russians regrouped behind the boulders, meeting the Indians with rapid musket fire, but the Tlingits kept advancing, led by a tall warrior in a Raven helmet. Lisyansky recognized Kot-le-an.

He was attired in a vest made of tightly placed bear ribs which could be shattered only by the direct hit of a bullet. His neck was protected by a thick wooden collar, reminding Lisyansky of a yoke used on oxen on the estate of his parents.

The young chief seemed invincible. He was armed with a huge Russian sledge hammer, which he wielded as if it were a medieval mace. Whoever came in reach of the hammer fell, his skull crushed.

From his vantage point on the bridge of the *Neva*, Lisyansky could clearly see that Kot-le-an was making his way toward Baranov, who lay on the ground behind a boulder, apparently wounded, surrounded by a handful of *promyshleniki*.

Timofei, too, saw the approaching Kot-le-an. He grabbed his musket by the barrel, ready to meet Kot-le-an in hand-to-hand combat. There was no time to load his gun; he had to use it the Tlingit way, as a club. He rose in front of his *nachalnik*, ready to die defending him.

Captain Lisyansky waited no longer. "Rapid fire starboard! Aim point blank at the woods!" he shouted. The deafening salvos from several cannons drowned the howl of the Tlingits. The cannoneers worked fast, loading the guns with well-drilled precision.

As the smoke dispersed, Lisyansky could see the Indians retreating, led by Kot-le-an himself. "Cease fire!"

The Russians did not pursue the enemy. They too, retreated, carrying their wounded and dead back to the camp.

Dreading that Baranov might have been killed, Lisyansky called for a launch and a detail of armed sailors. They rowed him ashore.

Baranov was stretched on a blanket, bleeding profusely, glowering at the men around him, furious at his failure.

"Thank God! You're alive!" Lisyansky exclaimed as he jumped into the shallows, not waiting for the launch to stop, his elegant soft leather boots filling with water.

"Those goddamned bastards!" Baranov cursed, his voice weak but less determined. "What are our losses?" he demanded, turning his head to Timofei.

"Ten dead and twenty-six wounded."

Baranov groaned. "Good Lord! Ten dead...twenty-six wounded..." He closed his eyes, suddenly looking very old.

Lisyansky knelt at his side and took his hand. "Let me take you to my ship so that my surgeon may attend to your wound," he said gently. Baranov did not protest.

The captain signaled the sailors to carry the Governor into the launch.

The Tlingits in the *kekoor* shouted triumphantly as they saw the sailors carry Baranov on an improvised stretcher. Mocking the Russians, they suspended the headless body of a sailor over the wall of the *kekoor*. It was pierced by arrows, impaled on a spear. From a distance it looked as if the sailor stood stiffly at attention, the square collar of his navy blouse moving gently with the breeze around the stump of his neck. The unfortunate cannoneer sent by Lisyansky to help Baranov's men was caught in the ill-fated attack. Now, headless, he hung over the Tlingit parapets as a grim warning to his fellow Russians.

The ship's surgeon removed the lead slug from Baranov's left shoulder, and cleansed the wound that had been, giving him much pain.

"I'll give you a sedative, Excellency. You need a rest," he suggested, but Baranov declined the offer. Tormented by his failure to capture the *kekoor*, Baranov was unable to rest. Swallowing his pride, he admitted to Lisyansky that his strategy had failed.

"I am a *promyshlenik*, not a Generalissimo," he tried to joke, a bitter smile cracking his ashen face. 'Please, Captain, take command. You're a military man, you know what to do."

Lisyansky took over without hesitation. It became a matter of desperate need that the Tlingits would be expelled from the island. A sailor was sent to the *Yermak* to bring Baranov's maps and Timofei, who perhaps knew the island better than anyone, was assigned as an aide-de-camp to the captain.

Lisyansky pored over the maps. He was convinced that only by intensive artillery barrage would the Tlingits be dislodged from the *kekoor*. It was impossible to storm the fort by land without heavy losses.

Lisyansky consulted with his officers. It was decided to transfer several of the *Neva's* guns to the other ships, to equalize their fire power; then move all the ships as close to shore as possible without running them on the rocks. Lisyansky appointed four of his officers as temporary skippers of Baranov's homemade navy.

Slowly the ships were maneuvered toward the treacherous shore. When they were repositioned, Lisyansky said, "Commence artillery barrage!" The command was repeated on all ships, like a diminishing echo.

The shells exploded, sounding like thunder, but not reaching the fortifications, only splintering the solid rocks below the *kekoor*.

"We're wasting ammunition. The ships should be still closer to shore," Lisyansky thought to himself.

"We can't get any closer, sir. The depth soundings are already alarming," the first mate said, as if reading his thoughts.

"Continue the barrage. At least it will prevent the Indians from leaving the fort for a counterattack."

"Aye-aye, sir."

Lisyansky went down to the infirmary. He needed Baranov's advice.

Baranov was resting, fighting off drowsiness. The ship's doctor did manage to give him a sedative in a glass of port. Baranov's face was flushed. "You are wasting your ammunition," he said with effort, his tongue feeling wooden. "Bring the guns closer to shore."

Lisyansky began to explain why it was impossible, but Baranov continued, "You don't have to move the ships. Just the guns," he said weakly. "Place them on rafts. Float the rafts like log caravans on the Volga."

Lisyansky saw immediately the advantages of Baranov's suggestion. "How long do you suppose it would take to build such rafts?"

"A day." Baranov closed his eyes, falling asleep.

Lisyansky turned to Timofei. "Do you know what he had meant?"

"Yes sir. Alexander Andreyevich thought of doing it last year, when we did not have any ships. The Aleuts will cut the trees and move the logs to the beach. They will float them and tie them into rafts. They are experts at that. Then we'll place the cannons on the rafts and the *baidarki* will tow them close to shore."

"An excellent idea!" Lisyansky exclaimed, grasping the idea.

A party of *promyshleniki* and two hundred Aleuts began immediately to cut trees on the fringes of their camp. Sailors from the *Neva*, armed with loaded muskets with fixed bayonets, formed a protective arc around them, aiming their weapons at the wild underbrush of the forest. The ships' guns continued to pound at the forest beyond, preventing the Ravens from leaving their stronghold to attack the woodcutters.

All day long the men felled huge trees, chopping off their branches, then rolling the trunks to the water's edge where another party of Aleuts pushed the logs into the water, floating them in the shallows. Balancing on the slippery logs, the Aleuts expertly tied them together with sealgut ropes, forming sturdy unsinkable rafts.

Lisyansky watched them from the bridge of the *Neva*. By evening, four rafts were ready, bouncing over the high tide like children's toys.

Lisyansky went below decks to the infirmary once more, to report to Baranov.

The Governor was awake. He greeted the captain with a weak smile. "I understand you have finished the rafts. Well done. Tomorrow you can place the cannons. No use working in the dark. The bastards are well aware of what we are doing. They might yet agree to our terms, now that they know what's coming to them. I am going to my ship." With the help of Timofei, Baranov rose to his feet.

"Thank you, Captain. Without your doctor I might have bled to death," he smiled at Lisyansky.

"Shouldn't you stay, at least until you feel better?"

"I do feel better," Baranov said. "I must go."

Lisyansky did not insist. By now he knew how stubborn the old man could be.

Lisyansky decided to follow his example. Leaving orders

to continue the bombardment through the night, he retired to his cabin. He opened his journal, bound in dark morocco leather and began writing down his impressions of the past day.

"They are very clever, the Tlingits," he wrote with grudging admiration. "Without any knowledge of engineering they have built their fortifications as impenetrable as any medieval castle."

Chapter 25

The guns pounded at the forest hiding the Tlingit *kekoor* throughout the night, inflicting no serious damage, but at least preventing the Ravens from slipping up on the Aleut encampment on the beach.

At dawn the cannons were placed on the rafts. The gunners from the *Neva* jumped down to the rafts, water lapping at their bare feet. The sailors passed the round cannon balls from hand to hand, placing them on a thick pile of fir branches spread on rafts to keep the ammunition dry. Sixteen *baidarki* towed the rafts toward the shore.

A rain of arrows from the forest met the rafts halfway. Several gunners fell, some seriously wounded. The Tlingits aimed only at the gunners, ignoring the Aleuts.

"Bastards!" Baranov shouted furiously from the bridge of the *Yermak*.

A longboat from the *Neva* picked up the wounded. Lisyansky replaced them with another complement of sailors. The rafts continued their slow perilous advance toward the shore, until they reached their positions. Several more gunners fell, the victims of the Ravens' accurate aim.

"Commence fire," Lisyansky said quietly, watching the rafts reach the shore. The order was repeated by his mate as a signalman raised the appropriate combination of flags along the mast of the frigate. Four heavy cannons on the rafts were loaded. The bombardment began. With each discharge, the cannons rocked the rafts. The water rose through the cracks between the logs, reaching up to the gunners' ankles.

Within minutes the devastating results of the concentrated close-range fire became evident. The breastworks surrounding the fort began to split. The Russians could see the

loose sand and stones filling the spaces between the breastworks rise above the *kekoor* like an eruption of a volcano,
spitting down a shower of debris. The explosions shook
the ground, sending reverberations over the sea in increasing
concentric circles, rocking the ships at anchor some distance
away. Orange tongues of flame soon protruded between the
logs of the *kekoor* licking them rapaciously, as tall columns of
dark smoke curled into the sky. The forest around the fort
became singed, many tall trees were sliced in two.

Still the Indians would not surrender.

"They are truly remarkable!" Lisyansky thought, torn
between vexation and admiration for the defenders.

The Russians battered the *kekoor* all through the day.
Toward sunset a lookout from the *Neva* shouted that a white
flag had been hoisted over the fort.

Lisyansky stopped the bombardment. A strange stillness
fell upon the sea and the Aleut camp on the beach. After
hours of explosions when the air and earth trembled, when the
sea heaved in fountains of spray with each misfired shell, one
became suddenly aware of the stillness that followed. Small
sounds could be heard: a bird chirped on a mast, a rope
flapped against the yardarm. A flock of seagulls driven away
by the bombardment returned, crying as they swooped down
to the waves. Human voices were heard, calling from one ship
to another...

Lisyansky scanned the smoking forest through his telescope. The white flag of surrender was attached to the tall
heraldic totem pole, still intact, rising defiantly above the
decimated forest. The Raven on top of the pole held it in
its beak, as if proclaiming, "Your Eagle wins, but I am not
defeated!"

"A canoe under a white flag! Starboard, aft!" the lookout
yelled. Lisyansky lowered his telescope. A small canoe under
an improvised white flag, a European shirt, (Lisyansky could
clearly see its flapping sleeves), was approaching the ship.

"Invite Governor Baranov to join us," Lisyansky said to
his adjutant without removing the telescope from his eye.

"I am here already," Baranov swung his leg over the railing, not bothering with the proper entrance. "I presumed
that the messenger would be sent to the most imposing ship,
so I anticipated his arrival!" He was in excellent spirits, even
though still pale, his left arm in a sling.

The canoe approached the frigate and the sailors drew it

to the ship with hooks on long poles. An old Indian scampered up the ladder.

Baranov recognized him as one of the natives once living in Fort St. Michael.

"The children of Raven move out," the Indian addressed Baranov ignoring the others. "The children of Raven want no more war. The children of Raven sing song when they go away. Listen to their song." The old man showed no signs of humility one would expect of the vanquished. He stood erect, facing the Russians boldly.

Baranov listened to him in silence. He did not ask any questions, did not demand any more hostages. He bent his head low as if to say "so be it," to which the Indian reacted with the same gesture.

Lisyansky was deeply moved by the dignity of these two adversaries, the old Russian Governor who after all his blustery threats accepted the victory humbly and the old Tlinglit, who took his defeat bravely. "Now we'll have the truce," Lisyansky thought.

The Indian vaulted the railing, landing on his feet in his canoe, flaunting his agility. He paddled back to the island, maneuvering among the rafts, paying no attention to the Russians. Once ashore, he lifted his canoe over his head and vanished into the thicket.

"What do we do now?" Lisyansky turned to Baranov.

"We wait. We wait for their song. But most of all, we stay alert," Baranov said. "They are still capable of treachery."

The darkness descended quickly. The ships lighted their lanterns. On the beach, the Aleuts doubled their bonfires. They did not believe that the Ravens would keep their word and leave the island.

Not a sound came from the forest.

"I'll go back to the *Yermak*," Baranov said. "No use my being under foot." Timofei paddled him back to his flagship.

The people were tense, straining to hear the song of the Tlingits. But nothing could be heard, only an occasional mournful cry of a seagull, a lap of water against the ship, a rustle of wind among the rigging.

The night fell. The dark October clouds shifted constantly, the moon vainly trying to break through their cover. No one could sleep.

A shrill cry of alert from the *Rostislav* suddenly pierced

the night, shattering the silence, breaking the tension of taut nerves.

"Indians, starboard!"

"I knew it!" Baranov exploded, his face red with fury. "I knew that I could not trust the savages! I knew they would try to sneak up on us!"

"Where are they?" Lisyansky yelled from his ship. "I can see nothing!"

"Starboard of me, the *Rostislav*," shouted Lieutenant Arbuzov, the temporary skipper, the last on the starboard flank. "There are a dozen or more big war canoes!" He sounded the general alarm.

"Fire on them!" Baranov yelled. "Don't wait! Fire on the bastards!" More than anyone Baranov knew the danger should the Tlingits be able to slip between the vessels. They would have climbed aboard the ships, silent and deadly as panthers, cutting the throats of the sentries, swooping down on the defenders in a wave of knife-wielding terror. A terrible hand-to-hand battle would have ensued, its outcome not necessarily certain; the Ravens were ready to sacrifice their lives.

"*Fire* on the damned savages!" Baranov bellowed to the gunners, peering into the darkness. All he could see were the dim outlines of the *Neva* and the *Ekaterina* alongside his flagship.

"We'll hit one another, sir," the artillery officer shouted back. "We can't see a thing!"

"Shit!" Baranov swore, exasperated.

Miraculously, the moon sailed out from the clouds, momentarily illuminating the sea, making the Tlingit war party clearly visible.

"*Rostislav*, fire point blank! Starboard batteries!" Lisyansky commanded calmly through a megaphone from the bridge of the *Neva*.

"Fire point blank, starboard batteries," repeated Lieutenant Arbuzov.

The cannons of the *Rostislav* roared. Tall pillars of water rose into the air, capsizing several canoes. The shots followed in rapid succession, forcing the remaining canoes to turn around. The *promyshleniki* lined up along the bulwarks of the *Rostislav* firing their muskets at the Indians struggling in the water. The warriors, those still afloat, paddled back to the shore. They did not bother to pick up the survivors. In their retreat they left them to swim to safety by themselves or to be drowned. The Russians, excited by the carnage, bent on bloody revenge, knew no mercy.

"Hold all fire!" Lisyansky commanded. *Promyshleniki* lowered their muskets with disappointment. In the ensuing silence there was suddenly heard a mournful sound floating from the forest.

"The song!" Lisyansky cried out with the exuberance of a young midshipman. "I hear the song!"

A strange, long-vibrating note reached the Russians on the ships and the Aleuts on shore. Woeful, it grew in volume. It swelled, then subsided, sounding at times like a howl of wolves in the dead of winter, then like a lament of mourners at a wake, bringing a spine-tingling chill to the listeners.

The *promyshleniki* reacted to the song with the shout of victory, "*OO-RRAH*," but the sorrowful wail from the *kekoor* continued, muffling the boisterous hunters. Subdued by the Ravens' lament, they fell silent.

Suddenly the funereal chant of defeat ceased. An unnatural stillness spread over the Aleut encampment on the beach and the ships at anchor. People waited for the sun to rise and uncover the mysteries of the night. As the horizon over the sea turned pink, bursting shortly into bright red and orange colors of the rising sun, Baranov motioned Timofei to paddle him once more to the *Neva*.

"With God's help, this is the end! Let's go ashore," he said to Lisyansky. Leaving the guards aboard the ship, the captain and his officers and men, all heavily armed, followed Baranov ashore in a flotilla of launches and *baidarki*.

Tension gripped everyone. The men scaled the precipitous approaches to the *kekoor*. The scouts cut a path through the thorny underbrush as the men cautiously advanced clutching at their weapons, ready to shoot at the first sign of ambush.

Baranov pointed to the sky. It was covered with flocks of black birds circling over the *kekoor*.

"Ravens," he pointed, turning to Lisyansky. "Prepare yourself for a grim sight."

Chapter 26

As the Russians and Aleuts climbed toward the *kekoor*, Baranov struggled through pain and weakness to keep up. The others shed their coats but Baranov shivered, his face ashen.

Suddenly he sank down on a boulder. "Don't wait for me; go ahead!" he snapped, furious at his weakness.

"No Alexander Andreyevich, we won't go without you. We all shall rest. We want *you* to lead us to the *kekoor*," Lisyansky said. Baranov nodded without speaking. He was touched by Lisyansky's understanding of the importance that he, the Governor, should lead his men to the conquered fort.

The men halted. There was no need to hurry any more. The Ravens were gone.

The palisade entrance, an opening large enough for only one person, was blocked by a huge tree stump. Timofei and a half-dozen Aleuts climbed over the ten-foot high breastwork and pried the stump away.

Baranov stepped through the opening. "Timosha, the flag!" he said brusquely over his shoulder. Timofei hoisted himself to the tip of the parapet and attached the Russian double-headed eagle to one of the remaining logs. A shout of *oo-rrah* rolled down to the troops on the beach and the crews on the ships. They returned the cheer and added salvos of cannon fire.

As he climbed down from the parapet, Timofei heard a moan from somewhere beneath his feet. He peered into a mass of broken branches and split remnants of logs which once were a part of the stockade. "Who's there?" he asked in

Tlingit. He saw a movement and heard a weak voice, but he could not distinguish the words. He picked his way through the tangle and found a woman, covered with dirt and blood.

Her face was hidden under matted dark hair with a lone wilted flower entangled in its mass. Timofei could clearly see her huge bulging belly which she hugged with both her hands as if trying to protect it. Something about the flower in her thick hair was familiar. Gently, he turned the woman over and brushed her hair off her face. It was Marinka.

Timofei tore a kerchief from his neck and pressed it firmly against the gaping wound on her head. The kerchief instantly became soaked with blood.

Marinka opened her eyes slowly. She seemed not to be surprised at seeing him before her. "I am with child," she whispered, her dry, cracked lips barely moving.

"Yes, yes, I know," Timofei said gently. He noticed with horror that Marinka's legs had been shattered into a mass of jagged bones and torn flesh.

"The child is dead," she continued. "I don't feel it move." She seemed beyond pain. Her voice grew weaker.

Timofei's thoughts whirled. He knew he should hate this woman who had betrayed them all, but this pitiful creature was beyond his hatred. He spoke to her in Russian, stroking her blood-soaked hair, saying soft words of comfort from his childhood.

Marinka seemed to understand. She watched his face.

Suddenly she shuddered and closed her eyes. Timofei kissed them, as he used to do in the years of his happiness. Marinka's face moved in a weak smile. She remembered.

"You good man," she whispered with effort. "My good white man..."

Her face contorted violently. Then she fell quiet.

Timofei cradled her for a few moments, surprised at the tears that ran down his face.

Finally, he stood up and selected four logs from the shattered palisade to form a bier where he placed Marinka's body. He covered her thickly with sand and dried spruce branches. Near by he saw a clump of daisies which somehow had survived the bombardment. He strewed them atop the branches. Then, striking sparks from his flint into a pile of tinder, he lit the funeral pyre. The dry branches caught at once. Soon the whole bier was engulfed in flames. Timofei stood bareheaded, praying silently.

The fire and smoke rose high, attracting several *promysh-leniki*.

"What are you doing?" they shouted to Timofei from the palisade above, but seeing his face, they retreated, one by one. "It must have been his Indian woman, whatever was her name," one of them said.

While the unrestrained *promyshleniki* and Aleuts looted the fort, Lisyansky surveyed what was left of the defenses and the well-constructed houses which could have easily accommodated a hundred or more people each. Like all Tlingit houses, they were decorated with intertwined symbolic animals and birds. At first glance it seemed to him that both sides were identical, but upon closer examination, he had discovered that each side had different images. He had never seen anything more intriguing, Lisyansky thought.

"It's magnificent!" he exclaimed enthusiastically, turning to his officers. "It's better than anything we saw in the Brazils or in the South seas! I never suspected that the Tlingits were such fine artists! What a wealth of imagination! What beauty!"

"If you like their paintings so much, wait until you see their carvings," Baranov smiled. "The Tlingits are excellent carvers." Lisyansky noticed that Baranov was speaking of the Tlingits with pride, as if they were his own men. "He has forgotten his enmity already," Lisyansky thought.

They had to bend low to enter the house. The top of the entrance was at the height of their chests. They squeezed through the opening one at a time, crowding on the platform inside the entrance. The sailors fingered their loaded muskets, still on the alert for an ambush.

But the house was empty.

The Russians cautiously advanced toward the fire-pit, still glowing in the dimness of the windowless house. There, on a platform near the smoldering fire, lay the bodies of thirty infants, neatly arranged in three rows.

The Russians gasped, staring at the tiny copper-brown bodies. Some were strangled, others had their throats slashed, the wounds gaping like open mouths.

"Dear Lord!" Lisyansky blanched, making the sign of the cross and baring his head.

"This must have been what they were chanting about last

night," Baranov said in a low voice. "They were murdering their infants." He, too, was ashen.

"But why? Why would they want to kill their own children?" Lisyansky asked, his voice shaky.

"They killed them for the survival of the tribe. The infants were killed so they would not cry and reveal the escape," Baranov explained. "They expected that we would kill everyone, just as they would have, if they had won."

"They judge us by their own standards...It's too horrible to comprehend!" Lisyansky shuddered.

"As the Tlingits see it, the children died to save the tribe," Baranov said.

Lisyansky had enough. "I must leave," he said to Baranov. "I feel sick."

Baranov glanced at the captain. Lisyansky's face had a greenish cast. "Yes, we had all better go now. But first, we must bury the infants," he said gruffly.

Lisyansky stepped over the threshold filling his lungs with fresh salty air, squinting in the bright sunshine after the darkness of the dwelling, feeling as if he had just escaped from a dungeon.

Once outside, he felt better. He looked around, encompassing in one sweeping glance the dramatic panorama of the bay with the ships at anchor and the colorful *kwan* houses behind him, soon to be burned to the ground as a final gesture of retaliation. He thought that it was a pity that the houses must be destroyed. But of course, it had to be done. The stronghold had to be leveled as a lesson to all Indians.

Baranov assigned the grim task of burying the infants to the Aleuts. They dug a large common grave, dumping the bodies into it two and three at a time. The tiny bodies made a smacking sound as they landed one atop another.

"No, no!" Baranov cried indignantly. "Don't throw them down like sacks of potatoes! Lay them down *gently*, they are babies!" The Aleuts, grinning good-naturedly, lined the dead infants in several rows. "You like it better?" the foreman asked.

"Yes," Baranov said. "That's much better." He took off his hat and made the sign of the cross. "I want to say a prayer for the children," he said to the priest who had accompanied the *promyshleniki* from the Kodiak Island and had come now to the fort. "Although they were heathen, they were still the children of our Lord."

The priest stepped back. "Go ahead, Governor, pray for them."

"Dear Lord, although they were heathen-born, they were Your children, O Lord. Bless the innocent babes, O Lord. Receive them unto You. As for these bastards," he pointed to a pile of Indian bodies, "punish their souls, send them to Hell for what they have done to our brothers and Your faithful servants. Amen."

Lisyansky was shaken by Baranov's prayer, but recognizing Baranov's peasant origins, Lisyansky thought that perhaps the prayer was right, after all. It expressed exactly the feelings of his men.

"Burn the damned place," Baranov said to Ivan Kuskov, as he turned his back on the *kekoor*. "I think this is where I shall build my new residence," he murmured, his thoughts already on the future. He turned to Lisyansky. "You know, I don't hate these bastards. After all, we pushed them off their land, even though we paid them well for it. Perhaps, if I were in their place I would have done the same, tried to get back my land...I wish there were a way to live in peace with them!"

Halfway down the path they saw Timofei. He was sitting on a boulder, his face distorted by sorrow.

"I am sorry, Timosha," Baranov said kindly. "I know you once loved the woman." Timofei nodded, saying nothing, falling in step behind his *nachalnik*.

In the camp below, the *promyshleniki* were already dividing the spoils. Cedarbark blankets, carved utensils, storage boxes made of bentwood, all decorated with Tlingit designs, were strewn over the pebbles near the water's edge. The Aleuts milled about, waiting for their share.

As Baranov, Lisyansky and the officers returned to their ships, the first tongues of flame leaped along the breastworks of the *kekoor*. Soon the whole fortress was ablaze. Billowing coils of dark smoke rose simultaneously in several places.

A flock of ravens took off from the burning *kekoor* and with harsh cries settled on the beach around the camp. The Aleuts threw stones at the birds fearful that the ravens were the black spirits of their dreaded enemy.

The glow over the Indian fortress remained orange throughout the night. The smell of burning was still in the air as Lisyansky bent over his chart table and wrote in India ink, BARANOV ISLAND, on his map of Russian America.

Chapter 27

Nikolai Rezanov stared at the craggy outline of Kodiak Island rising in the distance. He still brooded over the bitter memory of six wasted months of a frustrating mission to open trade with Japan. The Prince of Fisen, shogun of the island kingdom, had sent Nikolai and the crew of the *Nadezhda* out of Nagasaki Harbor in humiliation, all their gifts and proposals ignored.

When the *Nadezhda* returned to Kamchatka, Nikolai ordered the frigate to continue on her voyage around the world without him. He would sail for Russian America rather than return to St. Petersburg with nothing to report except the failure of his Japanese mission. He parted company with Captain Kruzenstern without much regret. He had never been able to establish a bond of friendship with Kruzenstern such as he had with Lisyansky. "That pompous ass is on his way to glory while I failed," Nikolai thought gloomily. "Let Kruzenstern take plaudits for the round the world voyage. He is a fine sailor, he deserves it. As for me..." Nikolai was not sure what he would do aside from inspecting the administration of the Russian-American Company. He needed time to think.

Now, six weeks later, he stared at the pitiful cluster of buildings that formed the village of Pavlovsk on Kodiak Island. "What can the Tsar's ambassador to the world achieve here, in this mudhole, that he could not do in Japan?" he mused to himself, a sarcastic smile tugging briefly at one corner of his mouth.

A longboat took him ashore along with Dr. Langsdorff and Ivan. Twenty new settlers paddled to land in *baidarki*.

A closer view of the settlement gave Nikolai exactly the same impression that Baranov, and later Timofei Tarakanov

had suffered in earlier years. There were still the rotting
wooden huts, a log church, a steam *banya*, warehouses, a forge
and carpenter shops, all dreary and weathered. Even the
sturdy two-story administration building that flew the flag of
the Russian-American Company could not relieve the desolate
look of the place.

To Nikolai's disappointment, Governor Baranov was not
in Pavlovsk. He was still in Novo-Arkhangelsk, building the
new fort.

As Nikolai explored the village, he was appalled by its
filth, refuse in the street and open outhouses surrounded by
clouds of buzzing flies. Most of the few hunters who remained
in Pavlovsk were drunk.

Nikolai refused to stay in the guest hut provided for him
by Baranov's deputy, Ivan Banner. He would return, instead,
to the ship. At least it was clean.

He began the inspection of the Company's books the following day. He found them to be meticulously kept, and Ivan
Banner, eager to help. But there was not much to see.

Nikolai could find no fault with Baranov's administration
of the Company, but he was shocked at the lack of provisions
in the commissary. The shelves were practically bare. Even
such staples as flour and sugar were gone.

"We're used to it, Your Excellency," Banner said. He
was a thin man with stooping shoulders, and a sad smile.
"It's our permanent curse. We can't raise food here. The
grain has no chance to sprout in this damn climate. It rots
in the ground. We depend on the ships from Russia. As you
know yourself, the ships get wrecked in storms. Governor
Baranov sometimes buys food from foreign captains, but we
can't always depend on that."

"How do you manage to survive?"

"We have adopted the native way of living. We eat fish.
There's plenty of fish in the sea. We have become so accustomed to eating only fish, that when we do have flour and
sugar and are able to bake bread—we get sick with stomach
cramps."

Nikolai could not imagine anyone living on such a diet.
He was grateful for the large supply of foods and spirits, once
intended for receptions in Japan, that Ivan had transferred
from the *Nadezhda* to the *Maria*.

But not everything was bleak in Palvovsk. Nikolai found
that there was a school for the children.

"Governor Baranov gave a thousand rubles from his own pocket to start the school," Banner said as he showed Nikolai into the log schoolhouse.

"You like the Governor, don't you?" Nikolai said with a smile, noting Banner's special warmth in saying Baranov's name.

"I love him. We all love him. He's like a father to us."

About twenty-five children of different ages were gathered in the room under the supervision of an old priest, Father Gehrman. He hurriedly moved a rough bench for Rezanov and Banner to sit on to watch his best students recite the Russian alphabet and then do sums on the blackboard, using an abacus made of seashells strung on sealgut thongs. The children showed their mixed Aleut and Russian parentage. Some were blond and pale-skinned but with dark, narrow eyes. Others had brown skins but blue eyes and stubby, turned-up Russian noses. Nikolai saw several girls among the students, a sight that would have been unusual in Russia.

"We even sent two of our best boys all the way to St. Petersburg to study navigation," Banner said proudly.

Nikolai could see that the Governor planned for the future, preparing the new generation to make a better life for themselves than their illiterate fathers and mothers had been able to do. Even so, Nikolai nearly broke into a grin when he thought of the cargo on the *Maria* that was waiting now to be unloaded. It consisted of over twelve hundred books in several languages, oil paintings and a collection of miniature ships, all from well-meaning St. Petersburg aristocrats. In addition, there was Nikolai's own collection of musical instruments, including a Stradivarius violin. "What a gift for a half-starved island of illiterates," he thought.

He decided to house the books on the shelves in the building for unmarried men and visiting crews. Between the windows he hung a portrait of the Tsar and other paintings. A carpenter from the *Maria* built two long trestle tables which were placed in the center of the room. One was to be used for maps and charts, the other to display a collection of miniature ships.

The creation of the library invigorated Nikolai. He resumed his writing. He sketched grandiose plans for the future of Russian America, assigning to himself a leading role in shaping it. "The American continent will mean far more to Russia than a trade agreement with an insignificant island such as Japan," he wrote in his journal. He began to devise the strategy for colonization of the lands along the Pacific. In his vision he could see Russian colonists, serfs and convicts and their families arriving on the new continent. He thought of wheat fields rippling in the wind like waves in the ocean of gold, women harvesting the crops, their colorful kerchiefs like wild flowers. He imagined villages, the church bells ringing from gold and blue onion-shaped belfries. He saw the American continent becoming *Russian America.*

"The serfs and convicts would be granted freedom, of course," he wrote. "There are thousands of convicts in Siberia, a ready-made population. Instead of keeping them in prisons, we'll resettle them in America without the right of returning to mother country, like the British do in Australia."

Feeling restless, he decided to sail for Novo-Arkhangelsk. He must meet the Governor, Alexander Baranov. He ordered Captain Khvostov to prepare the *Maria* to sail south.

In August, 1805, almost two years to the day since he had left St. Petersburg, Nikolai arrived in Novo-Arkhangelsk.

He stood on the bridge watching captain Khvostov tack the *Maria* into position to be towed to her moorings.

Dozens of small islands thickly covered with trees dotted the bay. From a distance they looked like furry green Cossack hats scattered over the surface of the sea. The shore of the main island, now marked on the charts as Baranov Island, was covered with hundreds of *baidarki.*

Despite the drizzling rain, the new fort was throbbing with life. Nikolai could hear the rhythmic pounding of sledge-hammers and the screeching of saws as the men prepared for another winter. As a military man, Nikolai could find no fault with the location of the fort. He turned his telescope toward the dock. Among the waiting crowd, he saw a short squat man dressed in native clothing, wearing a curly wig held to his head by a kerchief tied under his chin.

"Who's that comical little man in the wig?" he turned to Captain Khvostov.

"It is Baranov, the Governor."

"Hasn't anyone told him that wigs are out of fashion?" Nikolai smiled with amusement. The legendary Baranov certainly did not look impressive. He looked ridiculous.

"Don't let that wig deceive you, Sir. The Governor is a tough man. No one ever laughs at his wig. He wears it on special occasions, such as welcoming a new ship into the harbor," Captain Khvostov replied seriously.

"Ahoy, the *Maria*," Baranov yelled through his hands, held like a megaphone. "Who is the captain?"

"Lieutenant Nikolai Khvostov," the captain shouted in response. "I have a passenger, His High Excellency Chamberlain Nikolai Petrovich Rezanov."

"Welcome to Novo-Arkhangelsk!" Baranov waved enthusiastically.

Nikolai heard the grating of chains as the anchors dropped. Pulleys creaked and a longboat was lowered. Captain Khvostov, Rezanov, and Dr. Langsdorff climbed in. The sailors rowed them ashore.

Captain Khvostov stepped out of the boat and clicking his heels, saluted the Governor. "Your Excellency, may I introduce the Court Chamberlain, His High Excellency, Nikolai Petrovich Rezanov."

"Welcome, welcome," Baranov fussed, dismissing the formality. He was oblivious of his peculiar appearance. His wig was askew, dripping from the rain. The red calico kerchief tied under his chin to hold the wig in place made him look like a peasant woman.

Nikolai noticed that Baranov's hands were gnarled and swollen. They probably hurt for there was no strength in his handshake.

"We are honored, Your High Excellency. We never expected such an important visitor. I am afraid our accommodations here are not what you're accustomed to..." Baranov flustered.

"Don't worry, Your Excellency, I am quite tough. I'm a soldier. As for my friend, Dr. Langsdorff, he's still young and should be easily satisfied."

Baranov turned his attention to Dr. Langsdorff. "Welcome, welcome, Doctor! We are delighted to have a doctor among us."

Nikolai was given the best hut in the fort, but the roof leaked, the mica-covered windows rustled in the wind and the walls inside were wet and slimy. Rain seeped through every crack.

He moved in anyway. Ivan saw to the transporting of Nikolai's belongings from the ship, while the Aleuts patched the hut's roof, stuffed cracks in the walls with moss, and built a huge fire in the clay stove. Ivan spread Tatar rugs on the earthen floor and made a bed for his master on the *lezhanka*, using Nikolai's own goosedown comforters and pillows.

Bookshelves were built along the walls. Soon they were filled with Nikolai's favorite books and papers. His silver samovar was placed on a table covered with a Turkish shawl. A set of ivory combs and brushes was spread on a small table before Nikolai's silver traveling mirror. Under Ivan's watchful eye, the hut had been transfor ned into a comfortable home.

In the weeks that followed, Nikolai felt quite at home when he greeted Baranov and other visitors.

At one meeting, Nikolai took his violin out of its protective case and played several Italian sonatinas for his guests. The grizzled Governor dissolved in tears. The rare musical treat, added to Rezanov's brandy, overwhelmed Baranov.

Nikolai was delighted to have Baranov's company, after the years they had known one another only through letters. He heard in accurate detail the story of the Tlingit war.

"It was a costly victory, Nikolai Petrovich," Baranov ended, "and even now, our hunters have skirmishes with the Tlingits." Baranov looked into the fire with gloomy expression.

"Cheer up, Alexander Andreyevich," Nikolai said. "Perhaps some day the Indians will realize that we mean them no harm."

"I wish it were true," Baranov nodded his head sadly.

Winter was fast approaching. The torrential rains of autumn which fell in sheets of cold misery, were soon supplanted by the wet sticky snow. The evenings in Rezanov's warm hut became even more cherished occasions for his few friends. The rest of the men shivered in their hastily-built huts, plugging the cracks in their walls.

Then, once again the fort was under siege both inside and outside. Among the Russians scurvy made its appearance. No one knew what caused the outbreak. The only remedy which seemed to work against it was to eat fresh fruits and vegetables, which were always scarce. The warehouses of Novo-Arkhangelsk were even more barren than those in Pavlovsk and the new fort had twice as many people to feed. More than a thousand *promyshleniki* and Aleuts and their families dwelt now in Novo-Arkhangelsk.

Outside the fort, the Tlingits menaced again. Aleut fishing parties sent out to bring in the catch were ambushed.

Several brave *promyshleniki* who ventured outside to trap rabbits and squirrels, never returned.

The Tlingits grew bolder day by day. They paddled their menacing war canoes in full view of the fort, paying no heed to an occasional shot from the fort's guns. They knew that the Russians were getting short on ammunition and could not afford to waste it on a few canoes. They circled the island like a school of hungry sharks.

Nikolai kept loaded pistols by his bed. Ivan cleaned his own old Cossack pistols and kept them under his pillow at night. Attack seemed imminent.

Then a ship appeared. Maneuvering smartly among the islands dotting the bay, a fast, sleek American schooner, sheathed in copper, was fast approaching the harbor. She was named *Juno*.

The sight of the *Juno* and her guns instantly dispersed the Tlingits. The siege was lifted. The Children of the Raven vanished. The *promyshleniki* and the Aleuts felt free again to leave the fort to fish and hunt.

The *Juno* carried a full cargo of hard goods, ammunition and provisions, which Governor Baranov promptly bought. The ship's master, John D'Wolf and his crew, prepared to winter on Baranov Island.

Nikolai realized that one ship's cargo would not last long. Something drastic had to be done to prevent another siege and consequent slow starvation. It was then that Nikolai presented a plan that had been growing in his mind almost since the day he first saw the real situation of Russian America. He proposed to buy the *Juno* from her master, Captain John D'Wolf, and sail her to Spanish California to buy food from the missions.

"I don't think it would work. The Spanish don't trade with anyone," Baranov objected.

"There is no reason why we can't try to change their minds," Nikolai retorted. He offered Captain D'Wolf an irresistible price for the *Juno*, and D'Wolf, knowing that he would have to spend the winter in Novo-Arkhangelsk with an idle ship anyway, saw greater profit in selling the *Juno*. He agreed.

Nikolai renamed the ship the *Younona*, translating into Russian her given name. He made arrangements to send the *Juno* crew to the Sandwich Islands in the spring paying them handsomely for the inconvenience of finding their own berths home from there.

He decided to head the expedition himself, suggesting that the *Younona* explore the mouth of the Columbia River as well. According to his maps, the territory looked similar to southern Siberia, where the deltas of the mighty rivers made suitable sites for establishing new villages and towns. He was determined that they should explore the river; as far as he knew, it was still unclaimed by anyone.

He invited Baranov and the officers to a meeting at his hut. He served them English brandy and then began, looking at each man in turn. "Gentlemen, you'll all agree that we must find new sources of food. *Permanent* sources," he emphasized. "Even though we will survive this winter, what will happen to Novo-Arkhangelsk *next* winter? And the next? We cannot depend on ships from Russia to bring us our bare necessities. We must develop *local* sources of obtaining food!" Nikolai paused. Everyone waited for him to continue; but he shrewdly waited, letting the hopelessness of the situation sink in.

"What is your proposal, Nikolai Petrovich?" Baranov impatiently broke the silence.

"To abandon Novo-Arkhangelsk."

The men were stunned.

There was no turning back now. Nikolai continued, "Yes, we must *abandon* Novo-Arkhangelsk, and move the colony further south, perhaps to the mouth of the Columbia River."

"Abandon Novo-Arkhangelsk! Never!" Baranov exploded. He jumped to his feet, forgetting his painful arthritis. "We paid for this land with our blood. Our brothers were massacred trying to protect this fort and you want us to abandon it! I say, it's insane!"

"Not at all," Nikolai's voice was controlled. "I'll prove to you that this is the only logical solution." He turned to his work table and unrolled a map.

"As you can see, we have here an excellent chart of the Northwestern coast of America, made by Captain George Vancouver. My recommendation is to remove the entire garrison to the mainland, around here." He pointed to the mouth of the Columbia River. "We must stop our dependence on ships or primitive fishing and hunting. We must depend on *land* for survival, not on the sea. We must cultivate the soil, plant crops and raise cattle."

Baranov interrupted him impatiently. "You seem to forget, Nikolai Petrovich, that the land further south belongs to the Spanish Crown."

"The coastline—yes, but dear Alexander Andreyevich, as far as we know, the territory further *inland* belongs to no one," Nikolai replied calmly.

"Some years ago I presented this plan to Tsar Paul and he granted us full charter over any territory we might discover and claim for Russia. I recommend that we now take advantage of this permission and explore the land beyond the narrow coastal possessions of Spain. We *must* move inland! We must colonize on a large scale, bringing along whole families from Russia to populate our settlements. For that, we must be in a more temperate climate than Novo-Arkhangelsk or Pavlovsk. Above all, we must have arable land!"

"But Sir, wouldn't this represent an aggressive act against the British? After all, they have their interests in the Pacific as well," Captain Khvostov objected as Nikolai paused to look at the map.

"Not at all, Captain," Nikolai pointed to the map. "The way was open for the British to settle on the North Pacific as early as in the 1790s, but only a handful of them took advantage of the opportunity, settling mainly on the islands. I am suggesting moving further south, outflanking the British. The land beyond the coastline is still wide open for anyone who wishes to explore and claim it. I do not believe that the Spanish have the ability in exploring deeply into these territories. They have spread themselves too thin. They can't colonize these lands. But *we can!*"

"May I interrupt Your Excellency?" Baranov addressed Nikolai formally, obviously irritated. "It seems to me that you have no idea of the complications involved. Of course, I know nothing about diplomacy or about Spain. You are the diplomat and I am only an ignorant *promyshlenik.*" Baranov's tone became sarcastic.

"Let's suppose that you are right, and we do move south. What *I am* concerned with is just how are we going to manage such a resettlement. We don't have ships; our men are sick and exhausted by our war with the Tlingits. They can do no more, and I for one am unwilling to order them."

Nikolai was prepared for Baranov's objections. "Gentlemen, we are going to follow my plan and explore the territory around the Columbia River—or some other point deeper inland. The Tsar gave me the full powers to order such an expedition." He smiled. "All I'm asking now, dear Alexander Andreyevich, is that the *Younona* be outfitted for a journey of three or four months," he said, looking into Baranov's eyes imploringly.

"The Spaniards will not permit you ashore," said Captain D'Wolf, lighting his pipe. "They have never allowed my ship to anchor; not even for taking on fresh water."

"They'll allow *me*," Nikolai replied. "I carry the credentials of His Imperial Majesty's Envoy to the governments of the world. The Spanish will not deny me the right of paying them a courtesy call."

He closed the meeting. "That is all, gentlemen. I request that you prepare the *Younona* for the expedition. I appoint Lieutenant Khvostov as her captain, with Midshipman Davidov as the first mate. I would like to offer the position of the second mate to Captain D'Wolf. Dr. Langsdorff will accompany us as a naturalist to make notes of the flora and fauna and as my personal physician," Nikolai continued in his crisp tone. "I want the best man you can offer as my superintendent of cargo; he will be in charge of buying and storing provisions. Then I want a complement of thirty-five healthy men, the minimum needed to sail this ship."

He smiled. He appeared relaxed as he turned to Baranov. "Don't worry, Alexander Andreyevich, I won't start a war. All I want to do is to explore the territory further south."

Chapter 28

The *Younona* left Novo-Arkhangelsk at the end of February. Usually, it was the month of savage storms, but the *Younona* seemed to be sailing under the protection of kind spirits. She moved south rapidly, encountering only breezy but clear weather.

The fine sailing weather held as the ship passed Queen Charlotte's Islands and then the huge island named after Captain George Vancouver and on, to the mouth of the Columbia River. There the winds suddenly shifted. A powerful squall threatened to throw the ship straight onto the shoals.

Captain Khvostov put back to sea and lay off shore during the night. In the morning, he dispatched Timofei Tarakanov and Grishka, the Aleut, to search for a passage into the river.

Dr. Langsdorff, eager to be the first bona fide scientist to step on the shores of the great river, joined them.

Through strong off-shore currents, Timofei and Grishka paddled toward the bluish-gray line of the land. The *baidarka* pitched and dove into the waves, making Dr. Langsdorff instantly sick. He cursed himself, the boat and the impulse that had led him into this adventure. He slid to the bottom of the boat, moaning.

A bank of heavy fog slowly rolled toward the land in huge swirls, swallowing the tiny *baidarka*, and completely obscuring the shore.

Timofei and Grishka caught in the shroud of fog, wrestled with the sea. While they bobbed on the crests of the waves, they scanned the gray nothingness for a glow of light from the ship's lanterns. Veterans of years of foul weather, they knew their shipmates would be working to bring them back.

Even as he told the frightened doctor to be calm, Timofei

heard the muted thump of a small cannon. He turned the *baidarka* toward the sound. In a few moments another shot, louder now, told him he was headed in the right direction.

At long last, he heard voices. "Ahoy, *Younona*," he yelled.

"Ahoy!" the watchman called.

Steering the *baidarka* toward the watchman's voice, Timofei soon sensed the presence of the ship.

"Where are you?" the watchman shouted.

"Right here!" Timofei grinned into the fog as the *baidarka* gently bumped into the schooner's siding. Timofei guided his boat by touch along the ship's curved side, until he felt a rope ladder. He tied the *baidarka* to the ladder and helped Dr. Langsdorff to his feet.

"Can you climb up?" he asked the suffering physician in his halting English.

"Of course!" the doctor replied, but he could not find the slippery ladder in the gloom. He lost his footing and plunged into the water.

"I can't swim!" the doctor choked.

"Hold on!" Timofei shouted. "You *zhopa!*" he swore in Russian. The physician gulped and thrashed. Timofei dived into the water, and grabbed the drowning man by the collar. Langsdorff clutched him in panic, threatening to drown them both. Timofei crushed his huge fist against the side of Langsdorff's face, not caring where it landed. The doctor's body went limp.

Timofei probed for the net he knew Grishka would throw to guide him toward the *baidarka*. It was a dangerous method of rescue because the net could tangle around a swimmer, but it was quick. The Aleuts had taught Timofei how to use it. When he felt the *baidarka* close at hand, he clutched the bow to keep himself and the doctor afloat. "Lower the cargo net and haul him up," Timofei shouted to the invisible deckhands above. He heard the winches squeak as the cargo net slowly crept down until it touched the *baidarka*. Timofei rolled the doctor into it.

"Pull him up!" he yelled. The grating sound of the winch told him that the net was on its way up.

"Let's go," he muttered to Grishka, his teeth chattering. He grabbed the swinging rope ladder and climbed up, the Aleut behind him.

Captain Khvostov recommended to Nikolai that they

abandon the idea of entering the river. According to Vancouver's charts, the shoreline consisted of treacherous sand bars and shoals. There were sudden changes in the ocean floor and unpredictable currents. Perhaps in the summer, when the days were long, they could try again, but now, in March, it was too dangerous.

Nikolai was disappointed, but he agreed. He thought gloomily that his luck had deserted him since the death of Annushka. Nothing seemed to go right for him any more.

The weather changed again. The thick, foggy calm suddenly gave way to a howling stormy sea. Incessant rain lashed at the ship; lightening streaked across the black sky, illuminating the *Younona* for a few moments, making every object stand out sharply outlined before plunging the ship into darkness again.

Captain Khvostov skillfully maneuvered the battered schooner, keeping her riding into the wind. He remained on the bridge for two days, taking short catnaps slumped over his navigation instruments.

The *Younona* sailed on. Fog once more enveloped the ship. Captain Khvostov once more did not dare to leave the bridge. He prayed that the twenty-year-old Vancouver charts were accurate, and that there would be no unexpected surprises like rocks or uncharted islands jutting out of the sea.

On the twenty-seventh of March the fog finally lifted. A group of small craggy islands alive with millions of nesting birds appeared directly ahead of the ship. Their clamor could be heard from far away.

Consulting the Vancouver charts, Captain Khvostov concluded that it must have been the Farallones Islands. The *Younona* should be close to the Presidio de San Francisco, a small military fort and mission established on the northern extremity of the Spanish American empire.

It was a different coastline now. The hills were lower, less green than those in the north. There were snow-capped mountains in the distance, partly obscured by haze. The currents near the coast were swift, dragging the ship toward the shore. Captain Khvostov had to trim the sails and consult his charts constantly.

He watched the coast slowly passing by, noting the golden hills, thinking what perfect sites they would make for villages and towns. Then something caught his eye. Adjusting his telescope, he could clearly see cattle and horses grazing on a gently rolling hill. Rezanov and the others saw them too.

"Hurray!" yelled Davidov, throwing his cap into the air. They watched the grazing lands slowly becoming orchards and vineyards planted in neat rows, obviously well cared for.

"Your High Excellency, I suggest that we drop anchor and remain here until late afternoon," Captain Khvostov said to Rezanov. "Since we don't know whether we would be welcome here, we ought to watch the coast for any threatening signs before we anchor in their bay."

"A good suggestion," Nikolai agreed.

The *Younona* idled at anchor for several hours, the crew keeping a close watch on the coast. All was peaceful. In the evening, helped by a brisk wind, they sailed into the bay and dropped anchor.

Numerous squat whitewashed buildings surrounded by a palisade and a stockade, dotted the cliff above the strip of sandy dunes. It was the Presidio de San Francisco.

"Not much there," Nikolai said. "It looks even less substantial than Novo-Arkhangelsk."

"But at least the weather here is better. Just feel how warm it is! And look at that sunset!" Midshipman Davidov said exuberantly.

There was a commotion within the walls of the presidio. Tiny figures ran back and forth about the square: then the gates of the fortress swung open and several horsemen rode at full gallop toward the beach, stopping at the water's edge directly in front of the *Younona*. The men dismounted, gesticulating.

"Let them know who we are," Nikolai said. The captain commanded that the Grand Standard of His Imperial Majesty be unfurled, but the men on the beach appeared unimpressed.

"*Duraky!* the idiots don't recognize our flag. We are Russians!" the captain shouted. The men on the beach mounted their horses and galloped back to the presidio.

"I disagree with you, Captain," Nikolai said. "I think they acted wisely. It's getting dark. They obviously don't know who we are; they don't know our flag and have decided to wait until morning. Perhaps, they hoped we would be gone by morning. In any case, they did not fire on us, as I was afraid they might. It is a good omen. Let's rest and see what they'll do in the morning."

Next morning, Nikolai saw through the open door of his cabin the brilliant sky and heard the cries of the seagulls.

Captain Khvostov entered with a perfunctory knock on the door frame. He was beaming.

"Well, Nikolai Petrovich, today is the day," he said brightly. "Today we shall know whether we succeed in Spanish California or..."

"We cannot think of failure, Captain," Nikolai cut in. "We *will* succeed. One way or another. We will bring food back to Novo-Arkhangelsk. If necessary, we'll raid the presidio, although I would rather not think of that now." Nikolai liked Khvostov. The captain, although only twenty-six years old, was already an experienced navigator. And a fine companion, Nikolai thought.

Nikolai's mind was racing impatiently while Ivan shaved him. When the servant finished, Nikolai quickly donned an official Court uniform with gold epaulets and a sword.

"Please dispatch Midshipman Davidov, Dr. Langsdorff and the necessary company of sailors ashore for a preliminary parley. Everything will depend upon the proper conduct of this delicate mission. Dr. Langsdorff will carry out the actual negotiations for our landing. He's the linguist. The sailors must present themselves as if they were on review by His Imperial Majesty himself!" Nikolai commanded brusquely.

"Yes, sir!" Captain Khvostov saluted, understanding that the informality had ended.

"Spaniards are a very proud people. I want our men of rank to show the greatest degree of respect toward the officers of the garrison. Even an *exaggerated* degree of respect," Nikolai added emphatically. "Make certain the officers and men are dressed in clean uniforms and polished boots. I want the Spaniards to think that our visit is strictly ceremonial. We will request permission to refill our water barrels and buy fresh provisions for the crew. That's all. Once we are allowed ashore, I'll take over the diplomatic negotiations."

Khvostov saluted and left. He selected four men, Timofei among them, to accompany Dr. Langsdorff ashore.

Midshipman Davidov and the doctor appeared on the bridge, having changed into fresh garments, the young officer wearing a short ceremonial sword at his side, his dark side whiskers freshly combed.

They stepped into the launch; the sailors lowered their

oars. The first Russian emissaries to land on the soil of Alta California were on their way.

Chapter 29

Nikolai observed the presidio through his telescope. He saw a group of soldiers canter down the hill toward the beach. As they reached the bottom of the hill, he was able to distinguish two riders at the head of the group—a monk attired in a gray habit and a young man astride a magnificent golden stallion with a flowing mane and tail of such an unusual shade that it looked almost white. The animal was lavishly caparisoned with a handsome saddle, headgear and stirrups of tooled silver, which sparkled, reflecting the sun. It produced a strange effect, as if the horse were sprinkled with hundreds of tiny stars.

In contrast, the monk rode a pot-bellied nag with protruding hip bones and seemingly no saddle. A dozen uniformed men in leather jerkins and leggings, armed with muskets and lances, followed.

Nikolai turned his attention to the Russian boat. Midshipman Davidov stood erect at the stern, his arms folded over his chest in the required naval stance. Dr. Langsdorff, looking somber in his frock coat and a floppy beret of the Heidelberg Medical Society, sat on the passenger's bench.

"He reminds me of Dr. Faustus," the captain said to Nikolai.

"*After* his transformation, I presume," Nikolai retorted with a smile.

The sailors now leaped out, two on each side of the boat. They froze at attention, their hands raised in a perfect salute.

Nikolai glanced at Captain Khvostov. "Can you believe that those men have never seen service on a naval vessel? They are simple *promyshleniki!*"

The captain grinned. "I am impressed!"

The leader of the Spanish party and the monk dismounted. Nikolai readjusted his telescope. The leader was a very young man, practically a boy. He wore knee boots with raised heels and huge silver spurs in the shape of a star, his hands encased in leather gloves with elbow-high cuffs like the gloves of musketeers in old Flemish paintings. His face was shaded by a wide brimmed hat with a cockade and a plume.

"What a colorful young gentleman," Nikolai commented. "He must be an aide-de-camp."

Midshipman Davidov and the young Spaniard saluted one another. The Russian sailors stood stiffly by and the Spanish escort fidgeted astride their horses. The monk and Dr. Langsdorff shook hands. The observers aboard the *Younona* could see Dr. Langsdorff smile and bow, pointing to the ship and then to himself, but the Spaniards seemed not to understand. Their faces were blank.

"It looks as if they don't understand one another," D'Wolf said, puffing on his pipe. "What languages do your emissaries speak?"

"French, English, German, and of course, Russian," Nikolai replied.

"No Spanish?"

"I think they have found a common tongue!" Captain Khvostov interrupted quietly. "Watch their agitation!"

Indeed, the little group ashore came alive. The corpulent monk slapped himself heartily on his thighs and the faces of the others were suddenly wreathed in smiles.

The contact had been established. Shortly the Russians returned to the boat. The monk walking with Langsdorff, gesticulated wildly, his cassock sleeves flying about like the wings of a fat gray pigeon.

The sailors raised their oars to a vertical position in a salute. The midshipman and the doctor stepped into the boat.

The youth and the monk remained at the water's edge, one waving his hat, the other a red bandana kerchief. The horsemen, in loose formation, joined them, riding into the shallows, the horses pawing at the water.

"Judging by the friendly parting, our envoys were successful in their mission," Nikolai said, folding his telescope.

Davidov and Langsdorff were brimming with smiles. The

doctor, bursting with excitement, was eager to relay the details of their meeting with the Spaniards.

"Who is the young man in the hat?" Nikolai began at once.

"He is Lieutenant Don Luis Argüello, the son of the commander of the presidio. He is presently in charge of the garrison during his father's absence," Midshipman Davidov reported.

"Are we allowed ashore?"

"Yes, sir. We have been invited to join the family of Don Luis for a cup of chocolate."

"What? *A cup of chocolate?*" Nikolai's eyebrows rose in surprise.

Dr. Langsdorff felt that the mission owed its success entirely to him. He hurried to explain. "Yes, Your Excellency. It is their custom, the equivalent of being invited to tea. The young gentleman was most gracious. He expressed his desire to entertain you and all the officers in the home of his parents."

"Could it be a ploy?" Nikolai asked suspiciously.

"No, no, Your Excellency. The padre assured me that this is their custom." Dr. Langsdorff pursed his lips. "Of course, I was unable to speak to Don Luis directly. The young man does not speak anything but Spanish, but..."

"Oh, yes," Nikolai interrupted. "What language *did you speak with the Spaniards?*"

"Latin, Your Excellency. We tried French and English to no avail. We spoke German and I even uttered a few words of Japanese," the doctor smiled modestly. "And Midshipman Davidov tried Russian. Finally, I thought of Latin...a priest would know Latin, I thought."

"You should have seen how the old padre jumped," Davidov laughed. "He was so delighted!"

Langsdorff's cheeks reddened with pleasure. "I explained to Father Uriá who you were, Your Excellency. He assured me that Don Luis had full authority to allow us ashore. Meanwhile, we are invited this afternoon for a cup of chocolate with Doña Ignacia, the mother of Don Luis. He will meet us at the landing later and escort us to the presidio!"

"So, you don't suppose they might have some diabolical plot to kidnap us while we are indulging ourselves in drinking chocolate, do you?" Rezanov smiled.

"No, Excellency," Langsdorff replied, failing to recognize the intended humor.

"Splendid!" Nikolai said. "I want all of you gentlemen to accompany me ashore. Mr. D'Wolf will have to stay aboard." He turned to the Yankee captain. "I hope you don't mind."

"Not at all." D'Wolf said easily. "I'll pretend that the *Younona* is still the *Juno* and I am still her master."

They laughed, full of optimism.

Nikolai continued, "Be ready in half an hour, gentlemen, wearing your uniforms, complete with decorations. I also want four more sailors. They should be armed but remain at the boat."

"*Slushayst*, Sir!" the captain saluted. "With your permission, I'll leave now to change." He left the bridge. Nikolai turned to the American.

"Mr. D'Wolf, I would appreciate your keeping an eye on the presidio. In case of trouble, don't try to rescue us. Make a run for the Sandwich Islands. Sell the cargo, buy provisions and bring them back to Baranov."

"Do you trust me that much?" D'Wolf grinned.

"Yes, I do."

Captain Khvostov returned to the bridge. He had shaved and changed into a handsome uniform of the Russian Imperial Navy, with its gold fringed epaulets, shiny buttons and a *kortik*, a short ceremonial sword.

"Let's go, gentlemen," Nikolai said. "*S Bogom!* Let's hope that this glorious sunshine is a good omen for our mission."

He stepped into the waiting longboat.

They were met at the edge of the water by the youthful officer and the priest. The soldiers held the bridles of several extra horses which had been brought down from the presidio.

"*Estoy muy honorado, Señor Comandante,*" Nikolai greeted the young man. He stretched his hand out with a bright smile.

"*Oh, usted habla español!*" Don Luis gushed. He was delighted. "*Es muy afortunado para nosotros!*"

Nikolai bowed slightly. "*Si,*" he said, "*Hablo español pero no bastante bien.*"

Don Luis and Father Uriá were quick to reassure him. "*Usted habla muy bien!*"

"That won't do," Nikolai thought. To forestall the useless exchange of banalities, he said with exaggerated politeness, "It is very gracious of you, Don Luis, to invite us to your home." Everyone bowed.

The priest gestured for the soldiers to bring the horses. Nikolai leaped into the saddle with ease, immediately mastering his nervous Arabian gelding. The Spaniards were impressed. They appreciated good horsemanship.

Nikolai felt good astride his horse, but Dr. Langsdorff had great difficulty. Having never been astride a horse he couldn't get his foot into the stirrup. He was finally aided into his saddle by two soldiers who lifted him unceremoniously over the horse's back.

Nikolai and Don Luis rode together at the head of the cavalcade. The young Spaniard was ill at ease and to cover up, spoke rapidly about several subjects at once. Nikolai found it difficult to follow his conversation. His own Spanish weak, Nikolai smiled warmly most of the time, nodding now and then. As the subject turned to horses, he assured Don Luis that even the Russian Tsar himself would have been impressed by the Spanish horses. They were superb.

By the time the cavalcade reached the presidio, Don Luis had become an admirer of Chamberlain Nikolai Rezanov.

The *Presidio de San Francisco* built on high ground commanding the bay, was surrounded by roughly made adobe walls that were in need of repair and whitewash. Inside the walls, low buildings were arranged around the dusty plaza and its fountain. Two long, squat buildings on one side of the plaza were the barracks for the garrison; neat pyramids of old-fashioned muskets were stacked in front of the barracks and groups of casually uniformed soldiers idled nearby.

Across from the barracks the Russians saw a sprawling whitewashed building surrounded by a broad veranda that was shaded by a trellis of climbing roses. Among the rosebuds Nikolai noted several bird cages that held song birds. A few lean dogs slept in the shade of the veranda. Naked Indian children played nearby, digging in the dusty earth.

At the side of the plaza, stood a small chapel made of adobe brick, freshly whitewashed to a dazzling brightness. These simple adobe buildings, with several smaller houses on the periphery of the plaza, comprised the settlement.

A profusion of flowers gladdened Nikolai's eye. The flowers spilled over the railings of balconies, or crowded the steps of the houses. The houses looked modest, perhaps deceptively so on the exterior, but they certainly looked more substantial than anything in Russian America. "This settlement had been built at least fifty years before any of ours," Nikolai thought, observing every detail.

Scrambling chickens, cackling nervously, scattered from under the horses' hooves as the cavalcade cantered toward the main house.

Don Luis dismounted, a wide smile lighting up his boyish face. "*Mi casa es su casa*," he said.

Nikolai bowed with a smile. He noticed women's bright dresses and heard stifled whispers from behind the rose trellises.

For the first time in many months, he suddenly felt cheerful. "I am going to enjoy this visit," he thought. He dismounted and tossed the reins of his horse to a soldier who had hastened to his side.

Don Luis noted this. He vowed to himself that thenceforth he, too, would toss the reins to a groom with the same aristocratic nonchalance.

Don Luis dashed ahead to open the doors. Before he reached the veranda, the door was flung open wide by Maria de la Concepción de Arguëllo.

She was a slim, raven-haired girl. Her dark eyes were fringed by long, thick curving lashes, her milky-white skin seeming even paler in contrast to the darkness of her hair. She was dressed simply, in a red calico frock, her small firm breasts pushing against the tight bodice. Her luxuriant, glossy hair streamed down her back and was held away from her smooth oval face by a narrow red ribbon.

"Your Excellency, my sister Maria Concepción," Don Luis introduced the girl.

"*Enchanté.*" Nikolai took her delicate hand into his and raised it to his lips. "She probably doesn't speak French," he thought. "*Encantado*," he repeated in Spanish. "We are honored, señorita, to be in your company." She is *exquisite*, he thought.

The girl curtsied and blushed, but replied with cool composure. "On the contrary, Señor. It is our honor to have you among us. Come with me and meet our mother. She is waiting."

Chapter 30

The girl led the Russians into a large room with a stone tile floor. It was full of light reflected from the whitewashed walls, the sun streaming in through the open windows. The ceiling was low; the tall Russians could almost touch the exposed beams of dark timber which ran from one end of the *sala* to the other. The stark room was sparsely furnished with rough-hewn tables and high-backed chairs. A plaster statue of a Madonna painted in strong colors, stood in a special niche, a votive light flickering at her feet.

A fat green parrot sat on a perch, staring belligerently at the visitors through the bars of his black circular cage.

Doña Ignacia de Argüello rose from her chair at the window to greet the visitors. She was a handsome, stout woman dressed in black, her hair showing traces of silver. Her skin was still smooth and flawless.

Unlike her daughter she felt shy with the visitors, allowing Don Luis and Father Uriá to introduce the rest of her family. The names of the children clicked on unendingly as they bowed or curtsied, but Nikolai paid attention to only one, Maria Marcella Concepción.

"You may call me Concha," she said smiling. "Everyone does. I prefer it that way."

"Concha...Conchita..." Nikolai repeated slowly, savoring the name, rolling it on his tongue, almost tasting it.

Doña Ignacia presently left the *sala* taking along all the younger children, leaving Concha and Don Luis to entertain the guests while awaiting the arrival of the refreshments.

Nikolai found Concha delightful. He talked only to her, not bothering to translate their conversation to the others, turning toward Father Uriá only out of politeness.

Señora Argüello returned, carrying a tray of sweets. Behind her marched the servants dressed in loose white shirts and trousers tied around their ankles. The attire reminded the guests of Russian peasants' shapeless undergarments.

The servants brought in several heavy silver trays with a large silver kettle, a cream pitcher, a sugar bowl, and massive silver spoons. By the look of pride on Señora Argüello's face, Nikolai guessed that the silver service was the family heirloom. He immediately expressed his admiration for the fine silver.

Doña Ignacia's face radiated with pleasure. "It was a part of my dowry," she said, adding with pride, "I was born a *Moraga of Spain*."

Nikolai had never heard of the Moragas, but he pretended to be impressed. "Clearly, the Moragas were famous for their beautiful women," he said smiling.

The barefooted servants passed little cups of steaming chocolate to the visitors who now were seated around the table. Señora Argüello presided, pouring from the heavy silver kettle, careful that not a drop splattered on the white cloth covering the table.

Concha sat primly at the other end of the table, her hands folded on her lap, glancing now and then at Nikolai.

"What brought you to our shores, Señor?" she suddenly asked.

Nikolai expected this question, but he was surprised that it came from Concha.

Their eyes met. "A disaster brought us here, Señorita," he replied, deciding to risk telling the truth. Well, *almost* the truth, he thought. "We were battered by the sea for days; our crew became exhausted and sick. We are in great need of fresh water and food. But now I am most grateful that the storms brought us to the hospitable shores of Alta California!" He smiled gallantly at both Concha and her mother.

They were pleased.

Father Uriá observed Rezanov closely. Suspicious by nature, he searched for the *real* meaning behind Nikolai's smooth words.

"We will send fresh water and food to your crew at once!" Don Luis exclaimed enthusiastically. "Just tell us what you need. We have plenty of everything!"

"Thank you, Don Luis. You are most generous." Nikolai bowed to the young man ceremoniously. He turned his attention to Señora de Argüello. "We are most grateful for your gracious hospitality, Señora," he bent over her hand and raised it to his lips. It was time to leave. The first step of his mission had been taken.

Doña Ignacia blushed; it had been a long time since her hand had been kissed by so handsome a gentleman. The officers and Dr. Langsdorff each brushed her hand with their lips, clicking their heels.

"Do come back tomorrow," she stammered, unaccustomed to such courtly manners.

"We'll be most honored."

Concha saw them to the door. "*Hasta mañana,*" she addressed them all, but her eyes were on Nikolai Rezanov.

Don Luis and Father Uriá accompanied the Russians to the beach where the ship's longboat awaited them. The sailors sprang to attention.

Don Luis stared longingly at the ship. Reading his mind, Nikolai asked casually, "Perhaps, Don Luis, you and the padre would like to visit the ship?"

"I would like it very much!" the young Spaniard exclaimed eagerly. Then, checking himself, he turned toward the padre for approval.

Father Uriá nodded.

"Good." Nikolai smiled. "We'll send the boat for you tomorrow morning. Afterward, we will pay our respects to the charming ladies."

"*Por supuesto!* Meanwhile, my men will bring the supplies that I promised you," Don Luis replied exuberantly.

"Thank you, my friend," Nikolai stepped into the boat. "*Hasta luego, Don Luis. Hasta la vista, Padre.*"

"*Hasta mañana, Señor Altissimus Cancellarius. Vayan con Dios, Señores,*" the priest made the sign of the cross, blessing the Russians.

The sailors raised their oars in salute, then dipped them into the water evenly and smoothly, in unison. They, too, understood the importance of impressing the Spaniards.

"We must cultivate the Spaniards very carefully," Nikolai instructed the officers who gathered on the bridge of the *Younona.* "No one must mention trade. I want to win the trust of Don Luis and the priest, make them our allies before we meet with the Governor of Alta California."

"Permit me, Your High Excellency, to inform you of what I have learned from Father Uriá," Dr. Langsdorff raised his hand like a schoolboy.

"Certainly, Doctor."

"There is an edict from the King of Spain, Carlos IV, prohibiting trade between Spanish America and foreign countries, that is except France, who is their ally. Father Uriá suspects that we came here with a proposal to trade. Indirectly, he had warned me of their laws."

Nikolai winced. "What did you tell him?" he demanded sharply.

"I told the padre that Your Excellency, being interested in scientific discoveries, had outfitted his expedition for the purpose of compiling an atlas of the flora and fauna of the Pacific." He stopped, suddenly embarrassed that he had used his own interest in the natural sciences as an excuse for the *Younona* expedition.

"What a marvelous idea!" Nikolai exclaimed unexpectedly. "Doctor Langsdorff, you have just given us the best reason for being in the Spanish waters!" He turned to the officers. "You know now, gentlemen, why we are here. My dear Doctor, collect your samples of flowers and butterflies to your heart's content. What else did the padre say?"

"He pointed out that the presidio and the other Spanish forts are independent of the mother country. The missions raise enough crops and cattle to supply themselves and the forts. In fact, they send surplus to Mexico and Spain."

"Please continue."

Dr. Langsdorff, overwhelmed by unusual praise from Rezanov, resumed, "The priest also told me that he is Don Luis' tutor. He dearly loves the young man. He described him as an honorable officer, respected by the natives and the soldiers of the garrison. The young lady, Señorita Concepción, is the apple of her father's eye. And of the Governor's. He is her Godfather. She just turned fifteen—last month, to be precise. She has had several proposals of marriage from local officers, but refused them all. Father Uriá would like to see her married to someone at Court in Madrid, he says, or at least in Mexico."

"I agree with the padre. She is too good for the local blockheads. She deserves a better future," Nikolai said, rather more quickly than he had intended.

"That's about all that I was able to learn," Dr. Langsdorff concluded.

"And that is quite a good deal, Doctor," Nikolai said.

The watch called from the bridge. Several heavily laden wagons were approaching the beach.

Nikolai turned to the captain. "Please arrange to receive the cargo and prepare the ship for the visit of our friends tomorrow. Dr. Langsdorff's collections of dried flowers and dissected birds must be prominently displayed. I also wish not be disturbed until tomorrow."

Nikolai locked the door of his cabin and stretched on his bed, his arms folded behind his head.

"Perhaps my luck is changing." He thought of the events of the day. "It was a risk to come here, but worth it." He needed to achieve some spectacular feat to wipe out his diplomatic failure in Japan. Establishing trade relations with Alta California would do it. "Now I only need to convince the Spaniards they would benefit from trade with Russian America. It will open up the whole Western hemisphere for Russia!" he thought. "What is little Japan compared to the Americas!"

Concha could not sleep for thinking of Nikolai Rezanov. She had never met anyone as exciting as the tall handsome Russian diplomat, she thought. She went in her mind through the first moments of their meeting. She had watched him through the rose trellis as he rode with her brother across the plaza. He sat a horse with elegant ease and it was the first thing Concha had noticed about him. As the riders dismounted, she became fascinated by the height of the blond stranger. The men of her acquaintance were all of much shorter stature.

Later, in the house, Concha found herself staring at the Russian. "He has such beautiful blue eyes," she thought. "I have never seen such eyes before. They sparkle, when he laughs, then become sad and distant the next moment..."

Concha tossed on her narrow bed. "He's the kind of man I would like to marry someday," she thought.

She got up and flung her window open. The fresh air rushed into the room cooling her face. Concha stared at the ship anchored in the bay at the foot of the presidio. The *Younona* looked like an intricate, fragile toy, bathed in the bright moonlight. Concha could clearly see her rigging with its furled sails. Light shone through several portholes and Concha wondered if one might be in Rezanov's cabin.

"I wonder what he's thinking right now," Concha thought. She knew that she made a good impression on the Russian diplomat. "Perhaps, he's thinking of me also... No. This is impossible. He has more important matters on his mind." She returned to her bed but sleep evaded her. "It must have been so awful for Señor Rezanov to sail for weeks, battered by storms," she thought.

"I wonder how it feels to sail on a ship..."

Concha had been raised at the presidio and knew nothing of the outside world. Her Godfather, Don José Arillaga, favored her among the Argüello children, and when the priests had taught her to read, he began to add to her education.

Whenever he visited the presidio, he taught Concha history and geography, pointing out on a globe different countries, seas and rivers. He stirred her imagination, creating in her a longing to know more about the world outside the presidio. "How I wish I could see the Cathedral in Toledo, or hear zarzuela performed at the theatre in Madrid!" Concha sighed.

She knew that she would never see any of these wonders if she remained at the presidio in Alta California. She dreamt of Madrid. Her only chance of escaping the dreary destiny as the wife of a garrison officer would be through a marriage to some official at the Court.

No such official had ever visited the Presidio de San Francisco.

When Concha turned thirteen, the first proposal of marriage was presented to her father. Commander Argüello rejected the suitor without even mentioning the proposal to Concha. There were two or three other attempts by the officers of the garrison to win Concha's hand, but each was refused by the family.

Concha stared at the *Younona* through her window, thinking that St. Petersburg must be even more magnificent than Madrid.

Suddenly she had a disturbing thought. "I wonder if he's married?"

Early the following morning Nikolai amused himself by observing the plaza through his telescope.

A faint peal of bells drifted from the presidio. Presently

several gray-cassocked monks crossed the plaza and entered the chapel. A group of white-clad Indians crowded in behind them.

Nikolai saw several women leave the Argüello house, walking toward the chapel. It was impossible to see their faces from this distance, but he assumed that the lady in black was Señora de Argüello. Next to her walked a slim woman in a bright red dress. Nikolai knew at once it was Concha.

A feeling of warm pleasure enveloped him. It was reminiscent of his youth when the scent of pines or the trill of a lark would produce a sudden lightness of heart. He had not experienced such youthful joy in years. "I will see her again in a few hours," he thought.

The women disappeared inside the chapel. Nikolai suddenly felt ravenously hungry. To Ivan's pleasure, he wolfed down a large breakfast.

An hour later, a launch was sent for Don Luis and Father Uriá. Two younger Argüello brothers came along as well.

The boat arrived on the starboard side of the *Younona* and a new wooden ladder was lowered for the visitors.

Nikolai greeted his guests at the rail. He led them to the bridge where they drank a toast in fiery vodka with Captain Khvostov, his officers and Dr. Langsdorff. Nikolai had decided to save all formality and ceremony for his meeting with the Governor. As he escorted his guests around the ship, Nikolai drew their attention to Dr. Langsdorff's collection of dried plants, dissected birds and small animals, but Don Luis hardly glanced at them.

Casually, Nikolai pointed out the latest models of long-range cannons, saying matter-of-factly, "As long as the ship is equipped with these fine artillery pieces, she is well protected against any encounter on the high seas or on land!" The Spaniards were impressed. Don Luis enviously eyed the guns. He knew that their own ancient cannons were no match for the Russians'.

Finally, Nikolai stopped at a trap door. "Down there is our cargo. But I don't suppose you are interested in seeing that," he said off-handedly.

"Oh, but we are!" Don Luis protested.

"In that case, allow me to show you the way." A sailor lifted the trap door and Nikolai quickly climbed down. The Spaniards followed.

Like a good merchant, Nikolai demonstrated his wares. One by one he opened the long boxes bursting with bolts of woolen and cotton cloth and even exquisite silks.

"We have barrels of nails and dozens of crates of various tools. This is just a small sample of our cargo, " Nikolai said.

Don Luis was unable to control his curiosity. "What are you going to do with this cargo?"

"The usual. We'll trade it with the Indians along the coast. Or we'll sail to the Sandwich Islands and trade with the Hawaiian King."

"What will you trade it for? What can the Indians give you that you need?" demanded Don Luis.

"They can give me *food,*" Nikolai said carefully. "I did not mention it yesterday, for I thought it was inappropriate with the ladies present, but our colony in Novo-Arkhangelsk is in great need of food."

Father Uriá and Don Luis exchanged quick glances. Nikolai pretended not to notice. He continued, "Our new settlement is under siege by the Tlingit Indians. The colony in Novo-Arkhangelsk is almost starving. Supply ships sent from Russia never arrived. They were wrecked by storms. That is why we must barter our fine cargo for food."

"We have plenty of food right here in Alta California!" Don Luis blurted out.

Nikolai smiled bitterly. "I know, *amigo*, and I am grateful to you for sharing it with us, but we need more, much more. We need to empty our holds of merchandise and fill them with food for Novo-Arkhangelsk. I would gladly exchange my cargo with you, *amigo*, but I know that you are forbidden to trade with foreigners." He put his arm around the young man's shoulder. "Yes, *mis amigos*," he continued, "there is nothing that I would like more, but alas, I don't want to repay your hospitality by placing you in jeopardy with your own king."

The Spaniards hungrily eyed the boxes and crates full of precious goods. "Perhaps there is a way," Father Uriá responded cautiously.

Nikolai shrugged, "As the representative of His Majesty, the Emperor of Russia, I carry full plenipotentiary powers for opening diplomatic and trade relations." He allowed his words to sink in. He led his guests to the bridge.

He felt that Father Uriá was on his side. Perhaps he would aid him when the time came, he thought.

To cement their unspoken alliance, Nikolai presented Don Luis with a Russian fowling gun encrusted with mother-of-pearl and traced with gold. Father Uriá received a bolt of cloth of gold for the altar of his church, and the young Argüellos each received a pistol.

The visit over too soon, the Spaniards reluctantly stepped into the waiting longboat.

Chapter 31

In the days that followed, Doña Ignacia extended her invitations to include dinners. As the friendship between the Spaniards and Russians grew, everyone became aware of the flirtation between Nikolai and Concha. The family already knew that Nikolai was a widower, but only Concha dared to dream that there was more in Nikolai's interest in her than innocent flirtation.

While everyone awaited the arrival of Governor Arillaga, Father Uriá quietly spread the news about the *Younona's* cargo among the priests at the mission.

Don Luis similarly, described to the officers of the garrison the new weapons which the Russians were willing to trade for grain and beef. Soon every man at the presidio and the mission craved for the *Younona's* cargo. Still, there was no way of getting around the king's decree against trade. Only the Governor could circumvent the law, but as Nikolai had learned from Father Uriá, Governor Arillaga was a stubborn old man, proud of his adherence to the law.

"Is anything bothering you, Señor?" Concha whispered one day as Nikolai listened absentmindedly to Doña Ignacia reminiscing of her youth in Spain. "Perhaps I can help?"

"I doubt it, dear Concha. Yes, I am disturbed that I can't do anything to help our suffering people in Novo-Arkhangelsk. It's frustrating," Nikolai smiled sadly at Concha.

"But you are wrong, Señor. I *can* help you. Come with me to the patio; I have something very important to tell you." She led him to a small patio surrounded with flowering plants. She indicated a bench under a blossoming magnolia. "I overheard a conversation between Father Uriá and Father de la

Cueva. They say there is plenty of food *for sale*." She stressed the last two words.

Nikolai listened to Concha with mounting respect. This sheltered girl, who had never been beyond the walls of her little fort, spoke cooly about the ways of circumventing the laws of her country. "She's very clever," Nikolai thought.

"Father Uriá is going to suggest that you *buy* the food from the mission. Governor Arillaga cannot forbid the sale of surplus crops or livestock. The missions are free to sell their excess food to anyone. So, your buying it from the padres will be a private deal. No politics."

"What about my cargo?"

"The padres will *buy* your cargo with the gold you pay them for their provisions."

Nikolai shook his head in wonder. For days he had been wrestling with the dilemma and now Concha had presented him with so simple a solution.

He stood up and took her hand. "You are amazing, Señorita," he said, his lips brushing her smooth white hand.

Concha smiled. "That's not all. You should have your cargo seen by as many people as possible, especially the women," she continued. "*Before* the Governor arrives."

"You are a treasure!" Nikolai saw at once what she meant. "I envy the man who claims you for his own." Concha blushed. "You are very helpful to me, Concha," he continued. "I'll start by inviting the ladies to visit my ship."

When they returned to the *sala*, Nikolai bowed to Doña Ignacia. "Señora, you'll do me great honor if you and the ladies of the presidio would visit my ship. It's my only way to return a tiny bit of your hospitality. Please allow me the pleasure of entertaining you aboard the *Younona!*"

The two weeks in the sheltered waters of the Bay of San Francisco helped the crew of the *Younona* to get back on their feet. Freshly baked bread, vegetables and fruit, milk, eggs and meat furnished the cure they needed.

On the day of the women's visit to the *Younona*, the cargo boss, Timofei, placed long benches along the spotless upper deck, covering them with colorful Samarkand rugs, originally meant for the Mikado. He spread bolts of woolens and silks along with ribbons, scissors, mirrors, ornamental combs and strings of bright Italian beads. In addition there were pyramids of aromatic soaps, cooking utensils, several samovars and ornate chiming clocks.

The women arrived in a launch accompanied by Midshipmen Davidov and Don Luis.

Doña Ignacia, looking regal in her best black silk dress, her graying hair covered by a lace mantilla, introduced the women who curtsied self-consciously.

Nikolai led them to the deck, where tables were set with wine, cakes and fruit. He welcomed the visitors in Spanish in the name of the Russian Emperor. His voice trembling emotionally, he thanked Señora de Argüello and Don Luis for their generosity to his crew. The women felt tears welling in their eyes as he spoke.

"I love him," Concha thought, her own eyes moist.

The wine was champagne, unfamiliar to most of the women. They sipped it gingerly, watching the tiny bubbles rise to the rim of their glasses. The women were timid at first, but soon their inhibitions vanished and they began to chatter like a flock of sparrows, glancing at the displayed items, impatient to be invited to observe them closer.

The short repast over, Nikolai invited his guests to view the exhibit. "Do you suppose the people of the presidio might need some of these items?" he asked innocently.

"Señor, never in my life have I seen so many beautiful things! We need everything!" Doña Ignacia replied sincerely.

Nikolai motioned to Timofei to bring a basket of small souvenirs. Every woman found something to her liking—a ribbon, a small mirror, a handkerchief or a jar of rose water.

It was time to leave. Nikolai and the officers helped their guests into the boat.

"*Hasta mañana.* At the usual time, at our house," Concha whispered as Nikolai bent over her hand.

"I can hardly wait," he replied in a low voice.

She smiled and pressed his hand.

But Don Luis was at the ship the following morning with bad news.

During the night a messenger had arrived from Monterey, the capital of Alta California, bringing a letter from Governor Arillaga addressed to His High Excellency Chamberlain Nikolai Rezanov.

Don Luis looked gloomy. He too, had received a message from the Governor. The Russians were to be denied landing, the Governor wrote. But it was too late, Don Luis thought. "What am I to do?"

The message to Rezanov was written in French. Nikolai skipped over the long flowery salutations. The Governor suggested that there was no need for His Excellency to travel to Monterey to present his credentials. He would be arriving shortly at the presidio to do the honors to His Excellency in the name of His Most Catholic Majesty the King of Spain. Meanwhile, *he would hope that His High Excellency remain aboard his ship, for the modest accommodations of the presidio were unworthy of such a high personage.*

That was clear enough. "It could be worse," Nikolai thought. "He says 'don't land', but he doesn't say 'go away'!"

"Thank you for bringing the letter, *amigo*", he said to Don Luis. "I am looking forward to meeting the Governor," he smiled. "Meanwhile, isn't your mother waiting for us?" He motioned the young man toward the longboat.

Concha intercepted Nikolai on the steps of the house, "I must talk to you right away, Señor," she said at once. She led him to the back patio. "All the talk around the presidio is of your cargo and how much we need it!" She smiled, dimpling her smooth cheeks. She had a mischievous look on her face, which turned serious as she continued. "However, you must hurry. You must buy the food from the mission *before* the governor returns."

"Why is it so urgent?" he asked.

"Because..." she bit her lip and then said with determination, "because our two countries may be at war. Soon. If they are not already."

"Good Lord! Where did you get this information?"

"Governor Arillaga wrote to my brother not to allow your crew to land. He reminded Luis that Spain is an ally of France. And France is at war with England. And England is an ally of Russia. I don't know much about world affairs, but I thought that *you* would know what the Governor was referring to."

"I surely do, my lovely diplomat!" Nikolai said, raising her hand to his lips. "Thank you. I'll proceed immediately."

"Hurry! Once the monks know that we are at war with each other, they won't need to buy your cargo."

"I know, they'll confiscate it."

"Yes. Go to the mission today. Now. Don't delay. Make an agreement with the padres."

"Thank you, my guardian angel," Nikolai looked deeply into her dark eyes.

Concha blushed. "Go," she said, her voice suddenly shaky.

Nikolai cut short his visit with Doña Ignacia. "I must pay my respects to the padres at the mission," he said reverentially.

Accompanied by Father Uriá and Don Luis, the Russians rode out through the gates turning inland.

Concha waved her handkerchief from the steps.

"*Vaya con Dios!*" she cried. Nikolai lifted his plumed hat.

The Mission San Francisco de Asís was located several miles inland, facing the eastern hills and the valley below.

Nikolai and his entourage rode at an easy canter enjoying the gently rolling land where large herds of cattle grazed contentedly. In other pastures there were sheep, thousands of them, their thick winter coats dirty and matted; from a distance they looked like formations of boulders strewn over the green hills.

And then there were large herds of horses, sleek and beautiful, prized possessions of the Spaniards. Further along, Nikolai saw Arabian brooding mares and their young.

Father Uriá pointed to the herds. "They belong to the Argüello family. And the land too. As far as you can see."

Nikolai was impressed. He had not realized that the Argüellos were landowners. He looked closer at the land, well-planted with sprouting corn and blossoming orchards.

The mission loomed in the distance. Its church was an adobe structure with massive wooden double doors studded with heavy black iron nails. On each side of the doors two square columns, built as part of the wall, supported the second story with six similar columns under the sloping tile roof. Broad steps led to the great doors of the mission and a starkly plain gilded cross crowned the gabled roof.

The travelers entered through a side gate along the long wall encircling the mission. A wide cobblestoned plaza spread before them with a fountain that also served as a water trough for the horses. Chickens scampered away as the riders entered the plaza, but once the horses were tied to the rail, the chickens resumed their pecking, boldly walking under the horses' bellies.

The plaza was ringed by low adobe buildings, freshly whitewashed like the church and the surrounding wall. Tall, leafy trees shaded the plaza from the warm April sun. Groups of Indians camped in the shade of the trees. Nikolai noted that the Indians of California looked different from the Indians of Russian America. They were smaller, darker, and were dressed in sewn garments rather than in animal skins or cedarbark cloth. The women were attired in voluminous skirts and *rebozos*. Not one of them was bare-breasted. "The result of the missionary influence," Nikolai thought.

The priests met their guests cordially. Father Landaeta, the confessor of the Argüello family, invited them for a short prayer at their chapel. The statue of the Virgin, made of clay and garishly painted, dominated the modest chapel.

"It was probably made by an Indian convert," Nikolai thought.

The only expensive adornment in the chapel was a gold thread altar cloth, which Nikolai instantly recognized as his own gift to the mission.

After the prayer, the fathers led their guests to the refectory. A long narrow table was set with heavy pewter plates and goblets, coarse linen napkins, two-pronged forks and sharp narrow knives with wooden handles. In the center of the table were large platters piled high with roasted wild turkeys and chickens, freshly baked breads, yams and dishes of red peppers and beans. Jugs of honey, slabs of freshly churned butter were placed here and there, along with tall pitchers of young wines from the mission's own vineyards. It was the most lavish table that the Russians had seen in a long time.

"Such a variety of fresh foods!" Nikolai exclaimed. "Your hospitality is overwhelming!"

"We don't eat like this often, Your Excellency," Father Landaeta replied. "As a rule, we eat sparingly, indulging ourselves only at Christmas and on our patron saint's day, *el dia de San Francisco*. But the arrival of Your Excellency is such a great occasion! Señorita Concha informed us to expect you today."

Nikolai smiled. "That Concha!" he thought with delight.

The meal lasted more than two hours. The Franciscans were eager to learn about Rezanov's travels around the world—which Father Uriá had cleverly introduced as the main topic of conversation.

Finally, Father Landaeta said, rising from the table, "I would like to show you around the garden, Your Excellency."

He escorted Nikolai outside. "I wish to talk to you in privacy, Your Excellency. It is a very delicate subject." They walked slowly along the gallery, through the garden and out of the gate, pausing to admire the vista of rolling verdant hills.

"We have many God-given natural riches," Father Landaeta began softly. "We produce more than we consume, but our government forbids us to trade. It might have made sense decades ago, when this coast was wide open. Every ship then was suspected of being an enemy or a pirate, bent on conquest or pillage. But it is not so anymore. We have many presidios along the coast to guard our interests. We feel secure on the Pacific Coast. There is no reason not to trade our surplus grain and cattle with other countries. Yet—we allow our grain to rot, our cattle to die of old age, rather than trade..."

Father Landaeta paused, leading Nikolai to an old tree and inviting him to sit on the bench beneath it. Sitting next to him, his hands clasped on his lap, Landaeta continued, "There is no law, however, against *selling* our crops or cattle. We do it all the time between the mission and presidio. I think we've found the way of obtaining your cargo without breaking the law." He paused.

Nikolai allowed Landaeta his moment of triumph. "Yes, Father, I'm listening."

"It is very simple. We propose that you *buy* from us everything you need. Then, in turn, we'll buy your cargo with the money you have paid us for our provisions!"

"Brilliant! It is absolutely brilliant!" Nikolai exclaimed, pretending surprise. "We must conclude our exchange as soon as possible," he said, shaking Landaeta's hand.

"I agree. Will tomorrow be soon enough?" Landaeta smiled.

"*Por supuesto,*" Nikolai made a courtly bow. "Tomorrow will be just right!"

Timofei Tarakanov was placed in charge of buying the mission's provisions and delivering the *Younona's* cargo.

The Russians awaited anxiously, but the day passed with no sign of the wagons.

Another day passed. There were no wagons with provisions. The Russians waited, growing uneasy.

"When do you expect the Governor to arrive?" Nikolai asked Concha next day.

"Any day now. The moment I know I'll send you a message," she murmured conspiratorially. Concha was enjoying her role as go-between. She was in love with Nikolai; his interests were becoming hers.

Four days had passed since Nikolai's visit to the mission. Furious, he suspected that his elaborate scheme had failed. If there was a war raging between Russia and Napoleon— and thus Spain, as the French ally—the padres might have already learned about it. Perhaps they were preparing now to confiscate his ship and its cargo. Irked, Nikolai tried to force the issue. He sent a message to the mission that he would like to talk to the padres.

The padres were impossible to locate. Father Uriá was reported to have left for Mission San José, while Father Landaeta remained incommunicado.

Exasperated, but unable to do anything about it, Nikolai distracted himself with visits to the presidio. In the presence of Concha he was able to forget his anxiety. Daily, he had his boat take him ashore where Don Luis would be waiting for him with the horses. Like everyone else in the Argüello household, Don Luis was aware of the growing attraction between Nikolai and Concha. "I wish Señor Nikolai would marry our Concha!" he thought. Being related to a high Russian official, an intimate of the Tsar, appealed to the ambitious young Spaniard. He already imagined himself at Court in St. Petersburg—as a general, perhaps, or an ambassador— dressed in a handsome gold embroidered uniform and plumed cockaded hat. If only Señor Nikolai and Concha would marry, he fantasized.

The *Younona* rocked gently at anchor in the middle of the bay. Food was plentiful, the weather was perfect, but the Russians grew more nervous with every passing day. There were no provisions delivered from the mission.

Early one evening several small children appeared on the beach, all riding a single little burro. They shouted and waved their arms, trying to attract the attention of the men aboard the *Younona.* The captain trained his telescope on the agitated children recognizing them as the younger Argüellos.

"Call His Excellency to the bridge," the captain turned to a sailor on duty.

"The Argüello children are on the beach. They probably have a message for us," the captain said as Nikolai appeared on the bridge.

The older boy was waving his arms, shouting in a high thin voice. Nikolai was able to distinguish a few words: "*Mi hermana...El Gobernador...Mañana...*"

It was enough for Nikolai.

He shouted through his cupped hands, "*Muchas gracias, muchachos, vayan con Dios! Entiendo su mensaje.*" Turning to the officers, he said, "Well, gentlemen, tomorrow Governor Jose Arillaga is expected to arrive. Prepare the *Younona* to sail if necessary."

Chapter 32

Next morning the Russians observed the arrival of Governor Arillaga. A detachment of cavalry rode slowly along the dusty road, escorting a heavy carriage drawn by four large horses. The soldiers were armed with long lances and leather shields, in addition to muskets and pistols. They wore round hats and chest coverings made of tooled leather. There was something medieval about their attire, Nikolai thought, as if Cortéz himself might have appeared momentarily.

"Now we wait for the Governor's summons," he thought. Pacing the bridge, he weighed his choices. "Should the Governor order the *Younona* to leave, or worse, open fire on her, I could wipe the presidio off the cliff. But we would still leave empty-handed...Our crew is too small to go ashore and seize what we need. And then, of course, there is Concha."

She had become very important to Nikolai. For the first time since the death of Annushka, he actually desired a woman. Fantasies about Concha often filled his mind, crowding out the thoughts of everything else.

He had no doubt that Concha was in love with him, with that romantic passionate love only very young girls can feel.

His fantasies of Concha had acquired a new meaning since his first glimpse of the Argüello lands. She would receive some of those lands as part of her dowry. Were he to marry Concha, there would be nothing to prevent him from building a Russian settlement on her land. There would be no need to fight with the natives. No need to risk lives. The land would be *his*, already cultivated, waiting for the Russian colonists to nourish it further.

"Should I marry Concha? It makes no difference to me whether she remains a Roman Catholic," he thought.

"It will be a great political coup if I establish a legal foothold on the American continent," he thought, pacing the bridge as was his habit. "The Tsar will give me permission to marry Concha, I am sure. He will see at once the advantages of such a marriage. Should I propose? She is a lovely creature. I want her..."

He forced himself to return to reality. "I'm being romantic...I might never see her again should the *Younona* be ordered tc leave..."

Nikolai turned to captain Khvostov. "Can we make it to the Sandwich Islands with this crew?"

"We will be short-handed," Khvostov began. "As you know, we lost four men to scurvy at the beginning of our journey."

"Can we make it?" Nikolai snapped.

"Yes," Khvostov replied, feeling hot blood rush to his face. It was the first time Rezanov's temper had been directed at him.

"Make ready to depart at a moment's notice." Nikolai wanted no doubt about the urgency of the situation and his tone made it clear.

"Aye-aye, sir." Khovstov was at attention. Nikolai nodded and turned away.

A lookout shouted, "Boat approaching! Starboard fore!" Khvostov and Rezanov quickly snapped their telescopes into position.

A rowboat moved slowly toward the ship rowed awkwardly by two uniformed soldiers who struggled with the strong current. A stout friar in a Franciscan habit sat at the stern, a strand of black rosary beads in his pudgy hands and an enormous sombrero on his head for protection from the sun.

When they drew closer, the friar took his hat off, waving with it energetically at the Russians. "I bring you a message from His Excellency, Governor Arillaga," he shouted in Spanish, repeating it in Latin for good measure.

The ladder was lowered. The Spanish soldiers steadied the ladder as the padre climbed aboard.

"I am Father de la Cueva. I bring a personal invitation from the Governor of Alta California to join him at supper tonight at the home of Commandant Argüello." He bowed in a courtly manner, revealing a tonsure, smooth and pink.

"My officers and I are honored," Nikolai replied, return-

ing the bow and hiding the surge of relief he felt. "We will
be delighted to meet His Excellency and to express our gratitude to Señor Argüello for the hospitality afforded us by his
family."

Captain Khvostov watched narrowly and almost smiled
in admiration as Rezanov asked the priest, "Will you share a
glass of wine with us?"

"Indeed, I would! *Con mucho gusto!*" Father de la Cueva
smiled broadly tossing his sombrero to one of the soldiers.

Nikolai opened the door to his cabin, letting Father de la
Cueva pass. The officers and Dr. Langsdorff crowded behind.

"Never by the flicker of an eye did Rezanov let the priest
know how close we had come to losing everything," Khvostov
told the other officers later, shaking his head in admiration
of Nikolai's coolness.

Nikolai looked equally cool as he approached the Argüello
home in his court uniform, a blue moiré sash across his chest
with the star-burst Order of St. Andrew gleaming. The cor-
don and chain of the Order, studded with diamonds, was all
but hidden in the fine lace jabot that cascaded beneath his
chin. His blue velvet coat with a stiff high collar and knee
breeches were lavishly embroidered in gold and silver scrolls
as were his velvet slippers. He wore white silk stockings and
a white waistcoat. Over his shoulders was a dark velvet cloak
and on his head a plumed, cockaded hat.

"Let's go!" he said brusquely. "The governor's carriage
is waiting!"

Concha waited for Nikolai on the veranda, surrounded by
uniformed Spanish officers. She was smiling, first at one and
then the other, meeting their eyes, then looking away, making
them feel they had her full attention. She wore a close-fitting
many-tiered dress of old ivory-colored lace with a low decol-
lete. Her rich black hair, swept up in an elaborate coiffure by
her mother, was decorated with a fresh red rose. She wore a
lace mantilla and despite what her admirers thought, most of
her attention was on the plaza where she knew Nikolai would
be arriving.

Nikolai could see her, in his mind's eye, in St. Petersburg,
presiding over his own salon. "She was born to be at Court,"
he thought.

"Ah, here you are, Señor!" she exclaimed abandoning the
officers and coming down the steps to greet him.

"How beautiful you look tonight!" he said softly, bending

over her hand and pressing it lightly. "You make me jealous of all these splendid *caballeros* who have the pleasure of your company. If I were the ruler of the world I would exile them to that rocky island in the middle of the bay to have you all to myself."

Concha blushed but replied without hesitation, "All you need Señor, is to say one word, and I'll do anything you ask me to."

Nikolai suddenly felt the blood rushing to his head and pulsating wildly against his temples. "Do you really mean it?"

"I do mean it," Concha replied in a low voice, her eyes luminous.

"My dear girl," he said softly. "*Querida.*"

"Please come in, Señores. *El Gobernador* and my father are waiting," Don Luis dramatically flung open the great doors of his father's house.

"Later," Nikolai whispered to Concha. With a formal bow toward the Spanish officers on the veranda, he entered the house.

A change had taken place in the *sala.* The heavy table had been pushed against the wall and multi-colored straw mats spread on the uneven stone floor. The parrot in his circular cage was gone. At the far end of the room, seated in a high-backed carved chair, was an elderly man in Spanish court dress of black velvet. Several senior officers crowded around him.

Nikolai paused dramatically at the entrance. In his gloved hand he held his tightly rolled credentials with the Imperial Seal attached to a silken cord.

His officers stood stiffly three paces behind him, their plumed hats held in the crook of their left arms against their chests. Two steps further back stood Dr. Langsdorff dressed in formal attire, an academic beret firmly crowning his head.

The women of the Argüello family had taken seats along the walls, joining the garrison officers' wives already seated there, the older women in black, the younger ones in a dazzling array of bright colors. Nikolai noted that their finery was shabby, old-fashioned and obviously home made. "No wonder they are eager for our silks and laces," he thought briefly, turning his attention to the men.

"Welcome, Monsieur Rezanov, to the shores of Alta California," the Governor greeted him in French, rising from his chair with difficulty.

Nikolai bowed. The officers behind him clicked their heels. Dr. Langsdorff didn't know whether to bow like Rezanov, or to salute. Before he could resolve the dilemma, Nikolai handed the Governor his credentials.

"Permit me, Your Excellency, to convey the personal greetings of His Majesty the Emperor of all the Russias. I am your obedient servant." Nikolai, also speaking in French, bowed once more.

The Governor briefly glanced at the credentials and handed them to a stocky, swarthy senior officer who stood immediately behind him.

"Please sit down, Monsieur Rezanov," the Governor indicated an empty chair to his right. "We are honored to have the personal envoy of the Russian Emperor in our midst." Nikolai sat, his officers and Dr. Langsdorff taking their positions behind his chair.

The Governor, too, sat with obvious relief. Nikolai noticed that one of his feet was heavily bandaged.

"I wish to thank you, Your Excellency, for the hospitality afforded us during our visit to Alta California," Nikolai began formally. "Especially, I would like to thank Señor Commandante de Argüello and his lady for opening their hospitable home to us weary seafarers," he continued, switching into Spanish for the benefit of the Argüellos.

"Ah, the Señor speaks Spanish!" Arillaga was surprised, formality suddenly gone from his manner.

"Not as well as Your Excellency speaks French," Nikolai smiled. "One becomes rusty in a foreign tongue without practice."

Arillaga chuckled. "Perhaps you would enjoy speaking Spanish from now on. It will give you a chance to avoid becoming rusty. Besides, our host el Señor Commandante, will be able to participate in our discussions. Let me introduce him to you."

Nikolai rose, extending his hand to Concha's father.

Commandant Argüello was a stocky powerfully-built man of about forty-five. He had a dark complexion, different from the rest of his family and Nikolai suspected that he was of Mexican, rather than Spanish heritage. His jaws were square and he had a long black moustache. His smile was wide and friendly as he vigorously shook Nikolai's hand.

"Allow me to thank you for the hospitality extended to us by your deputy in command, Lieutenant Argüello," Nikolai said with sincerity.

"My son only performed his Christian duty, Señor. He could not have done less." They all bowed to one another again.

"*Bueno*. Enough formalities. Let's have a little wine to celebrate our meeting," said the Governor.

Doña Ignacia at once left the room to organize the refreshments. From the corner of his eye Nikolai saw Concha listening intently to the exchange among the men.

The official audience was over. The Spanish officers surrounded captain Khvostov and midshipman Davidov. Those who had met the Russians before and had entertained them in their quarters, greeted them with the familiarity of old friends. Dr. Langsdorff became the center of attention of the Latin-speaking priests who surrounded him in a mass of somber cassocks.

"If you don't mind, Señor, I'll remain seated. I have an acute attack of gout. I suffer excruciating pains!" The Governor extended his bandaged foot for Rezanov to see.

"Perhaps my physician can help, Your Excellency. I'll ask him to suggest a remedy."

"*Muchissimo gracias*." Arillaga relaxed. "I can no longer remember when we had a physician among us. Do you remember *ever* having a real physician in California, Don José Darió?" he asked the Commandant.

"No, *mi amigo*. The only physicians we have are the good padres and Indian *curanderos*," replied Concha's father.

"I am sure the learned fathers are excellent physicians," Nikolai smiled toward the padres, but to himself he thought, "The bastards! If they would only keep their promises!"

The Indian servants entered the *sala* bearing large trays with sweets and fruit, earthen jugs of wine and the familiar silver tea service. Untrained to serve at formal occasions, the servants clumsily passed the wine.

The Governor offered the first toast to the health of the Russian Emperor, Alexander.

Nikolai responded with a toast to the Spanish King, Carlos IV. The toasts followed one after another, the men standing in a semi-circle around the seated Governor. The ladies did not drink but were offered tiny cups of chocolate as they clustered around Doña Ignacia and Concha.

Several native musicians entered the *sala* carrying their guitars, drums and Indian flutes. The air of excitement and anticipation suddenly permeated the room. This feeling was well known to Nikolai, although he no longer experienced it himself. But he remembered it well. He remembered his young bride Annushka glowing with anticipation, waiting for the orchestra to strike the first chords of the Grand Polonaise which opened the balls at Court. He remembered her small hand, gloved in white kid, trembling over his as he led her to their place in the procession directly after the Princes of the Blood.

Only three years ago...

That feeling of anticipation was here too, among these young Spanish women and the officers of the garrison. It shone on the face of Concha, whose eyes had been riveted on him.

The servants removed the straw rugs, exposing the stone floor, as the musicians struck their instruments. Music, strange to the Russians, filled the *sala*. The unusual rhythms, like pulsating blood in one's temples, sounded almost savage. Several young women, Concha among them, left their seats at the wall and one by one entered the center of the room stomping their high heels rhythmically against the tile floor.

The young women moved in a stately manner, their backs straight, their arms raised gracefully over their heads, accentuating the stomping of their feet with the clicking sound of castañets.

Nikolai watched the fandango, the regal yet primitive dance, with fascination.

Concha danced with deep concentration. Not once did a smile break on her lovely face. Not once did a frivolous glance escape from under her arched brows. She manipulated her voluminous ruffled skirts with grace, her castañets clicking rhythmically.

Several young officers soon joined the girls. They too held their backs ramrod straight, their boots striking out the rhythm on the resounding floor. They danced around the girls, never touching them, but looking passionately into their proud upturned faces.

Nikolai suddenly felt jealous of the handsome young officer dancing opposite Concha, twirling around her, consuming her with his passionate dark eyes, his boots beating fast against the tile. And Concha, both sensuous and demure, her white neck curved like a swan's, so lovely, so desirable...

"How do you like the fandango, Señor?" It was Concha's father.

"Breathtaking! So different from anything that I have ever seen! Señorita Concha is a superb dancer!"

The music reached a frenzied crescendo as the dancers twirled and tapped their heels even faster. Then abruptly it ended. "Olé," the audience shouted.

An Indian began to sing. It was a complicated melody full of half tones and wails. It was a song devoid of any distinctive melody, barbaric and raw. Nikolai, brought up in the tradition of baroque music of Vivaldi, Bach and Mozart, felt assaulted by it. And yet, he liked it. In its plaintive sound he could hear the yearning of his own soul, furious yearnings for power, and dominance. And for the love of a woman.

As if knowing how he felt, Concha came to his side. Her face was flushed with the dance and she fanned herself rapidly. Her full lips were partly open as she breathed shallowly.

"She's not a child. She's a woman, ready to be loved," Nikolai thought, watching her.

The singer stopped and the musicians struck their guitars again. The familiar melody of a quadrille fran caise filled the *sala*.

"I know how to dance the quadrille," Concha said. "Would you like to dance with me?"

"I'd be delighted!" Nikolai felt suddenly carefree. Turning to the Governor, he said, "May I have your permission, Your Excellency to take my sword off?"

"But of course, *amigo*. How else can you dance?" Arillaga chuckled. Nikolai unbuckled his ceremonial sword. He took Concha's ungloved hand into his and led her to the center of the room. As the other couples began to assemble for the quadrille, Nikolai removed his white gloves. He wanted to feel the warmth of Concha's hand, to touch her skin, to be one with her. "My God, I'm acting like a young lad!" he thought, bemused.

A supper was served later in the open gallery. The musicians continued to strum and sing, but the guests' interests were now focused on food.

The women seated themselves opposite the men at a long table covered with a colorful tablecloth. Rezanov was placed between the Governor and the Commandant, facing Doña

Ignacia and the other senior ladies. Concha was far away, at the end of the table among the unmarried girls and children. Despite the distance, their eyes still often met.

Servants brought in a continuous flow of huge platters of roasted meat, partridge stuffed with maize and almonds, followed by trays of baked breads and cakes and pyramids of tortillas.

Nikolai hated drinking and gorging feasts when an intelligent conversation was reduced to shouted banalities between bites of food and sips of wine.

As if reading his thoughts, Arillaga turned to him, saying in French, "Do relax, Monsieur Rezanov. Tomorrow we'll discuss our affairs. I know precisely what you want." The old man smiled but there was no promise in his eyes. Nikolai did not like it. "He will never agree to trade," he thought in discouragement.

At last the banquet was over. The guests moved to a walled patio filled with flowers. The water splashed in the fountain and the floral fragrance mixed pleasantly with the sea air.

The musicians, standing in the arched doorways, strummed their guitars softly. Nikolai searched for Concha in the crowd.

"I wanted to talk to you all evening," he said, offering her his arm and leading her slowly toward the fountain. The murmur of the water would make it impossible for others to overhear their conversation.

"I know. I've been waiting." He could not resist the temptation to tease her.

"Oh? Perhaps you know also what I was going to say?"

"Yes, I think so." She raised her luminous eyes to him. They were full of trust. Nikolai had a lump in his throat.

"I want you to marry me," he said quietly.

"I kept praying you would say that," she replied. "I love you."

"Conchita..." he was suddenly speechless. "I've done it!" he thought as he squeezed her hand tightly, his throat dry. "I must talk to your father," he said.

"No, not yet, *querido*. Give him a chance to get to know you the way my mother and brothers do. I'll tell you when you can talk to him."

"Do you really want to marry me?" he asked in a low

voice. "I am so much older than you...I am forty-two. I could be your father."

"I don't care! I've been in love with you from the moment I met you. I loved you even before I knew that you were free," she whispered fiercely.

"Your Excellency," the Governor raised his voice above the noise of conversation and laughter. "I beg your indulgence, Sir, but I must retire. Your physician recommends that I rest." He stood with visible difficulty. He patted Concha on her cheek and shaking hands with Nikolai, left the patio accompanied by two of his aides.

It was a signal for the Russians to leave also.

"Until tomorrow," Concha whispered from behind her fan.

Nikolai paused before the padres, hoping for an explanation why the provisions were not yet delivered, but the padres offered only superficial pleasantries.

The Argüello family followed the Russians to the plaza.

"*Hasta la vista, señores, regresen mañana a la misma hora para tomar una taza de chocolate!*" Señora de Argüello kept saying cordially, as the Russians settled in the governor's carriage.

Nikolai saluted the ladies. Concha, hiding her face from her parents behind her fan, formed a kiss with her lips.

For that moment, Nikolai forgot about trade and priests and diplomacy. It was enough to know that Concha would be his.

Chapter 33

"What have I done!" Nikolai thought later that night in the privacy of his cabin. "I proposed marriage to a woman I hardly know, who's young enough to be my daughter!" He knew that he desired Concha more than he had ever desired any woman, including Annushka, but did he love Concha?

Nikolai always prided himself on being able to face the most shattering truths about himself. Would he be interested in marrying Concha if he had not seen the Argüello land, he asked himself. Yes, he thought. Now that he had been accepted by Concha he felt as if he had wanted to marry her even before he became aware of the Argüellos' holdings.

"I am a lucky man," he thought. "Concha loves me. She gave me another chance for happiness."

Next morning, the Governor sent a message that he was ill.

Nikolai had to be patient. He decided to concentrate on winning the friendship of Concha's father.

It proved to be much simpler than he had anticipated. Eager to show off his horses, Commandant Argüello invited him to spend a day on the family horse ranch nearby. Nikolai readily accepted the invitation. Accompanied by Don Luis and an aide, they rode to the ranch.

The well-groomed horses, snorting joyously, trotted along. The road twisted along the low hills covered with a bright quilt of wild flowers. Somewhere high above their heads a lark sang, filling the sky with his trills. They rode at an easy pace, Nikolai noting the fields of sprouting corn and winter wheat with an appreciative eye. He gazed at the bountiful landscape, thinking that some of it might soon be his.

The *ranchito*, as Argüello affectionately called it, was huge. Aside from its orchards and cultivated fields, it contained a special arena for training horses, enclosed on three sides by the adobe walled stalls. Indian grooms lived in a small house facing the arena on the fourth side. Beyond the walls, spread endless pastures enclosed by long wooden fences.

"I wanted to show you something very unusual," Argüello said. "I have several horses here, who are trained in the old method of the Spanish riding school. Have you ever seen it?"

"Bring Alcazar," Argüello called to the Indian groom who approached. The groom rushed into one of the stables and presently came out leading an Arabian stallion with a gleaming chestnut coat.

Nikolai gazed in admiration as Argüello approached the stallion, patted its neck affectionately and, reaching into his pocket, produced a piece of dark sugar. He offered it to Alcazar. The horse neighed gently, and scooped up the sugar with its soft pink lips.

Nikolai nodded and smiled. He and Concha's father would be friends.

When the groom finished saddling Alcazar, the Commandant walked the horse to the center of the ring. He jumped into the saddle, showing surprising lightness despite his stocky body and rode Alcazar around the arena, making the horse step sideways, criss-crossing its legs at a precise height angle as he trotted; then changing the gait again, he made the horse repeat several figures at different speeds. At the end of the faultless performance, Argüello made his stallion kneel on one leg and lower his head to the ground in a graceful bow.

Nikolai applauded. "May I try one of your horses? *Dressage* is very popular in St. Petersburg."

"Oh, then you know how to ride in the old Spanish way?" Argüello innocently believed only Spanish horsemen knew the art.

"I was privileged to learn when I was in Her Majesty's Horse Guards," Nikolai replied.

"*Bueno*. Bring out Duchessa," Argüello commanded.

The groom scampered back to the stables and shortly brought out a milky-white mare, already saddled. Her pink nostrils quivered as she followed the groom skittishly. Her small delicate head moved nervously and she trembled with excitement.

Nikolai walked slowly toward Duchessa, making soothing sounds with his tongue. He too, caressed her neck and muzzle, feeling her tremble even more under his touch.

"Now, now, little white dove," he whispered gently. "you are going to show them what you can do!" He slipped into the saddle, certain the horse would obey.

He patted Duchessa once more and then spurred her into a sudden gallop around the arena. He wanted to relax the horse, and at the same time, learn about her responsiveness. When he was satisfied, he turned her toward the center of the arena. He guided her through several classic figures of the *haute ecole.*

Duchessa obeyed him flawlessly. "*Que bonita muchacha!*" Nikolai patted Duchessa's neck.

"Señor, you would do honor to our old art even if you were to appear before the Spanish King!" Argüello exclaimed as Nikolai dismounted.

"I must return the compliment, Señor," Rezanov retorted, giving the reins to the groom. "The Russian Emperor would have been impressed by your performance. He's a connoisseur of *dressage*. He rides that way himself."

Argüello was flattered. "I would like to see that," he said.

"Perhaps it could be arranged someday," Nikolai smiled.

Hours later, after a meal in the shade of the oaks, the Commandant began uneasily. "I am aware, Señor, of your desire to trade with us. My son informed me of your needs, but my hands are tied. I must respect the Governor's wishes. The best I can do is to continue to supply your crew with all the food you need while you're here in Alta California. I can do no more."

"Thank you for your frankness," Nikolai said. He knew that he had made a friend of Concha's father. "I could ask for nothing more."

It was almost dark when they returned to the presidio.

Concha intercepted Nikolai before he could pay his respects to Doña Ignacia. The Governor was indeed indisposed, she hurried to report. "However," she whispered, "there is tremendous pressure on him to change his attitude. He is besieged by the women, who beg him to permit the barter of the presidio surplus food for the Russian cargo. But so far the Governor refused their pleas. He insists on his lifelong obedience to the law. He's very stubborn."

Nikolai's spirits sank. Now, it seemed, only the priests could save Novo-Arkhangelsk. But the priests remained silent.

Concha kept Nikolai well informed. She told him that Arillaga had sent a courier to the Viceroy in Mexico for special instructions. It was also she who disclosed that her father had argued with the Governor on behalf of the Russians. But even Concha could not find out why the priests were procrastinating. Nikolai fumed with impatience. He was no nearer his goal now that he had been six weeks before.

Inaction made him reckless. Well, there was one thing he could accomplish. He decided on a bold move.

"I am going to ask your father for your hand in marriage," he told Concha the following evening.

She paled.

"You haven't changed your mind, have you?" he asked in alarm.

"No, *querido*, I love you. But it's much too soon. My father might refuse."

"We'll have to take the chance." Nikolai said, his blue eyes steely with determination. "If you are willing to fight by my side, he won't refuse."

"I am willing," she whispered.

Next day, Nikolai arrived at the Argüello's house alone. The chocolate was already steaming in its silver pot and the children waited impatiently for their portions of the sweet drink. Nikolai noticed that Governor Arillaga was absent from the company. Obviously, he avoided him.

"I would like to have a word with you in private, Señor Commandante," Nikolai said, bowing formally to Concha's father.

Commander Argüello readily stood up. "Please come to my study," he said, opening the door. He indicated a chair next to a roughly-hewn desk, taking his own seat behind the desk.

"Yes, Your Excellency, what can I do for you?" he inquired pleasantly. "Won't you sit down?"

"No, *gracias*," Nikolai remained standing. "Señor Argüello, I humbly request the honor of having the hand of your daughter, Maria Concepción, in marriage," he bowed.

The Commandant appeared stunned.

Nikolai waited. At last Argüello cleared his throat, "You confound me, Señor. I don't know what to say...I must think..."

"By all means," Nikolai said easily. "I await your answer on my ship, Señor Commandante." He bowed and left the room.

In the *sala* he kissed Doña Ignacia's hand. "I must leave at once," he said. "Thank you for your hospitality." He turned to Concha and kissed her hand without a word. Then he left the room. Don Luis ran after him. The women heard the diminishing sound of horsehooves as they rode away.

Concha's face drained of color. Her hand trembled as she poured herself a glass of lemonade. The door of Argüello's study flung open and he appeared in its frame.

"The Russian wants to marry Concha," he announced, still stunned by the proposal. The women kept silent. He broke the silence, addressing them both. "Have you nothing to say?"

"*Santissima Virgen,*" Doña Ignacia whispered.

"I do," Concha said bravely. Trying to keep the tremor out of her voice she said, "I love Señor Rezanov. I beg you Papá to give your consent to our marriage."

It was a sleepless night in the Argüello household.

The Commandant, Doña Ignacia and three of their eldest sons gathered around the long table in the *sala*. Concha was sent to her room to await their decision.

"*Who is this Rezanov?*" Argüello asked in distress. It bothered him that he liked the man, but what if this Russian were an adventurer? How could any father entrust his daughter to such a man?

Doña Ignacia also was going through painful moments of soul-searching. She blamed herself for having contributed to Concha's falling in love with Nikolai. She should have known better; she should have better supervised her daughter. Instead she had allowed her to be in the constant company of the handsome diplomat. It flattered her that such a worldly man was losing his head over her daughter. But she kept her thoughts to herself now, afraid of her husband's wrath.

The younger Argüellos had no reservations about Nikolai. They already imagined themselves his aides-de-camp, living in St. Petersburg. They were eager to leave the presidio for a more exciting life outside its walls. They urged their father to give his consent to the marriage.

But Argüello was listening to them only partially. "The young are so impulsive and shallow! They see only one side of the coin, the bright, sparkling side which promises adventure," he thought.

"He's too old for Concha. He's almost three times her age," Argüello brought out his strongest argument. But Don Luis quickly challenged. "You've told us yourself, Papá, it's better for the marriage when the man is older. Remember?" Argüello had to agree that indeed, he had said that to his sons at the engagement party of their fifty-year-old uncle who was to marry a fourteen year-old girl.

"He's not a Catholic. The Church will never allow such a marriage," Argüello tried.

Doña Ignacia suddenly spoke. "Señor Rezanov's religion is very much like ours. Russians go to confession, take communion, and pray to the Virgin. Only they call her the Mother of God. And they believe in Heaven and Hell. Señor Rezanov told me that."

Argüello sighed deeply. It appeared to him that his entire family wanted Concha to be married to the Russian.

"Then there is the language," he began, but his sons smiled. "Nikolai speaks Spanish and French too, Father. Russian nobles all speak many languages. And we'll learn them too."

Don Luis put his arm around his father's shoulders. "Papá, it will be good for everyone to be related to Señor Rezanov. He will see to it that our presidio never lacks anything. He'll send us shiploads of goods from all over the world—once he's our relative. And Concha, she'll have an exciting life in St. Petersburg. But what will she have here? A dull life on a military post. She loves this Russian. Don't break her heart, Papá!"

Argüello listened to his son's pleas, astonished at his family's unanimous support for Nikolai. Even his wife, who had never expressed her opinion, good wife that she was, even she seemed to favor the marriage.

"We'll never see our Concha if she goes to Russia," he

brought the last argument, already surrendering to his family's pressure.

"If she marries someone from Madrid, or even Mexico, we'll never see her either," Doña Ignacia murmured, dabbing her eyes with a handkerchief. "It's the duty of a wife to follow her husband."

Finally Argüello said wearily, "This is too difficult a problem to solve without the advice of Don José. He is Concha's Godfather. He will know best the consequences of Concha's marriage to a foreigner."

Doña Ignacia sighed with relief. "Yes, he's so wise. Let the Governor tell us what to do."

Alone in her room Concha paced the floor. She tried to rest on her narrow bed only to jump up and start pacing again. She could barely hear the murmur of voices from the *sala*, the thick walls muffling the sound.

Time dragged. Unable to endure the suspense, Concha burst into the *sala*. The family members were still seated where she had left them, her mother's eyes puffy from crying, her father's face brooding. Concha thought he looked bewildered. She quickly glanced at Don Luis, her best friend in the family, but he averted his eyes. Obviously nothing had been decided.

She ran to her father and knelt before his chair. She grasped his rough tobacco-stained hands and covered them with kisses.

"Papá, *querido*, please let me marry Nikolai. I love him, Papá." She began to sob.

Doña Ignacia emitted a long wail, worthy of her Indian servants, as she too, burst into tears. Only moments before she supported Nikolai's proposal, but the realization that indeed she might never see Concha again overwhelmed her.

"Conchita, *hija mia*, we'll lose you forever," she wailed, swaying from side to side.

Argüello grimaced. He never knew what to do about tears.

"We'll talk to Don José tomorrow," he said meekly, patting Concha's head.

"Don José? Why should Don José decide who I am to marry?" Concha challenged. She crouched at her father's feet, suddenly humble and pleading.

"You always told me Papá, that you loved me. You always told me that your main purpose in life was to make us happy," she indicated herself and her brothers.

"I believed you. Until now, you *did* make me happy. But why did you suddenly change? Why don't you want me to be happy now? Don't you love me anymore?"

"Conchita! Don't talk like that to your father!" Doña Ignacia cried out.

"What have I done, Papá, to deserve such a punishment? Have I been a bad daughter? Have I been disobedient? Why do you want to deny me my happiness?"

"Go to your room, *chica*," Argüello said wearily.

"No, Papá. I won't go to my room. I am not a little girl anymore. I want to marry Nikolai and I shall, even if Don José disapproves," she said with quiet dignity, standing up. "I won't beg anymore, Papá. If you want me to be happy, you'll give your permission for us to marry."

"I want you to be happy," Argüello whispered, surrendering.

"Papá!" Concha threw herself into his arms, tears of joy running down her cheeks.

The Governor realized that Rezanov had outwitted him. He knew it the moment Argüello had informed him of Nikolai's proposal and of Concha's determination to marry him.

The old Governor stretched on his bed, his ailing foot propped up on several pillows. A light breeze from the bay moved the straw shade on his open window. Through its loosely woven design he could see the sparkling water and the Russian ship anchored below the cliff.

He began to chuckle. He no longer had to deny his people the goods they needed. "He's very clever, this Russian," Arillaga thought. "He solved his problem, my problem and got the prettiest girl in California, all in one stroke."

From the deck of the *Younona* Nikolai watched a large cavalcade leave the presidio early next morning escorted by a platoon of soldiers. He presumed correctly that the family was on its way to the mission. He took it as a good omen. Had he been rejected, he would have received a formal letter of refusal by now. Instead, the Argüellos were going to the mission, perhaps for a blessing. He watched the carriage and its escort disappear beyond the hills. There was nothing else to do but wait.

Nikolai gave free reign to his imagination. He thought of the rich lands beyond the hills. In his mind he already saw blond men and women and tow-headed children bustling in the verdant fields and pastures. He imagined the sound of bells from the onion-shaped belfries of the churches that would be built. He saw the Russian Imperial eagle spreading its wide wings over the American continent, and finally, he saw himself, titled and celebrated as the builder of the new Pacific Empire, his beautiful Concha at his side.

Chapter 34

Concha sat in the corner of the carriage, her head against its cracked leather upholstery. She kept her eyes closed, pretending to be asleep.

She was determined that nothing would stop her from becoming Nikolai's wife. Should the padres oppose the marriage, she would run away and marry Nikolai aboard the *Younona*. Captain Khvostov could marry them; she had heard that captains were empowered to perform marriages aboard their ships.

The rhythmic creak of the old carriage with its cradle-like rocking movement, the monotonous clopping sound of the horses' hooves upon the country road, had a hypnotic effect on Concha. She began to doze.

"I am Doña Maria Concepción, Contessa de Rezanov y Moraga," she whispered as an image of herself curtsying before the Russian Tsar floated through her consciousness.

The priests were expecting them. Argüello knew they learned about everything that went on at the presidio through the Indians who traveled between the mission and the presidio every day.

Concha was sent to Father Landaeta, who was waiting for her in the confessional. Her parents closeted themselves with Fathers Uriá and de la Cueva.

The priests advised the family to accept the proposal, but postpone the wedding until permission to marry was obtained from the Pope. They suggested a year's delay.

"This is the best thing that could have happened to us all, Señor Commandante," Father Uriá lowered his voice confidentially. "Conchita will never find anyone more important than this Russian. Besides, through him our presidio will acquire the attention of the Russian Tsar himself, the richest monarch in the world! We will trade with Russia without breaking the law because we'll be trading with your family, Señor!"

"Then you have no objection to this marriage?"

"None. It will be beneficial for all concerned."

"But what if the Pope won't allow it?" Doña Ignacia asked timidly.

"Don't worry, Señora. The Pope will bless the union. We live in the nineteenth century, Señora; we have become much more tolerant of one another's religion. Concha will remain Catholic of course, and their children will be raised as Catholics."

The fathers smiled at the Argüellos encouragingly.

Concha returned from confession radiant with happiness. Father Landaeta had no objections to her marriage to Nikolai.

She was euphoric. There were smiles again on her parents' faces, although her mother's eyes were still veiled in tears. The priests were full of good wishes, smiling fondly at her. Concha wanted to embrace the whole world.

She was not told, however, that her wedding would be delayed for a year.

The Russians on the *Younona* were tense. No one was allowed ashore. The captain was prepared to take the ship out to sea. Without exchanging confidences with Rezanov, the captain suspected that the fate of their expedition depended on Argüello's consent to Nikolai's proposal of marriage.

The officers discussed the situation. They could not comprehend Rezanov's motives in proposing marriage to Concha.

"She's a beauty, of course, but it's hardly enough reason to marry her," Khvostov said.

"I agree, it is rather odd that such an ambitious man would want to tie himself to an uneducated foreigner," Davidov said. He had learned from Don Luis about Nikolai's proposal. At the time, Davidov had barely managed to hide his astonishment; such a misalliance was too obvious. Even he, the son of a minor noble family with little wealth, would not have considered marrying someone like Concha. But Rezanov! "He must have lost his head over her," Davidov suggested.

"A wagon train is approaching," a lookout called out from the crow's nest on the mast.

"Any soldiers? Cannon?" Khvostov shouted.

"No, sir, only the oxen pulling a dozen large wagons. The monks are driving."

"The monks! Thank God!" Khvostov knocked on Rezanov's door. "Nikolai Petrovich! A wagon train is approaching. I believe it's our long overdue delivery from the mission."

Nikolai flung his door open. The front of his silk shirt was unbuttoned down to his waist, the curly hair on his chest golden in the bright sun of the afternoon.

A smile slowly spread over his lean face as he grabbed Khvostov's hand. "At last!"

The captain vigorously shook his hand. "Congratulations, Sir! I wish many years of happiness to you and Señorita Concha!"

"You *know*?" Nikolai was taken aback. He thought no one knew about his proposal.

"Yes, Nikolai Petrovich. We all know. Don Luis could not contain himself and told us. Congratulations!"

Nikolai flushed, embarrassed. "Wait, wait, Captain. I haven't heard yet from her father. But I do believe that the delivery of the provisions is a good sign."

"Of course, Nikolai Petrovich. This is exactly how I see it. *Mnogy leta!*"

The wagon train slowly descended to the beach. Timofei Tarakanov was already waiting with a boat for the priests. They came aboard the *Younona* with a list of items they intended to buy, written in Latin.

Dr. Langsdorff immediately assumed his role as an interpreter. The sailors began to unload the wagons.

Then other crates, filled with hardware and items needed by the mission, had been placed in the nets and swung over the bulwarks into the waiting boats. The wagons were reloaded. The powerful oxen strained and pulled as the wagons creaked, rolling slowly on their great wooden wheels back to the mission.

The monks offered no explanation why they had procrastinated with their deliveries. Nikolai decided not to ask. "The food is here and there will be more to come; but I'm sure they were scheming to get my cargo for nothing! They *knew* about the war!"

The officers toasted one another with vodka, celebrating the successful conclusion of their deal with the mission.

Suddenly a lookout shouted that a group of horsemen had appeared on the beach. The Russians recognized Commandant Argüello and Don Luis among the riders.

A launch was hastily lowered to bring the guests aboard.

"May I have a word with you in private, Your Excellency," Argüello requested formally. Nikolai showed him to his cabin and gently closed the door.

"I am proud to welcome you into my family...Nikolai," Argüello stammered pronouncing Rezanov's name.

"Thank you José Darió," Nikolai said shaking his hand.

"I'm glad you didn't call me Papá," Argüello laughed.

"Likely because I am your junior by two or three years only, " Nikolai grinned.

Concha waited impatiently for Nikolai's arrival. She had pried from her mother that her wedding would be postponed for a year.

A whole year! It was a lifetime. Concha was unwilling to wait that long and she needed Nikolai's support against her parents' decision.

"We must wait," Nikolai admonished her gently. "Don't cry *querida*, my dearest one. The two years will pass so fast that you won't even notice!"

"Two years?" Concha jumped to her feet in anger. "My mother said it was to be one year!"

"No, my darling. It will have to be at least two years," he said with a sigh. "It will take that long to sail back to Russia and then return to Alta California. I would like nothing better than to marry you now, at this very minute but it's impossible. We must wait until all the necessary permissions are granted. It takes time."

"Why do we need further permission?" she demanded. "My parents have agreed, the Governor has agreed, my father-confessor has no objection. Who else is there who must meddle in our love for one another?"

Nikolai smiled indulgently before replying. "*Querida, oiga*, listen to me. There are two serious obstacles that we must face. The difference in our religions is one, but equally important is the other. It's against the law in my country to marry a foreigner. Without solving these two problems, our marriage will be invalid in the eyes of your Church and my country."

Concha dissolved in sobs. A wave of tenderness swept over Nikolai as he comforted the forlorn girl. "Don't cry, *querida*. Your father has agreed that we become officially betrothed right away so we can be together as much as possible. But the sooner I leave for Russia the sooner I'll return. Time will pass quickly. At your age two years means nothing," he continued, kissing her wet face and cold little hands. "Let's go back to the family. We must plan our engagement party. I want it to be the finest, the biggest fiesta in Alta California, full of music and dancing!"

Concha nodded, finally smiling through her still wet eyes. "*te amo querido*," she whispered.

"I love you too," he replied, kissing her mouth for the first time.

The Indian runners spread the news of the engagement of Concha to the Russian envoy and delivered the invitations to the fiesta. The guests began to prepare for the long journey, some from as far as the missions of San Juan Capistrano and San Diego.

Meanwhile, Argüello invited Nikolai to move ashore and stay with his family in their spacious house. Nikolai accepted gladly. To stay under the same roof with Concha, it would be heaven, he thought, amused at his sudden youthful sentiments.

Concha and Doña Ignacia locked themselves in Concha's room surrounded by other female members of their household, working on a gown, which Concha designed herself, following Nikolai's description of St. Petersburg's fashion. She planned to surprise Nikolai with her creation and prove to everyone that she would make a perfect consort for the Ambassador of the Imperial Court.

The guests began to arrive days before the celebration. They were quickly accommodated within the garrison and among the neighboring ranchos. Their Indian servants were allowed to camp on the plaza. Soon the plaza was dotted with dozens of colorful tents. At night it was ablaze with campfires, reeking with odors of people, horses, cooking, all mixed with the faint scent of nightblooming jasmine.

Mountains of food had been prepared and huge quantities of wine in stone jugs were stored along the galleries where long tables were set for two hundred guests. The furniture in the *sala* was moved around to clear the space for dancing.

At dusk the guests began to gather on the plaza. The din of the rapid Spanish voices and the neighing of the horses filled the air but once inside the Argüello garden, the guests quieted down.

Finally, everyone had arrived. Don Luis signaled, and the great doors of the house were closed.

The women curtsied before the Governor seated at the far end of the *sala*, then proceeded to the row of chairs against the walls, glancing discretely at Rezanov. The men, bowing to the Governor and the Russians, remained standing, spreading deeper into the *sala*.

Nikolai and his officers, all wearing their parade uniforms, sat next to the Governor. Nikolai was growing impatient. The whole day he had not seen Concha. Where was she? He kept glancing at the door to the family's private quarters, waiting for her to enter. "I am behaving like a lovelorn fool," he thought wryly, amazed at himself.

The Governor rose from his chair with an effort and introduced Nikolai and his entourage. Then, taking his seat again, he motioned to Commandant Argüello, "Carry on, this is your fiesta, *viejito!*"

Concha's father greeted his guests cordially. "This is a happy occasion, *amigos*," he said. "I have given my consent to the marriage of my daughter Maria Concepción to Señor Nikolai Rezanov."

Concha, accompanied by her mother, entered the *sala*. There was a low murmur of voices as the guests reacted to her appearance. She wore a straight-flowing, high-waisted white satin gown with a low decolletage in dramatic contrast to the ruffled dresses of bright colors of other young women. No girl at the presidio had ever dared to wear such a low decolletage which showed the tops of her small firm breasts. Concha's glossy black hair cascaded down her back, arranged with simplicity in the manner of the goddess Juno-Younona, so different from the corkscrew curls of other women. She wore no jewelry but a few fresh sprigs of jasmine in her hair.

"She's truly breathtakingly beautiful," Nikolai thought. "She'll shine at the Court."

Concha stopped in front of her father. He took her by the hand and led her to Nikolai who had left his seat and stood waiting.

"Conchita, do you wish to marry Señor Rezanov?" Argüello asked.

"I do, Father," she replied in a cool clear voice.

"And you, Señor, do you wish to marry my daughter?"

"Indeed, I do," Nikolai said smiling. "I thank you for giving me your permission. And yours, Doña Ignacia." He bowed to Concha's mother.

"*Bueno*! I proclaim that my daughter is betrothed to Señor Nikolai Rezanov. Now let's celebrate!"

The banquet began. Native servants passed the dishes over the heads of the tightly packed guests.

Concha sat through the banquet with a demure smile, raising her glass in response to every toast but not drinking herself.

"She has the makings of a great lady," Nikolai thought proudly, watching his fiancée. "She knows intuitively how to conduct herself in public."

"I wish this were our wedding day," Concha whispered to Nikolai taking his hand under the table.

"I have a gift for you," he said. "It is a ring, a very special ring. It was given to me many years ago by Catherine the Great when I was a Guards officer." He slipped a gold ring with a large emerald surrounded by diamonds off his finger. "It's too big for you *querida*. I'll have it made smaller."

"It's magnificent," she whispered admiring the ring. "But don't make it smaller. I'll wear it around my neck as a talisman. When we are married, I'll return it to you. You'll give me another ring, made just for me. But I'll cherish this one until your return." She kissed the ring. Then she strung it on a narrow velvet ribbon from her coiffure and tied the ribbon around her neck. The ring slipped out of sight below the neckline of her dress and hung between her breasts. Nikolai imagined it nestled close to her heart, taking warmth from her body.

"I want you to love me forever. Promise?" Concha said in a low voice.

"I promise," Nikolai replied.

The musicians filed into the *sala* and the dancing began. Nikolai and Concha led the dancers in the French Quadrille. Concha gazed at Nikolai, oblivious of others. "I am so happy," she sighed as he whirled her in the first figure of the dance.

The quadrille over, the servants passed tiny glasses of lemonade to the perspiring dancers. Nikolai beckoned to Don Luis. It was time to spring his surprise on the guests. Don Luis, Nikolai's accomplice, quietly left the *sala*.

Next moment, the doors flung open and a band of Russians burst into the room with shrill Tatar whistles. They were led by Timofei, running fast in a squatting position, throwing his legs in front of him, a huge smile on his handsome face, the black patch over his wasted eye giving him a devil-may-care appearance.

Behind him came several more men from the crew of the *Younona*, also *v prisyadki*, strumming their balalaiki. They whistled and hooted, filling the *sala* with Russian exuberance. They were dressed in new red and blue and yellow shirts with embroidered collars, sashed with multicolored tasseled cords. They looked strong, towering over the more delicate statured Spaniards.

Nikolai winked at his officers. The surprise was well received by their hosts.

"Can you do this?" Concha asked, indicating some daring movement of Timofei's dance.

Nikolai laughed. "Heavens, no! This requires a special talent that I don't possess. Besides, only the lower classes dance in such a way. Too bad, but the nobility have adopted the European dances, waltzes, mazurkas, minuets and turn their noses at the truly *Russian dances.*"

"Too bad. I like your peasant dances. When we have our children, let's teach them all the dances and songs of our two countries," she said.

"*Querida,*" he whispered, thinking, "she's going to make me very happy!"

Two days after the fiesta Nikolai paced the Argüello garden, waiting for the last guests to depart. "We must be on our way back to Novo-Arkhangelsk," he thought. The ship was fully laden with provisions, waiting only for a few heads of cattle and sheep to be herded from the mission. It was time to leave, yet Nikolai stalled with announcing his decision to Concha.

Then a courier arrived with secret letters from the Viceroy in Mexico.

Governor Arillaga brooded over the letters, secluding himself in his room.

Nikolai paced the gallery, an uneasy feeling of disaster gnawing at him. It was no more a secret that Russia and Spain were at war, each being an ally of the opposing parties.

He heard footsteps along the gallery. Argüello entered, his face grim. "I was looking for you Nikolai. Please join me in Don José's room."

Nikolai bowed to his future father-in-law and followed him to the Governor's quarters.

"Come in, *amigo*," Arillaga greeted him with a false joviality. He was sitting near the window, his ailing foot propped on a footstool. "I want to confide in you the news concerning us all, but especially you, who are so far away from your native shores."

Nikolai took a chair opposite the Governor.

"There are several dispatches, most of them at least six months old," the Governor began. "The first one deals with Spanish affairs and affects you only indirectly. On October 21, 1805, to be exact, the Spanish and French fleets were jointly defeated by England in a great naval battle at Trafalgar. We lost twenty or more ships of the line. This, alas, ends our Spanish superiority on the seas. But it was a costly victory for the British as well. Along with several of their ships, they lost Horatio Nelson, their best admiral," the governor continued. "We have been harassed by Lord Nelson for years, so his death, for Spain at least, is good news. It almost balances our loss of ships." He sighed. "How barbaric that we must rejoice at another's death."

Nikolai remained silent. He was waiting for the other news, perhaps the news about Russia.

"The other dispatch concerns your country, Don Nikolai," continued Arillaga. "Apparently, in December, 1805 there was a battle near the village of Austerlitz between Napoleon Bonaparte and the Emperors of Austria and Russia. The European newspapers refer to it as 'the battle of the three Emperors.' *Entonces*, Napoleon was the victor. He made the Austrians plead for a separate peace and forced your Tsar to flee for his life. The newspapers say that Tsar Alexander barely escaped, riding through the night, accompanied only by two or three of his aides. I don't know how true it is. As you know, the newspapers tend to exaggerate." He poured a glass of water and gulped it thirstily. He detested being the bearer of bad news.

Nikolai was silent. The youthful face of Tsar Alexander

floated before his mind's eye. "It's all very grave, Your Excellency," he finally said. "However, I do hope that the situation might have changed. The battle of Austerlitz, when did you say it was fought?"

"Last year, December 2, 1805."

"Perhaps now, in May, 1806, six months later, a peace treaty has already been signed by France. It's entirely possible."

"I certainly hope so," Arillaga agreed. "Don José Darió and I have already decided to treat the situation as if the peace treaty has been indeed arranged. Since we have no orders regarding your ship, we will ignore the state of war between our countries."

"Nikolai is one of my own family," said Argüello.

"Precisely," the Governor nodded.

"Thank you for your confidence, Don José," Nikolai tried to smile but there was no joy in his voice as he continued, "I must leave for Russia immediately. I will have to cross the Asian continent by land now, instead of sailing along the trade routes...In case our hopes for a peace treaty have been premature," he added.

The three men stared at the globe. Argüello broke their silence. "Yes, *mi hijo*, you must leave. *Vaya con Dios.* Does Concha know?"

"Not yet," Nikolai said sadly.

Long after the house grew quiet for the night, Concha slipped into Nikolai's room.

It was dark, the rain beating loudly against the tile roof.

Nikolai was unaware of Concha's presence until she touched his face with her lips. He awoke with a start.

"Sh-sh!" she whispered, kneeling at the side of his bed. "I came to say goodbye."

He could not see her features. Her long nightdress was a barely visible shape in the darkness of the room.

"I couldn't sleep," she continued in a low voice. "I had to be with you." She threw herself on his chest. He could smell the fragrance of her hair which spilled over his face. He embraced her, searching for her lips. It was the first time that he had really held her in his arms, kissing her as he had so often yearned to do.

"You must go, *querida*," he whispered hoarsely. "No one

must know of this visit. Go, darling, before someone discovers you."

"I love you so much!" she breathed against his chest, unwilling to leave.

"I love you too. But you must leave."

Concha obeyed. She slipped out of his room as silently as she had appeared.

Nikolai was eager to be on his way. He stood on the bridge of the *Younona*, invigorated by the rising brisk wind, feeling well-rested.

The crew, too, felt good. The men sang as they pulled the ropes raising the sails, happy that they were homeward bound. They smiled at one another as the anchors crept up and the *Younona*, towed by her two longboats, moved slowly on toward the open sea.

Nikolai trained his telescope on the presidio. He saw a group of riders gallop out of the gates toward the cliff opposite the rocks, alive with barking sealions. He could clearly distinguish Argüello and Don Luis among the horsemen, but his eyes were on Concha. She was attired in her familiar red dress riding sidesaddle.

Nikolai smiled. "How she has changed," he thought. A child only two months ago, she had matured under his very eyes. He watched her galloping alone, way ahead of the group. Her long dark hair was loose, undone by the wind.

Concha reached the cliff's highest point ahead of the others. Deliberately alone, she reined her horse roughly, waiting for the ship to pass below.

As the *Younona* reached the cliff, the presidio saluted her departure with seven evenly spaced salvos. Nikolai saw small puffs of smoke from the shore battery. The echo repeated the sound, disturbing the sealions who plunged off the rocks into the water, climbing one over another, barking and thrashing.

The *Younona* replied to the salute with her own guns. Captain Khvostov raised signal flags bidding farewell to the presidio, but no one ashore understood naval language.

Nikolai saw Concha turn her horse abruptly and gallop down the hill out of sight.

A great feeling of loss engulfed him as he returned to his cabin.

"Make sail!" the captain shouted as the tow lines were gathered and the longboats were raised aboard the ship.

The *Younona* surged northward.

Chapter 35

Four months after the *Younona* had left Novo-Arkhangelsk, she was again within sight of Baranov Island.

The fort on the shore looked deserted. Observing it through his telescope, Nikolai could detect no signs of human presence, no smoke curling over the roofs. The crew lined up along the bulwarks, watching anxiously as the familiar shoreline slowly unfolded before them. They could clearly see the tall hemlocks spreading down to the edge of the water, the tide crushing at their feet, their gnarled roots awash in white foam.

The ship glided closer to the island, rounding the cape, coming into full view of the fort. It had the forlorn appearance of a deserted ghost town.

The *Younona* announced her arrival by a cannon shot. The blast rippled the water, bounced off the cliffs and returned its echo. A flock of ravens took off with harsh cries.

A group of men appeared on the shore. They climbed into several *baidarki* paddling with obvious effort toward the *Younona*. Lines were thrown to the men in the *baidarki* and the *Younona* was towed into the harbor. She was home.

Nikolai folded his telescope. He saw Governor Baranov in a one-man *baidarka* leave the landing, on his way to the ship.

Baranov climbed the ladder, puffing heavily. His face was haggard, covered with stubble. His wispy white hair, limp and greasy, reached to his hunched shoulders. His clothes were malodorous and needed mending. He was also drunk.

Nikolai ignored his appearance. He clasped the old man to his chest. "Alexander Andreyevich, your suffering is over. We've brought you plenty of provisions," he exclaimed.

"That's good," Baranov said apathetically. He was unsteady on his feet.

Nikolai put a protective arm around his shoulders, leading him to his cabin where Ivan had already arranged a table of *zakuski*, tidbits of smoked meats, cheese and bread and a bottle of vodka. Nikolai signaled Ivan to remove the vodka. "Tea," he said quietly. "Plenty of strong tea."

Baranov dropped heavily into the chair riveted to the floor.

"You probably want to know what happened here in your absence," he stammered. "The moment the *Younona* was out of sight, the savages were back. They laid seige to the fort. The bastards never gave up. They knew that we must hunt or fish to survive. They would spring on us, killing, killing everyone...even the dogs..." he sobbed. His nose turned red and he wiped it on his sleeve. "There are less than three dozen Russians left in Novo-Arkhangelsk. The rest are dead of scurvy or starvation, or the savages got them. And the Aleuts..." He paused and then sobbed, "I don't even count our losses among the Aleuts. They are practically wiped out. We waited for a ship, *any ship*. But none came. I have never seen such vicious storms as we have had these past months! I was sure that you on the *Younona* had perished also." His face puckered in a pitiful grimace.

"Dear Alexander Andreyevich, don't cry...We brought you tons of food! And we'll send another ship to California for more provisions. I made marvelous arrangements with the Spaniards! Your troubles are over, forever!"

But the old man continued to weep.

"We brought you live chickens, and cows, and sheep. You can start breeding livestock again," Nikolai tried once more, talking soothingly as if to a child.

"Chickens, cows, and sheep," the Governor repeated lethargically. "Breeding stock..." His head dropped to the table. He was asleep.

"What a sad display," Dr. Langsdorff said. "What must his men think?"

"He's filthy and drunk and pitiful, but he is the toughest man of us all!" Timofei said. "That's what we think!"

The next day Baranov proved the truth of Timofei's words. He arrived at Nikolai's hut for dinner sober, clean-shaven, long hair trimmed and combed and his worn-out native clothing mended by the devoted Timofei.

"You saved our hides, Nikolai Petrovich," he said. "The sight of the *Younona* chased the savages away. And the food you brought will save us again."

"From now on, Alexander Andreyevich, you'll have a steady supply of provisions from Alta California. Let me tell you my news." Nikolai poured a small amount of cognac into two glasses offering one to Baranov. Then he outlined his ambitious plans for Alta California.

The Governor was less than enthusiastic. "I would prefer to colonize some unclaimed land where we deal only with the savages. We have experience in taming them," he began choosing his words carefully. "The Spanish government would strongly object to our moving in on their territories, even though technically the land would be yours. If you excuse my saying so, Nikolai Petrovich, I think your plan is impractical."

He paused. Nikolai saw that the Governor had more to say.

"I do think, however, that we ought to send a ship or two to explore the coast *north* of the Spanish territory. Your land in Alta California will be very useful as a friendly harbor; I do not believe, however, that we ought to build a Russian settlement on your land. It still will be within the borders of a *foreign* country. Besides, we don't have enough men to spare for such a monumental undertaking. First we must recruit new people to come to Russian America. And not just to hunt for furs. We are beyond that. I want to have whole families; I want to have Russian women here. I want Russian children. It will be years, though, before we can populate America with our own people," he concluded with a sigh.

Nikolai was disappointed with Baranov's reaction. "No use talking to him," he thought. "It's not up to him anyway to decide the future of this territory." He said aloud, "The Tsar will see the advantages."

The evening ended with both of them annoyed.

Back in his hut that night, Baranov confided his thoughts to Timofei Tarakanov. "Rezanov must be insane to think that he can get away with such a scheme! Spain will declare war on us!"

Timofei smiled thinly. "I like his idea. I have had enough of this damned climate where nothing grows. His plan might work."

Baranov snorted. "Not in a thousand years! I truly disapprove of his plans, including his decision to marry that Spanish girl. As if there are not enough Russian women to go around. Why does he need to marry a foreigner?" he grumbled.

He appeared in Nikolai's hut several days later wearing his official tri-cornered hat. "Your Excellency, I respectfully request that I be given permission to leave Russian America next May. I've been here for sixteen years. Please advise the Company to send a replacement for me." He bowed. Then, removing his hat he sat down heavily on a chair, his spurt of formality gone. Pouring himself a glass of Nikolai's cognac, he gulped it down.

"Why, Alexander Andreyevich?" Nikolai inquired gently. "In my mind you and the Russian-American Company are synonymous."

"You are flattering me," Baranov smiled wryly, pleased nevertheless. "Just the same, I won't stay beyond next May. I am tired. I want to spend my last days back in Russia. I want to die on *Russian* soil."

That night Nikolai noted in his journal:..."He insists that he will not stay longer than next May...I am sorry that we must lose such an excellent man. It is a pity we cannot keep him here." Deep in his mind, however, Nikolai thought that perhaps it was for the best. He would see to it that the new Governor would be in full accord with his plans for the future. Perhaps the old man had outlived his usefulness...

Nikolai was eager to leave but he had to wait for a ship that would take him back to Siberia. The *Younona* was being refurbished and the new tender, which Nikolai had ordered to be built while he was in California, was still far from being completed. He fumed, realizing that the longer he waited, the more dangerous it would become to cross Siberia on horseback.

Then a ship appeared on the horizon, a Yankee schooner, the *Peacock*. She brought along a group of craftsmen from New England whom Baranov had contracted three years previously to help the Russians in their new industry—the shipbuilding.

In no time the work on the tender was completed. She was named the *Avoss*, meaning in Russian "Perhaps".

The *Peacock* also brought disturbing news that the whole

of Europe was caught in the web of Napoleon's wars of conquest. The old alliances between friends were broken, new treaties were signed, only to be broken six months later.

Nikolai listened to the Americans, knowing already quite a lot about Napoleon's campaigns from his meeting with Governor Arillaga. However, one item of the news brought by the Yankees had nothing to do with wars in Europe. It shattered forever Nikolai's hopes of exploring the Columbia River. He was too late.

Apparently, an expedition had been sent in 1804 by the American President, Thomas Jefferson, to explore the newly acquired Louisiana Purchase territories bought from France. The explorers, led by Meriweather Lewis and William Clark, had reached the Pacific Ocean in November, 1805, by sailing along the Missouri, the Snake, and the Columbia rivers. They established a small fort on the coast. The Columbia River had become a Yankee territory.

"It's July, 1806, now," Nikolai thought in disappointment. "The Yankees have outflanked us. And Spain, as well. They have been on the Pacific for *eight* months and we had no knowledge of it!" He paced the floor of his hut.

"At least, we have a foothold in Spanish California," he thought. Visions of Argüello's rich land appeared before him. He felt suddenly cheerful.

"By the time the Americans send their settlers across the continent, I'll have several shiploads of Russians already living in California," he thought, full of optimism.

Nikolai decided to leave immediately for Kamchatka aboard the *Avoss*. Midshipman Davidov, whom he had promoted to lieutenant, was to be her captain.

Nothing more detained Nikolai in Novo-Arkhangelsk. He bade farewell to the men of his California expedition. He would miss them, he thought. He would especially miss Timofei Tarakanov. He wished that he could pry him away from Baranov into his own service. "Why don't you come with me to St. Petersburg, Timofei?" he said. "I'll pay well. You'll live in my house as my steward."

Timofei shook his head. "No, Your Excellency. I must stay with Alexander Andreyevich. When you return, I'll sail with you to California. I'll dance at your wedding, Your Excellency!" They embraced as equals.

Nikolai was disappointed that Dr. Langsdorff chose not

to accompany him. He asked to be released from his contract. Nikolai suspected that Langsdorff was afraid of crossing the ocean sailing on a tiny tender. Reluctantly, he signed the papers that would permit Langsdorff's passage through various provinces of continental Russia at some future date.

Nikolai stepped aboard the *Avoss*, eager to be on his way. He had left letters for Concha and Governor Arillaga to be sent to California with the first ship going south.

The *Avoss* turned into the wind, and tacked out of the bay; she was too small to need towing.

Nikolai waved from the bridge. It occurred to him that perhaps he would never see Baranov again. "By the time I return on my way to claim Concha, the Governor will have been replaced." Nikolai felt sad that their paths might never cross again.

"I know so little about him," he thought. "I have never talked to him about his wife. I have never seen her nor their children..." But it was too late now.

Slowly the small islands surrounding Novo-Arkhangelsk disappeared in the translucent eerie light of northern summer. Two thousand miles of ocean lay ahead.

Chapter 36

Nikolai's accommodations on the *Avoss* were primitive. The little tender was not meant to be a luxury ship. He shared a cabin with the captain, while the first mate shared the only other cabin with Ivan. The rest of the six-man crew slept in the holds, sharing alternately the same three hammocks.

Nikolai occupied his time working on three manuscripts which he had begun at the start of the circumnavigational voyage. One was an account of his expedition on the *Nadezhda*; another, a Russian-Japanese dictionary, and the third, a Russian-Aleut booklet of useful words, on which he worked during the previous winter in Novo-Arkhangelsk. All three projects had been neglected by him while he was in California. Now, feeling ambitious once more, he worked on them in earnest.

In September, after four weeks of exceptionally good sailing weather, the *Avoss* sighted the rugged outline of the Kamchatka peninsula, and shortly, she put in at Petropavlovsk-on-Kamchatka.

She remained there only long enough to stock fresh water and food, Nikolai impatient to move on while the weather held. They sailed around the southern tip of Kamchatka and into the Sea of Okhotsk.

At once the *Avoss* was caught in a vicious storm, which tossed her over the waves like a paper boat. Cold rain flogged her mercilessly, punishing the vessel and crew for venturing out on the high seas so late in the season. When at last, a week later, she limped into Okhotsk harbor, her sails were torn to shreds, her mast split in half and her bilges full of water. The crew, half-dead from prolonged seasickness, had to be helped ashore.

But it was Nikolai who suffered most. He was in agonizing pain from his reactivated ulcer, plagued by new symptoms of dizziness, his chest torn by a heavy cough.

He stayed locked in his cabin for several days, preferring it to any of the flea-infested huts ashore, allowing only Ivan near him. He was ill and he despised himself for being infirm.

Ivan nursed him tenderly. He had been totally devoted to Nikolai. They grew up together, as "milk brothers", Ivan's mother being Nikolai's wet nurse.

As a young lad, Ivan had followed Nikolai to St. Petersburg becoming his valet and orderly while Nikolai served in the Guards. Ivan had no personal life but Nikolai's. Nikolai responded to Ivan's loyalty with affection. Were they of the same social class, they would have been close friends. But a broad gulf separated masters and servants. They could love one another, but they could never be intimate.

It was already the end of September when Nikolai began to feel better. "We must be on our way," he said to Ivan. "Find out if we can hire a decent convoy."

The commander of the Okhotsk garrison came aboard the *Avoss* to try to persuade Rezanov to postpone his journey until spring. "It's lethal in your condition, Your Excellency," he exclaimed. "You must winter with us!"

"No, my friend. I have already lost too much time. I leave at once," Nikolai said. "I must be in St. Petersburg as soon as possible."

On the last day of September the convoy was finally assembled. Nikolai mounted a shaggy, snub-nosed, shortlegged Siberian horse and trotted out of the stockade with his Cossacks and a supply train. By offering exorbitant bribes to the Cossacks, Nikolai hired two dozen men and sixty horses to escort him across Siberia.

Lieutenant Davidov and the commander of the garrison watched his departure.

"I feel I am watching a man leave for a duel from which I know he will not return," the commander said.

"Chamberlain Rezanov is a remarkable man," Davidov smiled. "I remember how we doubted that he could trade with the Spaniards. We even made bets against him. He fooled us then. Perhaps he will fool us again."

"Siberia is brutal," was all the commander would say.

Day after day, Rezanov and his Cossacks plodded across the Siberian coastal range climbing up to the summits, then descending into deep canyons. Sometimes they covered no more than five miles a day in torrential rains that drenched them to the skins and turned narrow mountain paths into raging streams. On such days they pitched their tents on high ground at night and awakened in the morning to find themselves surrounded by turbulent rivulets. They went without hot food for days, chewing dry strips of meat or fish for Nikolai was unwilling to let the Yakut guides spend extra time finding dry wood and erecting shelters for fires.

Through it all, Nikolai drove himself to near exhaustion. But he ignored the aches in his body, begrudging even the few hours of sleep needed by his men and horses.

He slept very little himself. His mind was bursting with schemes for the colonization of America.

"Alta California first, then the rest of the coast and finally, the interior," he muttered to himself.

He thought again of the Lewis and Clark expedition to the Pacific. "It would take years for the Yankees to send their settlers to the new territories. Whichever way they go, by land or around Cape Horn, it will take at least two years to arrive in numbers...We are already on the Pacific. It will take us no more than six weeks to settle in Alta California," he thought. "Success depends entirely on how soon I reach St. Petersburg and get the Tsar's orders."

He drove the men and beasts mercilessly, as he drove himself.

Ivan had never seen his master in such a mood. This was even beyond the fierce Rezanov impatience he had known all his life. Was his master trying to kill himself?

The Cossacks had not expected such stamina in an aristocrat who was almost twice their age and rumored to be seriously ill. But none of them complained. They knew there was safety in speed. They had to reach Yakutsk before winter caught them.

Snow was falling by the time they reached the banks of the great Aldan River. The waters rolled with a steely glint and the river roared as it rushed between huge boulders. Even in good weather crossings were dangerous, the Yakut guides knew, and now the river was swollen to a torrent with autumn rains.

A Yakut threw a stick into the water to test its velocity. Instantly, the stick was picked up by the torrent and swirling madly, carried along, disappearing among the boulders.

"Once we cross the river, the trip should be easy," Nikolai thought. Beyond the river lay the flatlands of the great tundra and then, Yakutsk, a real town with stone-built houses, the end of the first leg of their journey.

The Yakuts ventured across the ford, setting two ropes to mark the safe path. The Cossacks edged into the torrent, men clinging to the guide ropes, using their knees to urge their horses forward. The animals rolled their eyes as they struggled to find footing.

Nikolai's mare slipped, ducked her head and panicked. Nikolai tried to calm her, but it was no use. The mare floundered and tangled herself in the ropes. The other horses, frightened by her thrashing, broke through the guidelines, swimming toward the shore, kicking frantically.

Nikolai lost his grip on the rope and freed the mare to reach the shore on her own. He jumped into the water. He was a strong swimmer, but his water-soaked winter clothing pulled him down. Hooves of panicked horses thudded against his ribs and arms with paralyzing force. He began to sink. He had time for only one frantic shout for help before the water closed over his head.

Several Cossacks jumped back into the river. Dodging among the crazed horses, they raced to reach Nikolai before he was kicked to death by the panicked animals.

Nikolai felt a hand seize his collar. Then a strong arm caught him across the chest and he felt himself being pulled through the water. He was too weak to help or struggle. He could only gasp for breath each time his face emerged from the current.

Then other hands were clutching at him, lifting him, pulling him on the shore.

"God bless you, *bratzi*," Nikolai choked. Then he collapsed on the frozen ground.

When Nikolai regained consciousness, he found himself in a Yakut hut, Ivan by his side with a tin cup of strong hot tea.

"Where are we?" Nikolai whispered weakly.

"Thank the Good Lord, Your Excellency is better!" Ivan

made the sign of the cross fervently. "We are in the *yurta* of the Yakut chief. We have been here a week."

"A whole week!" Nikolai tried to rise. He felt faint and fell back against the pillows covered with wolf skins.

"You are very ill, Your Excellency," Ivan began, carefully tucking a blanket around Nikolai's shoulders. "You have fever. You were delirious and the Cossack *sotnick* and I thought we had better stop at the Yakut village and wait until you are better."

Nikolai felt too weak to argue, but he felt a wave of despair. "A whole week! By now we could have been in Yakutsk!" He drifted into sleep again.

The next day Nikolai made one feeble attempt to rise before he admitted to himself that he was unable to travel.

He allowed Ivan to fuss over him. He drank *kumys*, mare's milk, which the Yakuts swore would cure all ills. And he slept again.

After another week, he was still feeble, but able to take some interest in life around him.

He began to write a special journal for Concha, to educate her about Russia. Someday, he thought, we'll read it together.

He wrote: "My host, an old, bad-smelling Yakut, has only a dozen long hairs growing in his chin. He has a habit of stroking these few hairs as if they were a luxuriant beard. His head is clean-shaven and he always wears an embroidered skullcap trimmed with a broad band of red fox. He tells me that he has four wives but I am not allowed to see them. One of the wives chews his food for him for he has no teeth. I must confess, I am not eager to see his ladies and watch them chew his food for him. The old man is quite enough!"

"Oh, but I must describe the *yurta*! It is a large circular hut covered with turf and, alas, horse dung. This last substance makes its presence known at all times, but especially when all the people and their animals are crowded in for the night. The *yurta* is divided into two parts: the large one is for the animals, such as sheep, goats, dogs, and a few scrappy chickens. The smaller part is for people, at least two dozen of them. There are no windows in the *yurta* and the air grows very heavy. In the center there is a huge pile of sooty stones, where the children tend the fire. Smoke escapes through a hole in the roof, but enough of it remains in the *yurta* to make me choke. My host is not sure how many children he has with his four wives. He pointed to his own ten fingers and gestured three times. I presumed it meant that he had thirty children."

"Looking at the possessions of the old man, I couldn't help but think of the Indians and the Aleuts in Russian America. Compared to them my host is rich as Croesus! He has hundreds of horses and flocks of sheep and goats. He has colorful rugs spread over the straw on the earthen floor. Every summer he takes his brood to the steppes where he constructs a summer *yurta* made of animal hides. He is a true nomad, following his herds of horses as they graze. But in the winter his *yurta* becomes his castle, his hacienda, his palace!"

He reread his description and then folded the pages into an envelope. He pressed the crest of his ring firmly into a drop of hot wax, sealing the envelope.

Another week and Nikolai was on his feet again.

A cough still racked his thin body, but he ordered the convoy to be ready to depart the next day.

Two Cossacks helped him mount and then rode stirrup to stirrup with him to help him stay in the saddle.

The *sotnick* shook his head in desperation, "The man is sick; he'll die if he doesn't slow down!"

"You can't argue with him," Ivan shook his head. "I have served him since we both were boys. I know how stubborn he is. He listens to no one once he has made up his mind."

They rode in silence.

Snow fell often now. The Yakut guides followed a path marked by barely visible poles set in the ground at irregular intervals. There were no roads, only flat white *tundra* without a human settlement for hundreds of miles. They camped around the fires at night, listening to the howl of *tundra* wolves. Rivers were ice bound now; the crossing became easier.

Then the land changed slowly from the flat *tundra* to the foothills of a tall mountain range, and then to the treacherous terrain of sheer cliffs and narrow paths. The unshod horses' hooves barely made a sound on the paths covered with a thick padding of pine needles and snow. The *sotnick* kept the pack horses tied in groups of five; should one stumble on the icy path, the other four would prevent it from falling down the precipice.

Four and a half months had passed since the convoy left

Okhotsk. The men felt as if they had been traveling forever. The sense of time had vanished; one day was exactly like the next. Then one day the travelers stared out into the valley of the Lena River and glimpsed the onion-shaped copper domes of the Yakutsk monastery. They sparkled like bright lights, beckoning to the weary men.

Besides the monastery, Yakutsk consisted of only a few stone houses of the local authorities, a prison and two or three crooked streets of log huts under rotting thatched roofs, but to the men it was warmth, food, and shelter. They cheered and hastened their pace.

Nikolai stayed at the monastery as the guest of the Bishop only long enough to buy new horses, dismiss his Yakut guides and hire more Cossacks. He bought a deep sleigh which Ivan lined with bearskins to create a soft, warm bed for his master. Ivan himself was going to ride with the driver directly in front. The convoy would be following the course of the Lena River, riding over the ice toward Irkutsk, more than thirteen hundred miles southwest.

The hospitable monks gathered on the bank of the river to see Rezanov off. They carried church banners and a holy icon, while the Bishop blessed the travelers. Nikolai knelt with difficulty before the icon, the Cossacks of the convoy next to him. The Bishop intoned the prayers, the monks responded in unison and the Archdeacon swung his censer. Nikolai kissed the cold surface of the silver *riza* which enclosed the stern image of Christ. He had to be helped to stand up again.

"Nikolai Petrovich, don't go!" the Bishop urged. "Stay with us. You're ill. We'll take good care of you. Stay until spring when you can sail to Irkutsk in comfort, on rafts."

"No, Holy Father, I can't stay. The future of Russia may depend on the speed with which I reach the Tsar."

The old Bishop looked into Nikolai's eyes for a long moment, then sighed. "You are an obstinate man, Nikolai Petrovich. God be with you."

The Cossacks mounted and the caravan cautiously descended from the steep river bank to the ice-bound Lena.

Nikolai relaxed. He felt warm and cozy, like a child in a cradle. He watched the banks of the Lena slowly change their configuration, becoming steep and rugged. The fine snow dust flying from under the horses' hooves stung his cheeks, but he liked it. It cooled his burning face. He was feverish again.

The sky was deep-blue and cloudless. Nikolai watched the landscape soon become one dark forest as the river entered the *taiga*. Clouds of white vapor formed about the horses' muzzles; they snorted and raced along the smooth surface of the river.

Nikolai was at peace with himself. He realized that he was gravely ill, but he refused to think of it.

The convoy followed the frozen Lena for several weeks. At night the men camped under a canopy of ancient hemlocks, Nikolai sleeping in his sleigh, wrapped in furs.

The temperature dropped until the party seemed to travel in a cloud of vapor from the breath of the horses and men.

At night, Nikolai huddled in his sleigh, listening to the trees groan, and occasionally snap under the weight of the snow. Often he could hear the cry of wolves under the empty sky. They sounded sad and forlorn.

At bivouacs the Cossacks fished through holes in the ice-bound river. Within minutes the fish were solidly frozen. The men shattered them against the trees to make them easier to clean. They ate the fish raw with a pinch of coarse salt and dry mustard seeds while Ivan boiled portions of it for his master.

Occasionally the men came upon a great Siberian bear, taking advantage of the fishing holes left by the Cossacks. The bear would break the new ice forming over the holes, dipping his huge paws into the water, sometimes coming up with a fish. Most of the time, the bear came up with nothing; the holes were too deep and the sluggish fish stayed close to the bottom.

Nikolai ate without tasting anything. If he spoke it was to say "We must get an early start."

Irkutsk, it seemed to him, was still far away.

Chapter 37

Several weeks later, the caravan rode into Irkutsk and directly to Governor's mansion. Nikolai wanted to shake off the hands that supported him while he struggled up the steps, but even if he could have, he knew he could not stand without aid. To the worried Governor he could only say, "I am not well, Your Excellency. I would like to consult a physician right away."

"Of course, of course!" The rotund Governor's chins shook as he snapped orders to family and servants. The sight of Nikolai's gaunt face and burning eyes alarmed him.

When the doctor arrived, Nikolai was already washed, shaved and sleeping, propped against several soft pillows in a high brass bed.

He stirred slightly at the doctor's touch, and opened his eyes. "When can I leave," he asked. His lips were pale, his skin waxy.

"No travel for you until spring," the doctor said, squeezing Nikolai's bony wrist for emphasis. "You must have food and rest. You're exhausted. You must stay in Irkutsk until the end of winter."

Nikolai stared at him and shook his head imperceptibly. Then he fell asleep again.

The members of the Governor's family took it upon themselves to nurse their visitor back to health. Every few minutes there was someone entering Nikolai's room on tiptoe carrying a cup of hot soup or a plate of *pirozhki*, a glass of warm milk or sugar cakes. This went on until the doctor insisted that only Ivan was to serve Rezanov. The Governor was permitted to visit for ten minutes daily, but the other members of the family were forbidden to enter the patient's room.

The doctor's common sense remedy began to work. Nikolai began to feel stronger and improved health caused him to realize how ill he had been.

"Tell the Governor I want to update my will," he told Ivan. "Go on, fool," he smiled. "And don't look so gloomy. I am far from dead."

As Ivan left the room, Nikolai wondered if he had told the truth. Disturbing premonitions of death filled his mind. He was still very ill. Never before had he suffered from such dizziness, he thought. Any slight physical exertion left him panting. "A valid will is a good idea," he told himself. "The journey ahead is still very hard and I am in poor condition."

In the presence of the Governor he dictated a clause to his will that granted freedom to his loyal Ivan in six months. He wondered if Ivan would want to continue as a servant once he had gained his freedom. It would be a big change for them both to be separated after a lifetime together.

At the end of the second week, Nikolai's fever was gone and so was his persistent cough. The doctor insisted that he stay in bed until his dizzy spells were gone.

A week later, Nikolai gave orders to resume the journey. To quiet the Governor's pleading, he agreed to take along a physician.

"I have spoken to the doctor and he will accompany me as far as Krasnoyarsk. Perhaps there I can hire another physician who will continue with me to St. Petersburg."

Although it was still possible to travel by sleigh, Nikolai decided to ride. He could move faster. He cut his escort to twelve Cossacks and thirty pack horses. The original *sotnick* remained, bent on seeing him through to the end of the journey.

For the first three days the convoy rode along a track through the *taiga* marked by official black and white striped posts at regular intervals. The travelers made about seven miles a day, despite the deep snow. The doctor feared that the pace was too swift for his patient, but Nikolai ignored pleas to slow down.

During the fourth day a savage *purga* bore down on them. The Cossacks unloaded the horses and built a barricade around the animals with their packs. Drifts formed over the packs, making a wall to shelter the horses. Within this double wall of packs and animals, the men huddled while the blizzard tried to bury them.

The animals stood motionless, as snow built up on the felt blankets the Cossacks had spread over them. The men struggled to build a campfire, which flickered erratically one moment, only to be blown out by a gust in the next.

No one could survive without fire. Should the *purga* continue for more than twelve hours, as it often did, they would be doomed. All of them, men and beasts, would perish silently, slowly freezing to death. The Siberian *purga* granted no mercy.

Nikolai felt the icy wind reach even through his great sable *shuba*. He reached into its deep pocket and took out a bottle of cognac. A large gulp of the brandy seemed to spread warmth through his chilled body. Even though no one had seen him take the drink, it never occurred to him to save the cognac for himself. The unwritten law of the Siberian traveler was to share equally. He held out the bottle to the doctor to pass on to the others. When the bottle was returned to Nikolai, it was empty.

The *purga* lasted them throughout the night, but by morning the wind died down and the sun shone again. "Thank God," said the *sotnick*, "Sometimes these blizzards last three or four days."

Even though the blizzard had stopped, travel was impossible. The little camp was buried under ten-feet high drifts.

But Nikolai pressed the Cossacks to repack. Only when the *sotnick* said, "We can pack, but we cannot move," did Nikolai seem to understand the trail was buried and impassable.

They were forced to remain at the camp for three days, slowly enlarging the radius of their bivouac by building large fires to melt back the drifts.

Nikolai tried to relax, but he felt more irritable with every passing hour. Despite himself, he began to pace back and forth between the campfires with his hands clasped behind his back, his long *shuba* trailing behind him. His gaunt face, with its burning eyes, looked possessed. "At times he looks insane," the doctor thought.

Finally, the *sotnick* announced that they could try to resume the journey. Cautiously probing the snow with long poles, they made their way back to the trail hidden under deep drifts that reached to the horses' shoulders.

They moved in a single file, laboriously fighting for every

inch. The horses strained, plowing their way through the drifts, the Cossacks using long poles as levers to help the animals. Nikolai raged silently. He knew he was feverish again by the dizziness that almost overwhelmed him while he tried to stay in the saddle.

Then almost as sudden as the *purga*, warm winds blew rain clouds from Mongolia, bringing the promise of spring. The torrential rains melted the snow faster than the rays of the pale winter sun.

"It's false spring, Excellency," the *sotnick* said, "but it may save us." They would travel fast and reach Krasnoyarsk before the next *purga* closed the roads once again.

It was the beginning of March.

Nikolai rode through the downpour in the middle of the convoy, concentrating his physical and mental powers on one objective, to reach Krasnoyarsk. He could not think beyond that. Reaching Krasnoyarsk became the most important goal of his existence. His thoughts of Concha became infrequent. He often whispered her name, but he could not recall her face; it mingled in his mind with Annushka's face. He rode, thinking only of Krasnoyarsk, as if the city had a magical power to restore his health and rejuvenate his spirit. Even St. Petersburg had become something far in the distant future. To reach *Krasnoyarsk* was his only goal.

After a week of hard riding the black mud under their horses' hooves began to change color; it acquired a faint reddish tint.

"I think we are approaching Krasnoyarsk," said the doctor, hoping to cheer Nikolai. "The soil there has a red color."

The words had an electrifying effect on Rezanov. "We must hurry! We must hurry!" he thought. "We must beat the *purga!*" He stared at the doctor wildly, then whipped his horse savagely. The animal neighed and burst into a frantic gallop.

"Wait, wait!" shouted the doctor, whipping his own horse, but Nikolai was far ahead.

The Cossacks rushed in pursuit. They galloped at a breakneck speed, the mud flying from under the horses' hooves, splattering them with large red splotches. The rain dissolved the mud into rivulets streaming down their faces like blood.

Suddenly, Nikolai slipped. His body hit the ground but

his leg was caught in a stirrup. The horse bolted on, dragging his body.

The Cossacks whipped their horses until they overtook the terrified animal and stopped it. They lifted the unconscious Rezanov and placed him on a felt *burka* spread at the side of the road. He was bleeding from a deep gash on the crown of his head, his face battered, the ankle that had caught in the stirrup, twisted at a strange angle.

"God Almighty, why are You punishing us! What have we done to deserve such a calamity!" Ivan cried, wringing his hands, falling on his knees next to his master at the side of the road. Tears streamed down his unshaven face, mixing with the rain and mud, disappearing in his soggy beard.

"Get my bag!" the doctor shouted to the Cossacks who crowded around the fallen Nikolai. They looked bewildered, their bearded faces pale under layers of splattered mud. "Hurry!" the doctor yelled. The men rushed to unload his medical chest.

The doctor cleaned and bandaged the wound on Nikolai's head, washed and dressed the other cuts and bruises. He set the bone in his ankle and made a splint to support it. Then he soaked a handkerchief with spirits of ammonia and held it under Nikolai's nose to bring him back to consciousness. Nikolai's eyelids fluttered, but he remained unconscious.

"He's in shock," the doctor said. "We must get him to Krasnoyarsk!"

They placed Nikolai on a sling of several *burki* tied between two pack-horses.

The *sotnick* sent two men to ride ahead, to alert the Governor of the province and request help. The rest of the convoy inched along trying to spare the injured man more misery.

Nikolai floated in and out of consciousness, burning with high fever one moment, shivering with chills the next, delirious, unable to swallow anything but a few spoonfuls of broth which Ivan boiled for him at every stop.

"He's dying," the doctor said quietly to the *sotnick*. "If we don't get him into a warm house and give him proper care he'll be dead in a few days."

"Has he a chance if we get him to Krasnoyarsk?"

The doctor shrugged his shoulders. "Who knows? It's all in God's hands..."

They trudged doggedly ahead for another week.

Concha celebrated her sixteenth birthday quietly along with her family at the hacienda. "It's almost a year since I met Nikolai," she thought as she woke up that morning to the patter of rain on the roof. "It was raining also, the day we had said good-bye."

For weeks Concha had been depressed, struggling with the debilitating feeling of jealousy. She imagined Nikolai as having already arrived in St. Petersburg, being surrounded by his friends, his children and dazzling women. She saw him dancing at the Palace balls.

Doña Ignacia watched her daughter with alarm. Concha had lost weight, her delicate face becoming gaunt, her dark luminous eyes—lusterless.

"*Que le pasa a te, hija*, what's the matter, child?" Doña Ignacia patted her head as if she were still a small girl. "I know, you miss Nikolai, but look, *querida*, a whole year has nearly passed! One more year and we'll be celebrating your wedding! Nikolai is probably already on his way back to California!"

Concha's eyes misted with tears. "I hope you're right Mamá...Sometimes I think that he has forgotten me..."

"Don't say that, *hija*! Nikolai loves you!" Doña Ignacia cried indignantly.

Concha smiled sadly. "I have this dreadful feeling that I'll never see him again..."

Doña Ignacia dissolved in tears.

A Cossack riding as lookout galloped back to the slowly moving convoy.

"There's a wide river ahead! It must be the Yenisei! We're near Krasnoyarsk!" he yelled excitedly.

Out of the frosty mist of the morning, the travelers soon saw the frozen expanse of the Yenisei River and, just beyond, many columns of smoke that marked Krasnoyarsk. Several churches with high onion-shaped belfries dominated the skyline of the city. Their gold and azure domes shone even in the cold mist of the winter.

A few hours later came the creaking sounds of carriage wheels and clopping of horses' hooves.

"It must be the *careta* for Nikolai Petrovich. Thank God!" Ivan exclaimed, making the sign of the cross.

A large old-fashioned carriage drawn by four Percheron horses dipped and rocked on huge springs as it approached.

It was surrounded by uniformed garrison soldiers, led by the two Cossacks from the convoy. The coachman and his helper perched precariously on a high seat swaying as the vehicle careened from side to side, sending cascades of mud from under its great wheels.

"Hurry, get the Chamberlain out of this damned weather," Ivan shouted at the coachman.

"He's not long for this world," the coachman said as he helped to lift Nikolai onto the broad cushioned seat of the carriage.

"You bastard!" Ivan shouted furiously. "You don't know him the way I do. He'll be fine as soon as we get him into a nice, warm bed."

The doctor and Ivan climbed in after him, settling on a seat opposite the patient.

"Gently!" Ivan yelled threateningly to the coachman through a small window above his seat.

"I'll do my best. This damned road is no good for anything but a Tatar goat!" the coachman replied.

Cautiously, he began to turn the *careta* around, his four horses responding as one. The soldiers and the Cossacks chopped tree branches, spreading them under the wheels to prevent them from sinking into the mud.

Inside the carriage, Nikolai lay pale and helpless.

The carriage and its escort pulled up in front of the Governor's mansion. The Governor and his family crowded at the entrance hall to watch Nikolai being carried into the best bedroom in the house.

Ivan and the doctor shooed everyone away. They undressed Nikolai and Ivan sponged his body with warm water and soap. Then they dressed him in clean nightclothes and tucked him in under a pile of feather-filled comforters.

The doctor touched Nikolai's wrist. The patient remained comatose, his body cold and his pulse rapid, thready and irregular.

A local doctor, who had been summoned, entered quickly. The two physicians shook hands and stood at Nikolai's bedside. The new physician glanced at Ivan, crouching on his knees in the corner, mumbling prayers before the icons.

"It's all right. He is the Chamberlain's serf. He won't bother us," said the doctor from Irkutsk.

They listened to Nikolai's weak heartbeat, probed the wound on his head and changed the bandages. The Krasnoyarsk physician said uncertainly, "He probably suffers from a severe brain injury."

"In addition to the fractured ankle, a bleeding ulcer, inflammation of the lungs and God knows what else," added the doctor from Irkutsk.

They stood helplessly looking at the patient, feeling inadequate, their medical training all but worthless.

Suddenly, Nikolai opened his eyes. He stared straight ahead, seeing no one. His hands began to move, fast, fast, the fingers touching the edge of the blankets, as if probing their quality.

Ivan made the broad sign of the cross and burst into tears.

"*Perebiraet*. He's fingering the blankets. His end has come. It's the sign," he sobbed.

"Don't talk nonsense," the Irkutsk physician snapped.

"No, Your Excellencies, Nikolai Petrovich is dying. Look! He's fingering again. *Perebiraet*. God save his soul."

The tree men watched Nikolai as he stared into space, his fingers probing, clutching at the edges of the bedclothes.

Then a long shudder shook his emaciated body as his fingers released the covers. "He's gone!" Ivan whispered and collapsed on his knees at the side of the bed.

The physicians each took Nikolai's wrists probing for a pulse.

There was none.

Ivan crossed himself and nearly blinded with tears, gently closed Nikolai's eyes.

Chapter 38

News of Nikolai Rezanov's death did not reach Russian America until the late autumn of 1807.

Governor Baranov was in Pavlovsk when the ship bringing the news arrived from Okhotsk. He immediately ordered a *panikhida* to be performed at the church in Rezanov's memory. He elbowed his way through the crowd of *promyshleniki* and Aleuts and knelt heavily before the altar. It was difficult for him to kneel. His joints ached and the nagging pain in his gnarled fingers made it difficult to make the sign of the cross.

"Rezanov was a good man," he thought. "I often failed to see eye to eye with him, but I'll miss him. *Russia* will miss him. He was a visionary."

He glanced at Timofei kneeling next to him, who wept uncontrollably, the tears rolling down his cheeks, gathering at the tip of his moustache, hanging like drops of melting ice.

Timofei was outraged that no one had prevented the senseless accident which led to Rezanov's death. "Surely, Rezanov shouldn't have been allowed to travel on horseback, sick as he was," Timofei thought. "It's more than a year since the *Younona* left the presidio in California...Poor Señorita Concha! She's waiting, not knowing that he's no more." Timofei wiped away his tears. He stood up and helped the Governor to his feet. They were the last to leave the church. They walked slowly toward Baranov's house, the mud squishing under their boots.

"You are welcome to come in for a *charka* of vodka," Baranov said stopping at the gate of his tiny garden.

"No, Alexander Andreyevich, thank you." Timofei wanted to be alone.

Baranov did not insist. He too needed to be alone to absorb the blow of Rezanov's death.

"All right, some other time..." He shuffled toward the door, the flimsy boardwalk bending under his weight.

With a pang of sorrow Timofei noted Baranov's stooped shoulders and the old-age shuffle. There was no spring to his step, no vigor in his countenance. Baranov was worn out.

Timofei leaned on the crooked picket fence surrounding the forlorn vegetable garden, watching Baranov disappear behind the door. Slowly, Timofei walked away. His thoughts switched to the presidio de San Francisco. In his mind's eye, he saw the white-washed *sala* and the enchanting child-woman dancing with haughty grace before the entranced visitors. He saw the aristocratic face of Rezanov melting into a warm smile as he gazed at his Concha.

He recalled Concha's tragic face as well, as she galloped to the high cliff for the last glimpse of the departing *Younona*. "Did she ever think that she would never see her betrothed again?" he thought. Feeling wretched, Timofei walked toward his own lonely lodgings.

Baranov sat heavily at his table, drinking alone, staring at the pile of unopened dispatches. He felt no interest in them. His thoughts were on the mutilated body of Rezanov as it must have been when the Cossacks had finally stopped his terrified horse and freed the fallen Rezanov.

"What a senseless end to a brilliant career! What a great loss for Russia!" he thought, gulping down another glass of vodka, reaching for the packet of dispatches with a sigh of resignation. They had to be read and dealt with.

The very first document changed his mood abruptly, clearing the fog of vodka from his head. It was the proclamation awarding him the Order of St. Anna, Second Class, for his "devoted services to the motherland." Eagerly he searched the dispatch pouch for the box containing the medal.

He tore the protective wrapping off impatiently and took out the elegant red velvet box. He snapped the lid open, and the beautiful enameled cross resting on a shiny moiré ribbon appeared before his eyes. "Calm down. It's only a medal," he told himself, aware that he was behaving like an excited child. His heart was pounding. He pressed his hand to his chest, as if to slow it down. He wished that Blossom were there to share his pleasure, but she and the children were visiting with her tribe.

"It must have been Rezanov's recommendation," he thought. "God rest his soul!" Tears of gratitude welled up in his eyes. He inhaled deeply, trying to control the sobs that began to shake his body. He stood up and crossed himself several times before the icons. He was again in full possession of himself.

Baranov decided to remain in Pavlovsk until spring. The settlement in Novo-Arkhangelsk was well run in his absence by Ivan Kuskov. Besides, he expected to be replaced in the spring.

The colonies were finally beginning to prosper. Ships were built in Novo-Arkhangelsk and several more of them were purchased from the British and the Yankees. Through Rezanov's agreement with the Admiralty, naval officers were permitted to sign up for a tour of duty in Russian America. Better ships and expert captains made a great difference in the rate of safe crossings of the Pacific, Baranov noted in his journal.

One of the captains who signed up with the Russian-American Company was Nikolai Isayevich Bulygin.

Captain Bulygin came out of an impoverished minor noble family, which comprised the majority of Russian service personnel. His parents long dead, Bulygin had no lands, no serfs, no estates to provide him with the funds needed to lead the life of a nobleman. He was fortunate to have been admitted to the Naval Academy through a petition of a distant relative.

He graduated with a rank of navigator and at once signed up to serve in Russian America.

"It's the age of great discoveries," Bulygin was full of optimism. "There are new islands and straits to be discovered, the way to achieve fame." The example of Captain Kruzenstern, another poor man who had commanded the first Russian expedition around the world only three years before, was constantly on Bulygin's mind. He dreamt of becoming famous. It was the only way for the penniless captain to become something more than a mere professional sailor.

Nikolai Bulygin was twenty-five years old. Six feet tall

and slenderly built, Bulygin had thick brown hair which he
wore cut short in the back but allowed to mingle with his
curly sideburns in front as was the fashion.

His nose was straight and a bit prominent, which gave
him an appearance of a Roman. He was shy with women
and to cover up, he smiled often, having been told that he
had an engaging smile and the most beautiful teeth. Were
he wealthy, he could have easily become a dandy, for he paid
great attention to his appearance, but his lack of funds made
it impossible for him to own more than one suit of clothes
and a short ceremonial sword.

This lack of funds was another reason why Bulygin had
signed up to sail the ships for the Russian-American Company
and re-enlisted again at the end of his first three year contract.
There was a chance to make good money. Eventually.

Bulygin was returning to Russian America after a short
leave. He rode in a post carriage across the Urals, toward
Irkutsk where he was to purchase supplies for the Russian
settlements in America.

He arrived in Irkutsk and promptly made his way to the
office of the local merchant Peter Gorbatov. He carried the
letters of introduction which he presented to Gorbatov.

The old man turned the letters in his hands and then
smiled in embarrassment. "I never learned how to read or
write, but my daughter here acts as my secretary." He
pointed to the young woman sitting primly on the high-
backed sofa.

Bulygin bowed to the young woman and handed her the
letters.

"They are from Governor Alexander Baranov," she said,
glancing at the letters.

"Ah, my good old friend," Gorbatov said. "He writes
only when he needs something!"

"Which is quite often," his daughter said with a smile.

From the corner of his eye the captain watched Gorbatov's daughter. Her eyes, which so startled him with their
deep violet color, were lowered now and her long curving
lashes seemed to cast a shadow on her smooth cheeks.

Anna was her name. She wore her hair uncovered, like a
girl. It fell over her shoulders in two heavy braids, the color
of ripe wheat, reaching well below her narrow waist. She was
almost as tall as Bulygin and she wore a European-style dress
with a rather low cut neckline.

Bulygin never expected to find such a fashionable dress in provincial Irkutsk. Anna looked as alluring as any young woman in St. Petersburg. Her father, on the contrary, was wearing a loose, high-collared red *kosovorotka*, girdled with a silken cord with long tassels. His coarse trousers were tucked into knee-high pleated boots, which squeaked as he walked.

"You stay at my house, sir," Gorbatov said. "Our only inn in Irkutsk is a fleabag, I am told. My house will be much more comfortable."

"Thank you. You're very kind."

"I'll go and tell the servants," Anna said with a fast glance at the captain. She left, her braids swinging across her straight back.

"We hardly ever see new faces around here," Gorbatov continued with a chuckle. "All we ever talk about here is wheat and pork, iron nails and sail canvas. Perhaps you would be willing to tell us about your travels, Captain."

"I'll do my best... I am not good at entertaining."

"You're heaven sent!" Gorbatov smiled. "My family will be delighted to have you with us!"

"It'll be my pleasure," Bulygin said, inclining his head and bowing slightly.

Chapter 39

Anna liked Bulygin from the moment she first saw him. She liked his lean, narrow frame which was in such contrast to the stout and stocky men of her father's circle. Even the young men of her age were already bulky, the stoutness being considered a sign of prosperity. She liked his shy smile and she really enjoyed listening to the stories of his voyages.

She listened to his descriptions of London and Copenhagen, thinking, "Was it possible that I could see such places some day?" She yearned to see the world beyond the frozen *taiga* and dull Irkutsk. She followed Bulygin's voyages on a large globe, tracing his route from England to St. Petersburg. "I envy you your travels," she sighed.

Although Anna's own father remained illiterate, she was well-educated. Gorbatov had high ambitions for his children. He had realized that only by becoming educated would his children, including his daughter, ever be able to rise above their station in life. He was inspired by his friend and mentor, Grigory Shelikhov, who had succeeded in marrying his own daughter to the late Chamberlain of the Court, an hereditary nobleman, Nikolai Rezanov.

Following the example of Shelikhov, Gorbatov imported tutors from Moscow to teach his children the necessary skills of reading and writing, and his daughter, in addition, the gentle arts of playing a clavichord, dancing and speaking French, the language of nobility.

Anna surpassed her brothers in learning, soon to become her father's bookkeeper. At sixteen she read voraciously, exhausting the limited supply of books in the town's library. Gorbatov began to order books for her from St. Petersburg. He was proud of his daughter.

After two weeks of enjoying Bulygin's stories in the company of her father and brothers, Anna wanted to know more about his personal life. She waited until they were alone in her father's study.

"It must be terrible for your wife when you are at sea," she said.

"I am not married, Anna Petrovna," Bulygin said, annoyed with himself for blushing. He had been attracted to Anna from the first day of their meeting, the attraction growing into infatuation.

"I knew it!" Anna thought. With a prescience of a much more mature woman than her sixteen years would warrant, she sensed that captain Bulygin was in love with her. She observed his discomfort, waiting for him to speak. He kept silent.

"He's too shy," Anna thought.

They stood near the globe on which the captain traced for her the route he was about to take when he would leave for Kodiak. Their hands almost touched.

"I want to marry him," Anna thought. "I've never met a finer or more interesting man... Or a better looking one..." Boldly, she put her hand over his.

"I know that you love me, Nikolai Isayevich," she said softly. "I want you to marry me. Go and ask my father for my hand... I promise, he won't refuse."

Because of Bulygin's impending departure for Russian America, the engagement, wedding and feast had been squeezed into a ten day period. The usual prenuptial meetings of the groom with the friends of the bride's father had to be eliminated.

The old log church shone with the flickering light of hundreds of wax candles. The light reflected on the gilded frames of the ancient icons, illuminating the stern faces of saints and martyrs peering down on the worshipers below.

The wedding guests crowded the church, each holding a lighted candle, waiting for the bride. She entered on the arm of her elder brother, her parents remaining in the house as demanded by tradition. She was dressed in a white brocade *sarafan* embroidered with seed pearls and silver thread. A high *kokoshnick* encrusted with pearls, made her look almost as tall as her bridegroom. Bulygin met her half way along the aisle.

A murmur of appreciative voices greeted the young couple. "They are so handsome," the guests whispered.

A bearded priest in a tall gilded mitre and heavily embroidered robes intoned the vows of marriage in a deep basso, which the archdeacon echoed in a high tenor. As Bulygin and Anna exchanged rings, the choir, hidden in the wings, sang *mnogy leta.*

The priest covered their clasped hands with a cloth of gold and led them three times around the *analoi*, upon which rested an old massive Bible. Four wedding attendants, changing every few minutes, held the golden crowns of matrimony over their heads throughout the ceremony.

At last the long service was over. The Bulygins, followed by the guests, left the church.

In the church yard a *troika* of white horses decorated with white pom-poms and ribbons, waited for the Bulygins. An old Cossack in a shaggy fur hat with a long peacock feather, was perched on the seat in front of the carriage. He bowed to the young couple.

Bulygin threw a handful of coins to a crowd of beggars for good luck. The guests settled in their own carriages and set off to Gorbatov's house for the wedding feast.

Anna astonished the family when a few days after the wedding she announced that she would accompany her husband to Kodiak.

"But *golubushka*, you can't do that!" her father cried throwing his hands above his head in a gesture of desperation. "It isn't done! No woman has ever set her foot in that wild country!"

"You forgot Natalia Shelikhova. She went to the Aleutian Islands more than twenty years ago," Anna smiled. She felt capable of enduring a long journey across Siberia and then over the ocean, to Kodiak Island. She saw no reason to be separated from her husband for three years just because no woman since Natalia had ever ventured to travel to Russian America.

No amount of tears from her mother, no persuasion by her father about the dangers of such a voyage would change her mind. She was determined to accompany her husband.

Bulygin was delighted by Anna's decision. Very few women would sacrifice comfort and security to follow their men, he thought. He was proud of this proof of her love, although he knew that there was another powerful reason for her decision. Anna was eager for adventure. She yearned to see other lands, other people than those of her dull, provincial Irkutsk.

Although he could see many difficulties in traveling with a woman, the pleasures of Anna's company outweighed his apprehensions. He was ecstatic about Anna. Making love to her had become the most significant part of his life. He had never been in love before. At twenty-five he had very limited experience with women. Too poor to afford a permanent mistress, he had visited brothels, now and then, finding little pleasure in bought encounters, feeling soiled after these brief visits, terrified of disease.

His love for Anna opened the gates for new feelings which flooded his whole being. For the first time in his life, Bulygin felt tenderness toward a woman. Loving Anna, feasting upon her young luscious body, he felt as if he were shedding his dry pedantic nature like a snake sheds its skin. He was emerging as a new person. He was becoming romantic.

The Bulygins departed from Irkutsk amidst the tears and lamentations of Anna's family. They were to travel along the Lena, living in a spacious cabin built atop a raft to be towed by a galley, rowed by a band of convicts, chained to one another at their ankles.

Peter Gorbatov waved his handkerchief as the galley and the raft slowly reached the middle of the wide river. The galley picked up speed aided by the swift current, soon disappearing beyond the bend.

Gorbatov fought the tears welling up in his eyes. His beloved daughter, his *golubushka* Anna, was gone...

Chapter 40

Anna enjoyed the slow river journey. Bundled up in a warm sable coat, her lap covered with a wolfskin blanket, she rested on a heap of animal skins spread on the raft, watching the never-changing scenery. It was still quite cold in early May, but the river was free of ice and the *taiga* on both shores was coming to life after the long winter. The maples and the cottonwoods, covered with buds, were bursting, ready to open. They stood out against the dark green of the old hemlocks and tall cedars, stretching their slender, still naked arms to the warming sun, rejoicing in spring.

The convicts sang as they rowed, the sound of their voices audible for miles along the wide, placid river.

Anna loved these melancholy songs. She sang along with the convicts, feeling sad and happy simultaneously. Bulygin did not share her love for these plaintive songs, but he enjoyed listening to her clear sweet voice. "I am a lucky man," he thought.

At night the huge canopy of the heavens spread over their heads as they lay in each other's arms, gazing at the stars through the tiny windows of their cabin.

"I have never dreamt that such happiness could exist," Bulygin thought as he caressed Anna's breasts under her long linen shift.

Anna always responded to his touch. She knew the convention. The "nice" women merely tolerated this part of their marriage, but her nature wouldn't permit this hypocrisy. Without false modesty she allowed her husband to explore her body, as she explored his, with curiosity. They caressed one another passionately, but always in the darkness, both having been brought up in the belief that nakedness was forbidden even with one's spouse.

As the days stretched into weeks, Anna began to invite two or three young Cossacks to her raft for tea. She presided over a stout copper *samovar* as the Cossacks joked with her in their broad Siberian dialect, which Bulygin often found incomprehensible. At such times his imagination tormented him as he would fantasize the Cossacks abandoning the galley to its fate, abducting his beloved, and disappearing with her into their dark *taiga*. Or, he fantasized a mutiny among the convicts, visualizing how they would murder him and the Cossacks, and carry off his Anna. But the worst of these terrible fantasies was the image of Anna responding to another man's touch.

Anna was ignorant of his torment. She saw in the young Cossacks her own brothers. She felt sorry for these lads who were so far away from their families. She felt sorry for the convicts as well, and wished that she could invite them to her raft, but she was afraid of them. She had been taught since childhood that all convicts were murderers and bandits. She was accustomed to seeing long caravans of them trudging along in chains on their way to the *ostrogs* near the Arctic circle or in Kamchatka. She was moved to tears by their emaciated faces, dirty, barely covered bodies, half-shaven heads and their swollen feet. It pained her that she could do nothing but offer them a few rubles and pray for their souls.

The convicts towing her raft were no exception. Anna sent food to them and persuaded her husband to distribute vodka among them at least once a week. It was about all she could do for them.

The men's shackles were never removed but an affinity of sorts had developed between them and the Cossacks. The young Cossacks helped the wretched prisoners build their campfires when the raft and the galley would come to shore for the night. They often shared their rations and even vodka with the convicts, curling up around the fires for the night not far from one another.

Bulygin, watching their encampment from his cabin on the raft, often thought that he could not distinguish who were the guards and who were the guarded.

By the beginning of June, six weeks after they left Gorbatov's house, the travelers reached Yakutsk. The first leg of their long journey was completed.

Bulygin planned to spend two weeks in Yakutsk, outfitting for their trek across the coastal mountain ranges to the sea of Okhotsk. He wished to buy pack horses and hire another Cossack convoy along with several Yakut guides. He knew that the trip across the mountains would be far more dangerous than their placid journey along the Lena.

Like all important visitors to Yakutsk, the Bulygins were invited to stay at the local monastery, as special guests of the bishop.

Anna decided to use her time by learning how to ride a horse. She begged the old bishop to lend her one from the monastery stables, until he relented.

She learned to ride quickly, sitting the horse astride to Bulygin's initial horror. But Anna was persistent.

"Please, darling, don't argue," she begged. "I'll be more comfortable astride, and I'll wear trousers. They are more practical than all these skirts." She pointed to her voluminous petticoats.

Bulygin tried to object, but she covered his mouth gently with her hand.

"Sh-sh-sh...I have decided. I'll ride astride and I'll wear men's clothing."

Surrendering, Bulygin kissed the hand covering his mouth.

The Bulygins bade good-bye to the hospitable old bishop, ready to begin their long trek over the mountains of the Dzhugdzhur range toward the sea of Okhotsk.

Anna was warmly dressed in several layers of clothing, a combination of the native Yakut attire of a cotton shirt, leather breeches and a short cotton-padded kaftan tightly belted with a Cossack military belt. She wore Yakut boots made of horsehide so closely sewn as to be waterproof. In her saddle bags, she carried additional winter clothing. Although they were to cross the Dzhugdzhur range in the middle of the summer, it was always like winter at high altitudes.

She plaited her long blond hair into multitudes of thin braids following the custom of the Yakut women. It would be impossible to keep her hair washed and brushed while on the trail, she thought. Should lice attack her, which was quite possible, it would be easier to find along the exposed skin created by parting her hair every one-half inch.

"I must be ready for *anything!*" she told her husband.

She felt at ease in a saddle, perched on the back of her shaggy horse, not much larger than a pony. She watched the Cossacks as they harnessed the pack horses with special wooden frames from which vertical planks rose on each side to support the load of two bales of equal weight. The pack horses were roped in groups of five, each to be led in a single file by a mounted Yakut guide.

The Yakuts led the horses onto the *parom,* and two row boats, manned by the Cossacks, towed it across to the eastern bank of the Lena.

The town of Yakutsk looked attractive from the opposite shore of the Lena. Built on high ground and surrounded by wooden stockades and watchtowers, the town looked charming, Anna thought. The copper domes of the three stone-built churches sparkled in the sun. Even the old wooden churches looked picturesque, their shingle-covered, onion-shaped domes crowned with shining crosses.

"How charming the town looks from this distance," Anna said squinting in the sun. "It looks like a fairytale city..."

"You look like a fairytale Tatar princess yourself," Bulygin murmured kissing Anna's ear peeking out from a cascade of dozens of thin braids. "I like your new appearance."

Anna smiled. "You don't mind my wearing trousers?"

"No. You look beautiful even in trousers!"

"I am certainly more comfortable in them," she laughed.

The convoy mounted. Bulygin gave the signal to move. Their hazardous journey across the Dzugdzhur range was about to begin.

Anna enjoyed her ride. But as the first hour went by, her arms and shoulders began to ache. Soon, her legs began to hurt as well. She glanced at the *sotnick* riding at the head of the column, hoping that he would signal a stop. But the old Cossack led the caravan at a steady pace.

It was Bulygin who finally suggested that they dismount and walk alongside their horses. He too, suffered from pain in his legs and back. He helped Anna down.

"I think we had better rest," Anna decided for both of them. "Nikita Stepanovich, please halt the convoy. I must rest!" she declared to the *sotnick*. "As you know, I am a novice rider."

"And I am out of practice," Bulygin joined her sheepishly.

The Cossack chuckled into his beard. He had expected that Anna would beg for mercy much sooner.

"Halt!" he shouted, raising his arm. The convoy stopped.

"No need to worry, Your Excellency," he reassured her. "But take my advice, get right back on the horse after the rest. It will hurt, but you must stay in the saddle. I'll fix a back rest for you that ought to help." He made a roll of a bearskin and tied it behind Anna's saddle.

Shortly, he insisted that they must continue. He lifted Anna into the saddle and she gripped the horse's flanks with her aching thighs. She was determined to ignore the pain.

The Cossacks were impressed. "She's tough!" They nodded approvingly. "She'll be no trouble on the trail."

When at last the caravan reached its first camp site, Anna had to be lifted off her horse, but she limped to her tent refusing assistance.

As the days went by, she felt less pain, until at last she began to fully enjoy the journey.

No longer saddle-sore, she often joined the *sotnick* at the head of the convoy. The old man was full of tales about the Yakuts, the nomads of Eastern Siberia, known for their great herds of horses.

"See those horse hairs hanging in the bushes?" he asked her once as they approached a narrow pass.

"Yakuts hang them on bushes as an offering to the mountain spirits for permission to enter the forbidden territory. By the time our guides have made a trip to Okhotsk and back, their horses' tails and manes will be gone. Plucked naked!"

"Poor horses!" Anna smiled. "Tell me more about the Yakuts," she urged.

"Well...Did I ever tell you that the Yakuts are afraid of bears? When they meet a bear, they bow, take their hats off and address the bear as *toyon*, a mighty chief. They beseech him not to harm them and beg him to let them pass. If the bear doesn't move, then of course they kill him without much ceremony," he laughed.

"Yakuts are good guides, aren't they?" Bulygin joined Anna and the old Cossack, listening to their conversation.

"The best. They know this region as a man knows the palm of his hand. And in the winter, they know best how to make a shelter in the snow and how to survive. We have learned a lot from the Yakuts."

The three of them rode at the head of the convoy along the shallow stream. During the rainy season the stream was a roaring cascade, but now the water barely reached above the horses' hooves. The horses enjoyed walking in the shallow water. It cooled their bruised legs, the soft sand cushioning their unshod hooves.

The craggy formations of the Stanovoy ridge, shaded in purple hues, rose vertically around them. Sometimes the path between the rocks grew so narrow that the riders' shoulders brushed against the mountainsides.

"How long before we reach Okhotsk?" Anna turned to the *sotnick*, repeating the question she had been asking for the past two weeks.

"Perhaps three more weeks if the weather holds. Are you bored with our company?" he glanced at her sideways, teasingly. He liked Anna.

"No, I am not bored," Anna laughed. "How can I be bored when I have a companion as good as you, Nikita Stepanovich?"

Bulygin, riding next to his wife, shifted in his saddle uneasily. He disliked Anna's camaraderie with the *sotnick*.

The weather favored the travelers, remaining bright and crisp. The Cossacks hunted, providing them with fresh deer meat, or sometimes wild duck and geese, which the Yakuts cooked over an open fire during their nightly stops. At times Anna felt that the journey was unreal and would never end, that they would ride in and out of the canyons, over the rocky paths until the end of their lives, as in a dream.

Then the weather had suddenly changed. Ominous clouds hid the mountains and a torrential rain descended upon the earth with a vengeance. Thunder reverberated among the narrow canyons. Within minutes the path under the horses' hooves was awash, swiftly becoming a torrent.

The *sotnick* signaled for a halt. The path was too narrow to set up camp. A scout was sent to search for a suitable place where they could open their tents and unload their pack horses.

They waited, watching the swirling waters rising around their horses' legs.

Time crawled interminably. Finally the Yakut returned. He had found a small clearing, out of the path of the rushing water. He led the caravan toward it, cautiously moving the pack horses over the steep course, hidden by the rushing torrent. If even one horse had lost its footing and fallen over the edge, the whole *svyazka*, tied to one another, would follow.

The Yakut held the rope to his *svyazka* in his teeth, while he probed ahead with a long pole, guiding his horse with his knees. The other Yakuts followed him in similar fashion. Soon the Cossacks too, began to move slowly, one by one, the *sotnick* leading Anna's horse.

The storm began to subside. The thunder, less violent now, sounded like the booming of siege cannons, heard from afar. The sky began to brighten as patches of blue appeared above the mountains, contrasting sharply with the dark heavy clouds. Then, the sun peeked from around the clouds, illuminating the mountaintops. A rainbow formed a lovely arch linking the top of one mountain with another.

The travelers reached the clearing and struck camp. Below them, at the foot of the mountain, was the swollen Akachan River.

From their camp the river looked like a broad lake with clusters of trees protruding from its surface like green islands.

Anna stared at the flooded valley with a feeling close to panic. "I have never seen anything so awesome! How can we possibly cross this water?" she whispered, but the old Cossack heard her.

"Don't worry, Anna Petrovna, I'll see to it that you cross the river without getting your boots wet!" he chuckled good-naturedly. "Even if I have to carry you on my back!"

They remained at their camp for a week, watching the Akachan slowly recede. Finally the *sotnick* gave the order to mount up.

The caravan cautiously made its way down to the rock-strewn bank covered with mud and the debris of broken trees. They paused, astounded to see many up-rooted trees which had floated along the river during the flood, being now caught by the clusters of trees on the shores. With the river receding, the uprooted trunks had become entangled in the branches of the living trees. They hung precariously above the receding water.

The Cossacks pulled several uprooted trees across the narrowed river, covering them thickly with fir branches, creating an improvised bridge. The Yakuts unloaded the pack horses and led them into the water. The Cossacks crossed the river over the flimsy bridge, carrying the packs on their heads. Anna and Bulygin followed. As the *sotnick* had promised, Anna's boots did not get wet.

Once across the river their path became easier. Almost every night now they stayed at posting stations, changing horses regularly. Finally, six weeks after they had left Yakutsk, they caught their first sight of the sea. They gazed at it, glistening in the distance, steely-gray.

Okhotsk, their destination, was within sight.

Chapter 41

The schooner *Vladimir* was about to weigh anchor, when the Company agent ashore signaled that passengers had just arrived from Yakutsk and the *Vladimir* was to wait.

Captain Petrov swore. "Who can be going to the colonies so late in the year?" he thought. "Whoever they may be, I don't intend to waste another day in Okhotsk!"

Were it up to him, Petrov would never sail into the treacherous waters of Okhotsk. The town was built on a spit of land, in the delta of the rivers Okhota and Kukhtui, which formed one mouth, where they emptied into the Sea of Okhotsk. Ships putting in at the town could enter the Okhota only at high tide.

Many were wrecked in the delta, because of the constantly changing currents between the river and the sea. The town itself was often flooded as the river rose at high tide, spilling over the crooked streets.

Petrov detested the town's dirty, rotting wooden houses, its mudcovered streets and the gray columns of chained prisoners that shuffled along them.

He disliked the free citizens of Okhotsk as well. He considered the men drunkards and scoundrels and the women not much better. Yet, he had to choose his crew from these men. Only the threat of floggings kept them in line.

Petrov's frustration turned to dismay when he learned that his passengers would be Nikolai Bulygin and wife. He was about to bellow his objections when he caught sight of Anna as she hesitated at the narrow gangplank.

She smiled and strode up the flimsy board ramp. By now she was used to men's reaction to her beauty and Captain Petrov's expression was easy to read. In a matter of minutes he offered her his own cabin and moved his gear to the mates' cabin.

Anna had never seen an oceangoing vessel before. She was pleased with her tiny cabin with its two narrow bunks built with raised sides like a child's cradle. She strolled around the open deck and the captain's bridge with its spoked wheel. She stared up at the tall masts with the lookout's crow's next on top of one of them and the sails, gathered neatly under the yards, feeling excited, like a child. She chatted with the crew, the wind playing with the strands of her wheat colored hair. The men had followed her every move since she first appeared.

Captain Petrov knew exactly what he must do next. There was danger for Anna and it must be eliminated he thought. He called the men together on the deck below the bridge. They stared up at him with vodka-dulled faces.

"If any of you bastards try *to touch the lady,* you will be hanged!" Petrov stared at each face in turn, his eyes hard. Then he snapped, "Dismissed!"

Anna had never thought that anyone would want to harm her. The thought of rape never entered her mind. But the tone of Petrov's voice was such that she stepped closer to her husband. He placed a protective arm over her shoulders, fingering the handle of his pistol.

From the beginning of the voyage Anna felt seasick. She lay in her bunk, unable to eat, vomiting until only bile remained. She felt weak as an infant.

Bulygin nursed her tenderly, washing her face and changing her clothing. He fed her miniscule amounts of warm porridge and made her sip strong camomile tea. When at last Anna was able to retain a small amount of food, he knew that the worst was over.

The *Vladimir* was caught in a vicious storm along the western coast of the Kamchatka Peninsula. Battered by gale force winds, the ship pitched and rolled for three days and nights. Then the winds died completely. The ship lay becalmed, near the Kurile Islands, lost in the dense fog. Captain Petrov furled the sails waiting for the new wind to disperse the fog.

After her days of illness, Anna finally emerged on deck. She looked pale and thin, her cheekbones more prominent and her face even more beautiful with the loss of its childlike roundness. Captain Petrov placed an old rattan chair on the bridge for her. Sitting there she watched the daily routine of the ship.

The wind rose again and the *Vladimir* sailed on. The weather grew cold and Anna donned her sable coat. She liked to stay on the bridge despite the chilly air. She watched the sea birds, the gulls, the petrels, and cormorants as they flew over the ship, sometimes resting on its rigging. One day the *Vladimir* was joined by a school of whales blowing spouts of water. The captain reassured her that they had nothing to fear. The whales were friendly creatures if left alone.

It began to snow. The *Vladimir* sailed past the islands of the Aleutian chain, some of them denuded of all vegetation by the brutal winds, while others were covered thickly by coniferous trees. Anna was fascinated by the scenery, and thrilled by the sight of a smoking volcano glimpsed through the mists.

"I have never seen such good sailing weather so late in the season!" Petrov exclaimed one morning after they had been at sea for over four weeks. "You must have brought us luck," he smiled at Anna. "If we continue this way, we'll be in Kodiak within a week."

"And none too soon! Although I no longer get sick, I have had enough sailing. I can't understand how anybody can *love the sea!*" she said.

The men laughed. "No woman could possibly ever understand that!" Bulygin replied. "It's the challenge, the conquest, the danger!"

"And the seasickness," Anna laughed.

The *Vladimir* skimmed the sea like a pelican. However, their luck changed as they came within sight of Kodiak Island. The wind died down once again, and the becalmed seas barely rippled beneath the ship.

A faint sound of a cannon from Pavlovsk settlement acknowledged their presence within the Kodiak waters. Soon several *baidarki* appeared to tow the ship into the harbor.

Anna watched from the bridge as the *baidarki* reached the *Vladimir* and a bearded Russian *promyshlenik* and several Aleuts climbed aboard. They brought a huge rectangular *pirog*, still warm from the oven, its crust stuffed with fish and rice, a gift from Governor Baranov. There was also a note welcoming the ship to Pavlovsk.

The captain divided the *pirog* to serve everyone and issued a *charka* of vodka for every man to celebrate their safe arrival. "With God's help we made it, *bratzi!*" he said, tossing the vodka down his throat in one gulp. "There's no truth in the old saying that a woman aboard a ship brings misfortune!"

Governor Baranov waited at the landing, staring at the ship through a curtain of slowly falling wet snow, watching as the *Vladimir* was pulled to her moorings in the harbor. The sight of a ship still excited him, although he hardly ever ventured out to sea now, leaving the daily administration of various settlements in the hands of his deputies. He preferred to remain in his cozy, disorderly office, getting ready for retirement, but still thinking about expansion of Russian interests on the American continent. He never gave up his dream for a truly *Russian* America.

"If only Rezanov had lived to marry his Spanish beauty!" Baranov thought. "We could have had the whole Alta California in our pocket by now!"

Yet he did not let the loss of Rezanov's influence stop him. Stubborn as ever, Baranov commenced to develop his own strategy. Following Rezanov's basic plan, he purchased two new ships from the Yankees and the British, to chart the waters around the mouth of the Columbia River and Gray's Harbor. As far as he knew, the territory there was still unclaimed. Meanwhile, he wrote detailed letters to his superiors, explaining his plan. He knew these letters would remain long undelivered because there would be no more ships leaving for Russia until the next spring, but it did not bother him. By the time his letters reached St. Petersburg, the first part of the expansion plan would already be underway.

Squinting, Baranov readjusted his telescope, watching the *Vladimir* reach her moorings and drop anchor. "I wish the bastards would hurry," he muttered, his fingers stiff around the cold tube of the telescope. It began to drizzle, the wet snow turning into rain.

Baranov shivered. He pulled his *shapka* closer over his ears, touching the soggy fur with distaste.

He saw a longboat lowered and several people climb down into it. Several more piled into the surrounding *baidarki*. The small flotilla slowly moved toward the shore. Soon Baranov was able to see two men in naval officers' uniforms. "Good, they finally *did* send me the naval officers!" he grumbled, his spirits rising considerably. He needed qualified captains to sail his new ships. Now they were here, at last!

The lightweight *baidarki* were the first to reach the landing.

"Who's the master of the ship?" Baranov demanded from a man who jumped on the landing.

"Captain Petrov, sir."

"Any passengers?"

"Yes, sir. Captain Bulygin and his wife." Baranov nodded in recognition of Bulygin's name. "I remember him. So, he's married now and he brought a wife along, eh. Who is she, a creole or an Indian?"

"Neither, sir. She's a Russian lady from Irkutsk. A *beautiful lady.*"

"Beautiful, you say?" Baranov chuckled, his irritability suddenly vanishing. "A beautiful *Russian* lady, eh?" The young man saluted and hurried to catch up with the others on their way to the communal barracks.

The ship's boat edged alongside the landing. Two young men in naval lieutenants uniforms vaulted up from the boat onto the landing. They saluted the Governor, who raised his hand to his wet *shapka* without looking at them. His eyes were on Anna. Wrapped in a bearskin blanket, she sat on a pile of cushions at the bottom of the boat, her face pink from the cold, her eyes sparkling.

The officers helped her to the dock. Although she was dressed in men's clothing, with her hair plaited into two thick braids, Baranov thought he had never seen a woman more beautiful. She smiled at the Governor, and murmured, "I am so honored to meet such a legendary man at last! I am well rewarded for the rigors of our journey from Irkutsk. I've heard so much about you from my father!"

"Madame, the pleasure is solely mine!" Baranov replied and raised her mittened hand to his lips.

The Bulygins were given the best quarters, an old hut with a leaky roof. It had two rooms, one of which was filled with neatly stacked piles of dry, sawed logs. The other had a clay stove with a *lezhanka.* A roughhewn table and two hard benches were the only pieces of furniture. The tiny windows covered with mica, allowed little light to penetrate the gloomy dampness of the hut. "Aren't you sorry now that you came with me?" Bulygin asked, afraid that Anna might say "yes."

"No," she replied without hesitation. "This is nothing!" She made a sweeping gesture with her hands indicating the empty room. "I'll fix this hovel into a cozy place in no time. I can live anywhere, as long as I am with you!" She smiled and her cheeks dimpled.

"You are my treasure," he murmured, wanting to embrace her, yet hesitating in the presence of the Aleut women.

"Of course!" Anna laughed. "Now your treasure will start the fire."

Despite the fire, they spent their first night sleeping fully clothed on the still cold *lezhanka*. It would take two or three days for the bricks to be thoroughly warmed.

In the morning, Bulygin was in an irritable mood. Their luggage had still not been brought ashore. The rising wind made it impossible to send a boat to the ship. He paced the empty room, feeling utterly helpless.

There was a knock on the ill-fitting door and the Governor entered, his back bent, his fur hat plastered with wet snow, which began to melt and drip over his turned-up collar. His pale-blue eyes were ringed in red as if he had not slept for a long time. His sparse white hair surrounded his head like ruffled feathers.

"A thought occurred to me," he said, as if continuing an interrupted conversation, seating himself on a hard bench and taking off his wet *shapka*. "As I met you yesterday, Anna Petrovna, I realized what a miserable place our settlement must be for a lady. I was wrong when I thought that we were ready to bring Russian women to America," he mumbled as if to himself. Anna and Bulygin waited for him to continue. "I am used to Pavlovsk, but to you it must look terrible."

"Well...Not really." Anna was caught by surprise.

"Don't deny it, my dear, *it is terrible*," he said wearily. "You'll hibernate here like bears until spring. So, I have a proposal. You must occupy yourself with something useful." He took his parka off. "It's getting warm," he said.

"I agree, Alexander Andreyevich, but what exactly do you have in mind?" Anna could not imagine what useful occupation could be found for her on the island where she was the only white woman.

"Anna Petrovna, you must forgive an old man, but I want

to exploit your presence here. I need your help!" He looked at her imploringly, his eyes veiled with sadness.

"What can I do?"

"First, you can give me a glass of hot tea. While we sip it, I'll tell you what you can do," he replied.

"Of course! Please forgive me." Anna hurried to the storeroom to order an Aleut woman to boil water in a samovar.

The Governor faced Bulygin. "I need your consent, Captain," he said lowering his voice. "I propose that Anna Petrovna teach our native girls the gentle arts, such as sewing and embroidery. The winter is long and she soon will be bored among so many men. Women need companionship of their own gender. Just as men do."

"I can hardly think that native girls are suitable companions for a lady," Bulygin objected.

"They are children, my dear Captain," Baranov replied without offence. "The mixed-blood children. We call them 'creoles'. They will worship Anna Petrovna!"

"Who will worship me?" Anna entered the room carrying a tin of English biscuits.

"The children, Anna Petrovna, the little creole girls who are half-Russian, yet who don't know *how to be Russian*. Their mothers can't teach them; they are native women. And their fathers, although they are Russians, can't teach their daughters sewing or embroidering. Without you the little girls will have no chance of being anything but half-breeds. The girls need you, Anna Petrovna!" He looked at her in such a mournful, pleading way, she laughed. The great Governor begging a favor from her!

"Yes," Anna said simply.

"But, Anechka..." Bulygin began to object.

"Darling, I want to do it," Anna said softly but with a steely note in her voice. Bulygin said no more.

An Aleut brought in the samovar and placed it in the middle of the table as another woman brought a tray with tall glasses.

"I am sorry, Alexander Andreyevich, but we have little to offer you," Anna apologized. "Our baggage has not yet been brought from the ship and we have only this tin of old English biscuits. Not even sugar! And we don't have glass holders!"

"Don't worry, Anna Petrovna, I did not come here for

a banquet," Baranov reassured her. "I came here to talk to you and your husband. As to the supplies, I'll see to it that you lack nothing."

Chapter 42

Three weeks passed quickly. Anna bustled about transforming their damp dwelling into a warm, comfortable house. The leaky roof was fixed, the cracks in the walls patched with dry moss and hemp, the holes in the floor plugged with tarred wads of rope. Baranov had sent them three large bearskins to spread on the floor and two foxskin blankets.

A bag of bullrushes served them as a mattress. Anna brought along linen sheets and plump goosedown pillows, which made their *lezhanka* as comfortable as her bed in her father's house. She spread an embroidered shawl on the table and draped linen towels, edged in coarse lace, around the windows in traditional peasant style.

Captain Petrov presented her with the rattan chair on which she had spent so many hours aboard his ship, adding to it a brightly embroidered cushion, a parting gift from his mother.

The bitter winter started early. Huge drifts piled up against the Bulygins' door, isolating them in their house.

"I hate this place!" Bulygin complained, pacing the hut.

"I'm used to being imprisoned by snow," Anna said with a smile. "In Irkutsk we have it every winter."

"Well I'm not. I am accustomed to more civilized conditions."

When at last the storms quieted down, Baranov appeared at the Bulygins' door holding two young girls by their hands.

"Here...They are Masha and Olya." he said brusquely. "If they misbehave, whip them."

"Alexander Andreyevich! What are you saying! I am not going to *whip* anybody."

The children clung to one another, shyly peeking at Anna from under the hoods of their furry parkas.

"I'll be going now," Baranov said. "I would like Captain Bulygin to accompany me to my office. We have much to discuss in preparation for his journey in the spring."

Bulygin bowed, barely hiding his displeasure. He was reluctant to leave their warm nest and trudge through the snow to the Governor's office.

"He'll be back in a couple of hours," Baranov promised, winking at Anna. "You need a little respite from one another!" The men left before Anna thought of a proper reply.

"He's right. We need a little time apart, even just to realize how much we miss one another!" she thought. She turned her attention to the children. "Come over here. Sit with me by the fire. My name is Anna Petrovna."

The girls took their outer garments off and bashfully lowered themselves to the very edge of the bench, touching shoulders as if afraid to lose contact with one another.

"They look like little nestlings," Anna thought. "How old are you?" she asked.

"Ten," one of them whispered.

"I'm nine," the other followed, almost inaudibly. "We'll have some tea and cookies, first," Anna smiled, expecting the girls to smile in return. But they merely stared. Their dark eyes watched Anna's every movement as she opened a cupboard and placed three cups and saucers on a tray. She called to her servant to boil water and bring it when it was ready. Then she placed a handful of cookies on a platter and set it on the table.

"All right girls, let's sit down," she said brightly, pointing to the bench at the table. Awkwardly, the children sat at the table, their eyes never leaving her face.

"How can I make them talk?" Anna thought, discouraged by their silence. "Have some cookies."

They stared at the platter making no move.

"Have a cookie," she urged, taking one herself.

Timidly, the children stretched their thin hands toward the platter, their eyes still on her, distrustful.

"Eat!" Anna ordered sharply. They began to nibble, biting off tiny pieces, holding the cookies all but hidden inside their fists.

The Aleut woman brought the samovar in and Anna busied herself with making tea. The children watched her closely.

"You eat just like squirrels!" Anna laughed, deciding to take another approach. "You know—crunch, crunch, crunch." She made a funny face, trying to look like a squirrel. The girls smiled thinly.

"Why don't you talk to me?" Anna insisted. "Has a cat gotten your tongue?" The children shook their heads and stuck out their tongues.

"If you don't want to talk, then I will. I'll tell you about myself when I was your age." She began, telling them about growing up in Irkutsk, about her parents and her brothers, about her dog, Polkan, and her fears when once she thought he was lost.

"Did you find him?" Masha suddenly broke her silence.

"Yes, someone found him wandering around and brought him back to me."

"We have a dog," little Olya volunteered. "Her name is Snezhinka."

"What a lovely name! Snezhinka! Is she white and fluffy, like a snowflake?"

"Yes," Olya said shyly.

The ice was broken. By the time Bulygin returned, the children were chatting with Anna as if they had known her all their lives. "I can see you made another conquest," he said, shaking the snow off his parka.

Anna smiled. "All right, girls, run along now!" she kissed the children's round cheeks. She waved from the door as they disappeared in the swirling snow.

"I enjoyed myself...I look forward to their return visit." Anna said. "Did you have a good time with the Governor?"

"Not I. I had to suffer his reminiscences," Bulygin retorted. Anna laughed and kissed him.

"Did you miss me?" he asked.

"I had no chance to think of you," she confessed. "I was busy concentrating on my "conquest" of the children's hearts," she laughed.

Masha and Olya returned the next day with three more girls. A few days later, four more girls joined the group.

Bulygin resented the intrusion. He did not want to share Anna with anyone. He wanted her thoughts, her pleasures, her concerns to belong only to him. He would go to Baranov's office the moment the girls arrived. Even Baranov's ramblings were better than watching Anna enjoying herself with others.

The winter dragged on. Anna was oblivious of the depressing darkness. She was happy. She thought that she was pregnant, but hesitated to confide in her husband, waiting for more proof, cherishing her delicious secret, before raising his expectations. She ignored the winds howling in the chimney, feeling safe inside her snug little house. She was a *sibiryachka*, accustomed to harsh winters. She had learned to endure the dark winter months by preparing for the future. All her friends had spent their winters in the isolation of their homes. They made lace and embroidered tablecloths and towels, which eventually would become part of their dowry. They were supervised by older women, who worked alongside them, embroidering shirts for their husbands and sons, while the grandmothers, ruling over them all, knitted soft warm shawls. There was always plenty of sweets and much tea drinking at such gatherings. Men were not allowed to be present at these *devichniki* but Anna's younger brothers often sneaked in, hiding under the table covered with a long velvet mantel, waiting for Anna to pass sweets under the table.

Anna smiled, remembering those winter gatherings at her father's house. Once or twice a week, she and her mother visited the homes of her aunts and cousins, bringing their work with them, gliding along in a *troika*, arriving glowing from frost, her mother downing a silver *charka* of vodka offered by the hostess to chase the cold. A blizzard might rage outside, but the women were safe within their small circle, listening to old Siberian folktales told by someone's ancient nurse, or singing sad Siberian songs in close harmony.

Anna tried to recreate the same atmosphere of warmth for her pupils. She taught them the songs she had loved since her childhood. They would sing together, one group baking cookies, the other learning how to cut a pattern for a dress or to hem a skirt. Anna went from one girl to another, correcting a stitch here, congratulating a shy baker there, encouraging everyone with a pat on the head.

Some weeks later, Bulygin found lice in his hair.

"No more! Enough! I won't allow these dirty half-breeds into my house anymore!" he shouted.

Anna had never seen him angry. It frightened her. "But Kolya, dearest, be reasonable, it might not be the children's fault. It could be that our own servants brought in the lice," she protested.

"I forbid you to have these creoles in my house!" he pounded on the table. The sound of his fist against the wood reinforced his anger.

Anna's eyes welled with tears, but she proudly gathered herself up.

"Don't *ever* shout at me," she whispered, trembling. "I can understand your concern about finding lice, but it is not fair to blame it on the children!" Anna's face was suddenly drained of its color.

Bulygin was instantly repentant. "I am sorry. I didn't mean to shout at you. Please forgive me, my darling, my dearest, my precious, I didn't mean to upset you." He fell on his knees, searching for her hands and covering them with kisses.

"I know how much you enjoy teaching these girls. But I'm worried about your health. You're looking so tired lately."

Anna glanced at him quickly. "Does he know that I am pregnant?" she thought. "No...How could he? But he's right. I must be careful now. Fifteen girls are too many; they do *tire* me. Perhaps you're right," she said aloud.

He nodded, waiting.

"I'll select four most capable girls and train them to be the teachers of the others. The Governor will be pleased as well. He is already bemoaning the coming of spring when we would be gone from Kodiak. He is afraid his plans to train the girls in 'the womanly arts', as he calls it, will collapse with our departure."

"Yes, it is *definite* now that we will be leaving for Novo-Arkhangelsk in the early summer."

"I'll be half over my pregnancy by the time we sail," Anna thought. "I hope I won't be seasick again!" To Bulygin she said, "I wish there were some other way to travel than by ship."

Bulygin smiled at her. "You'll love sailing in the summer! The seas are calm, and we'll be going south, toward a much more temperate climate."

Their quarrel was forgotten. Anna called for a samovar. She debated briefly with herself whether to tell him about her pregnancy, but decided to wait a little longer. "I must be *absolutely sure!*" she thought.

Anna shivered on the warm *lezhanka*, unable to get warm under a cover of blankets and furs. She knew now that she was no longer pregnant. The blood flow of a miscarriage was massive and Anna felt spent at the end of four days. She was glad that she had not confided in her husband. "He would have been so disappointed," she thought.

"It's for the best," she told herself. "This is no place for a white woman to have babies. There are no doctors, no midwives...Who would have delivered my baby?" she thought, trying to convince herself that she was really *glad* that there was no baby. But she cried quietly nevertheless, mourning her unborn child.

Spring had arrived suddenly. Only the night before, heavy snowflakes kept falling on the ground, but by morning the warm winds from the south transformed them into raindrops, melting the snow.

It rained for several days, and when it finally stopped, instead of snow, there was mud. But it was spring. The sun peered from behind the black clouds, and days began to lighten and to lengthen.

The mood of the people brightened as well. Anna, slowly recovering from her miscarriage, resumed her work with the four chosen girls. Soon they were ready to teach the others.

Baranov was delighted. "If it were up to me, Anna Petrovna, I would give you the Order of St. Catherine! How can I ever thank you enough?"

Anna smiled. She seldom smiled now. Her painful recovery from the miscarriage was followed by a depression, which she was just beginning to overcome.

"The success of my pupils is gratifying enough, Alexander Andreyevich," she said.

"In another month you'll be sailing to Novo-Arkhangelsk," Baranov continued. "I am sending two ships there. I have a special assignment for them, a voyage of exploration!"

"A voyage of exploration?"

"Yes, my lady, a voyage that may change Russian destiny!" Baranov said with a faraway look in his watery eyes.

Chapter 43

Two ships left Pavlovsk with the first winds of May, Bulygin in command of the *Nikolai* and Petrov the captain of the *Kodiak*.

Anna fully enjoyed her voyage this time. The weather was perfect, as her husband had promised it would be, and she suffered no seasickness. Bulygin was happy also. He was doing the kind of work he loved and his treasure, his Anna was at his side.

The two ships sailing in tandem, often raced one another, challenging the competence of their captains and the crew against each other, the losers saluting the winners with a salvo from their ship's cannons.

It took nearly three weeks for the ships to reach Novo-Arkhangelsk.

The capital of Russian America was fortified with stout logs set close together and backed by more than sixty cannons. Governor Baranov had sworn that never again would the Indians take this town.

Novo-Arkhangelsk now had several streets bordered by squat log houses and the onion-domed church under construction. At the water's edge there were carpenters' shops, sailmaking sheds, a blacksmithy and forges. There was a new warehouse next to a *zapruda* where dozens of tree trunks floated, to prevent them from cracking in the sun. In time the logs would be removed from the *zapruda*, dried and hewn into perfectly straight masts and yards. Further along the shore, stood curing sheds where sheathing planks for the ships were prepared. The air was filled with the biting smell of hot wet wood mixed with the scent of melting tree sap.

The dream of Governor Baranov to have a real shipyard

had finally come true. Three ships in different phases of construction were surrounded by scaffolds. The Yankee shipwrights whom the Governor had hired from Boston, scurried around the vessels, their Russian apprentices at their heels. The air rang with the sound of hammers and the wheezing of saws.

"Our own Russian ships built right here, where they are needed!" Bulygin exclaimed.

Anna stepped onto the rickety landing jutting out into the sea. The wind whipped about her, flattening her skirts around her legs. She grabbed at the skirts with one hand while with the other she struggled to keep her hair from falling down to her shoulders. Unsuccessful, she gave up and laughed, as she looked back at her husband.

"Hurry up, before the wind blows me away!" she cried.

He offered her his hand, but she declined, laughing, indicating her billowing skirts that she now had to hold down with both hands, abandoning her hair. It cascaded over her shoulders in a heavy golden mass, the wind whipping it up into a shimmering halo.

On shore, Timofei and Ivan Kuskov, stood on the balcony of the Governor's new residence watching the disembarking travelers through their telescopes.

"A Russian lady! I'd better go down and greet her," Kuskov said limping down the hill. He was crippled during a battle with the Tlingits some years before.

"Aren't you going?" he shouted, seeing that Timofei had remained on the balcony.

"You go. I'll join you later." Timofei did not want to relinquish the observation post that allowed him to spy on the new arrival without her being aware of it. He watched the mysterious woman and the group of men surrounding her.

"She is young," he reflected. "Only young women have such bright hair." His heart was pounding as he refocused his telescope. Her face, suddenly very near, made him hold his breath. She was *beautiful*. The most beautiful woman he had ever seen. More beautiful than any portrait of a court lady. He was right, she was young, no more than eighteen. Timofei could clearly see her shiny white teeth as she laughed and struggled against the stubborn wind. He saw Kuskov hurry toward the new arrivals, bowing to the woman and saluting the two men in naval uniform, who were obviously the captains of the ships. Kuskov led them toward the Governor's residence where special rooms were always ready for important visitors. Folding his telescope, Timofei left the balcony.

By her clothes he knew the golden-haired stranger was a lady. Whoever she was—she was not for him.

Anna liked Novo-Arkhangelsk from the first moment she saw the green lushness of the island, the peculiar formations of the surrounding archipelago of miniscule islands dotting Sitka Sound, the lofty cone of Edgecumbe volcano in the distance. She was delighted that the fort had the appearance of a town, rather than a military outpost. It reminded her of Russian towns in Siberia.

The Bulygins were given the best room in the Governor's residence, facing the bay. It was furnished in European style with a mirrored armoir and a broad bed, so high, one had to use a small stepstool to get into it.

Anna bounced on the bed like a child. "I like it so much!" she exclaimed happily, turning to her husband. "Look, real goosedown pillows and Holland linen sheets!"

Bulygin smiled. "I am so glad you're not disappointed, my darling. I was afraid your taste for adventure would turn sour after living in such primitive conditions."

"Primitive conditions? No more! This is not Pavlovsk. I have never seen such a lovely bed! No even in Irkutsk!" she exclaimed. "And it was not just my 'taste for adventure' that made me follow you to America. I wanted to be with you."

Bulygin held her, thinking once again what a lucky man he was.

"And so, here we are, in Novo-Arkhangelsk, together!" he said caressing Anna's luxuriant hair.

"I like Novo-Arkhangelsk!" Anna wiggled out of his arms and unfastened her cumbersome petticoats. "Even the weather here seems to be better than in Pavlovsk. Much warmer."

Bulygin did not reply. He watched as one petticoat after another fell at her feet, surrounding her with a ring of coarse white lace, like frothy foam on top of the waves. To his eyes Anna was a Venus stepping out of the sea. He felt desire welling up in him. How he would love to tear Anna's corset off and carry her to the tall bed! But it was impossible. It was daytime. The brilliant sun poured through the uncurtained windows, sharply illuminating every object. They could not make love in broad daylight. It was not done. They must wait for the night. He looked away from her.

Reading his thoughts, Anna smiled. She was about to slip a fresh dress over her head, but changed her mind. Instead, she unlaced her corset and freed her breasts. Round and firm, their pale nipples stood erect. She pulled a string and untied her pantaloons. "Look at me," she whispered. She pressed her soft lips against his and kissed him, slowly and sensuously. "We don't have to wait until dark," she murmured. "Besides, there is no real darkness here in the summer." She caressed his face with small kisses, until Bulygin found himself struggling with the buttons of his tunic, his fingers refusing to obey him. Anna helped him, unbuttoning one button at a time, looking deeply into his eyes. "Take off *all* your clothes," she whispered.

Clumsily he shed his tunic, hesitating to unbutton his trousers in front of her. Understanding, Anna turned her head away. Hastily he shed the rest of his clothes.

The sun bathed the room in its rays. It was the first time they had seen one another in the nude, as they made love tenderly, without the cover of darkness.

By the time Timofei was introduced to Anna three days after her arrival, he already knew that she was the bride of Captain Nikolai Bulygin, the master of the *Nikolai*.

He felt strangely relieved that Anna was unobtainable. Yet, he could not get her out of his mind. He had not seen a Russian woman since he had left the Cossack village twelve years ago, and he had *never* seen such a perfect beauty as Anna Petrovna Bulygina. Even Concha seemed only an exquisite child in comparison to the lush beauty of Anna.

A few days after the arrival of the ships a routine was established among the captains, their officers and a few chosen *promyshleniki* who began to gather at the Governor's residence every evening. They limited their drinking to gentlemanly quantities, staring at the captain's wife as if enchanted, listening to her sing in a soft girlish voice as she accompanied herself on the clavichord, recently purchased from an English captain.

Timofei attended all these evenings leaning against a doorway at the back of the room, always first to leave at the end of the little recital, terrified that he might betray his passion.

Anna was aware of Timofei nonetheless. It was impossible to overlook the tallest and the most powerfully built man among the *promyshleniki*. He was also the most handsome. The black patch over his eye added to his attractiveness.

Anna was curious about this romantic-looking figure. "Why is he so sad?" she thought, "and why does he avoid me?"

She spent the summer waiting for her husband and captain Petrov to prepare their ships for the next voyage. The *Kodiak* was to sail south into the waters of Spanish America, while Bulygin on the *Nikolai*, was to update Vancouver's charts of the coast along the mouth of the Columbia River.

Anna watched the outfitting of the *Nikolai* with personal interest. The brig was to be her home for several months and she was planning ways to make it comfortable.

Ivan Kuskov recommended that she take along her two Aleut women. Although Bulygin would rather have had two extra deck hands to add to the seventeen man crew, he allowed the two women to take bunks behind a curtain in the crew's quarters.

A day before the departure Kuskov presented Anna with a fluffy, white puppy. She promptly named the dog Snezhinka, in honor of her first pupils in Pavlovsk.

The ship was equipped with the latest survey instruments bought from the British. Captain Bulygin looked forward to working with them.

In her holds were stowed sacks of glass beads, bolts of calico cloth, hunting knives, and boxes of brass buttons for trade with the natives along the way.

Ivan Kuskov appointed Timofei to be in charge of the cargo on the *Nikolai*. It would be his responsibility to trade with the natives and to supervise the supplies, as he had done for Rezanov.

Timofei liked to be a part of a sailing crew, but the presence of Anna would add complications, he thought. It would be difficult for him to be in daily contact with her, yet he longed for that nearness.

The brig was ready for departure. The crew on the *Nikolai* was in high spirits. The voyage promised to be easy, although there were only seventeen men to work the brig. But seventeen good men, including a cabin boy, could manage her, Bulygin thought.

Kuskov watched the *Nikolai* sail away. He was to follow her within ten days on the *Kodiak* under Captain Petrov commanding his Okhotsk crew. The two ships were scheduled to meet in December in Gray's Harbor, a territory nominally belonging to the Spanish, but unprotected by them and therefore open for claim by an enterprising explorer.

He made the sign of the cross over the departing ship, wishing the *Nikolai* a safe journey. Then he spat over his left shoulder. He was superstitious about women aboard the ship.

Chapter 44

The brig took into the wind like a seagull. Her white sails taut, she skimmed the waves, gliding over the green ocean.

"What a beautiful day!" Anna thought as she stood leaning on the railing, watching the sea open under the ship's prow. The foam created intricate patterns as it separated under the bow, leaving two even sections on each side of the cut. The foam reminded her of delicate lace.

As the days passed she spent many pleasant hours on deck. She liked to watch the men as they clambered up and down the rigging, working the sails. The weather was still warm and the sure-footed sailors, hanging over the yards, wore nothing but their coarse canvas trousers.

The men felt inhibited by Anna. They were warned to watch their language and Timofei had threatened to crack the skull of the first man who relieved himself over the rail in her presence. She was a *barynya*, not a coarse woman, they had been warned. Yet, Timofei avoided her.

It became a challenge to Anna to win his friendship. She had heard he was a good singer, so she decided to approach him through music. She remembered the nights around the campfire in Siberia, singing with the Cossacks. How pleasant it would be if she could get the sailors to sing too.

She called to Timofei as she sat on the deck, sketching the shoreline.

"Mr. Tarakanov, I have a favor to ask," she began with a smile. "I hope you won't refuse."

"Anything you wish will be done, Anna Petrovna."

"Good. I want you to sing. I've heard that you play the balalaika and that you sing and dance. I've heard that you made a great impression on everyone when you sang and danced at Chamberlain Rezanov's party in Spanish California."

Timofei blushed under his sunburn. "It was a special occasion, the Chamberlain's engagement party."

"Do you mean I'm not special enough?" Anna teased.

"Oh, no, no...Anything you want, I'll do gladly!" Timofei stammered.

"Good. I want you to bring your balalaika. After supper, you and I will sing together. And then, after we practice, we'll make the crew sing with us."

She flashed a smile at him, then turned back to her sketch.

Timofei returned to the crew's quarters, feeling like a young lad after his first kiss. He took his balalaika off its hook above his hammock and gently plucked at its three strings. They reverberated under his finger, sounding thin and off-key. He tuned the instrument, turning the pins gently, listening closely until they were exactly right.

"To sing with Anna Petrovna! A gift from heaven!" he thought.

Whenever a lookout would spot an Indian village ashore, the *Nikolai* dropped her anchors close to the land. Furling her sails, the brig would announce her arrival to the tribe by firing a cannon shot.

The natives would converge on the brig in dozens of canoes, bringing fur pelts, smoked salmon and various items made of whalebone, or carved of wood, or woven of grass.

Timofei, who spoke several Indian dialects, established a strict rule permitting only three natives aboard ship at any one time. He did not trust the Indians. They were heavily armed with bows, arrows, and lances. Some even carried European muskets and American pistols as well. They could be dangerous in large concentrations. Timofei dealt with them fairly, but he was wary.

It also disturbed Timofei that Anna Petrovna saw the Indians as they climbed aboard, in flimsy loin-cloths, or nothing at all. Like all Russians, Timofei believed that it was a sin to submit a woman to the sight of male nakedness. To expose *Anna Petrovna*, to this wickedness was almost more than he could bear. Trying to shield her, Timofei confined trading to one part of the brig, but Anna was interested in unusual objects brought by the Indians. She moved freely among them, ignoring their nakedness.

She laughed, noticing Timofei's disturbed face as three totally nude men climbed aboard, their bodies gleaming with sweat and an application of halibut oil.

"Relax, Mr. Tarakanov," she chuckled, "I am a married woman. I *know* how a naked man looks!"

Despite her air of indifference, Anna was very much aware of masculine nakedness. The savages looked magnificent, she thought, knowing of course that she would never dare to confess this to anyone.

The survey of the shore continued. Bulygin compared his observations with Captain Vancouver's charts, made nearly twenty years earlier, finding them to be remarkably accurate.

The weather was still mild and pleasant, unseasonably warm for October, with just enough wind to make tacking easy. They finished charting the western shores of the Queen Charlotte Islands and proceeded further south, toward the big craggy island bearing the name of George Vancouver. Every evening, with the approach of darkness, the *Nikolai* retreated into the sea. There was safety in its vastness for the Indians ashore could never be completely trusted.

Anna was curious about the Indians. She was intrigued by the totems rising over the villages, eager to examine them in detail, having never seen anything quite like them. In Novo-Arkhangelsk all vestiges of Indian art had been destroyed after the island fell into Russian hands.

But Bulygin was adamant that she remain aboard. "There are not enough of us to protect you," he declared sternly. So, Anna watched the totem poles through his telescope, marveling at the mystery of their design, painting them in watercolors in her sketchbook.

By the end of October the *Nikolai* reached latitude 48 degrees, 22 minutes North at the Strait of Juan de Fuca, separating Vancouver Island from the mainland.

A chain of tall, green mountains rose before them. Thick forests covered the shores. It seemed that the trees grew right out of the rocks at water's edge.

Almost four weeks passed since the ship left Novo-Arkhangelsk. They were weeks of easy sailing, pleasant weather and profitable trade with natives who were surprisingly friendly.

"They are accustomed to trade with the British and the Yankees," Timofei explained to Bulygin.

But the lovely weather was not to last. A sudden dead calm fell on the waves. Not a sail stirred. The proud standard of the Empire and the flag of the Russian-American Company raised below it drooped lifelessly from the masthead. The air became oppressively heavy. The captain inspected every inch of the brig ordering the hatches to be battened down, seeing that every movable item be made fast. He felt ill, suffering from recurrent bronchitis which tore at his chest.

The crew was growing nervous. They were mostly *promyshleniki* who were accustomed to riding out the storms in their *baidarki* by passively surrendering to the mercy of the winds, allowing the waves to toss their light crafts as if they were chips of wood. But the same brave men felt uneasy on the ship. They felt trapped. The ship was large and the art of navigation was a mystery to them. They had to entrust their lives, blindly, to a captain who would know how to save them, they hoped.

When the storm finally hit the brig, the wind kept changing, whipping the waves into huge mountains, pushing the ship toward the shore, then away from it.

Sheets of slanting rain lashed at the men as they worked the sails. The ship groaned and shuddered, the gigantic waves breaking over her bow.

Anna huddled in her bunk. She prayed, holding onto its raised sides.

The tempest lashed at the brig for three days. When it finally began to subside, the *Nikolai* had been seriously damaged. Her foremast was split and Bulygin had it chopped down to prevent further damage to the ship. One of her longboats was torn off its davits, her sails were in shreds and she was listing. The strong currents pushed her toward the rocky shore. Bulygin inspected the ship, his worn face showing despair.

The ship drifted toward the rocks near shore. The current was too strong for oarsmen to tow the ship back to sea with the remaining longboat.

"We're going to smash," the men thought in terror, watching the saw-toothed shore grow even closer.

The captain ordered an anchor to be set, trying to halt

the movement of the brig. The ship shuddered, then continued to drag toward the rocks. A kedge anchor was dropped and it slowed her down, but Bulygin already knew that the anchors would not hold. The ship groaned, as if aware of her fate.

The situation grew more dangerous as a mantle of fog wrapped around the brig, obscuring the land and the ocean. A third anchor was set. Unable to see, Bulygin fought for his ship by some sixth sense, by responding to her every groan and vibration. He ordered the last anchor to be dropped. The ship stopped dragging. The anchors held! The captain breathed a sigh of cautious relief. But the brig suddenly jerked as two of her cables snapped, frayed against submerged rocks. The remaining two anchors were not enough to hold the brig against the powerful shoreward drift. It was only a matter of time now when the remaining cables would break. The *Nikolai* was doomed.

Two desperate hours passed, the captain and the men listening anxiously to every new sound. As a light wind began to rustle in the shreds of the sails, the fog partially lifted. But the wind could no longer help the unfortunate brig. She was helpless, like a bird with broken wings; she could not fly with the wind.

Bulygin knew that nothing could save the ship. He had to save the crew. He made his way quickly into his cabin.

"Anna," he said gently, trying not to frighten her. "We must abandon ship. Just gather warm clothes. Don't take anything else. I'll be back in a few minutes." He could not see her in the darkness, but he sensed her fear. Yet she sounded calm when she replied, "I'll be ready."

Bulygin returned to the deck. The fog had lifted completely. The ship had drifted within a few dozen yards of the desolate beach, separated from the sea by a barrier of protruding sharp rocks. The rocks were so close that Bulygin could clearly see nesting birds nervously watching the looming ship.

Presently, there was a grinding and tearing of planks and the brig shuddered. She was wedged into the rocks. It was only question of time before the heavy seas broke her apart.

The shore beyond the surf looked deserted. Bulygin sounded the alarm to abandon ship.

"Mr. Tarakanov, transfer ashore as much of our provisions and weapons as possible. Hurry, we don't have much time."

Timofei assessed the situation, eyeing the torn canvas still hanging on the broken spars. "We'll need it," he thought. "It will make a couple of tents. I hope we'll have time to strip it down. Hurry *bratzi*!" he shouted. "Grab your warm clothing, food, and guns! With God's help we will make it ashore! It's only a few dozen yards to the beach!"

Bulygin rushed to his cabin. Anna had already gathered two large bundles with their warmest clothing, changing into a man's attire. She looked calm, but she was in terror of the water for she could not swim.

There was a shift in the brig's angle of heel and a terrifying sound of tearing of the ship's planking. The hull had cracked.

"Hurry! Go on deck!" the captain shouted, rushing below to examine the damage. Anna moved to the deck, dragging her bundles behind her and clutching her little dog.

The men scattered around the brig gathering their belongings. Everyone realized that the ship would be split apart momentarily.

"Abandon ship!" the captain commanded, returning to the bridge.

Anna, holding Snezhinka in her arms, saw two *promyshleniki* jump into the surf, holding their guns high over their heads, hurrying to reach the shore before a wave caught up to them. Three more men slipped over the bulwarks and Anna saw them reaching the shore.

"You must go now!" Bulygin ordered Anna. "Mr. Tarakanov, please help my wife."

Timofei understood. The captain had to be the last one to leave the ship.

"The shore is near, Anna Petrovna. It shouldn't be hard to reach it," Timofei said calmly, sensing Anna's terror. "The trick is to slip between two breakers. Let me help you."

Timofei lifted Anna as if she were a small child. He stepped over the rail pausing on the rope ladder. He hesitated before jumping into the surf, waiting for the breaker to pass and split into a fine spray against the rocks. Then he jumped. The water reached well over his waist and he hoisted Anna even higher as he lunged through the surf toward the shore.

Anna shut her eyes. She felt safe in his strong arms. She

put her head on his shoulder, hiding her face in his curly hair, clinging to him for protection.

Momentarily he put her gently on the ground. Only then did she realize that she was still clutching tightly to her shivering puppy.

"Wait here," Timofei pointed to a flat rock. "I must return to the ship. *Bratzi*, watch over Anna Petrovna," he directed the men already ashore. "Build a fire, check your guns..."

Obediently, Anna sat on the boulder as Timofei waded back to the doomed ship. She released Snezhinka from her grip and the dog ran toward the surfline, barking, trying to catch the little wavelets as they retreated into the sea. Anna watched her carefree dog with a sad smile. Snezhinka's exuberance was such a contrast to the tragic predicament of the shipwrecked crew, she thought.

The *Nikolai* was hopelessly impaled on the rocks. The breakers pounded the ship with tremendous force, sounding like explosions of distant cannons, the waves engulfing her, then quickly breaking into frosty spray, rolling off her deck and sides, exposing her perforated hull until the next assault.

During these precious few seconds when the sea rolled off the wounded ship, the men hurried to jump into the surf, carrying ashore whatever they were able to grab. They returned to the ship at once to repeat the process.

Captain Bulygin and Timofei directed the men from the slanted bridge of the badly listing brig. The men pulled down the remnants of the sails, working feverishly against time. Finally, they formed a human chain and stood chest-high in the pounding surf, passing the crates of gunpowder and barrels of food from one to another. Those already ashore, dumped them in an ever-growing pile of salvaged supplies, Anna and her Aleut women working alongside the men.

"Careful, *bratzi*! Keep them dry!" Timofei shouted, watching the men pass muskets from one to another, holding them high over their heads. He kept glancing at the dark forest on the edge of the beach, expecting to see Indians creeping toward his shipwrecked comrades, but the broad beach was silent except for the cluster of survivors.

The falling darkness halted the salvaging operation. "With God's help, if the ship survives the night, we'll resume tomorrow," Captain Bulygin said to Timofei. "Let's go!"

They jumped into the surf, helping one another to stay on their feet.

The tide was running out. The murderous breakers were gone, supplanted by gently rolling shallow waves. Bulygin noted that the bottom of the sea at the shoreline was smooth and sandy between the exposed rocks.

"Perhaps we should continue unloading the ship," he said to Timofei. "Without the surf it ought to be easier."

"We must first set up sentries ashore," Timofei replied. He was thinking of Anna. He knew that she would be in greatest danger should the Indians attack. She would be their prize. The Indians were always fascinated with Anna's pale skin and golden hair. They tried to touch her whenever they came aboard the brig. Sometimes she allowed them to finger a strand of her hair, smiling at their reaction to its silkiness.

The Indians had offered Timofei the choicest otter skins in exchange for her.

He explained to them that Anna Petrovna was a "good luck woman" for the ship and not for sale. They understood that. They had many treasured good luck symbols themselves, with which they never parted. They accepted the idea that the white men had chosen a golden-haired woman as their talisman of safety.

Timofei had never mentioned the Indians' offers to the captain. He did not want to alarm him. He believed he could deal with the Indians himself. Although they understood the reason why Anna was not for sale, there was nothing to prevent them from trying to *steal* her should they have an opportunity.

Such an opportunity existed now. There was only a handful of Russians to protect Anna. A handful, against unknown numbers lurking in the dark forest.

Chapter 45

The shipwrecked crew gathered around the fire on the beach. They were all there, exhausted by their ordeal, but unharmed. They shivered in their wet clothes, not daring to take them off in Anna's presence.

"For God's sake, take your clothes off!" she cried angrily. "I won't look!" She turned her back to the men.

"Yes, *bratzi*, let's warm ourselves," Timofei said gruffly. He shed his own shirt, plastered against his wide chest. He jumped on one leg, then on the other, pulling off his soggy boots, and succeeding, peeled off his pants. The men and the Aleut women followed his example. All crowded around the fire, warming their naked bodies in the life-sustaining waves of heat.

"We must build several more campfires," Timofei said. "One is not enough to keep all of us warm and to dry out our clothes." The men began to rummage among the piles of supplies, searching for their belongings and spare clothing. It was almost an impossible task. Their personal belongings were buried under the mountains of salvaged goods.

Anna was the only fully clothed person among the survivors, having been carried ashore by Timofei. She sat on the flat stone, with her back toward the men. Suddenly she laughed. "This is really silly! Do I have to sit like that until you are dressed again?" She exclaimed as she turned around. The men, including her husband, hastily cupped their hands on their genitals. She ignored their gestures of modesty, saying simply, "We are all in trouble together."

The women brought armloads of driftwood and the men quickly built two more fires. They spread their clothing on the sand near the fires, hanging their boots on sticks around the perimeter. The boots, swollen with water, looked like misshapen miniature heads on elongated necks. As they began to dry in the intense heat, the sea water impregnating the leather turned into white salt crystals. It made the boots look even more like the shrunken heads of some grotesque albino tribe.

Captain Bulygin huddled on the rock near the fire, his arms locked across his chest, shivering, despite the heat of the fires. He felt ill, exhausted by cold and the strain of command, unable to concentrate on what had to be done. He merely nodded in agreement with Timofei's suggestions until Timofei began to give orders directly.

Timofei's first concern was the preparedness of their weapons. The muskets had to be dry and in readiness, should the camp be attacked.

"Check your guns, *bratzi*," he advised urgently. "It's only a question of time before the savages arrive. Even if they had missed seeing the crippled ship, I'm sure they will see the fires or smell the smoke and come to investigate."

"Perhaps they'll help us," Anna said.

"Perhaps. But we must be ready if they don't." He did not want to frighten her, yet he wanted to prepare her for the possibility of an attack.

Meanwhile, the men using the salvaged canvas, raised two tents and moved some of the supplies inside. They crowded inside as well, huddling together for warmth, sharing a few blankets against the cold autumn air.

Timofei set up four sentry posts around the perimeter of the camp, taking command of the first watch himself.

They spent an uneasy night.

Timofei, especially, felt the weight of responsibility. He stood watch, tended the fires, gathered driftwood and talked to the sentries.

"Cheer up, *bratzi*, tomorrow we'll explore the shore. Perhaps we can find a good spot and build a couple of huts. By spring, there will be many ships passing by. Someone will rescue us. Governor Baranov will never abandon us!" The men were eager to believe him. They clutched their muskets nervously, staring beyond the bright reflections of the campfires into the blackness of the silent forest.

In the morning it drizzled. The coast was blanketed with fog. The people peered into the fog, barely able to see the silhouette of their ship. She was still there, holding again.t the onslaught of the brutal sea.

Timofei stripped again, reverting to the Indian custom of wearing nothing.

The men followed his example. They waded into the cold sea, hoping to empty the ship of her supplies.

But they were too late. The ship's holds were flooded. She was listing so badly that her port side was almost at the water's level. As the tide began to rise once again, Timofei ordered the men back.

The sea came over the rail in a swish, like a shiny green curtain. Timofei jumped overboard.

Later in the day Timofei and several men cautiously ventured into the woods looking for high, dry ground, where they could build sturdy huts and settle in for the winter.

They trudged through the dense underbrush, the marshy water smacking loudly under their feet.

"Nothing but swamps," Timofei reported to the captain. "We must send scouts further inland, into the mountains."

Bulygin listened, his eyes half-closed. He was feverish, which made him feel as if he were floating. He heard Timofei's voice, one moment clear as a ship's bell, then muffled, as if coming from a great distance.

"It's only sixty-five miles to Gray's Harbor," he finally said hoarsely.

Timofei wasn't sure that he heard him correctly. "Sixty-five miles to...where? The captain must be delirious," he thought to himself.

"To Gray's Harbor," Bulygin repeated, raising his voice. "The *Kodiak* will be there, waiting for us next month at Gray's Harbor."

"And we can easily make it on foot!" Timofei exclaimed, grasping Bulygin's idea.

"Yes," the captain wheezed, shaken by a paroxysm of coughing, waving his hand, imploring them to be patient with him.

When his coughing had finally subsided, the captain continued with great effort, "Look at the map. There are no bays, no big rivers to cross between here and the harbor. It is probably possible to cover this distance on foot."

He pointed with a shaking finger to the approximate location of their shipwreck, drawing a line across the map towards Gray's Harbor. The map showed the outline of the shore around Cape Flattery, suggesting terrain unbroken by any large bodies of water. The inland area of the map was left blank by Vancouver, indicating that it had not been explored. "We must take a chance," Bulygin said, wearily moving his finger across the blank space.

"We can make it easily, sir!" Timofei exclaimed. "Sixty-five miles is nothing!" The *promyshleniki*, crowding around them, shouted their approval.

"We'll start toward Gray's Harbor tomorrow," the captain said closing his eyes, exhausted by his effort.

Anna put her hand over his forehead. It felt dry and hot. "He's very sick. He can't walk," she said quietly to Timofei.

"We'll wait. Don't worry, Anna Petrovna. A couple of days won't make any difference now. We'll get to Gray's Harbor, don't worry!"

The crew buoyed up by new hope, brightened. The men laughed, shouting encouragement to one another, playing with Snezhinka, feeling that the time for despair was over. In a day or two, they would be on their way to Gray's Harbor and a meeting with their compatriots. It had not occurred to them that the *Kodiak* might not be there, or even worse, that the ship's fate might have been similar to theirs.

If anyone thought of that, he kept it to himself.

In the morning the sun shone brightly for the first time in a week. The sea sparkled and shimmered, its surface rippling. The air felt crisply fresh, with a touch of frost.

The men and the Aleut women sifted through the salvaged supplies searching for blankets, spare boots and other items of clothing. Accustomed to the harsh lives of hunters they were undaunted by the prospect of crossing the unknown terrain on foot. They knew that they could cope with the icy winds and bitter cold as long as they moved toward their goal—Gray's Harbor.

Timofei divided the loads to be carried by every person, including Anna. The men were armed with two guns each, and carried pistols with ammunition for each of their weapons. The women were to carry spare clothing and blankets. The men constructed several litters, using odd pieces of broken spars and canvas to carry three kegs of gunpowder and shot, and barrels of food. Timofei ordered the rest of the goods to be thrown into the sea.

"The savages!" the sentry yelled.

Timofei jumped to his feet. "Keep calm, *bratzi* and for God's sake don't shoot!" he implored urgently. "Anna Petrovna, go to your tent." Anna quickly obeyed, joining her sick husband.

"I'll parley with them. Perhaps they're friendly." Timofei tossed his gun to one of the men, spreading his arms to show that he was not armed. He walked slowly toward the Indians.

With a broad smile he stopped within a few feet of the approaching Indians, stretching his hands to them in a universal gesture of friendship. The Indians, about fifty in all, stopped also. They were totally naked, their copper-colored bodies glistening with halibut oil. They wore no war paint.

They were armed with bows and arrows, shouldering long lances and heavy clubs. None of them carried guns to Timofei's relief.

"We are friends!" Timofei said in Tlingit dialect looking straight at the warrior at the head of the group. He hoped that the Tlingit word for "friend" would be understood by these men. "Friends...Good men...*Yak-ie kaa*," he repeated, smiling and nodding several times in the manner of the Tlingits.

A stockily built man wearing the conical hat of a chief and a cedarbark mantel, turned to his men and in a rapid flow of guttural words issued an order.

Then he and two of his warriors boldly followed Timofei into the camp. The rest of the Indians waited.

"Watch yourselves, *bratzi*," Timofei muttered to the Russians. "Be friendly!"

In the tent the Chief commenced a long speech in an unrecognizable dialect. Timofei decided to take the proceedings into his own hands. He reached into the sack containing glass beads and brass buttons which he had salvaged from the wreck for trading with the natives.

"Here," he said, proffering a string of blue beads to the Chief. "I am your friend. *Ax xooni*."

The Indian's face broke into a smile as he grabbed the beads, repeating the word *Ax xooni* and nodding.

The contact was established. Timofei handed strings of beads to the other two Indians. "Friends, friends," he kept saying, pointing to himself and to other Russians. The Indians nodded, smiling. Timofei gestured toward the small fire inviting his guests to sit down with him.

Suddenly there were angry shouts and the sounds of a scuffle. Timofei grabbed for his gun. The Indians jumped to their feet and dashed out of the tent.

The *promyshleniki*, greatly outnumbered, formed a circle around their salvaged supplies.

The Indians dashed around snatching blankets from the pile, rolling away barrels of smoked pork, pulling at the sacks of tea and sugar, spilling the contents on the sand.

"Stop it, stop it!" Timofei yelled. But it was too late. He saw one of his men fall, stunned by a blow on the head; then another, speared by a lance in his abdomen. He heard a shot as someone emptied his gun point blank, killing the attacker.

A rain of arrows descended on the Russians.

Timofei felt stinging pain in his right shoulder as an arrow pierced it.

The Indians were retreating under the concentrated musket fire, carrying their wounded.

Timofei staggered as he pulled the arrow out of his shoulder. "Bastards, damned savages!" he yelled. "I should have known better than to trust the bastards! Where is Anna Petrovna?" he thundered, holding his hand to his bleeding shoulder.

"I am here, I am safe." She appeared at the entrance of her tent. "You're wounded, Timosha!" she cried, as she ran toward him. It was the first time that she had called him by his diminutive name.

"Nothing serious," he replied. "But several are hurt. Sabachnikov got a nasty wound in the belly. They hit him with a spear."

"I saw it."

Timofei bent over Sabachnikov. The man was suffering great pain, the spear still in his abdomen. Timofei took hold of its handle and yanked it out with a quick motion. Sabachnikov screamed and then fell silent, his face drained of color. He lay in a puddle of blood, the sand under his body saturated. Sabachnikov was bleeding to death.

"We must stop the bleeding." Anna knelt on the sand next to him.

Several eager men came to her aid. They peeled off

Sabachnikov's garments, exposing an ugly gaping wound as it oozed blood in slow pulsating spurts.

Anna tore her long silk scarf off her neck and deftly bandaged the man. The scarf at once became impregnated with blood.

"Let me look at your wound, Timosha," Anna said. "Don't be such a hero."

"It's nothing. I am hardly bleeding now."

"Let me bandage it for you. What do we have that I can use?" She looked around helplessly. "I wish I had my petticoats now," she sighed, pointing to her Yakut leather trousers and boots.

"Here. Use this." One of the men tore a strip of his shirt. It was barely enough to go once over Timofei's muscular shoulder, but it covered the wound.

"We must leave at once," Timofei said. "The savages will be back with reinforcements." He posted double guards around the camp as he hurried to report to captain Bulygin.

"Can you walk, sir?"

"Of course I can walk," Bulygin replied indignantly, but a seizure of painful coughing doubled him up. "I'll walk," he managed to wheeze, wiping his moist brow with a handkerchief.

"We'll leave at once. The camp can't be defended."

Timofei returned to his men. "We'll carry Sabachnikov on a litter," he said. "It means we must abandon a keg of gunpowder or a barrel of pork. You decide, *bratzi* which it will be."

"The pork!" the men shouted. "We need gunpowder. We will hunt for our food."

"Right! Get ready, *bratzi*. Remember, we're on our way to meet the *Kodiak!*" he exclaimed heartily, pretending there was no doubt about this meeting. "Let's go!" he shouted. He slung the guns over his shoulders, his own and the captain's, and took his place at the head of the group. The men lifted the litter supporting the unconscious Sabachnikov while the others carried litters with kegs of gunpowder and shot. They fell into step, the wounded hobbling along with the help of their comrades, the captain and Anna in the middle of the column.

"Just like the convicts in Siberia," Anna thought with bitter humor, observing the ragged party as they slowly moved in single file away from the doomed ship.

Chapter 46

They followed the shoreline, bearing south. The landscape was desolate and beautiful, the sea framing the beach in white foam, beating hard against the sharp rocks. The beach was strewn with grotesquely twisted driftwood, bleached by the sea and the sun. Seagulls flew over their heads their sharp, mournful cries the only sounds competing with the surf pounding beyond the rocks.

They trudged ahead silently, Anna supporting her husband with her arm. At first he waved her away impatiently, stubbornly coping with his infirmity, but each attack of coughing left him weaker until he had to lean on her for support.

Toward evening they reached the end of the exposed shore. A dark, tall forest rose ahead. Timofei sent two men to scout the approaches to the forest. They returned shortly with the good news that the forest was dry.

"We'll camp for the night," Timofei decided.

They found a clearing along a narrow stream, bounded by towering dark cedars. The men chopped off tree branches and built several crude shelters, big enough for one or two people. Timofei made a shelter for the Bulygins. One had to crawl into it on all fours but once inside, it was cozy and could be warm if both openings of the *shalash* were covered with the fronds from the inside.

"We won't build a fire tonight," Timofei explained to Anna. "Keep your husband warm with blankets and brandy. Here..." He handed her a flask of English brandy.

"Thank you." Anna took the flask and crawled into the *shalash* after her husband. She knew that Timofei, who was adamant about what they were to carry, must have left something of his own personal belongings so that the captain would have his brandy.

"We'll change sentries every two hours. I'll take the first watch," Timofei said to the men. He assigned three other men to positions on the perimeter of the camp, making everyone check their guns before dispersing among their *shalashi*.

The night passed quietly, disturbed only by the hooting of an owl and the occasional howl of a coyote.

They listened uneasily to the night sounds, aware that the hoots and the howls might have been Indian signals. In the morning Timofei inspected their bivouac and decided that it was not defensible against attack. The clearing was surrounded by thick trees, providing perfect cover for the attackers while exposing the defenders. He gave the signal to move on.

Anna helped her husband to his feet. He staggered, stumbling over tree roots. She propped him up, encircling his waist with her arm and placing his arm across her shoulders.

"You're an angel," he whispered, his lips cracked and bleeding. She did not reply.

Timofei drove his little group mercilessly throughout the day. Their only chance of surviving a possible Indian attack was in finding a defensible position. Toward the evening, he decided to halt the group and scout the terrain ahead.

When he returned, he was pleased. He had found an abandoned cave full of dried salmon. The cave must have been used by the natives as a fishing camp for there was a salmon trap in the shallows of the stream. Timofei decided it was perfect for their purpose. The cave was deep, accommodating them all; its entrance was narrow, requiring only two sentries to guard it. The men built a campfire, the smoke escaping through the crevices in the rocks. They covered the stony floor with layers of hemlock fronds, aromatic and soft, spread their blankets on the boughs, and slept.

Anna tucked her husband under the blankets as if he were an infant. She looked at him with pity. He seemed to have shrunk and his face had all but disappeared under wild growth of hair.

An image of Timofei flashed through her mind. She saw herself bandaging his wounded shoulder, his bronzed skin smooth under her fingers. She saw his broad chest covered with curly golden hair and she thought how wonderful it must feel to put her head on his chest and fall asleep.

Disturbed by her thoughts, Anna squeezed Snezhinka in her arms, burying her face in the dog's soft fur.

"I love you Snezhinka," she whispered to the squirming dog.

They remained in the cave for several days, resting and healing their wounds. Captain Bulygin's violent seizures of coughing had eased, leaving a nagging pain in his chest.

Only Sabachnikov failed to show any improvement. Weakened by the loss of blood, he was barely alive. Anna changed his bandages, holding her breath against the odor exuding from his wound. Sabachnikov was dying as gangrene slowly ate away at his body.

"We can't stay here forever," Captain Bulygin declared one morning, resuming his command over their destinies. "We must be on our way to Gray's Harbor."

That afternoon the sentries brought in an old Indian woman who had suddenly appeared from the forest. She was dressed in a long cedarbark shift and was barefoot despite the patches of snow on the ground. Her gray hair was plaited into two thin braids that fell on each side of her wrinkled face.

"What's your name?" Timofei asked in Tlingit. To his relief she replied, "Tlingits called me Ka-too-woo." She told Timofei that when she was young she was given as a bride to a Tlingit warrior. When her husband was killed in a whaling accident, her tribe, the Quillayutes, bought her back because she was the Chief's sister.

"She says that she knows a short cut through the forest that will lead us to her village," Timofei translated.

"We don't want to go to her village," Bulygin snorted.

"True, sir, but she says there is a wide river ahead. We don't have it on our map. Her people live on the shore of the river. Perhaps we can buy canoes from them and reach Gray's Harbor by sea. It will be much faster and safer. I suggest that we follow the woman."

"Can we trust her?"

"We have no choice, sir. She told me that the Indians with whom we had the fight, are mad coyotes. Her tribe is at war with them. She called them thieves."

"Ask her if we can buy the canoes."

Timofei turned to the woman. Anna listened to the strange sounds of the clicking Tlingit dialect, thinking "I like the old woman. She has a kind face, like a wise grandmother."

"Well?" Bulygin asked impatiently.

"She says, sir, that there are many canoes in her village and if we are willing to pay—we can have several."

"Then let's go! Let's not waste any more time."

The *promyshleniki* gathered their sparse possessions. They picked up the litter with the dying Sabachnikov. Once more they were on the move.

"What day is it?" Bulygin suddenly asked. He had lost count of the days during the acute stages of his illness, when the days and nights had fused into one.

"November the seventh," Anna said.

"The seventh...Only a week since the shipwreck..." he said softly as if to himself.

The wind was rising. The tops of the tall trees swayed above their heads.

The forest moaned, full of whispers. Shaken by a sudden gust of wind into a fury of protest, it stood trembling again, waiting for the next upsurge of wind.

The path kept climbing up. They had to halt often to change the bearers of the heavy litters. The wretched Sabachnikov, barely alive, begged his comrades to put an end to his miseries.

Timofei watched Anna trudging ahead. She had lost weight, her face becoming gaunt, her eyes dulled and her lips chapped and cracked. She laughed no more. She shuffled along the path with a load of rolled blankets on her back.

Timofei thought of cheering her up but could find no words except the usual shallow expressions of encouragement. He wished that her husband would boost her morale, but the captain still seemed lost in his illness.

"We'll be in Gray's Harbor soon," Timofei said, adjusting his stride to hers. Anna looked at him blankly. "Anna Petrovna, hold on, just a few more days! We'll get boats at the village and we'll be in Gray's Harbor in no time!"

Toward the evening they reached the summit of the mountain and began their descent. Below, a wide river twisted looking like a silvery snake. Across the river stood several tribal houses, smoke rising above them, and beyond the bend the rapids churned in white foam.

The Quillayute woman pointed to the houses. "My village. The Raven people," she said proudly.

"Ravens again," Timofei thought. "No matter who the Indians are, they always have Ravens!"

"You wait here," Ka-too-woo said. "I'll go and tell my people to take you across the river."

"How are you going to cross it?"

"I have a canoe."

"Listen, Ka-too-woo, tell the Chief that we want to buy two large canoes. And this is for you. *Kaw oot.*" He gave her a necklace of multicolored beads. Ka-too-woo slipped the beads over her head. A slow smile spread over her wrinkled face.

"You look like a beautiful young woman, Ka-too-woo," Timofei said. A little flattery would do no harm, he thought.

Ka-too-woo cackled with delight, showing a row of yellowed teeth. Then she trotted toward the river as if she were indeed a young woman. Soon they saw her paddling a small canoe, the darkness swallowing the little craft.

It was snowing in the morning, the snow falling down in heavy wet flakes, mixed with rain. The Russians waited anxiously for Ka-too-woo.

"A canoe!" the sentry shouted, pointing at a small boat on the steely surface of the river, barely visible through the curtain of falling snow.

Ka-too-woo beached the canoe on the shore.

"Where are the boats?" Timofei demanded, as Ka-too-woo reached the camp.

Ka-too-woo pointed to the river. A large canoe was approaching the shore.

"It's not enough. We cannot take all our people across in just one boat."

"You can make two trips," she replied. "I'll take three people in my little boat," Ka-too-woo continued. "Three light-weight people," she pointed to Anna, one of the smaller Aleut women and the cabin boy, Kotelnikov.

"I would prefer that Anna Petrovna crosses the river in the big boat," Timofei said to Bulygin. "It's much sturdier."

"Nonsense," Anna said. "I'll go with the old grandma. Just let's get going!"

"I'll take eight men and follow her in the big boat," Bulygin ordered. "The rest of you wait here until we send the boat to pick you up." Bulygin was suddenly full of optimism. Even his cough seemed to disappear. He issued orders as to who was to cross the river with the first party.

The large canoe reached the shore. Two unarmed elderly Indians wearing Chilkat blankets over their cedarbark shirts helped the Russians to load the canoe, urging with gestures that the white men should place their muskets on the bottom. But the wary *promyshleniki* would not let their guns out of their hands. The guns gave them a feeling of security.

The Indians pushed the canoes into the water, jumping in themselves and paddling vigorously.

Timofei observed their progress through the telescope. It stopped snowing and he could clearly see the Quillayute village across the river. It was rather small, consisting of only six communal houses, but they were sturdily built, decorated with the tribal designs. On shore he could see several large whaling canoes, the type that could easily make the trip over the ocean to Gray's Harbor, even in November.

But the welcome sight of the boats was short-lived. Timofei suddenly became aware that something was wrong with the big canoe. He saw the *promyshleniki* flailing their arms as if reaching for balance. He heard shouts for help as the canoe began to sink. The two Indians jumped overboard, swimming toward the shore. The Russians, burdened by their guns and heavy backpacks, struggled with the canoe, trying to keep it afloat, but it was filling with water fast. Finally, the men gave up the struggle. They plunged into the icy water.

The small canoe with Anna reached the opposite shore. A crowd of Indians rushed at the occupants, surrounding Anna and the others in a howling mob.

Chapter 47

The men thrashed about in the swift current that carried them down the river. "Help, *bratzi!*" they yelled. Timofei and the others ran frantically along the river bank, several diving into the water, swimming toward their drowning comrades. Timofei saw Bulygin being drawn toward boulder-filled rapids.

"Hold on, captain!" Timofei shouted as he leaped into the river. The current picked up his body, pulling him down and swirling him around, but Timofei was a strong swimmer. With several powerful strokes he reached Bulygin. Encircling the captain's chest with his left arm, propping him up out of the water, Timofei turned him on his back. "Relax," he gasped, "let me do the work." He swam toward the shore, supporting the captain's head above the water in the crook of his arm.

It was exhausting to fight the current. With every foot of distance gained, they were swept diagonally farther along the river.

The men ran along the shore with long branches, ready to pull them out. Using all his great strength, Timofei gradually narrowed the distance to the shore until he could make a one-handed grab and catch one of the branches the men held out to him.

The *promyshleniki* pulled them ashore.

Timofei collapsed on the ground, panting shallowly.

"My wife?" the captain stammered between the bouts of coughing.

"She's gone," one of the men said.

"What happened? Why did the big canoe sink?" Timofei struggled to his feet, still unsteady.

"The bastards must have planned it that way. They had holes drilled in the big canoe and unplugged them in the middle of the river. We began to sink in seconds. We lost all our gear and most of the guns," the man, Petukhov replied.

Timofei looked at the captain. Bulygin lay prostrate on the ground, his face down, hidden by his folded hands.

"Sir?" Timofei touched him by the shoulder. Bulygin turned over. "I want to die," he whispered, closing his eyes. Timofei stood over him, helpless.

"We must ransom Anna Petrovna and the others," Timofei said to his men as they retreated to their old camp above the river.

Bulygin sat in front of the fire, his back bent, a figure of despair. He looked like an old man.

"How can we do it? We have nothing to offer as barter. Half of our gear is on the bottom of the river," Petukhov said.

Timofei was silent. He had never felt so helpless before. He was horror-stricken at the thought of Anna among the savages.

"They will turn her into a slave..." he thought. The vision of Anna as a helpless slave, repeatedly molested by some savage or passed among many, flashed before him. He squeezed his fists until his knuckles turned white.

"We *must* rescue Anna Petrovna!" he cried out, not caring anymore whether Bulygin or anyone else might guess his love for Anna.

"The canoes are on the river!" the sentry shouted. Three large whaling canoes filled with warriors pulled out from the Quillayute village.

"Take cover!" The *promyshleniki* fell to the ground, seeking cover behind the fallen trees and rocks. But the Indians were not trying to cross. Instead, they drove the canoes upstream with powerful strokes.

Timofei extended his telescope and focused it on the departing canoes. There was Anna, seated in the bottom of one of them, with her arms pinned to her body. "Dear God," he gasped, covering his face with his hands.

"She's there, isn't she?" Bulygin said in a strangely dead voice, staring into the fire.

"Yes," Timofei barely whispered.

"She would be better off dead." Bulygin turned his back to the river.

The canoes disappeared upstream beyond the bend.

"What shall we do now?" Petukhov said.

Timofei pulled himself together. "I think we must follow the river upstream and into the mountains. We must find a safe camp for the winter."

Timofei turned his mind to ways of finding Anna. The fate of the other hostages did not interest him. Marya, the Aleut woman, would work and copulate with the Indians just as she had worked and copulated with the Aleuts or with the Russians. As to Kotelnikov, he was a creole boy, half Russian, half Tlingit. He would adapt easily to life among the Quillayutes, or whoever he might be sold to. It was Anna, only Anna, who was on Timofei's mind. He could only imagine her despair at finding herself at the mercy of the Indians. The thought that she would be raped repeatedly made him livid with rage, not so much because of the actual act, but because of what it would do to her spirit. As a man in love, he suffered *her* pain and he lived *her* despair.

He thought that perhaps there was a way of finding out about Anna through Ka-too-woo. "The hag would know," he thought. But how could he get to Ka-too-woo? Obviously, it was impossible now. If he, or anyone else, went to her village for a parley, he would be seized without achieving anything. No, they must wait. Perhaps the old woman would come to them, knowing that they would be eager to bargain for Anna. She was clever, the old hag, Timofei thought, as he marched ahead of their diminished group.

Suddenly, the wretched Sabachnikov moaned, regaining consciousness. "Leave me, *bratzi*, don't bother to bury me. I'm dead." He sighed deeply and a quick shudder ran through his body. Sabachnikov was dead.

Timofei took a close look at Sabachnikov, whose mouth was drawn back exposing his teeth in a skull-like grin. His eyes were rolled back, showing their whites. Timofei gently closed his eyes with the palm of his hand.

"We'll do as he wishes. We'll leave him here," Timofei said, his voice unsteady. He placed Sabachnikov's hands on his chest, crossing them in the Russian Orthodox tradition.

"Take his boots off." he said quietly to Zuev. "Where he's gone he won't need them. For us the boots may save someone's life." Zuev pulled the boots off Sabachnikov's feet, holding his breath from the putrid odor of gangrene.

They quickly dug a shallow grave and lowered Sabach-nikov's body into it. "God forgive us for leaving our brother without a proper Christian burial," Timofei prayed, kneeling briefly at the grave as the men shoveled the earth over the body.

The group began to move once again.

At bivouac that night, Bulygin spoke to the men. "*Bratzi,* I can't command you. I'm disabled by my loss. I know nothing about Indians or survival in this cursed place, so I appoint Timofei Tarakanov as our commanding officer. Yours and mine. He will have the full responsibilities and privileges of commander." A sad smile crossed his face. "Privileges! How ridiculous it sounds!" he chuckled without mirth. "Do you agree with my choice? Do you want Tarakanov to be your leader?"

The men all nodded. There was a muttered chorus of "yeses."

"Mr. Tarakanov, you're our leader. You have been elected unanimously." He reached inside his coat pocket and withdrew a small notebook bound in red morocco leather and a pencil.

"I'll write an order of transfer of authority. We'll all sign it."

Timofei, the only one who could read and write, read the order aloud and then signed the acceptance. The *promysh-leniki* made crosses at the indicated places.

"You are the commander now, Mr. Tarakanov. You keep the document," Bulygin said wearily.

"Aye-aye, sir," Timofei saluted.

Ka-too-woo had forced Anna to drink a bitter potion and now Anna was in a daze, unaware of her surroundings. Her vision was blurred and she felt nauseous. She remembered nothing of the past. She was barely conscious.

The warriors lifted her out of the canoe. They untied her restraints and stood her up. She wavered and reeled, stumbling and falling, her legs wooden. They pulled her up roughly, leading her toward the tribal house. They pushed her through the opening of the house into a smoky semi-darkness. Anna reeled again, the faces of her captors jumping before her eyes. She tried to focus her vision but the images of human faces and animal snouts appeared before her. Rings of red and orange swam around as she tried to stay on her feet. Her knees buckled. She collapsed on the earthen floor.

She heard a din of guttural voices. Bright colors undulated before her, making her feel strangely placid one moment, then terrified of some danger which she could not name. She felt as if she were outside her body, floating in space. She was handled by many rough hands, but she had no power to resist.

When she came to, she was shivering. She reached for a blanket. There was none. She tried to get up but felt so dizzy that she fell back. The rough surface of the mat bruised her skin. She rubbed her bruise, suddenly becoming aware that she was naked.

Anna panicked. She had a vague recollection of something terrifying that had happened to her. What was it? She lay quietly, trying to focus her burning, aching eyes on some familiar object, finding none. She was surrounded by darkness. Only above her head, on the ceiling, could she see the faint reflection of a flickering fire. She touched her body again, inch by inch, feeling numbing pain in all her limbs, instinctively postponing the final discovery, the traces of dried semen between her thighs.

Then she remembered. "No!" she cried out loudly, "No! No!" She tried to jump to her feet and run, but stumbled in the darkness and fell on the prostrate body of her new master. He grunted, waking up. She felt her breasts being squeezed hard as the man rolled over her.

"No!" she screamed again, thrashing under his weight. The man paid no attention to her struggles. She felt him grow hard as he thrust himself brutally into her powerless body.

Timofei and the other survivors walked for three more days, moving deeper into the mountains. Finally, they found a small clearing that sloped gently toward the river.

It was perfect for setting up a camp. They cut down several dozen trees and built a square cabin with four corner protrusions for sentries. It was constructed like a miniature watch tower in Novo-Arkhangelsk, with slots for the gun barrels and boxes of ammunition at each sentry post.

By good luck they discovered a bank of red clay and dug enough of it to construct a rough stove with a stone chimney.

The cabin had one door and no windows, but they left

musket slits between the logs so they could defend the terrain around the hut.

The first really heavy snow fell in mid-December, almost burying their little cabin, but they were accustomed to deep snows. The men set traps for rabbits and squirrels, saving their ammunition for a possible Indian attack. They fished, but their catch was never enough. The meager supplies of food taken from the *Nikolai*, were long gone. The Aleuts, Nastasia and Yakov, hungrily eyed Snezhinka. During the night, when the Russians were asleep, the Aleuts slit Snezhinka's throat and skinned her carcass. Nastasia roasted the meat on a spit over an open fire, and as the aroma began to permeate the cabin, the men awoke.

No one scolded the Aleuts. They had done what was natural to them, with the best of intentions to help them all survive. Only Bulygin and Timofei refused their portions. They mourned the little dog. Snezhinka was the last thread tying them to Anna.

"We must find a way to get more food," Timofei thought. "Perhaps we should scout the territory further up the river." They had observed many small canoes traveling up and down the river, indicating that there were villages along its shores. Timofei decided to take a chance and send a couple of men to trade for food.

"Watch yourselves, *bratzi*," he said, giving the men most of the rations and a bag of trade goods.

The well-armed men departed and the remaining sixteen braced themselves for an anxious wait.

Chapter 48

The scouts, Zuev and Kormachev, returned to the camp, leading an Indian captive by a rope. They had tied his hands behind his back and encircled a rope around his ankles, making him walk in short shuffling steps.

"We grabbed a hostage!" Zuev crowed, full of youthful energy for the first time since the shipwreck. "We came upon this bastard as he was squatting to shit, so we grabbed him." The men broke out in raucous laughter, as if a dam had suddenly burst open and released the pressure accumulated behind it. They hooted, slapping themselves on their thighs, wiping the tears of laughter from their eyes.

The Indian stood erect, retaining his dignity, ignoring the hooting Russians.

"It was clever of you to capture a hostage, but did you bring any food?" Timofei grinned at his two scouts.

"Did we! Just look in that sack! We snatched all they had!" Kormachev boasted. "There were three of them. Two ran away the moment they saw us, but we grabbed this one."

"So, what have we got here?" Timofei emptied the contents of the bag in the snow. "Aha, we've got five large *kozhuchi*! It will hold us for a couple of days until the savages come to ransom their man. Well done, *bratzi*." He slapped the scouts on their backs.

The men cut the salmon into small parts, drawing lots for the most desirable middle sections.

"Bring the hostage inside," Timofei said. Zuev pushed the Indian toward the door. The man stumbled over the rope tying his feet and fell. Zuev lifted the butt of his gun, ready to hit him.

"Stop it!" Timofei raised his voice sharply.

"But this is a good for nothing savage!" Zuev exclaimed.

"Savage or not, we need this man. You think I don't know how you feel?" Timofei continued. "I, too, would like to wring his neck, just because he's a damned Indian! Who among you has lost an eye to them? Who of you has been a prisoner as I was? Use your heads, *bratzi*. Even though we hate them, we need their help. We must find allies among the Indians."

Grudgingly, the men agreed that Timofei was right. They untied the Indian's feet and led him into the cabin.

Timofei tried to talk to the prisoner in Tlingit but the man did not understand the dialect. To show that he meant him no harm, Timofei divided his own portion of fish into two equal parts and offered one to the captive.

The Indian refused his offer. He stared stoically ahead, ignoring Timofei's attempts to be friendly. Timofei shrugged his shoulders. "We'll have to wait for his tribesmen. Perhaps someone among them might speak Tlingit."

They did not have to wait long. Next day three warriors attired in long cedarbark shirts arrived at the Russian camp. They were armed with bows and arrows and carried heavy, intricately-carved clubs made of whalebone.

The emissaries were led by an elderly man. He began a long diatribe in a dialect unknown to the Russians.

"It's hopeless! I don't understand a word!" Timofei exclaimed. He pointed to his mouth and then to the remaining fish portions showing with a gesture that there was no more fish.

The old Indian nodded.

Timofei laughed. "That's it, old fellow! No - more - fish!"

Next, to make sure that the old Indian grasped the idea, Timofei pointed to each Russian and Aleut, holding two fingers each time. The Indian repeated Timofei's gestures, nodding his agreement.

The warriors departed. Within several hours, the old Indian returned with exactly thirty-two large salmon. The contact was made.

Timofei released the hostage, giving him and the old man three brass buttons each, as a payment.

After that, the old Indian regularly visited the Russian camp, bringing food, always receiving gifts in return. Trying to cultivate his friendship, Timofei began to learn from him Quillayute words.

"Perhaps with the help of the old man we can find out about Anna Petrovna," he thought.

Anna drifted into passive submission to her master. After the first few days when she fought him only to be struck down, beaten and then brutally raped, she gave up. Her buttocks and thighs were covered with welts raised by the sealgut strap that her master had used to whip her. One of her eyes was half closed from the blow of his fist. She was given some bitter tasting drink that made her indifferent to her fate. She was stripped of her clothing and kept naked, except for a cedarbark poncho that the Indians kept lifting, sometimes laughing, sometimes shaking their head in wonder, fascinated by the whiteness of her skin and the blondness of her hair.

She was held within the confines of a platform bordered by bentwood boxes containing food, facing a firepit kept constantly burning by the youths on guard. The house was dark and full of smoke, but it was warm. She was grateful for that.

She was given a watertight basket into which she could urinate and was taken out of the house once a day for her other call of nature, always followed by a group of women and children.

As the weeks unfolded, Anna, half-drugged most of the time, became used to the indignities of her new life. She recoiled in revulsion only once as she was given a basketful of stale urine in which to wash her hair, which was crawling with lice. She pushed it away.

With gestures she explained that she wanted hot water. The women brought her a bentwood box full of water into which they dropped several red-hot stones. Anna washed her long hair and then her body with the warm water. The women stood around her in a tight circle, holding Anna's poncho in front of the fire to keep it warm. It suddenly dawned on her that they were at her service! She pointed to her wet hair, gesturing that she wanted them to search for lice. At once several women began extracting the fat, blood-swollen lice from her hair, squashing them between their fingernails.

The Indian who nightly assaulted Anna was the chief of a small kwan belonging to the Quillayute tribe. Red Wolf was a strongly built man of about forty. He had bought Anna from Ka-too-woo for twenty Chilkat blankets and a bladder of whale oil.

Anna was a valuable possession. It thrilled Red Wolf to mount the white woman every night to the envy of the other men, although he did not experience any special gratification. A woman was a woman.

Anna, in rare moments when her mind was clear, dreaded that she might conceive. She prayed to die first. Her last glimpse of her husband and friends was to see them spilling from the sinking canoe. Her husband was dead and so were the others, all dead. There was no one left to help her.

Snowbound and bored in their small cabin, the men grew restless. Fights started over small matters, but mostly over the Aleut woman, Nastasia. Timofei decided to step in before someone was knifed. His solution was simple and direct, just like the thinking of the other *promyshleniki*.

"*Bratzi*, I know that we all need a woman..." he began. "I propose to establish a schedule when each of us can have Nastasia. I talked to her and she agreed."

"Keep me out of this," Bulygin interrupted indignantly, leaving the hut.

The men shouted their approval. "Go ahead, draw lots. But anyone bothering Nastasia out of his turn will be denied his time."

"I find it utterly disgusting!" Bulygin protested to Timofei later. "I never expected this of you, Mr. Tarakanov!"

"Sorry, sir, but the men are restless. You know, sir, the Aleuts think nothing of copulating. To them it's natural, not shameful. Honestly!"

"Barbaric!" Bulygin exclaimed. "I don't mean the Aleut woman. Perhaps she doesn't know any better, but it's *barbaric* that you, Christians, are willing to use her in such a shameful, degrading manner! How can *you* participate in such...such a debauchery?" Bulygin shook his head.

"I am a man, Captain. I, too, need a woman," Timofei replied with a shrug.

January and February passed and in early March they could smell spring in the air. It was six months since they left Novo-Arkhangelsk, months full of tragedy and despair.

But with the coming of spring, they began to hope again. Perhaps this year, 1809, would see them back home.

One morning the old Quillayute appeared in their camp with Ka-too-woo. The old woman smiled as if meeting a group of good friends. She announced that she could arrange for the exchange of Anna.

Timofei's heart skipped a beat. "Where is she?"

"Nearby." Ka-too-woo was evasive. "You can have her back in a few days if you pay."

"We'll give you all the beads we have!"

"We don't want beads. We want guns," she said curtly, retreating to the river and climbing into her canoe. The old man followed her.

"We want the guns," she shouted as she paddled away.

The Russians returned to their hut.

"Let's give them the damned guns!" Bulygin cried in agitation. He was feverish again, red blotches burning brightly on his cheekbones.

"We cannot hand our guns over to the savages," Timofei said. "The guns are our only protection."

"I don't care! Give them all they demand. I order it!" Bulygin shouted.

"I am the commanding officer here, by your own appointment, sir," Timofei raised his voice. "As much as I want to ransom Anna Petrovna, I must consider the safety of all. Personally, I don't trust Ka-too-woo. She might fool us again, once we give her our guns. But you decide, men. I'll abide by your decision." He left the hut. At once the door was flung open as Zuev appeared on the threshold.

His face was grim. "There's nothing to decide," he said. "We won't part with our guns. Sorry, Captain."

Bulygin turned his face away, tears rolling down his sunken cheeks.

Chapter 49

They waited anxiously for the return of Ka-too-woo. "She'll never bring Anna Petrovna. She was bluffing," Timofei thought as he scanned the river.

Bulygin sat slumped on the boulder near the water, coughing, spitting blood, waiting. He refused to leave his post.

At dawn on the third day, the men checked their guns as they once again lined up on the shore beside the steely river that glistened coldly in the gray morning. It began to drizzle and all were cold and wet before two small canoes appeared from beyond the bend. One person sat in the lead canoe and three in the other.

"Take cover," Timofei ordered urgently. "Don't shoot without my signal," he warned. The men dispersed, leaving Timofei and the captain alone on the shore.

The canoes stopped opposite the Russian camp, armed Quillayute warriors appeared on the far shore.

Timofei stared at the slumped form in the middle of the second canoe. He could not see her face beneath the conical cedar fiber hat, but his heart told him it was Anna.

Ka-too-woo reached the shore. "I'll take you to see the white woman," she said brusquely. "Climb in."

Timofei turned to his men who watched from behind the boulders.

"Come out, *bratzi*, we are in no position to take Anna Petrovna by force. Take care of our guns." He handed his pistol to Kormachev.

"We cannot go with the old witch, unarmed," Bulygin objected.

"We must. We are safer unarmed. Less temptation for

the savages across the river...They want our guns more than they want us." Reluctantly, Bulygin passed his pistol to Zuev and followed Timofei into the canoe.

Timofei felt tension swelling in him with every splash of the paddles. He stared ahead. They seemed barely to move toward the other canoe.

Bulygin, too, was tense. He was terrified to face his beloved wife after these months of captivity. "Will she be disfigured in any way?" he thought.

Ka-too-woo brought her canoe within three yards of the other and turned it around. "Here she is, your white woman," she said pointing with her paddle at the figure in the hat.

"Anna!" Bulygin cried in anguish, his voice cracking.

"Kolya!" Anna tried to rise but one of the Indian paddlers jerked her back and yanked the hat from her head.

Bulygin and Timofei gasped. Where was the beauty they had known? Before them was the gaunt face of a strange old woman, her sunken eyes dull and her lips cracked. Her hair, once so lustrous, looked ragged and lifeless. Even the expression on her face was that of a frightened animal, cornered without the means of escape.

"Anna Petrovna, you poor darling, you dear suffering lady! God bless you, you're alive!" Timofei cried out, his words tumbled over one another.

"Kolya, save me, for God's sake, save me! Timosha, save me, please, help me, save me, help me, save me," she begged, repeating the same words as if not knowing any others.

Bulygin began to sob. The Indians watched him stonily.

"You saw the woman," Ka-too-woo said, turning her canoe around. She began to paddle back toward the shore.

"Don't leave me!" Anna screamed. "Don't leave me!" She thrashed about trying to jump out of the boat. The Indian pulled her back roughly.

"We'll be back, I promise!" Timofei shouted, shaken by the encounter. Bulygin covered his face with his hands.

Ka-too-woo beached the canoe and Timofei helped the captain get out. Bulygin staggered, his vision blurred by tears.

The *promyshleniki* rushed toward them. "How is she? How's our Anna Petrovna?" They all talked at once.

"She has suffered much," Timofei replied briefly.

Ka-too-woo pulled at Timofei's sleeve impatiently. "Give me the guns."

"Listen, Ka-too-woo," Timofei made an effort to sound friendly. "We *cannot* give you the guns. We need the guns to hunt for food. But we'll give you anything else you want. Do you want this?" He proffered his telescope.

"I want the guns." She did not even look at the telescope.

"Don't be stubborn, Ka-too-woo. Would you like this pretty necklace?" He dangled a long string of colorful beads.

"I want the guns. Or we'll sell the white woman," she replied pushing the beads away contemptuously.

"Perhaps we can offer her Nastasia in exchange?" suggested Zuev who understood the Tlingit dialect.

"A brilliant idea!" Bulygin cried eagerly. "Of course, let's give them Nastasia and the beads and whatever else they want, but let's get my wife back!"

"We cannot deliberately deliver a human being into their hands," Timofei protested.

"Do you like it better that *my* wife remain in their hands? *My* wife, a Christian woman, is she worth the same to you as some Aleut, whom you made a whore for your men?" Bulygin was livid with fury.

"Give them Nastasia!" the men shouted.

Zuev dragged the frightened Nastasia out of the cabin and held her before Ka-too-woo. "We won't give you our guns, but take this woman," he said in Tlingit.

Ka-too-woo laughed. "I don't want her, she has no eyes," she snickered pointing to Nastasia's narrow-slit eyes. "I don't want a woman with black hair and no eyes. I want a white woman with yellow hair, with eyes the color of the spring sky." She turned away contemptuously and marched toward the river.

"Wait, wait!" the men shouted running after her, but she climbed into her canoe and with a few swift strokes, reached deep water.

"You won't *ever* see your white woman," she warned and paddled away.

The Russians watched helplessly as the two canoes forged upstream toward the bend in the river.

"Save me! Plea-a-se..." they heard Anna's long cry of torment as the boats vanished beyond the bend.

Anna collapsed on her mat in the Quillayute village. Having been so close to her husband and then snatched from him again broke her spirit completely. She had only one wish now—to die.

She lay motionless on her mat refusing to get up. She became covered with scabs of filth, her hair crawled with lice again. Her body itched and she scratched herself raw. She did not even notice that her master had stopped molesting her. She would eat a piece of fish if she were offered one, or eat nothing if she were forgotten. She ceased to know the difference.

The Chief brought a shaman to examine his captive. The shaman walked cautiously around Anna, lifting her blanket with a stick, poking his long rattle at her now and then. She stared at him with her lusterless eyes, hardly aware of his strange appearance.

The shaman danced around her chanting his incantations against the evil spirits. He shook his rattles, and sang in a high-pitched voice, his long mane of hair, stiff with ashes and goosedown whirled around him as he danced.

The Indians crouched on the ground around the platform, watching silently. The children crowded behind, their eyes filled with wonder, watching the medicine man exorcise the evil in the white woman. But Anna remained in her hopeless apathy.

"You must get rid of the white woman," the shaman declared. "She's cursed. Her flesh is like the flesh of the white fish rotting on the shore. Her hair is yellow, like the feathers of a nestling. Not at all like the hair of a good woman should be. Get rid of her. Kill her."

"My brother paid a good price for her," Ka-too-woo objected.

"Then sell her. Sell her to your enemies!" The shaman nodded wisely. "Let her bring bad luck to your enemies!"

It was decided by the tribe to hold a potlatch, extensively in honor of their visitor Ka-too-woo, the Chief's sister. To hide their intentions of getting rid of Anna as somebody cursed, the tribesmen took an oath to keep her infirmity secret. It would have been a terrible blow to their pride if their scheme became known. The chief, Utra-Makah, to whom they planned to give Anna at the potlatch, would have been insulted. He would have been justified to declare a war on them, even though the tribes were related to one another.

The Quillayutes sent a messenger to the Makah tribe,

which dwelt at the tip of Cape Flattery, inviting their Chief
and his kwan for a potlatch.

The women prepared Anna for her role as a gift. They
scrubbed her, picked off her lice, combed her hair and forced
her to eat. When she was allowed to return to her pallet, she
curled up on her mat, like an infant, falling instantly into a
deep, comatose sleep.

She was given back her clothes. She pulled on her soft
leather breeches and a cotton shirt and wiggled her toes inside
the warm fur-lined Yakut boots. The fact that her body
was covered again seemed to break loose the bond of her
indifference.

A new hope began to flicker in her mind. She knew now
that her husband was alive and the Russian camp was only
hours away. If she were to steal a canoe she could reach the
camp.

But her feeling of renewal was short-lived. The Quillayutes were preparing for some special occasion. Anna suspected that it would be a potlatch. She had learned from
Timofei about the potlatches, the strange ceremonies when a
Chief gave away his entire possessions or destroyed them to
demonstrate by his indifference that he cared nothing about
the loss of a dozen blankets or the death of a few slaves.

"The death of the slaves!" Anna thought, suddenly turning cold. Was it to be her fate to be sacrificed at a potlatch?
Was that the reason her master stopped molesting her? Was
he about to kill her?

Chapter 50

The guests arrived in twenty large canoes decorated with the designs of the eminent Makah whaling families. The elderly Chief Utra-Makah stood on the stern of the leading canoe. He wore ceremonial robes of cedarbark and a tall hat with a crown that rose like a three-part telescope. A copper pin pierced his nose and clusters of long dentalium shells dangled from his ears. His body was tattooed starting at his wrists, then leading to his shoulders, and over to his chest and back, descending to his buttocks, thighs and calves.

In the bow of the Chief's canoe stood a warrior wearing a carved mask of a raven and giant wings that he flapped as the canoe moved through the water. He was the Raven of the tribe, the best dancer who appeared at all important ceremonies.

Another figure, a shaman, crouched at the Chief's feet, beating a drum and chanting. The warriors repeated his chant in unison as they paddled. The shaman's face was painted in black stripes and his mane of matted hair was crowned with a wreath of cedarbark, dyed bright red. He wore only a short cedarbark apron and clusters of deer hooves around his ankles.

The women and children, all dressed in their best cedarbark clothing, rode in the other canoes.

The Quillayutes lined up along the riverbank, waiting for the Makahs to disembark. The tribes were similar in their language and general appearance, but despite intermarriages, each mistrusted the other.

The guests were led into the Chief's house, where the tribes settled around the fire, facing one another. The Chiefs sat together on a raised platform.

Anna was hidden, drugged, behind a pile of blankets. She thought dimly that it would be a good time to try to escape, yet lacked the energy to try.

The celebrations began with dances. Wearing masks of birds and animals, the dancers pranced before the fire, recounting the deeds of their ancestors. They turned and stomped in one great mass of shuffling feet, raising clouds of dust. Their shadows, grotesquely enlarged, jumped on the walls.

The dances continued for hours, interrupted only by the Quillayute women who brought in large wooden platters of salmon and halibut. The guests attacked the food, dunking chunks of fish into containers of hot olachen oil. With grunts of pleasure, they sipped oil from special ladles carved of mountain goats' horns. Later, these ladles would become the first items to be distributed at the potlatch.

The feasting lasted deep into the night.

Next morning the tribes resumed their festivities. Both tribes boasted of their descendance from their deities—the Ravens and the Wolves.

On the third day, the Quillayute children were brought in for the special ritual of tattooing. As a gesture of friendship, the best Makah artists traced dots and zigzags on the girls' chins and the boys' cheeks and arms. The children endured the pain stoically, only the very young daring to cry.

By the fifth day the fervor of the festivities slackened. The people were glutted with food, songs and dances. The guests waited impatiently for the gifts.

A long line of Quillayutes formed outside the house. Each person held onto a corner of a blanket, one in front and one behind. They entered the house in single file, forming an unbroken chain of people and blankets.

The showing of the blankets took several hours. Then came the canoes. The Quillayute Chief ordered them to be thrown into the fire. He watched stonily the destruction of his beautiful boats demonstrating to his guests that he was *so* rich that the loss of the canoes meant nothing to him.

Next, several bladders of halibut oil were poured over the fire. The oil made the flames leap up to the rafters, the dry boards threatening to catch fire, but Red Wolf smiled. "Only a wealthy Chief can afford to waste so much oil," he thought.

Finally, the time had come to present Anna. The Makahs

were told by Ka-too-woo that their hosts had a white slave woman among their possessions.

Utra-Makah was especially interested in the white slave. He had several profitable dealings with the ships sailing by his village. Only recently he had sold a shipwrecked white sailor to a ship's captain, who paid ransom for this prisoner. The price for a white woman, although not as high as a man, would still be good enough, Utra-Makah thought.

The old Chief had often fantasized of capturing a ship with all its white men. His warriors could easily overpower the crew were it not for the ships' cannons, he thought. They could destroy a village with one blast.

Utra-Makah could not comprehend such supernatural powers. Being a practical man, he decided to become a friend of the white man. He had profited greatly ever since. His village, high on the cliff on the northern tip of the peninsula, became a way station for many a white sailor captured by the coastal tribes. The natives would sell their white slaves to Utra-Makah, who in turn, would offer them to the captains of the ships.

As he waited to be shown the white woman, Utra-Makah anticipated another possible deal.

Anna was led by the women into the center before the fire. They combed her hair and let it fall over her shoulders, reaching down to her hips. The fire reflected in its gloss, making it look like gold, then changing it into red copper and silvery-blue. The Makahs have never seen such hair before.

Anna stared at the sea of garishly painted brown faces, recognizing no one, not even her master, Red Wolf.

Utra-Makah grunted, nodding his head, noting she was young and looked healthy. Perhaps he would keep her for himself. He had never seen a white woman before. He liked her hair; it looked soft, perhaps it was even softer than the best of cedar fibers. He motioned to his shaman to examine the white slave.

The shaman vaulted into the circle before the fire. He stomped his feet dancing around Anna, the deer-hoof rattles around his ankles making clicking sounds.

Anna stood stonily, submitting to the quick pokes of his fingers. The shaman touched her hair, squeezed her breasts and poked at her buttocks through her Yakut leather breeches. He propelled her roughly toward Utra-Makah and pushed her down to her knees before her new master, her hair sweeping the ground at the Chief's feet.

Utra-Makah rose. He adjusted his robes, paying no more attention to Anna. He was going to dance with his warriors, after which the potlatch would be over. He wanted to go home. The Makah women led Anna away.

The Quillayutes lined up along the shore, watching the Makahs' departure. Their potlatch was a great success. They had given away all their accumulated wealth, leaving for themselves only the bare minimum for survival. Their tribal honor was upheld. Now they would wait to see how well the Makahs reciprocated a year or two later. Now the Makahs' pride was at stake!

The great fleet of Makah whaling canoes glided away. The shaman began his chant and the warriors responded, paddling in unison. A soft rain mingled with mist rising over the river, soon obscured their departure.

By the end of April the *promyshleniki* finished building a boat. It could accommodate no more than six people with their gear, but they had already bought a whaling canoe from the old Quillayute which could carry the rest of them.

The old man volunteered to be their interpreter. Timofei hired him at once. He had proven himself to be trustworthy, Timofei thought. Throughout the winter he kept supplying the Russians with dried fish and halibut oil and as Timofei's own proficiency in Quillayute dialect grew, with the news about Anna. Through him the Russians learned that Anna had been given away at the potlatch to the Makahs.

As he rewarded the old man for his information Timofei asked "How far live the Makahs?"

"Very far..." he pointed north. "Utra-Makah is a great Chief. Ka-too-woo is his wife's sister."

In the first week of May, 1809, the Russians loaded their few remaining possessions into watertight baskets. There was not much to pack; their extra clothes, boots, and blankets were all bartered for food during the winter. Should they fail to reach Gray's Harbor this time, they had practically no chance of surviving another winter.

Their gunpowder and shot was almost gone. From now on there would be no hunting with guns, Timofei announced. They needed to preserve their ammunition for defense.

The old Indian arrived at the camp paddling a one-man canoe. He smiled broadly, announcing that he was ready to lead them.

The Russians sat down for a moment of silence as was the custom before any journey. Then, making the sign of the cross, they settled in their two boats, paddling down the river toward the ocean.

Anna was brought directly to Utra-Makah's house. There were several dozen people living in the house, all members of the Chief's extended family. The house was much larger than the one in the Quillayute village and its supporting posts were carved in heraldic designs of ravens and whales and beavers instead of the Quillayutes' eagles and wolves, but Anna failed to notice any difference between these images. She was living in a drugged fog. It was understood by all that Anna was to be Utra-Makah's private property.

The Chief's wife ordered two old women to attend Anna. They took her to a creek and washed her body with icy water.

That night Utra-Makah joined her on her mat, without the brutality of her former master.

Several days later, Utra-Makah made up his mind. He wasn't going to trade the white slave. He wanted her for himself.

Anna was no more given powerful potions to keep her docile. She was allowed to move freely about the village, although a crowd of children always trailed behind her.

One clear morning she saw the white sails of a ship. It startled her. She ran toward the cliff. A ship, a beautiful winged bird, skimming the waves like a seagull, was on her way north.

"*Korabl!*" Anna cried out, tears spilling over her cheeks like torrents breaking through a dam. But the ship grew smaller, disappearing in the shimmering sea.

Anna fell to the ground, sobbing.

The children tugged at her. She bent her head in resignation and wiped her tears. She allowed them to lead her back to the village.

She was shaken out of her apathy by the sight of the ship. She lived now for her trips to the shore where she scanned the sea for the sight of a sail. She began to take interest in her surroundings. It was summer now, warm and beautiful, and Anna noticed that she was barefoot, wearing the native cedarbark shirt.

She longed to see a ship again, her symbol of hope. And one day, a ship did appear. It anchored in the bay below the cliff. Utra-Makah at once departed to trade with the new arrivals. Anna watched from the cliff as Utra-Makah and several of his warriors climbed aboard the ship under the Union Jack. "Save me!" she screamed. The wind carried her anguished cry but not far enough to be heard. She watched helplessly until the ship weighed anchor. Her sails fully unfurled, the ship moved away, her crew unaware of Anna's presence.

Utra-Makah returned from his visit looking well-satisfied. In exchange for several dozen otter skins, he brought back two hunting knives, a bolt of calico cloth, and a suit of European clothes, complete with a formal stove-pipe pearl-gray hat.

He shed his cedarbark shirt and put on the jacket bought from the captain. He was barefoot and under his jacket he wore only a loin covering. To complete the picture, he tied a magnificent silk cravat around his neck and crowned himself with the top hat. He paraded proudly before Anna.

She almost burst out laughing, but caught herself in time. She knew that the Indians would not tolerate ridicule. She had heard that there was a custom of punishing anyone who laughed at the Chief. The lips of the culprit were pierced by sticks, sealing them together.

As she watched the parading Chief, she became aware that she was smiling. When was the last time that she had smiled? Probably while she was still aboard the *Nikolai*! The images of her husband, of Timofei and the others appeared before her, but instead of plunging her into despair, they gave her a new strength. She suddenly recalled Timofei's stories of his own captivity. The Indians often sold their white prisoners back to the white people. It was more profitable for them than to keep them as slaves. "Perhaps I can convince the Chief to sell me to the next ship," she thought, full of new optimism.

Inspired by her new hope, Anna decided to learn the Makah language so that she could communicate with the Chief. "I'll learn from the children. I'll draw pictures in the sand and learn the words. I must be able to talk to Utra-Makah!" With that goal in mind, Anna found herself humming.

Chapter 51

The old man led the canoes down the flooded river. Following him in the smaller of the two canoes Timofei kept struggling with a vague sense of danger. Like most *promyshleniki*, Timofei was accustomed to the ocean. Paddling along the flooded river with its hidden dangers of rapids and submerged rocks was a different matter. Timofei was nervous. He hoped that the old man knew his way.

The river flooded deeply into the lowlands, hiding the shores. Only the crowns of the submerged trees along its shores were visible, creating an impression that the river was studded with hundreds of small green islands. The Quillayute kept to the middle of the river, leading the canoes through the deeper waters.

Darkness fell. The old man nosed his canoe toward the shore. It was time to stop. They dragged their boats to high ground and built a fire. They were ravenously hungry. They attacked their meager rations like starving dogs, ripping the tough strips of dried fish with their teeth, swallowing half-chewed pieces without tasting them.

Bulygin was the only one who felt no hunger. He was ill again, the painful, lung-tearing cough bringing the taste of blood to his mouth. He was feverish, but by morning, the fever usually subsided, leaving him weak and moist with sticky perspiration. He knew that he was suffering from consumption. The signs of the dreaded malady were all there: the tearing cough, the fever, the sweat, and the blood.

Bulygin almost welcomed his infirmity. It was a proof that his life was not worth fighting for. He had lost his will for survival after his last encounter with Anna. He would welcome death, he thought. The sooner the better.

At sunrise the Russians resumed their trip. It was a sparkling morning, the trees just opening their delicate buds, their sticky tiny leaves covering the branches with faint green veils. The sun, reflected in the water, shimmered in hues of red and orange. The sky above the river was of a tender lavender, turning into a deep blue higher up. A chill hung in the air, but it was the pleasant chill of spring which would soon turn into warmth.

On the third day the travelers reached the spot where Anna and two others were abducted more than six months ago. Further downstream lay Ka-too-woo's village.

Timofei halted the boats. "I suggest we send the old man to negotiate on our behalf for permission to pass. Our only chance of reaching the sea lies in the good will of Ka-too-woo's tribe."

Zuev was the first to object to Timofei's suggestion. "For Christ's sake, we have the guns! Let's attack the bastards, sack and burn their damned village and get even with them! Let's fight our way through their cursed territory!"

Several *promyshleniki* joined him, but Kormachev took Timofei's side.

"Wait, *bratzi*, before we attack the bastards, let's send the old man to parley with them. Should he fail, we'll fight," he counselled.

The men argued among themselves, but eventually agreed to send the Quillayute to the village as their envoy. They pulled their canoes further ashore and hid them under the bushes.

They retreated into a cave imbedded in the rocky shore. Timofei examined the cave closely. He posted guards and, as usual, took the first watch himself.

The men did not dare to light a fire. They hoped the Indians had not seen them. No one spoke any longer of revenge. Such talk only demoralized them, presenting no practical solution.

The men dozed, waking up with a start, their empty bellies growling, reminding them that their last meal had been more than eighteen hours ago.

The drab morning slowly crept in, barely distinguishable from the night. Kormachev distributed their last supply of fish.

They waited for the return of their envoy, chewing grimly on the rancid fish.

Suddenly they heard the rhythmic splash of paddles. Through the layers of fog, a long slender canoe came into view, fast approaching. The men tensed.

"Steady, *bratzi*," Timofei warned. The men nervously clutched at their guns.

The canoe bumped gently against the low-slung branches of a half submerged tree.

"Cover me, *bratzi*," Timofei said, making the sign of the cross. He stepped out of the cave with outstretched hands to show that he was unarmed.

"You, the one-eyed giant!" he heard the familiar cackle as Ka-too-woo greeted him, broadly smiling.

"*Bratzi*, come out, the old hag is here," Timofei called to his compatriots. Cautiously, their guns cocked, the men emerged from the cave. Bulygin remained inside, unable to face the betrayer. The two Aleuts, always fearful of the Indians, held back too.

"You want to go to the sea, we'll let you," Ka-too-woo began at once. "Give us your guns—we will let you go to sea."

"I told you before, we need the guns to hunt for food," Timofei cried out in exasperation.

"We'll give you food," Ka-too-woo interrupted. "You give us beads, we give you food. You give us guns, we let you pass to the sea. If you don't—we'll kill you."

Timofei relayed her proposition to his comrades. "Let's not refuse her conditions outright. Perhaps we can give her a couple of guns after all. Without ammunition they are useless to us."

His proposal stunned the men. "We won't give up our guns!" they shouted.

Timofei ignored their outburst, turning back to the old woman. "I don't trust you, Ka-too-woo," he said. "You must prove that you'll keep your word. Bring me fifty big fish and I'll pay you one blue bead for each."

"And the guns?"

"Bring the fish first. We'll talk about the guns later."

"I'll bring the fish," Ka-too-woo replied, returning to her canoe. She pulled away from the shore, moving swiftly downstream.

"I suggest that we offer her two guns," Timofei said as

they returned to the cave. "We will break the mechanisms to make them useless. We won't miss the guns, *bratzi*. We have enough ammunition for only *three* guns! The rest of them just add weight to our gear."

Timofei's arguments fell on deaf ears. The *promyshleniki* could not comprehend the idea of surrendering their guns. The guns were extensions of themselves. As long as they had *some* ammunition, they would not part with any of their guns. They were firm about that.

They waited for Ka-too-woo's return. There was no further need to hide, so they built a fire. Kormachev suggested they make their cave into a camp. "Who knows how long we'll have to stay here. Might as well make it comfortable," he grinned as he went around chopping cedar fronds and spreading them over the rocky floor of the cave.

Ka-too-woo kept her word. The old Quillayute returned with fifty large salmon that evening, but Ka-too-woo did not appear herself.

The old man pointed to the woods surrounding the cave. He made a sweeping movement with both arms as if to encircle the whole landscape, then made a gesture as if he were stretching the string of a bow.

Timofei understood. The camp was surrounded. The Russians were under siege.

The old man returned to his canoe, indicating that he was ready to leave. Timofei paid him for his services, but the Indian still hesitated to leave. He turned to Timofei and pressing his finger to his lips, glanced around. He pointed to the bushes where the Russians had hidden their canoes.

He spread his hands wide, palms up, in a gesture of emptiness. His message was clear. Their canoes were stolen. They had become hostages of the tribe. The old man paddled away.

"We are surrounded," Timofei announced, returning to the cave.

"We must make a breakout!" Zuev shouted. "I say, let's make a break for the sea! Tonight!"

Timofei shook his head sadly. "We can't. We are trapped. Our boats are gone."

The men jumped up, crowding at the opening of the cave, but had to duck back as a shower of arrows fell around them.

"Bastards!"

"We must wait for Ka-too-woo's next move," Timofei said with quiet fury.

Chapter 52

Ka-too-woo was in no hurry. She waited, knowing that the Russians would soon run out of food again. When she thought that the time was ripe to press her demands, she arrived in their camp and boldly peered into the cave.

"You, one-eyed Chief," she called out. "I came to get the guns."

Timofei charged out of the cave like a bull. "You are a snake! You're worse than a she-skunk!" he cursed, trying to remember the most insulting Tlingit expressions.

She listened patiently to his outburst. When he had run out of invectives, she calmly sat down on a boulder.

"The white woman is in my village," she announced. The news stunned him, as she knew it would.

"She's been here for several days now. She belongs to Utra-Makah, the big Chief. He's visiting my brother, the Quillayute Chief."

Timofei swallowed hard, trying to keep his voice from trembling. "Can we see her?"

"I'll bring her." She threw down several bunches of small fish and extended her palm for the payment, preparing to leave.

"When will you bring the white woman?" Timofei rushed after her, but an arrow pierced the path between him and the departing Ka-too-woo. It quivered in the ground, reminding him that he was a captive.

"Sometime," Ka-too-woo replied, settling into her boat and paddling it toward the middle of the river. Timofei lowered himself heavily on the ground.

Zuev came out of the cave and sat on the ground next to

him. He squinted in the bright sunshine after the darkness of the cave. "I think it's a new trap," he said.

"Yes. I think so, too. We have nothing left to offer for Anna Petrovna's freedom. And Ka-too-woo knows it."

"Perhaps they mutilated Anna Petrovna and don't want her anymore. They'll throw her back to us to teach us a lesson."

Timofei shuddered at the thought.

They returned to the cave. It stunk from dampness and smoke. The men huddled around the smoldering fire, haggard and thin. Timofei and Zuev looked at them, both thinking, "how long will they endure?"

Ka-too-woo returned to the camp several days later. Without Anna. A flotilla of whaling canoes followed her, the Makah Chief standing in the bow of the leading boat with his arms folded across his chest. The Chief was attired in his European finery, wearing his formal pearl-gray top hat and no trousers. "Look at the bastard! I wish I could wring his neck!" Timofei spat furiously on the ground. He tightened his grip on his musket.

Utra-Makah disembarked and climbed the rocky path with deliberate slowness. The Russians waited, standing in a cluster, seeking protection in their closeness, their empty muskets presenting an appearance of force they knew did not exist.

Utra-Makah expressed no apprehension at the sight of the armed *promyshleniki*. He had enough warriors to wipe the Russians out at the wave of his hand. He glanced only fleetingly at their muskets, staring instead at Captain Bulygin's naval overcoat with its double rows of brass buttons, and torn but still shiny epaulets. He turned to Ka-too-woo, trotting at his side, and pointed to Bulygin's overcoat saying something in his clicking guttural dialect.

"The Chief says he wants the husband's coat," Ka-too-woo translated into Tlingit.

"The Chief likes your uniform, sir. He wants your coat," Timofei said to the captain.

"Of course, of course," Bulygin fussed, taking his overcoat off, his trembling fingers fumbling with the buttons. "Of course, anything, anything..." He began to cough again, expectorating blood spittle.

He handed his still warm coat to Ka-too-woo. The Chief

promptly put it on, glancing at the Russians as if seeking their approval, like a young boy in his first sailor suit. There was something innocent in his joy. Timofei found himself smiling.

"*Hach,* good!" he said in Quillayute, one of the few words that he had learned from his former guide. The Chief paraded proudly before the Russians. Then he spoke briefly to Ka-too-woo and departed with his warriors.

The Russians were perplexed. "What was the point of the Chief's visit?" Timofei thought. He turned to Ka-too-woo. "What did the Chief say?"

"He wants you to go with him to his village."

"What?"

"If you don't, you'll never make it to the sea," she smirked and trotted down the hill toward her boat.

"Where's the white woman?" Timofei shouted.

"With her master." Ka-too-woo paddled away.

Timofei conferred with Zuev.

"What shall we do? Perhaps we should follow the Chief...We are surrounded here. Without ammunition we cannot fight our way out. Not all Indians are savages. Some are quite decent." He thought of his captivity among the Tlingits after the sack of the old Fort St. Michael. Marinka's mother was certainly decent, he thought.

"I'd rather be dead than voluntarily follow the savages!" Zuev exclaimed.

Timofei sighed. "I know how you feel. Yet...We might find a way of escaping from Utra-Makah at some future time..." he added without much conviction.

Early next morning the Indians returned, bringing Anna. They sent her up the path alone.

She paused at the entrance to the cave. It was dark and she could barely see the outlines of the people inside.

"Anna!" Bulygin cried out from the depth of the cave. He slowly widened his eyes and then shut them closed. His recurrent fever often brought him images of Anna, pleasant while they lasted, but making the reality even more unbearable later. He was not told by Timofei and Zuev that Anna was nearby. He was too ill, they decided, to withstand another tragic encounter with his wife.

"Kolya, darling Kolya," he heard Anna's gentle voice.

She stepped into the cave. Timofei led her by the hand to Bulygin's pallet.

"Kolya, open your eyes, I'm real," she whispered.

Bulygin slowly opened his eyes. He rose to a half-sitting position and reached out to her. She fell into his arms, sobbing.

"Kolya, Kolya, my darling, you're ill," she kept saying, covering his emaciated face with kisses.

Timofei watched them with pity. They looked so pathetic, both thin, unkempt, Anna dressed in an Indian shirt barely reaching down to her knees, barefoot, her legs scratched and covered with insect bites. One would have never recognized the former lush beauty in this exhausted looking woman.

The *promyshleniki* surrounded them in a tight circle. They wept unashamedly at the reunion of the tragic couple. The low fire flickered, illuminating their bearded faces and sunken eyes.

Finally, Anna pulled herself together. "*Bratzi*, I have come here as a messenger," she said. "Please hear me out." She faced the men, bracing herself against the outburst of their anger which she knew would follow.

"I advise you to join the Makahs," she plunged in. "Utra-Makah is aware of your worth as white people and he intends to sell you to the white captains. If you go with me to his village, he'll eventually sell all of us to some British or Yankee captain. I saw the British ship myself...It was anchored near his village. On the other hand, even if you manage to escape from here and try to trudge through the rain forests and mountains, you'll be picked up by other tribes. The whole coast knows about you by now. You'll be killed if you fight, or captured by some other tribes, surely more cruel than the Makahs."

The *promyshleniki* listened to her with growing uneasiness. "She's right," many of them thought. "It's better to go with a friendly tribe and hope to be rescued than fight our way through the wilderness."

Anna continued, "I know it's degrading for my husband and for the rest of you to see that I, a white woman and Christian, speak for the savages. But it's a question of survival, *bratzi*. I resigned myself to being the Chief's whore."

Bulygin covered his face with his hands. "Don't say

that!" he cried out. "My wife—an Indian whore!" he recoiled from her. "Don't shame me before our people!"

Anna continued. "There was a time I prayed to die. I
was ill, I was cruelly abused, I thought that you were all
dead. Then many months later, I saw a British ship. It
was anchored right under the cliff of the Makah village. So
close! I could see the faces of the sailors, all white, like mine.
I watched Utra-Makah trade with the British. It was then
that I realized that I could be rescued! I began to learn the
Makah tongue to convey the idea to Utra-Makah. He was
already aware of the high ransom the captains paid for the
white prisoners. But he was not sure that a woman would
bring a high enough price. I convinced him that I would bring
an even higher ransom because I was the *only* white woman,
a great prize for the white men. Utra-Makah promised that
he would offer me in trade to the first ship that anchored in
his bay. Then he heard you were spotted on the river. He
decided it was his chance to trade not only one white woman
but a whole group of white people, so he took off for a visit
with the local Chief who is Ka-too-woo's brother. He took
me along to persuade you to join him."

Timofei listened attentively. "It makes sense," he
thought. "Utra-Makah is obviously a clever man. Perhaps
we ought to cast our lot with the Makahs," he thought as he
listened to Anna's arguments. "Her plan is certainly better
than anything I can think of."

"The summer will be over soon," Anna continued. "If
you don't reach Gray's Harbor within the next few weeks,
you're doomed. And you won't reach it, the Indians won't
let you. You won't survive another winter in these woods.
You have no blankets, no warm clothing. Not even beads to
trade for food. Nothing."

She paused, looking from one man to another, letting
the hopelessness of their predicament sink into their minds.
"No, *bratzi*, your only way of getting out of here is to join the
Makahs and wait to be ransomed by some passing ship."

"What if the Chief changes his mind and decides to keep
us?" Kormachev asked.

"He won't. He anticipates a great profit when he barters
us for goods with the white captains."

"What do you say, *bratzi*?" Timofei raised his head, facing the men. "I believe Anna Petrovna has the best solution.
Let's go with the Makahs. Even if no single ship can afford

to buy us all, the news of our captivity will surely reach Governor Baranov. He'll send a ship to rescue us, we know that! I intend to follow Anna Petrovna's plan."

Bulygin was the first to join Timofei in his momentous decision. It was months since the men had heard their captain express an opinion. He spoke now with a trace of his former authority.

"I agree with Mr. Tarakanov. Our only chance of gaining freedom is in being rescued by a ship. I'll go with him," he concluded shakily, without looking at Anna.

She wanted to embrace him but did not dare to. "He despises me," she thought. "He too, called me a whore."

"Who else wants to join us?" Timofei queried. "Speak up!" Ovchinnokov raised his hand, then Nastasia and Yakov, the Aleuts. The other men exchanged worried looks. The idea of surrendering to their enemies was repugnant to them.

"Anybody else?" Timofei was surprised so few were willing to take a chance. There was silence.

"No," Zuev replied firmly, assuming the leadership. "The rest of us are going to try our luck in reaching Gray's Harbor."

Anna smiled sadly. "You are making a mistake. You'll never reach the harbor. The savages are lying in wait for you all along the coast."

The men wavered but Zuev spoke again, cocky and arrogant. "Don't worry about us, Anna Petrovna. You go to your friends and wait to be ransomed. We'll send a ship for you as soon as we reach Gray's Harbor. We might come ourselves to bargain for your release," he added, bringing out laughter in his followers.

"I'll do my best to make Ka-too-woo return your boats," Anna said. "I must leave now. Will you come with me, Mr. Tarakanov, and explain your decision to Ka-too-woo? My knowledge of their language is very limited."

"Gladly." Timofei rose to his feet.

Ka-too-woo was waiting for them in a large canoe in the company of several armed warriors. "I knew that you would follow her!" she exclaimed. "You have your eye on her! Your one and only eye!" she laughed, delighted with her joke.

Timofei chuckled. "You're a wise old bird, Ka-too-woo! You should be called an owl, instead of a chickadee."

"What are you talking about?" Anna said.

"Just exchanging some pleasantries," he replied, feeling almost happy for the first time in many months.

Chapter 53

The Indians returned one of the canoes. Timofei wrested a promise from Ka-too-woo that his men would be allowed to proceed to the sea in exchange for several muskets. The Russians broke the mechanisms, making the guns useless. Ka-too-woo slung the guns across her shoulders and marched down the hill toward her canoe.

"They can go!" she shouted. "My people won't bother them."

The *promyshleniki* prepared to part company. Zuev's group loaded the canoe with a few dried fish bought from Ka-too-woo and a watertight basket of fresh water. They divided the remaining ammunition and secured their pistols inside their belts. They were ready to leave. They embraced the remaining people, tears sparkling in the eyes of many. All had a feeling they would never see one another again. Zuev embraced Timofei, kissing him on both cheeks three times as was the Russian custom.

"Be careful, Timosha," he said, his voice cracking, betraying his emotion.

"You too, Pavlusha. Take care of yourselves, *bratzi.*" Timofei embraced the departing men one after another.

Bulygin took Vancouver's map from his pocket. "I won't need it any longer. Take it. It shows the coast pretty accurately." He opened the map and pointed to Gray's Harbor. "Here it is. Gray's Harbor. We're approximately here." He made a mark on the map with his fingernail. "When you reach the sea, you must follow the coast, bearing directly south. Keep the coastline on your left; that way you won't get lost." He knew that none of them could read a map but they were accustomed to the sea, peerless in manipulating small boats.

"Well...*S Bogom!*" They all sat down on the ground for a moment of silent prayer, then the departing men climbed into their canoe. They waved to the tiny band remaining on shore, feeling free and brave as they picked up speed, paddling in unison.

Utra-Makah sent two warriors to fetch the remaining Russians. Timofei helped Bulygin into the boat. The captain was shaking with chills again. "Here, put it on," Timofei took off his coat. His teeth chattering, Bulygin put the coat on.

The canoe glided along the receding river toward the ocean following Utra-Makah in his boat. One could clearly see the floodmarks on the trees and on the sides of the porous rocks.

Timofei paddled with deep, even strokes, thinking of Anna. He remembered how he saw her for the first time, only a year ago. She was walking along the landing in Novo-Arkhangelsk, having just disembarked from the *Nikolai*, laughing, fighting the wind that was blowing at her skirts and hair. "Poor Anna Petrovna," he thought. "She has suffered more than any of us." He knew the captain was ashamed of her and would rather she was dead. There was a time when he, too, thought it would have been better if Anna were dead. But no more. He was grateful that she had survived, glad that she proved to be so strong.

He saw Ka-too-woo on the shore and raised his hand in farewell.

"Good luck to you, one-eyed Chief!" she yelled.

"You too, wise bird!" he shouted back. He settled back on his knees, ready to paddle with the rest of the Makahs. He felt that his life would take a turn for the better.

Captain Bulygin crouched on the bottom of the canoe, dying. His breath came out in short laborious spurts as he stared into the cloudless sky, his eyes seeing nothing. Snatches of thoughts crowded his mind. He thought of Anna, not the way he saw her last, gaunt and unkempt, but as she was when he first met her. "Anna, my love," he called, but his voice never rose above a whisper. "I am dying," he said, the feeling of relief suddenly enveloping him. He was free of pain, he felt no cold, although fine ocean mist covered his face as the canoe reached the sea. He closed his eyes, finally at peace.

The Indians were the first to discover that Bulygin was dead. They grabbed his body under the arms and by the legs and tossed it overboard.

"Dear God!" Timofei cried out. He made the sign of the cross. "May God rest his soul," he said. The other hostages murmured "Amen".

Timofei knew the Tlingit superstitions about the dead in their midst. The bodies were removed as soon as possible. Apparently, the Makahs were no different. They too, hurried to get rid of the dead.

Timofei became the personal property of Utra-Makah, while the others were dispersed among the members of the Chief's family.

The Chief spoke some Tlingit and Timofei was able to converse with him in a combination of Tlingit, Quillayute and sign language, which both of them found quite adequate.

Utra-Makah repeated his promise to trade his Russian captives at the first opportunity.

"It's only a matter of time now, and a single ship!" Timofei thought.

But the weather had changed. Storms churned the sea, gale winds uprooted the trees ashore. Rains pelted the sea and the land. The storms raged in the Pacific for two weeks. When they subsided and the cool, cloudy weather returned, the sea still looked angry, its waves capped with white curly foam. There were no ships.

Timofei seldom saw Anna. She was kept among the women. She took the death of her husband without much outward emotion. She had suffered so much already that nothing seemed to hurt her anymore. But deep inside, she bled from this wound most of all.

The summer was ending. Timofei had no idea what month it was, July or August, perhaps even early September, having long lost count of the days. He knew that summer was on the wane for the nights had grown longer and darker and the woods were full of ripened berries.

Several weeks passed. It was obvious there would be no more ships until the next spring.

One night Ka-too-woo reappeared in the village. She conferred with Utra-Makah, who sent a messenger to fetch Timofei.

"We go hunt whales tomorrow," Utra-Makah said. "Do you want to come with us?"

"Yes!" Timofei had been on whale hunts with the Aleuts before and the challenge of the hunt excited him. The whales did not surrender meekly, like seals or otters. They often took the lives of the hunters before they would submit to their fate. It was dangerous to bring down a whale and only the bravest were allowed to participate in the hunt.

"You come to the shore at dawn," Utra-Makah said, dismissing him.

Ka-too-woo waited for Timofei.

"Tomorrow you hunt whale, but tonight you can have your white woman," she said. "I'll bring her to you." Before he could reply, she was gone.

Timofei felt his face suddenly ablaze. Anna Petrovna was being passed on to him! The woman whom he had desired so passionately for so long, could be his tonight. But he knew he would not touch her. He *loved* Anna. He wanted her, but only if she were to give herself to him freely. He could not treat her as any woman, enjoying her body for its own sake. He loved her.

Ka-too-woo brought Anna to his pallet. "I keep my word," she laughed as she gave Anna a push.

Anna stumbled in the darkness and fell on all fours next to Timofei. Ka-too-woo, still cackling, left them alone.

"Did you hurt yourself?" Timofei whispered, helping Anna to sit up.

"No," she said. He could feel her tremble.

"I won't touch you, *golubushka* Anna Petrovna," he whispered tenderly. "Don't be afraid of me." She continued to tremble and he covered her with his blanket.

"I'm so glad that it's you, Timosha," she murmured. "Ka-too-woo told me that I was to sleep with another man tonight. I did not know it was to be you."

"Sh-sh-sh, *golubushka*...I won't touch you. I'll guard you. Go to sleep," he eased her onto his mat, tucking his blanket around her. A great feeling of tenderness toward Anna overwhelmed him. He did not need her body; the nearness of her was enough to fill him with a joyous feeling of happiness.

"I'm cold. Put your arms around me, Timosha," she said.

He encircled her in his arms, Anna resting her head on his broad chest.

He felt her fragile form in his arms. "Where's her voluptuous beauty?" he thought, loving her even more now that she was hurt, abused and emaciated. He thought she was asleep, when he suddenly heard her murmur in his ear, "I know you love me, Timosha. I knew it for a long time, even in Novo-Arkhangelsk, when you tried to avoid me. I always knew that you loved me. Take me. I know you want me."

"I can't. Not in this way..." he replied in a hoarse whisper.

"Take me, Timosha...I want you too. I *need* you to love me..." she continued to murmur against his ear as if hearing nothing of his words. She kissed his bare chest, clinging to him tightly along the full length of his body.

"Anna Petrovna, *golubushka*, please, don't...don't torment me," he pleaded.

"Love me, Timosha...I want you to love me..." she repeated. Timofei sought her mouth. "Yes...yes...yes..." she murmured.

They made love tenderly, his passion all but drowned in his great feeling of love for Anna. She clung to him even after they were spent, seeking safety in his embrace.

Early in the morning Ka-too-woo shook Timofei by the shoulder. "The whalers are ready to leave. Hurry!" Timofei kissed the sleeping Anna. She looked rosy like a child, fragile and vulnerable. "I'll protect her...She's mine now," he thought as he hurriedly left the house.

Ka-too-woo waited on the beach until the two whaling canoes departed for the hunt. Then she returned to the house and woke Anna roughly.

"You come with me. I'll bring you back next spring when the ships start coming again."

"I won't go!" Anna cried in terror. Something terrible was about to happen to her again.

Ka-too-woo laughed. "You want to be with the one-eyed white Chief, I know, but I want you to go to my brother's son." She grabbed Anna by the hand, her fingers digging into her flesh like the talons of a bird.

"Timosha!" Anna screamed, but he was not there to hear her.

Ka-too-woo pushed Anna along the path toward the

shore. Six young warriors waited for them in a canoe. They took off at once, heading south, hurrying to complete their two-day voyage before the next storm would make the sea a cauldron of heaving waves.

"Why did you take me away?" Anna cried.

"Because Utra-Makah wanted to make a gift to my brother's son."

"He sold me!"

"No. He just lent you to my brother's son for the winter. Like he lent you to the one-eyed white Chief. Utra-Makah is very generous. You'll be back with the first winds from the south."

Anna said no more, resigning herself to her fate.

Chapter 54

Timofei knelt in the large whaling canoe, one of the crew of eight men. A great privilege was granted him by Utra-Makah: participation in a whale hunt was the occupation of the bravest.

Timofei suspected that Utra-Makah was testing him. Perhaps he wanted to prove that no white man was a match for his warriors. Timofei did not care. He was euphoric with his sense of freedom. He sliced the water with his paddle in rhythm with the other six men. The harpooner, Utra-Makah himself, did not paddle. He stood in the bow, watching the sea for a spout of water that would indicate the presence of a whale. At his feet lay a wide, shallow basket with meticulously coiled line made of whale sinews. The line was attached to the tip of harpoon of elk horn. Upon striking the whale, the barb would remain in his body, while the shaft of the harpoon could be used again with another barb.

Each sinew line was precisely the length of five fathoms. At regular intervals it was studded with buoys made of whole sealskins turned inside out. Timofei helped to inflate the buoys by mouth, a most unpleasant procedure. In Russian America it was always done by the Aleuts.

The whalers were naked. Their hair was tied high on the tops of their heads into whalers' knots, Timofei conforming to the custom.

A second canoe followed at a short distance carrying the Chief's younger brother who was to strike the second blow at the whale.

Timofei knew that only the Chiefs could be harpooners. The Indians endowed the harpooners with mysterious powers, undisclosed to mere warriors. They trusted their Chiefs to follow the rigid purification rites before a hunt which would assure success.

Utra-Makah, standing on the bow, looked like an old wood carving. His every muscle was tense. He was a man in his fifties, still strong, still magnificent in these last years of his manhood. He still could deliver the fatal blow to his prey.

Utra-Makah raised his hand, pointing to a slender column of water rising in the distance. "*Chet-a-puk!*" The man in the stern steered the canoe around. The chase was on.

The whale was just under the surface, lolling leisurely in the warmer coastal waters. Timofei could clearly see his huge body as it drifted lazily, the whale probably dozing.

They approached the giant cetacean from the rear. Maneuvering the canoe to the creature's left side, they barely paddled so as not to startle the beast. Utra-Makah poised his harpoon at shoulder height. His right foot was firmly planted forward, his left resting on the bow thwart, balancing his body. He pivoted like a dancer, his taut muscles rippling, and struck, hitting the whale just below the left flipper.

The huge creature thrashed, as several more harpoons were thrown into his thick hide, each dagger-sharp barb attached to a line with buoys.

The whale fought them courageously. He rose up out of the water, the lines with their attached floats entwining him as if they were bead necklaces. He fell back into the water with a thunderous clash sending tons of water over the men, dragging the canoes out to sea at breathtaking speed, the men hanging precariously to the sides. Timofei knew that the beast would exhaust himself eventually and turn toward the shore, pulling the canoes along. Whales had a strange instinct which often drove them toward the beaches and to their deaths in the shallow waters. The natives took advantage of it allowing the beast to tow the canoes back to the land.

The whale raced, the two canoes attached to him by lines of bobbing floats. Swimming just under the surface of the sea, he flipped his huge tail, sending avalanches of water crashing over the flimsy boats and their puny crew.

Finally, the whale began to tire. His run became slower, his tail flipped out of the water no more. The men grinned at one another. They knew that before long the beast would give up his fight and turn toward the shore.

Timofei relaxed the tension in his shoulders.

Utra-Makah, who crouched low during the mad drag into the sea, rose to his feet again. He had a slender sharp lance in his hands which he was readying to plunge into the beast's heart.

The whale rolled once more. The creature was barely moving now, the water around him tinged with blood. It was time for the kill.

Utra-Makah slowly raised his narrow lance with the sharp bone point. He drove it home to the heart.

The whale spouted a tall column of blood and red bubbles appeared on the surface of the water. A convulsion ran through his great bulk. He expired within moments.

The Makahs shouted victoriously. They turned their canoes around, towing the dead whale toward the shore.

Timofei shouted along with them. The sea behind the boats reeked with blood. Flocks of seagulls appeared from nowhere, swooping into the wake of the whale. They cried sharply as if mourning the death of the great beast.

The sky darkened. A storm was approaching, the clouds hanging heavily over the sea. Timofei looked at the dead whale. "Forgive me, Lord's creature, for causing your death," he murmured superstitiously, still following the habit formed when he was a young lad.

The whole Makah population had been waiting on the beach. People ran into the surf helping to drag the immense carcass ashore. Crowds of admiring boys surrounded the whalers.

Timofei felt the muscles of his legs tremble and his shoulders ache. Utra-Makah put his arm around his shoulder. "I'm proud of you, one-eyed Chief!" he said with a broad smile.

Timofei grinned back and shook the Chief's hand in an European manner. "I am proud, too, Utra-Makah, to be with you and your men."

Timofei followed the whalers to a stream of sweet water to complete the ritual of the hunt by washing off the salt spray and splotches of whale blood. They accepted him as an equal.

There were open blisters on the palms of his hands and on his knees rubbed raw against the canoe. But the hands and the knees of the Indians were also covered with blisters and sores. Utra-Makah's legs bore the marks of rope burns where the line had hit him while uncoiling.

The men bathed, the water stinging their open wounds, soothing their bruises.

On the beach, the Makahs gathered around a large bonfire, hacking at the whale, cutting away blocks of blubber. They now had enough oil to last for several months, and plenty of blubber for weeks to come. They could take as much whale meat and blubber they wanted, the rest being arranged in rows on the special stands for later consumption as it would "ripen."

Timofei peered into the crowd of women, searching for Anna.

"The white woman is gone," Utra-Makah said. "Ka-too-woo took her away."

"Why?" Timofei turned around, paling.

"I promised her to my nephew," Utra-Makah said, adding with a sly smile, "when she returns in the spring, I'll give her to you." Timofei's short-lived happiness was crushed.

The warriors brought Anna to Ka-too-woo's village at the mouth of the river. The full moon illuminated the water, reflecting in it as if it were a column of shimmering silver. The tribal houses stood broodingly on the shore, their weather-beaten heraldic symbols softened by the moonlight.

The old woman guided Anna toward her dwelling. "You sleep here. In the morning we go to my brother's son. He lives quite far." She handed Anna a blanket.

Sleep evaded Anna. Her newly found fragile optimism was slipping away once again. Her tender night of love-making with Timofei was like a fantasy. Perhaps it never really happened...Perhaps it was something that she had invented to ward off the humiliation of being a mere chattel, passed on from man to man.

She must have dozed off. She was startled when Ka-too-woo shook her vigorously by the shoulder. "Get, up, yellow-haired woman. We have a long way to go!"

They made their way to the river. Ka-too-woo pulled her small canoe down the slope and into the water. "From now on we'll go alone," she said as they climbed into the canoe. "Here. Eat some fish." She handed Anna a large chunk of dried salmon.

They glided silently along the placid stretch of the river.

The eastern sky gradually burst out in a blaze of color but the thick forest on the banks of the river remained dark. The sun touched only the very tops of the trees, leaving the forest floor damp and cold.

Ka-too-woo steered toward the shore. "We'll go into the forest now."

They walked along the narrow path, pushing the low slung branches. The moss felt soft under Anna's bare feet, but she could feel the swampy water underneath it.

The rain forest was choked with vegetation. Out of every trunk of a fallen tree there rose slender shafts of new trees, all stretching out to the sky in search of light and warmth.

Ka-too-woo finally stopped. "We'll sleep here." She pointed to a thick tree split at its base into two parts. It created a niche, high enough for a person to walk in as if it were an arch. They spent the night inside the tree, Anna finding it quite comfortable, almost like sleeping in a huge, high-backed chair in her father's house.

They reached their destination two days later. It was a small forlorn village on the shore of a mountain lake.

"My nephew is too poor to buy a wife. But he's young. He'll lay with you more often than Utra-Makah," Ka-too-woo said. "Utra-Makah was not using you much, I've heard, so I suggested to send you for a short time to our nephew. Let a young fellow have his fill, eh?" she laughed lewdly. "Utra-Makah is a good uncle, no?" She was delighted with her cleverness.

"Ka-too-woo, please, take me back!" Anna begged, knowing it was useless. How could she explain to Ka-too-woo her shame and the feeling of degradation? The old woman would not understand.

Ka-too-woo smirked. "I'll take you back. In the spring."

A group of naked women and curious children surrounded them. Ka-too-woo spoke to them in a dialect that Anna did not recognize.

"My nephew has gone trapping. His mother will take care of you. I must go." She raised her arm in a farewell gesture.

"Don't go!" Anna cried, clutching to her cedarbark shirt. Ka-too-woo pulled her shirt away from Anna's desperate fingers. She left without another glance.

An old bent woman, deformed by rheumatism, grabbed Anna's wrist with her bony fingers. She was surprisingly strong as she dragged her inside the house. She pointed to a dirty mat before the fire and Anna knelt on it.

Timofei was crushed by Anna's new ordeal. "It surely will kill her this time," he thought in despair.

His spirits rose somewhat when four Russian prisoners were brought to Utra-Makah. They were part of the group who had departed with Zuev. They had been ambushed and driven upon the rocks where their boat was wrecked. They had to surrender. Eventually, their captors brought four of them to Utra-Makah, having sold the other eight to different coastal tribes.

Timofei invited his compatriots to share the *zemlyanka* which he had built for himself. The *zemlyanka* with its hinged door was a new kind of dwelling for the Makahs. They would come to visit, swing the door over and over again and gaze in wonder at the clay stove with a *lezhanka* on top and a chimney above the sod roof.

The Indians marveled at Timofei's cleverness. There was nothing that the one-eyed Chief could not do, they decided among themselves. He could fix anything that was broken. He could carve wooden bowls, adorned with life-like flowers and snowflakes. For the children he made wooden dolls which opened like boxes, revealing a surprise collection of even smaller figures inside each succeeding doll.

Timofei's capabilities made the Chief think that perhaps he should not give him up. He would exchange the other hostages, but perhaps he ought to keep the one-eyed giant for himself, Utra-Makah thought. The one-eyed Chief and the yellow-haired woman. Let them make some yellow-haired children for him!

Chapter 55

Anna's new master, Eagle Beak, was a young man in his early twenties. His name was well deserved. He had a large hooked nose which reminded her of the eagles seen on tribal totems. He was short of stature but broad at the shoulders, with long muscular arms. His sturdy short legs, his chest and his buttocks were covered with a continuous tattoo. As he moved, his body exuded raw power, the tattoos expanding or contracting as if they had a life of their own. Watching him, Anna was seized with terror. She cowered under her blanket.

Eagle Beak took possession of her immediately. He had never seen a white woman before and having one in his power gave him a feeling of omnipotence. Aroused by the paleness of her skin and the shiny mass of her golden hair, he grunted like a boar. He tore the blanket off her and roughly yanked her to her knees. He pounced on her, pushing her on all fours. He mounted her from the back, burying his face in her unraveled hair.

A small circle of curious spectators squatted around them, watching their Chief and his new woman.

"No!" Anna screamed, mortified at being taken like a dog, her nudity exposed, but Eagle Beak, holding her firmly by the shoulders only increased his thrusts. She collapsed, sobbing.

As the days followed, Eagle Beak's repeated brutal assaults gripped Anna with constant terror. She tried to blot out the faces of the watching tribesmen, but they were always there, real or imagined, witnessing her humiliation.

Snow fell on the ground. The Indians, prevented from their daily fishing forays by a storm raging over the lake, remained in their houses. During that time of idleness, Eagle

Beak generously shared Anna with the other men of the tribe. His mother would fetch her at his fireside and lead her to one or another house, depositing her before the master of the moment.

Anna's degradation was complete.

The winter dragged on. Anna spent her days curled up under her blanket, like in the days of her captivity in Red Wolf's village. At night, she was inevitably claimed by Eagle Beak or one of his men. She dimly remembered that she must endure until spring, but why—she did not remember. Was it her father to whom she would be returned in the spring? She did not know. She thought of herself as still a little girl, sleeping in front of a stove in her father's house. At other times she waited for Timofei to tell her what she was to do next. She never thought of her husband, locking him out of her consciousness, but Timofei appeared in her deranged thoughts as a beacon of safety.

She became pregnant but she was not aware of it. The functions of her body or its cleanliness long ceased to concern her.

Months passed. The women soon noticed Anna's condition, pointing to her with giggles. Anna watched them in torpor, not associating their laughter with herself nor noticing her changing figure. She had not talked to anyone for months, not understanding their dialect. She talked to herself, but these conversations were fragmentary, her mind filled with strange images, often frightening, or with waves of color, moving and undulating, accompanied by strident and clashing sounds. She was on the brink of insanity.

The winds of spring brought rains. When the sun had reappeared again from behind the moisture laden clouds, the women took Anna to the lake to wash the filth off her body and to clear her hair of lice in preparation for Ka-too-woo's return. The women dressed her in a new cedarbark shirt and braided her hair in a long braid, decorating it with seashells. They were reluctant for her to leave, curious to see what kind of child she would produce.

Ka-too-woo arrived while the snow was still on the ground but the running waters undermined it from below, making it look gray and porous like dampened sugar. She worried when Anna failed to recognize her.

"Don't you remember me? I'm Ka-too-woo. I told you that I would return. I'll take you back to Utra-Makah."

Anna looked at her with vacuous eyes.

"Utra-Makah and the one-eyed Chief. Remember him? He's waiting for you."

"One-eyed Chief..." Anna repeated, not comprehending.

"She has lost her mind!" Ka-too-woo turned to her nephew. "What have you done to her? Did you beat her, or have you starved her?"

"I treated her well. I did not even make her work," Eagle Beak replied proudly.

"I believe you. How long has she been with child?"

"Five or six moons," the women replied.

"Whose child is it?" No one could tell.

Anna stared at Ka-too-woo as the recognition of the old woman gradually began to penetrate the fog in her mind.

"Ka-too-woo...You came for me," she said slowly, the Makah words floating to the top of her consciousness as bubbles of air rise to the surface of a swamp.

"Yes, I came to take you back." Ka-too-woo, not ever given to emotion, felt stirrings of pity. She could not understand what might have caused Anna's confused state but whatever it was, Anna looked pitiful. "White people are so weak," she thought.

"We'll start at sunrise," she said to Anna. "Sleep now." Anna curled up smiling, obedient as a child. She allowed Ka-too-woo to tuck her in as if she were her mother and she a tiny girl, safe in her parental house.

The women gathered around Anna, filling the basket she was to carry with various small gifts, seashells and tiny carved figures, toys for her unborn child. She stood among them with a vacant expression, but Ka-too-woo nodded her head approvingly. She was sure now that Anna had not been mistreated by her nephew's tribe.

Ka-too-woo touched Anna's shoulder. "Let's go." She stuck a basket into her hands and waved to the women, turning toward the forest. Anna followed.

The quiet forest was still covered with patches of snow but the path was clear, winding like a dark thread. Ka-too-woo walked at a brisk pace and Anna soon began to lag behind. She stopped, leaning on a tree.

"All right, let's rest for a while," Ka-too-woo said over her shoulder. She stretched out on dry moss under the tree. Anna lay down next to her, content to be with her.

"I am glad that you came back, Mother," she said slowly. "Where were you all this time? I missed you!"

Ka-too-woo looked at her sharply. "The white woman has lost her mind," she thought. "I am not your mother...My name is Ka-too-woo," she said.

Anna shook her head. Her mother's face was before her. Then, some other images began to surface from the abyss of her clouded mind. She saw herself as a child, riding in a *troika*, with her father driving and she clinging to him, half-frightened, half-exhilarated by the fast gallop. She saw herself floating on a raft along the placid river in the company of a dear person wearing a coat with many shiny buttons. "My husband..." she thought, trying to make out his face but seeing only the curly golden beard and the black patch of Timofei's visage.

She did not notice that Ka-too-woo had resumed their journey. She followed her, like a puppy.

They stopped for the night and slept inside a burned-out tree.

"I remember!" Anna suddenly exclaimed as she crawled out of the cramped space the next morning, her body stiff and aching. "I had slept in a burned tree before. Only it was a different tree. It was quite comfortable."

Ka-too-woo chuckled. "It's the same tree. You weren't heavy with child then."

"Heavy with child..." Anna repeated. "It was long ago. I lost the child." The image of herself suffering on the *lezhanka* in her hut in Pavlovsk appeared briefly in her mind.

"You are heavy with child now," Ka-too-woo said. "An Indian child." Anna placed her hands on her abdomen, instantly becoming aware of the hard bulge. As if jolted, the fog lifted from her mind, exposing the reality in its harsh light.

She remembered everything. The memories streaked through her mind like lightening illuminating a dark sky, splitting it open, allowing new pain to enter her consciousness.

"I am pregnant," she whispered, her brow beading with sweat. "I can't go back," she panicked. "I am truly a whore now."

She followed the old woman along the path, her mind

lucid, as if it had never been deranged. She knew that she could never return to her people. She would be shunned, ridiculed, forever humiliated. She would be condemned. Her own family would turn away from her in shame. Her father would curse her to hell. She could not face her people.

She knew now what she must do.

Chapter 56

The Russian hostages living under the benevolent protection of Utra-Makah had no reason to complain. They were well treated by the tribe, allowed to participate in all its activities, hunting and fishing. They had plenty to eat, their masters sharing with them as if they were kin and not slaves.

Old Utra-Makah was a clever man. He bought the remaining Russians, one by one, from the different tribes, until all of them were concentrated in his village.

Spring had finally arrived, and stayed. The meadows around the village burst out with flowers and the trees donned the green mantles of new leaves. The air vibrated with the song of small birds and the buzz of insects. The sea below the cliff looked smooth and sapphire-blue after the months of angry storms.

Timofei waited impatiently for Anna's return, but day after day passed until he began to suspect that something terrible must have happened to her.

The Russians anxiously watched the horizon. With the coming of spring, any day now a ship might appear, bringing their liberation. But the immense ocean was empty, no white sail breaking the monotony of its expanse.

Timofei began to work on a kite that he was making for the children. It was to be a large kite made of the thinnest lining of seal stomach, stretched and dried to parchment transparency, with a long tail made of a tough sealgut thread.

When it was finally completed, Timofei climbed a rock on a windy northwest point of the cliff. While a crowd of children watched, he felt the wind tug at the kite as he lifted it over his head. As it soared, the children became transfixed, silent with reverence.

Their reaction puzzled Timofei. He had expected yells of excitement, but the children stared at him in awe. He shrugged his shoulders, winding the long string around a spool, bringing the kite down. He was disappointed at their lack of enthusiasm.

That night Utra-Makah demanded to know how Timofei was able to reach the sun. The children had reported that the one-eyed Chief talked to the sun.

Timofei chuckled, thinking that there was no harm in making Utra-Makah believe that he indeed could communicate with the sun. "I'll talk to the sun again, tomorrow, if you wish."

In the morning, the villagers gathered at the approaches to the rock. They sat on the ground wrapped in their fringed blankets, waiting patiently for the great miracle of communion with the sun.

Timofei lifted the kite over his head again. A gust of wind snatched the kite from him, blowing it higher and higher, as if indeed, it were going to reach the sun.

"What are you telling the sun?" Utra-Makah said watching the kite soar.

"I beseech it to bring me home to my people," Timofei replied.

"Ko-rabl!" Kormachev yelled running toward Timofei's *zemlyanka*. "There's a ship!"

The *promyshleniki* dashed toward the beach. They could clearly see a two-masted ship, but it appeared that she had no intention of approaching the shore. She sailed at full speed parallel to the shore, her course straight north.

"She's going away! Don't leave us!" Zuev cried, waving his arms as if the sailors aboard could see him. "Don't leave us!" he yelled hysterically.

Timofei was seized with a sudden idea. "Help me, *bratzi*," he shouted, grabbing his kite and running toward the rock. The men picked up the slack of the string, grasping his plan. They ran with him, as he released the kite into a gust of wind. The kite soared and dived over the ocean, its parchment-like surface glistening in the sun. The *promyshleniki* prayed that someone aboard the ship would notice it.

Suddenly Zuev yelled, "They're tacking! They saw the kite! They're changing course!"

The ship was turning, tacking towards the shore.

"*Oo-rrah!*" shouted the Russians, embracing, jumping up and down like children.

The *Lydia*, an American brig under the command of Captain Brown, dropped anchors in the bay below the village.

At once Utra-Makah prepared for his visit to the ship. He donned Bulygin's naval overcoat and placed his silk top hat on his head. His warriors paddled him and Timofei to the brig.

As the canoe reached the ship, Timofei found himself fighting tears, unable to hide his emotion at being so close to liberation. He climbed up the flimsy rope ladder.

"Good Lord in Heaven, thank You for my deliverance!" he exclaimed in English, allowing the tears to run freely down his face.

"Who are you?" Captain Brown stared at him in astonishment. "You're obviously not an Indian!"

"No, sir, I'm Russian. From the *Nikolai*."

"Good God! The *Nikolai*! She was lost more than two years ago!"

"Yes, sir. I'm one of the survivors."

"God bless you, son!"

Utra-Makah had finally delivered all his Russian prisoners to the *Lydia*. Anna was not among them.

"Where's the yellow-haired woman?" Timofei demanded. His heart suddenly felt cold.

"She hasn't come back. Maybe she liked it with my nephew," Utra-Makah said.

Blood rushed to Timofei's face but he controlled himself. He turned to Captain Brown. "Please don't leave yet, sir. The widow of our captain is still missing."

The captain nodded. "Sure, son, I'll wait two more days. That should be time enough."

Utra-Makah and his warriors departed, their canoes laden with American blankets, pearl buttons and hunting knives.

Timofei scanned the ocean through a borrowed spyglass. Any moment he expected to see a tiny canoe bearing Anna and Ka-too-woo, but the calm ocean was empty.

Two days passed. There was no Anna.

"We must be on our way, son," the captain said to Timofei. "Every day spent idling costs the shipowners money. We can pick up the captain's widow on the way back from Novo-Arkhangelsk, in a couple of months."

"No! If you leave her behind, I'll stay also," Timofei blurted.

Captain Brown looked closely at Timofei. The young man's face was flushed and contorted in pain.

"He's in love with the captain's widow," the captain thought.

Timofei lifted his head. "I beg of you, Captain, as one Christian to another, give me three more days. I'll search for her myself. If I don't return, then sail without me."

"How are you going to find her?"

"The Chief will help me. He knows where she is."

"Do you trust him that much?"

"Yes, sir. Utra-Makah is an honorable man. Besides, it's in his own interest. He expects a great profit in selling the white woman to you."

Captain Brown's leathery face stretched into a grin. "What the hell, son! A few more days won't make that much difference. The weather is pretty good this time of year. We'll catch up, somehow. Go ahead. Find her, but remember, if you're not back in three days, I'll weigh anchor."

"Yes, sir. Thank you, sir!" Timofei shook the captain's hand vigorously. "I'm on my way!"

A longboat was lowered and the sailors rowed Timofei ashore.

"Why are you back, one-eyed Chief?" Utra-Makah greeted Timofei. "Don't you want to go with your people?"

"I do, my friend, I do, but first I must find the yellow-haired woman."

"She'll be back soon."

"But the ship will be gone!"

"I'll sell her to another ship."

"No, Utra-Makah, you must let her go with *this* ship. Help me get her back."

Utra-Makah laughed. "I know. You want to sleep with this woman."

"Yes, I want to sleep with her," Timofei said, thinking

how easy it had become to say it, while only a few months before he barely dared to admit it, even to himself.

"I'll send a scout to my nephew's village. It will take no more than three days."

"Three days! Three days is all I have before the ship sails!"

Utra-Makah shrugged his shoulders with indifference. It did not matter to him when Anna would be sold to the white people, now or later. He would make a good profit, one way or another.

"I want to go with the scout," Timofei said.

"Go, you're a free man," Utra-Makah said with another shrug.

Timofei stripped off his new clothing given to him by the sailors of the *Lydia*. "Keep it," he said, handing his clothes to Utra-Makah. "In return, give me your six best men and the fastest canoe."

"You'll never make it in three days. Instead, ask the white Chief of the floating house to take you there. He can sail faster than any canoe."

"The captain would never agree to alter his course and sail south," Timofei thought. His spirits—so high a few moments before at the prospect of finding Anna—now sank to a new depth.

"You go this way," Utra-Makah continued as he pointed south. "There will be a great river. Ka-too-woo's village is there. Get a scout in the village. He'll take you to the forest, until you come to a lake. My nephew Eagle Beak's village is there."

Timofei reached for his clothing. "No, it's mine now," Utra-Makah declared, intercepting his hand. He gathered Timofei's shirt and trousers. "I gave you good advice."

"I must return to the ship and talk to the captain," Timofei said.

"I'll take you." Utra-Makah was eager as ever to visit the white man's floating house.

Captain Brown listened to Timofei's impassioned plea with sympathy. He had pondered Anna's predicament after Timofei's departure. He had thought of his own wife and daughter and of the ransom he would have paid for their freedom had they become prisoners of the Indians. No price would have been too high, he thought. As Timofei talked, the captain made a decision: he would delay his departure for as long as it took to find the captain's widow.

"I know the river you're talking about," Captain Brown said. "We passed it on our way north. It's impossible to sail up the river. Too rocky. But I'd be willing to anchor near its mouth and wait while you go ashore."

Timofei beamed. "God bless you, sir!" he cried falling to his knees and trying to kiss the captain's hand.

"No...no...I'm glad to do it," the captain stammered in embarrassment, hiding his hands behind his back. "These Russians!" he thought, "such strange traditions..."

"Make sail!" he commanded.

Utra-Makah scampered back to his canoe, a new bead necklace dangling over his chest. He watched as the *Lydia's* sails snapped, filling with the wind, billowing out. The ship tacked, setting her course directly south.

Anna dragged behind Ka-too-woo, her every step a painful effort, her mind clouded again. She saw herself as a little girl hunting for mushrooms with her nurse on the outskirts of the great *taiga* ...The nurse was way ahead on the narrow path and little Anna was tired and fearful that she would get lost...

"*Nyanya*, where are you?" Anna called, her eyes filling with tears.

"I'm scared!" She huddled under the tree, sobbing.

Ka-too-woo stopped and looked back. Anna was crouching under the tree like a frightened rabbit. Angrily, Ka-too-woo walked back. She tried to pull Anna to her feet, but Anna fought with her, throwing herself on the ground as if in a childish tantrum.

"I won't go, I'm tired. Carry me, *nyanya*," she sobbed.

Ka-too-woo stood over her helplessly, not understanding the Russian.

"The evil spirits have invaded her again," Ka-too-woo thought. She spread her blanket on the ground and gestured for Anna to lie down. Obediently, Anna curled up on the blanket, her tears forgotten, a thumb in her mouth, falling asleep instantly.

They stayed under the tree for the rest of the day and the

night. In the morning, Anna was calm again as they resumed their trek.

"Look, there's a ship!" Ka-too-woo pointed to the ocean as they stopped to rest on the high bank of the river. Directly below them was a stretch of calm deep water. Further on, there were the rapids, and still further, beyond the bend, the river emptied into the dark ocean.

Anna stared at the ship, her mind dimly aware of the details. The ship looked tiny from that distance, but Anna could clearly see its furled sails. The ship was at anchor.

"I don't have to go all the way to Utra-Makah's village," Ka-too-woo thought, eager to get rid of Anna. "I can trade the yellow-haired woman right here, with this ship...I'll settle it with Utra-Makah later." Ka-too-woo began calculating what she should demand in exchange for Anna. Should the yellow-haired woman be worth more because of the child, another worker, or less, another mouth to feed? Ka-too-woo could not decide. She did not know how white people valued children.

Anna stared at the ship, mesmerized. She felt no joy, had no clear thoughts, only a vague feeling of shame.

"They'll curse me...My father will curse me..." she whispered.

A feeling of dread pressed on her, suffocating her with growing terror. The ship threatened her.

"Let's go," Ka-too-woo tugged at her impatiently.

They made their way down to the water's edge. Ka-too-woo dragged her canoe out of its hiding place. Anna watched her apathetically, making no move to help.

"Aren't you happy to be near your people?" Ka-too-woo said.

Anna did not hear her. Her head was full of noises, snatches of Russian and Makah words, all senseless. She vaguely remembered that she had seen a ship but it was gone now. It could not be seen from the lower riverbank.

"Look! The one-eyed Chief! He came to fetch you!" Ka-too-woo suddenly yelled, pointing to the river. A canoe was moving up through the rapids. Two men paddled it, one with bright golden hair, shiny in the sun.

"Timosha!" Anna whimpered, her mind a fog of confusion. "Don't leave me, wait for me!" she shouted in her mind, unaware that the canoe was moving toward her and not away from her. "Wait for me!" She staggered toward the water.

Ka-too-woo was busily loading her bundles into the canoe, mumbling to herself. The floating house must have been sent to pick up the yellow-haired woman. Utra-Makah must've completed his deal with the white people. She did not notice that Anna stepped into the water.

Anna dropped her Indian blanket and it instantly floated away, picked up by the fast moving current. The water swirled around Anna's legs, rising up to her waist as she made several more steps.

"Wait for me! Don't leave me!" she cried silently, as she walked still deeper into the swirling river.

"What are you doing?" Ka-too-woo yelled as she turned around. Anna continued walking.

Timofei saw Anna. "Get back!" he shouted. The paddle bowed under his desperate stroke and the canoe struggled against the current.

Anna smiled. She made another step, oblivious of the freezing water. It was almost over her shoulders now. Anna abandoned herself to the river. It picked her up, carrying her swiftly away, toward the rapids. She did not struggle.

Ka-too-woo pushed her canoe into the water. The two canoes raced in pursuit. Timofei saw Anna disappear, then emerge in the surging current.

Ka-too-woo in her canoe and Timofei and the Indian scout in theirs, paddled frantically, aiming toward the point where the river churned against huge rocks, its waters white with foam. Anna's body was caught in the boulders, her golden hair undone and floating about her like seaweed at high tide. Her battered face was peaceful, her eyes shut.

Ka-too-woo turned her canoe around and headed back to the shore.

Timofei leaped out of his canoe landing on a large boulder. He knew in his heart she was dead but he lunged toward her, ignoring the danger, trying to catch her body before it was swept away through the rapids. The river raged at his feet. He cradled Anna's dead body in his arms.

He collapsed on the boulder, weeping. "Anna... Golubushka... So close to freedom... God, why do You punish me so!" he cried out.

"You, one-eyed Chief, are you going to stay on the rocks?" Ka-too-woo called from the shore.

Timofei wiped his eyes. The scout was waiting for him, holding the boat from being swept away by paddling in the lee of a boulder. Timofei lifted Anna's body into the canoe. At least she would get a Christian burial. He thought of his short-lived happiness. Anna...she had carried a child of someone else... she was snatched from him by unrelenting fate.

"You wanted the yellow-haired woman badly," Ka-too-woo said, meeting him on the shore. "She was no good. She was possessed by evil spirits. Even when she belonged to Red Wolf, she was possessed. This is why he got rid of her," she added.

Timofei stared at Ka-too-woo, half-hearing, but understanding from her tone that she was trying to make him feel better in the only way she knew. He unbuckled a knife from his American belt and handed it to Ka-too-woo.

"Good luck, old woman," he said, turning his back on the river, on the Indian scout and on Ka-too-woo. He paddled alone now toward the ship, out of sight beyond the bend.

EPILOGUE

In the years that followed Timofei Tarakanov's miraculous rescue, the Russian dream of an American empire continued to grow. Although the Russian-American Company sorely missed the influence of Nikolai Rezanov, wily old Governor Alexander Baranov picked up Rezanov's dream of a Russian settlement in Alta California. He sent Ivan Kuskov aboard the *Kodiak* in 1808 to reconnoiter the area around Bodega Bay, north of the presidio de San Francisco. More fortunate than the doomed crew of the *Nikolai*, Ivan Kuskov and his men wintered in Gray's Harbor as scheduled.

In the spring, they explored the coast around Bodega Bay and found a suitable site for building a fort.

The territory had been claimed by the Spanish crown by right of discovery but the Russians gambled that Spain, bled white by Napoleon's wars and spread thin in the New World, would be unwilling to press the issue of Russian encroachment.

In 1812 a small Russian contingent arrived at the site of the future Fort Ross. Kuskov bargained with the local Kashia Pomo Indian Chief for a piece of land on a high bluff over the ocean and bought it for "three blankets, three pairs of trousers, three hoes, two axes and several bags of glass beads."

Timofei Tarakanov was among the men who had sailed with Kuskov to built the fort. Years later, Timofei wrote his recollections of the wreck of the *Nikolai* and the tragic story of Anna Petrovna. Captain Vasily Golovnin, visiting Russian America at the time, included Timofei's story in his book of *Remarkable Shipwrecks.*

No one knows who brought the shattering news of Rezanov's death to Concepción Argüello. It could have been Kuskov in 1808 or even Timofei Tarakanov in 1812. A passing sea captain might have also brought the news.

Concha was devastated. She locked herself in her room. When she finally reemerged, she was a different woman. Gaunt and pale, her eyes rimmed in red, she was nevertheless composed. She announced to her family that she would become a *beata*, a woman devoted to good works, who followed the laws of the sisterhood of nuns. She had renounced marriage, vowing to remain a virgin.

When years later, the Dominican Order had established its first convent near Monterey, Concha was among its first novitiates. She entered the convent when she was about sixty and died a nun, still devoted to good works and the memory of her fiance.

She was buried in Benecia, California, where one can still visit her grave.

Throughout this period Alexander Baranov endured. Under his leadership, twenty-four Russian settlements were built, scattered among the islands and on the northern shores of the mainland. Some were no more than two or three huts, while the others, like Novo-Arkhangelsk, Pavlovsk and Fort Rossia (Fort Ross) became substantial towns.

The Indians presented no more problems. Even Kot-le-an made peace with Baranov.

The old Governor began his attempts to retire as early as 1806, but each time he was on the verge of leaving, his successor would perish on his way to America. Baranov finally became convinced that it was God's will that he remain at his post. He stopped asking to be replaced.

The new directors in St. Petersburg, however, thought differently. Despite the huge profits from the fur trade, which Baranov had created for them, they felt the time had come to transfer the management of the colonies from civilian to naval control. Russian America was about to become a base for a growing navy.

Baranov protested in vain, but without Nikolai Rezanov to fight for him in St. Petersburg, it was a losing battle. His enemies spread rumors that he had grown enormously wealthy by stealing from the Company. A special investigator was sent to inspect Baranov's records.

Unaware of the cloud of suspicion hanging over his head, the Governor readily submitted the records of his twenty-eight years of administration. He had nothing to hide. If anything, he had spent his own funds, establishing schools and orphanages, paying for them out of his own pocket. He had given away most of his shares in the Company as rewards to his men. He was no richer than when he had first arrived in Russian America in 1790.

The Company inspector, Kirill Khlebnikov, concluded that the books were kept meticulously. During the months of the audit, Khlebnikov learned to admire Baranov. Eventually, it was he who wrote the only biography of that remarkable man.

Khlebnikov submitted his findings to Captain Leontii Hegemeister who was secretly appointed by the Company to replace Baranov as *Glavny Pravitel.* But instead of being pleased that there was no thievery, Hegemeister announced that Baranov was fired without pension. With stupefying ingratitude, the new directors threw him out, without even a letter of appreciation.

Baranov was deeply hurt. His only wish now was to leave the Company and return to Russia.

He asked Blossom if she would accompany him. She declined. They had been living apart for several years. People gossiped that her mind had become unstable ever since she had tried to kill their son. She had become very pious, spending hours on her knees before the icons.

Baranov prepared to leave America forever, having celebrated the wedding of his and Blossom's daughter Irina to a naval lieutenant, Semen Yanovsky.

Nothing could keep him in America any longer, Baranov thought. He was seventy-two. His daughter was settled, his son Antipatr was about to enter the Naval Academy in St. Petersburg as a cadet, fulfilling a dream for father and son alike.

Baranov boarded the schooner *Kutuzov* under the command of the same Captain Leontii Hegemeister, who had caused him so much dismay.

Hegemeister had grown bored with the administration of the colonies. He was a seagoing man, ill at ease with the *promyshleniki* and the natives. Hegemeister had left young Lieutenant Yanovsky, Baranov's own son-in-law, to administer the colonies while he seized the chance to command the *Kutuzov* on a voyage around the world.

The news of Baranov's departure galvanized Russian America. Hundreds of *promyshleniki* and Aleuts with their families hurried to Novo-Arkhangelsk to bid goodbye to their beloved *nachalnick*. They paddled their *baidarki* day and night and were joined by the Tlingits. The warriors, led by Kot-le-an, arrived at the fort in an armada of war canoes.

Hegemeister nervously paced the deck of the *Kutuzov*. He never expected such an outpouring of affection for his predecessor. He watched as Baranov, sobbing uncontrollably, embraced his men, kissed their bearded faces and blessed their children.

Baranov had a special farewell embrace for Kot-le-an. He squeezed the younger man in his arms, and said, "Forgive me, Chief. Perhaps we should have left you Ravens alone. Perhaps you should've remained untamed."

Kot-le-an replied, "You did not tame us. Your cannons did."

Hegemeister had had enough of this outpouring of emotion. He gave the command to weigh anchor.

It was December 1, 1818, when Baranov saw Novo-Arkhangelsk for the last time.

But he never reached Russia. He died of tropical fever near Batavia, and was buried at sea in the Indian Ocean in April, 1819.

Meanwhile, the Russian-American Company's board of directors in St. Petersburg had taken a new course. Delighted with their great profits from the fur trade, they voted huge bonuses for themselves, giving control over the colonies to the naval command under a new twenty-year charter.

Dozens of career officers signed up for tours of duty, bringing their families along to Novo-Arkhangelsk, the capital of Russian America. New buildings sprang up, not leaky, drafty huts, but well-built European-style two story houses. Sidewalks were laid and the central street was covered with gravel. A church was finally completed and a priest arrived bringing along gilded icons and reliquaries. The church was named St. Michael's.

Nikolai Rezanov's dream of creating an oasis of culture on the Pacific was becoming a reality. His modest library was expanded to include several hundred new volumes; his collection of curiosities became the basis for a little museum.

The foreign captains visiting the fort began to refer to Novo-Arkhangelsk as "the Paris of the Pacific".

Tsar Alexander, who was keenly involved in the progress of Russian expansion while Rezanov was still alive, at first continued his support of the colonies, but, exhausted by his wars with Napoleon, he seemed to lose interest in his Pacific empire.

By the time the "Corsican scourge" was forced into exile on the Island of Elba, Russian America was far from Alexander's thoughts. His once lofty plans gathered dust in the offices of the various ministries.

Alexander died in 1825 on a religious pilgrimage in Taganrog, near the Sea of Azov, leaving no heir. His younger brother, Nikolai, succeeded him as the Tsar.

Nikolai's reign began with the bloody suppression of the Decembrists, a group of liberals who had staged a revolt demanding social reforms. The five leaders of the rebellion, all scions of noble families, were hanged. One of them, a poet, Kondratii Ryleyev, was the manager of the St. Petersburg offices of the Russian-American Company.

Nikolai I ruled Russia for thirty years, during which time the colonies on the Pacific prospered, despite the Tsar's lack of personal involvement. Fort Ross, however, had proved to be an unprofitable enterprise.

Built in less than a year, Fort Ross rose on a bluff some 110 feet above the sea, with a long staircase of 116 steps leading to the rocky shore below, where the wharfs and toolsheds were constructed. But the harbor was non-existent. The approaches to Fort Rossia were strewn with submerged rocks and the ships had to anchor some distance away.

Ivan Kuskov, its builder and the first administrator, fought valiantly to keep the fort going, but the fur-bearing animals had disappeared from its waters, destroyed by indiscriminate hunting. The Kashia Pomo Indians, who were so good at weaving and basketry, proved to be uninspired farmers. Crop failures followed year after year, helped by thousands of gophers who chewed the tender roots before they had a chance to develop. The settlers still had to depend on ships to bring their basic supplies from the mother country.

The directors of the Company had had enough. They voted to sell Fort Ross.

It was sold in 1841 to a rich landowner from the Sacramento River valley, one John Sutter, for 30,000 Spanish piasters.

In 1974, under the direction of California Department of Parks and Recreation, Fort Ross was painstakingly restored to be enjoyed by contemporary visitors.

Although the Russians were no longer in California, they were still active on the Pacific.

But the profits of the Company were declining. The fur-bearing animals, which once teemed in the waters of the northern Pacific, were practically gone. Nevertheless, the Company's charter was renewed for the third time, for another twenty years, although the United States was moving westward at a fast rate, and Russia was too far extended to stop the expansion. Many in St. Petersburg began to favor getting rid of the settlements in America.

The new Tsar, Alexander II, having lost the Crimean War, was licking the wounds inflicted upon his Empire by the combined forces of England, France and Turkey. Several of his ministers advised that the colonies in America had become too expensive and had outlived their usefulness.

Alexander agreed to the sale of Russian America to the United States for the sum of seven million two hundred thousand dollars.

The deed was signed on October 18, 1867 in Novo-Arkhangelsk. The city was renamed Sitka and the country became known as Alaska, an Aleut word meaning "continent". Some say that it was an Indian word meaning "big country".

The Ravens, the Eagles, the Bears, and the Wolves had become known collectively as the *Americans.*

REFERENCES

Bergamini, John, THE TRAGIC DYNASTY, A HISTORY OF THE ROMANOVS, Putnam, New York, 1969

Bancroft, H.H. HISTORY OF ALASKA, San Francisco, 1886

Bancroft, H.H. HISTORY OF CALIFORNIA, Santa Barbara, 1963

Chevigny, Hector, RUSSIAN AMERICA, THE GREAT ALASKAN ADVENTURE 1741-1867, Balantine, New York, 1973

Davidov, G.I. TWO VOYAGES TO RUSSIAN AMERICA 1802-1807, edited by Richard A. Pierce, Limestone Press, Kingston, Ontario, 1977

Dmytryshin, B. IMPERIAL RUSSIA, A SOURCE BOOK, 1700-1917, Holt, Rinehart and Winston, New York, 1967

Gibson, James R. IMPERIAL RUSSIA IN FRONTIER AMERICA, Oxford University Press, New York, 1976

Golovnin, V.M. VOYAGE ON THE SLOOP DIANA FROM KRONSTADT TO KAMCHATKA 1807-1808 and DESCRIPTION OF NOTABLE SHIPWRECKS SUFFERED BY RUSSIAN NAVIGATORS, St. Petersburg, 1822

Golovnin, V.M. AROUND THE WORLD ON THE KAMCHATKA 1817-1819, University Press of Hawaii, 1979

Hays, H.R. CHILDREN OF THE RAVEN, McGraw-Hill, New York, 1975

Ivashnikov, N.A. RUSSIAN ROUND-THE-WORLD VOYAGES 1803-1849, edited by Richard A. Pierce, Limestone Press, Kingston, Ontario, 1975

Khlebnikov, K.T. BARANOV, CHIEF MANAGER OF THE RUSSIAN COLONIES IN AMERICA, edited by Richard A. Pierce, Limestone Press, Kingston, Ontario, 1973

Khlebnikov, K.T. COLONIAL RUSSIAN AMERICA 1817-1832, Oregon Historical Society, Portland, 1976

Krause, Aurel, THE TLINGIT INDIANS, University of Washington Press, Seattle, 1955

Kruzenstern, A.I., VOYAGE AUTOUR DU MONDE, Paris, 1821

Lisyansky, Urey, VOYAGE AROUND THE WORLD IN THE YEARS 1803, 1804, 1805 and 1806, London, 1814

Madariaga, de, Isabel, RUSSIA IN THE AGE OF CATHERINE THE GREAT, Yale University Press, New Haven, 1981

Makarova, R.V. RUSSIANS ON THE PACIFIC, edited by Richard A. Pierce, Limestone Press, Kingston, Ontario, 1975

THE MEMOIRS OF CATHERINE THE GREAT, edited by Dominique Maroger, Hamish Hamilton, London, 1955

Mitchell Mairin, HISTOIRE MARITIME DE LA RUSSIE, Deux Rives

Saum, Lewis O. THE FUR TRADER AND THE INDIAN, University of Washington Press, Seattle, 1965

Sister Jane, S.H.F., CONCEPCIÓN ARGUELLO, unpublished MA Thesis, University of San Francisco, 1962

Shelikhov, Grigory, A VOYAGE TO AMERICA, edited by Richard A. Pierce, Limestone Press, Kingston, Ontario, 1981

Tikhmenev, P.A. A HISTORY OF RUSSIAN-AMERICAN COMPANY, University of Washington Press, Seattle, 1978

Troyat, Henri, ALEXANDER OF RUSSIA, E.P. Dutton, New York, 1982

Yarmolinsky, Avrahm, SOME RAMBLING NOTES ON THE RUSSIAN COLUMBUS, Bulletin of the New York Public Library, 1927